Chapter 28

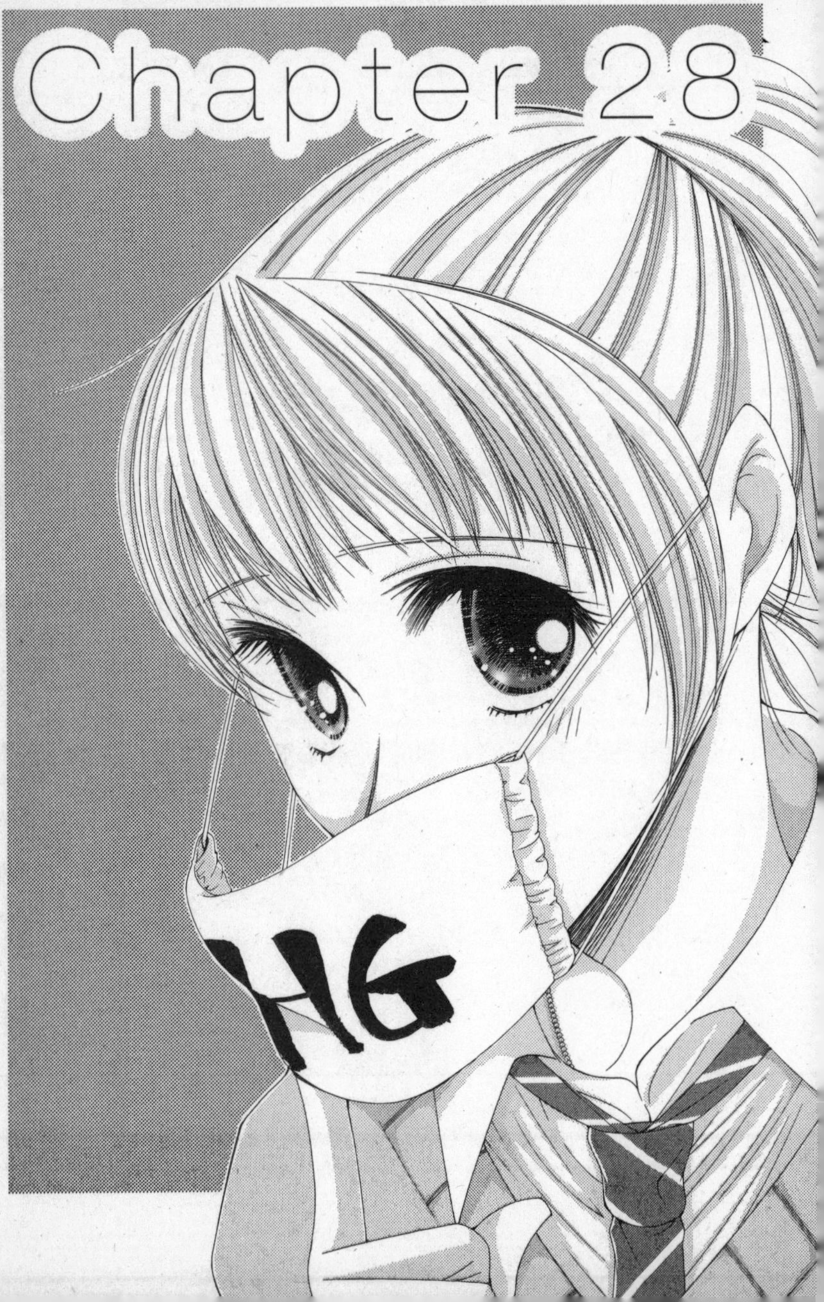
HG

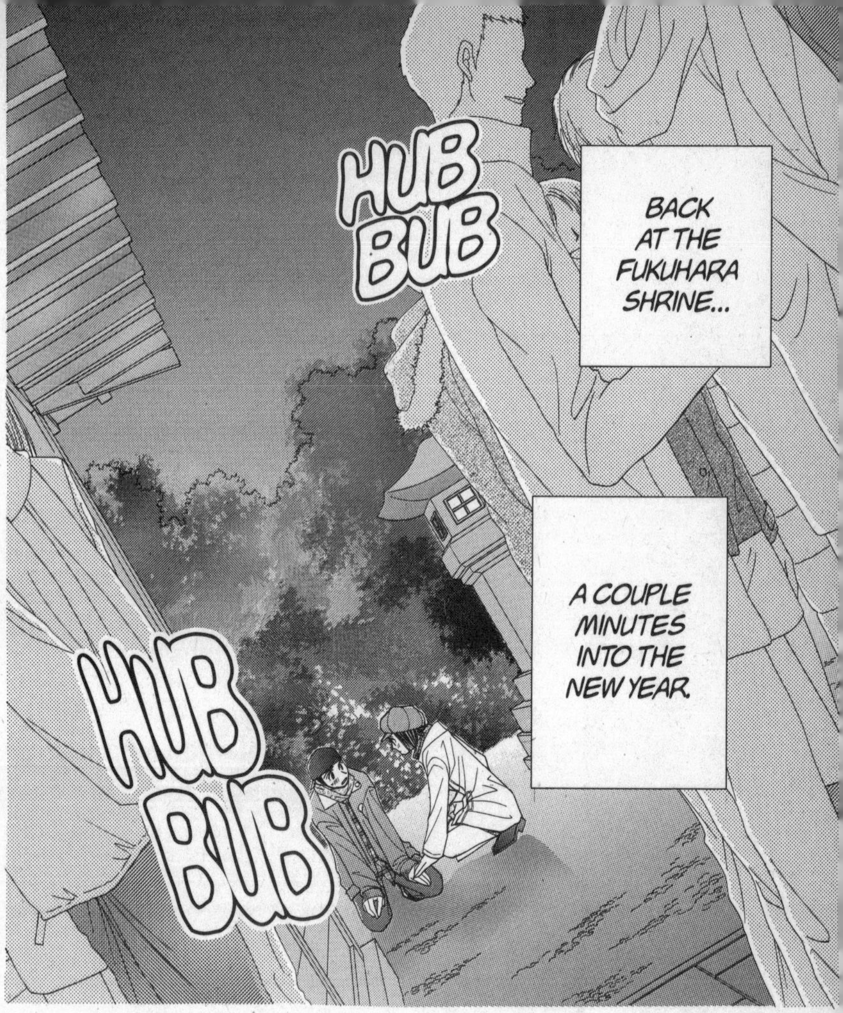
BACK AT THE FUKUHARA SHRINE...
HUB BUB
A COUPLE MINUTES INTO THE NEW YEAR.
HUB BUB

hot gimmick

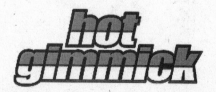

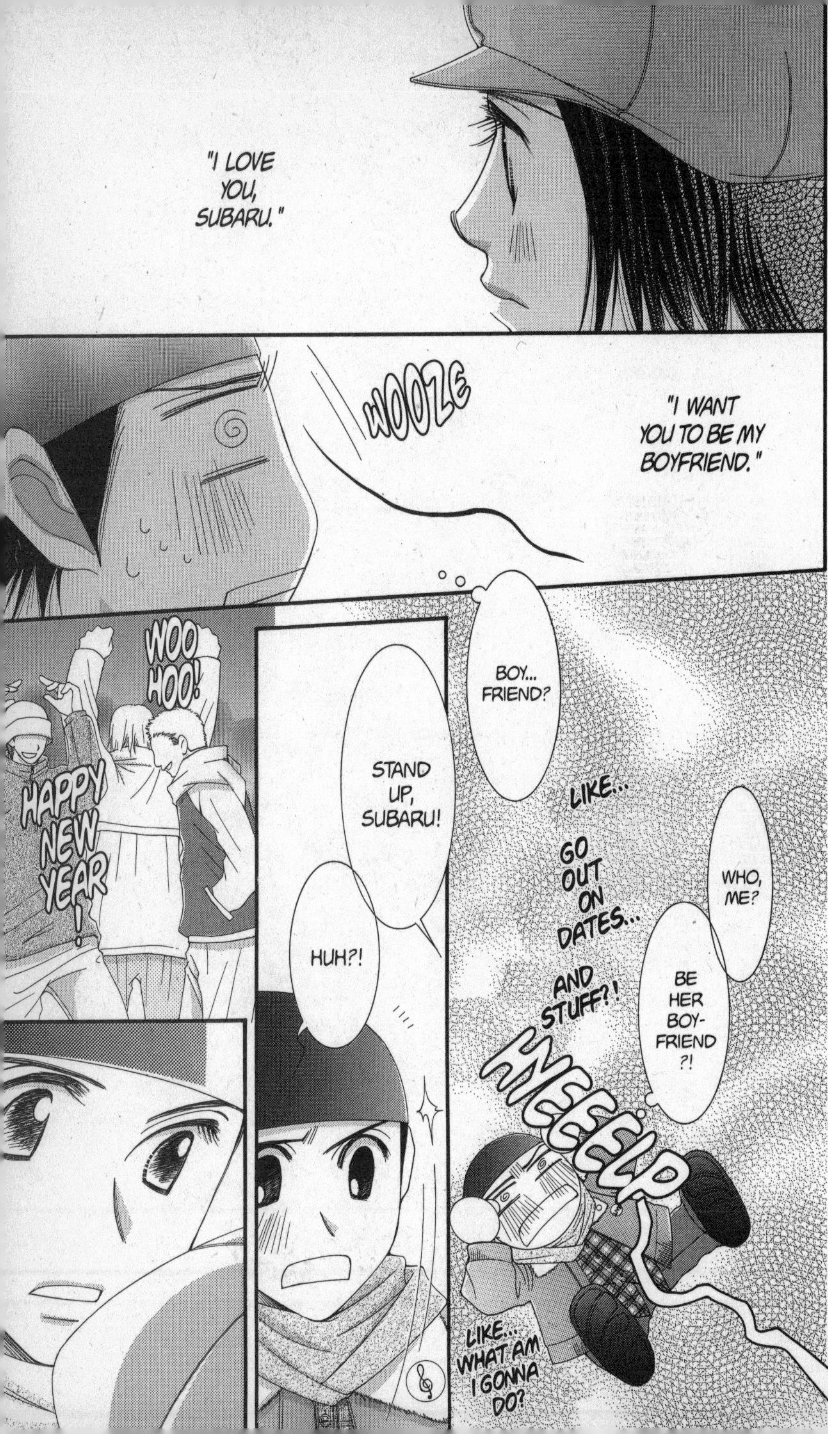
"I LOVE YOU, SUBARU."
"I WANT YOU TO BE MY BOYFRIEND."
WOOZE
BOY... FRIEND?
WHO, ME?
LIKE...
GO OUT ON DATES...
AND STUFF?!
BE HER BOY-FRIEND?!
HYEEELP
LIKE... WHAT AM I GONNA DO?
STAND UP, SUBARU!
HUH?!
WOO HOO!
HAPPY NEW YEAR!

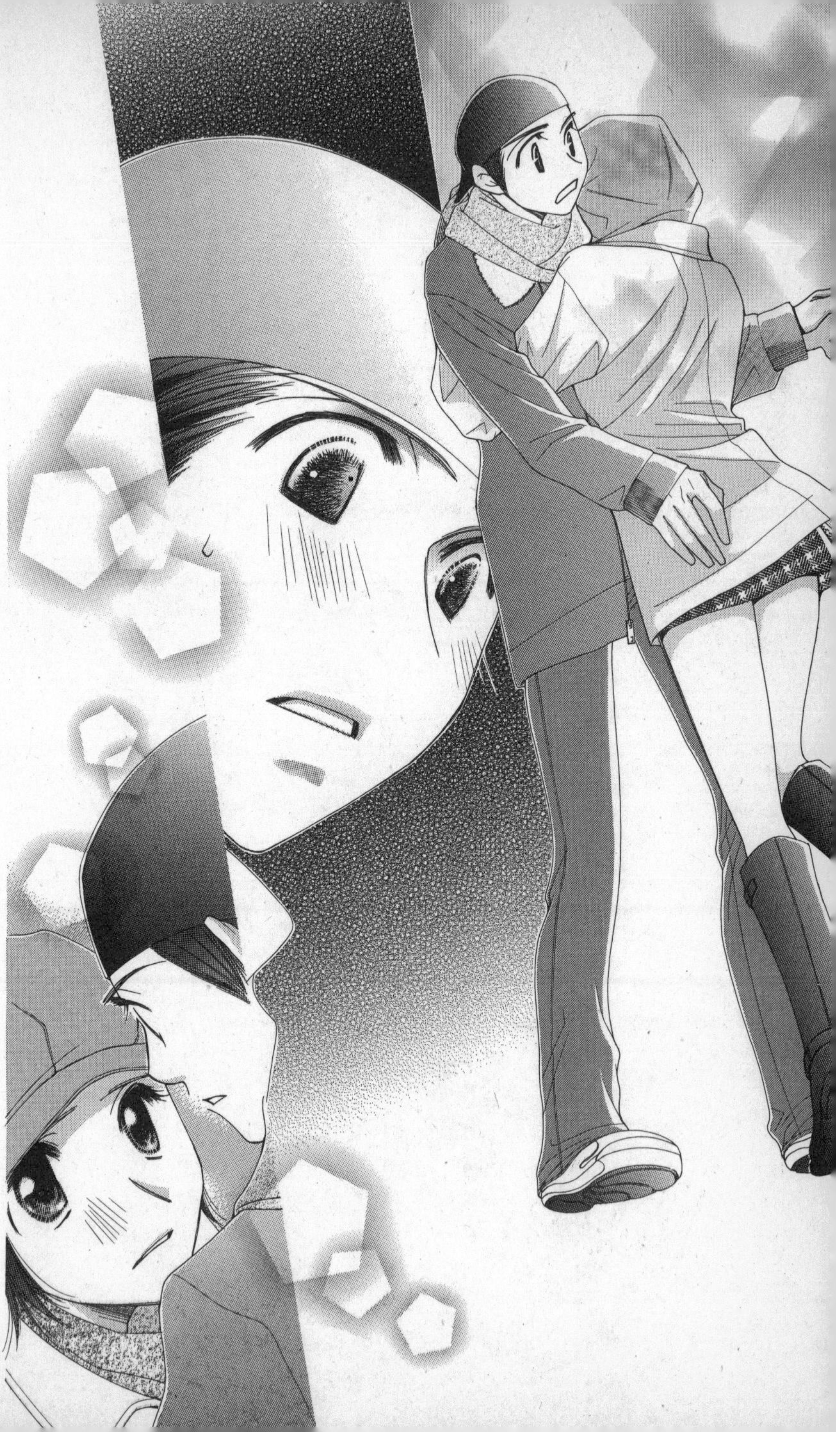

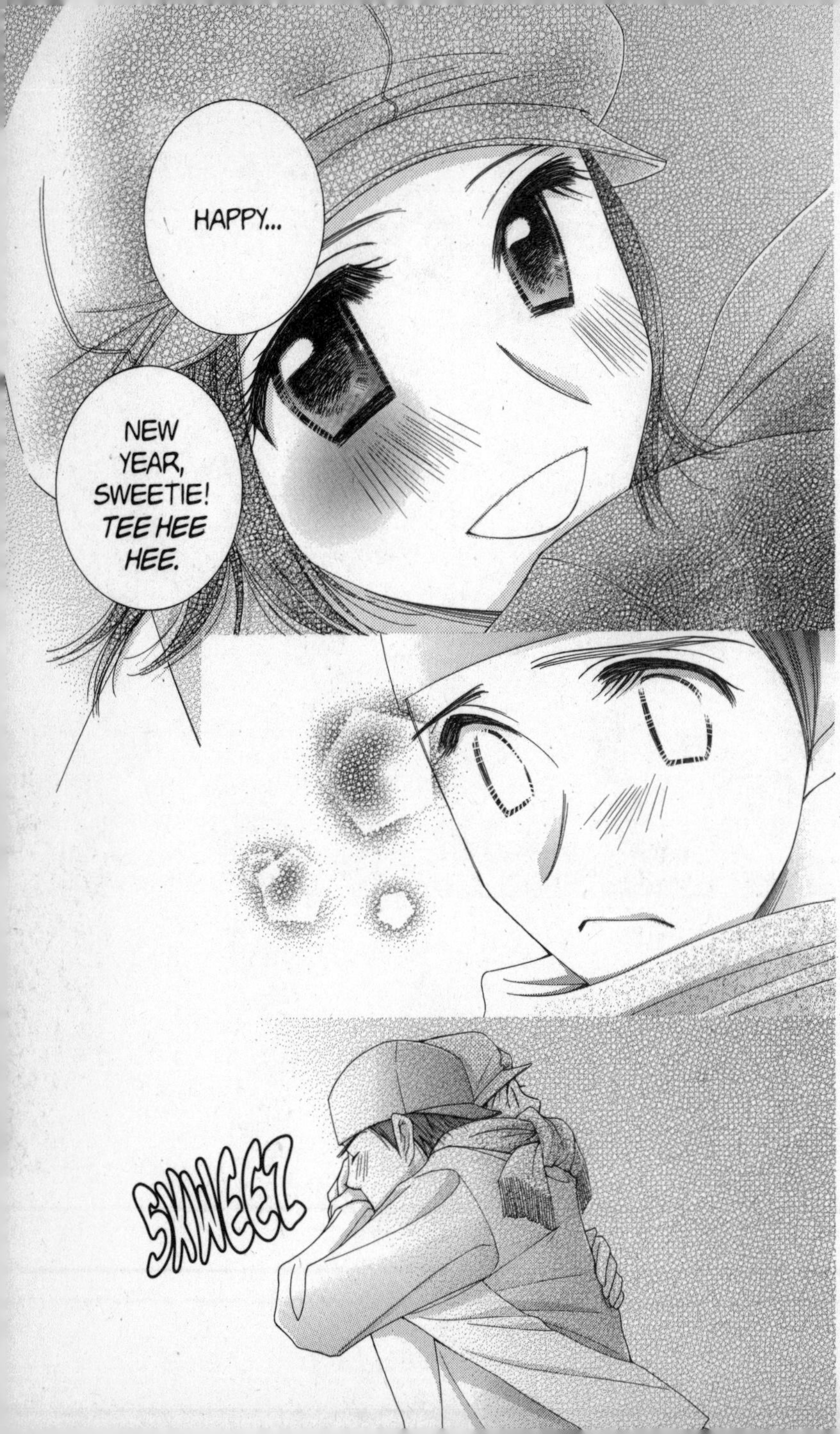
HAPPY...
NEW YEAR, SWEETIE! TEE HEE HEE.
SKWEEZ

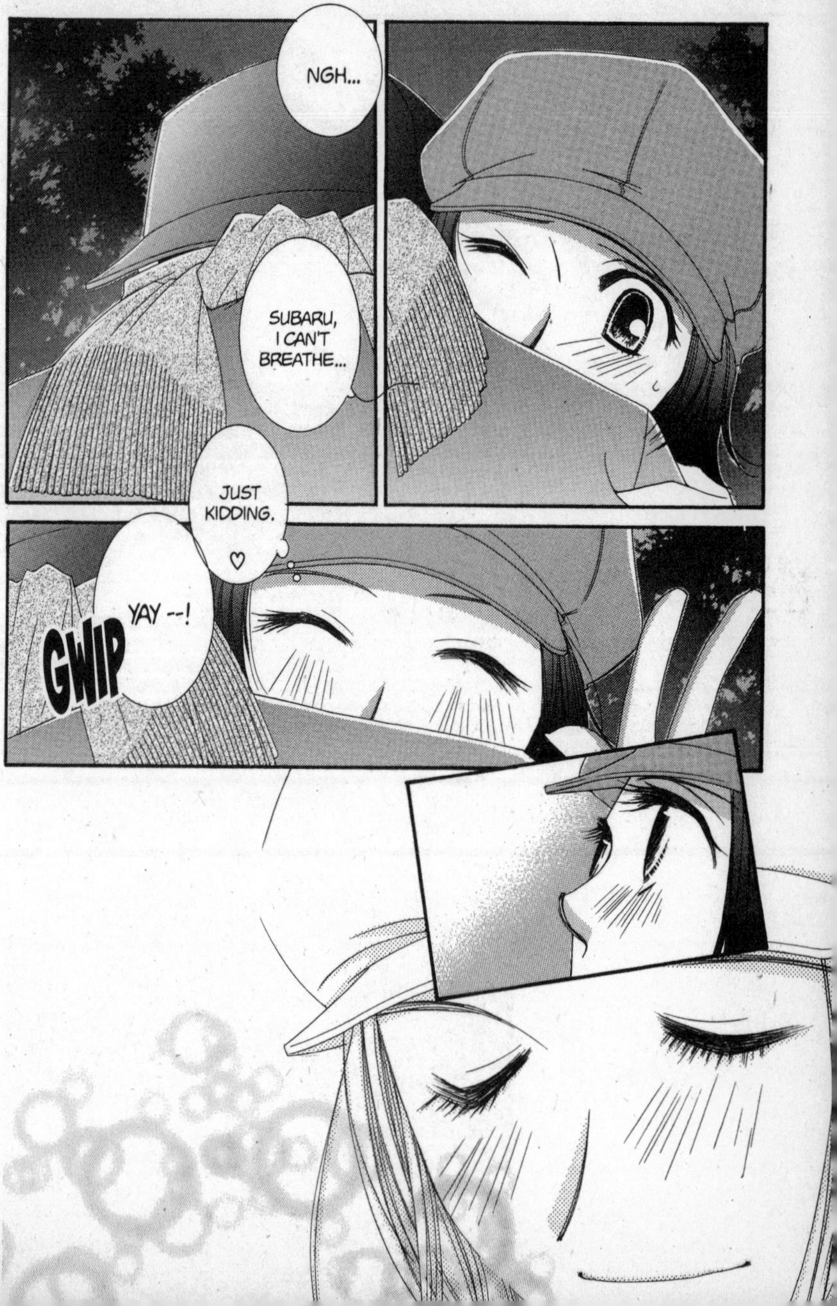
NGH...
SUBARU, I CAN'T BREATHE...
JUST KIDDING. ♡
YAY --!
GWIP

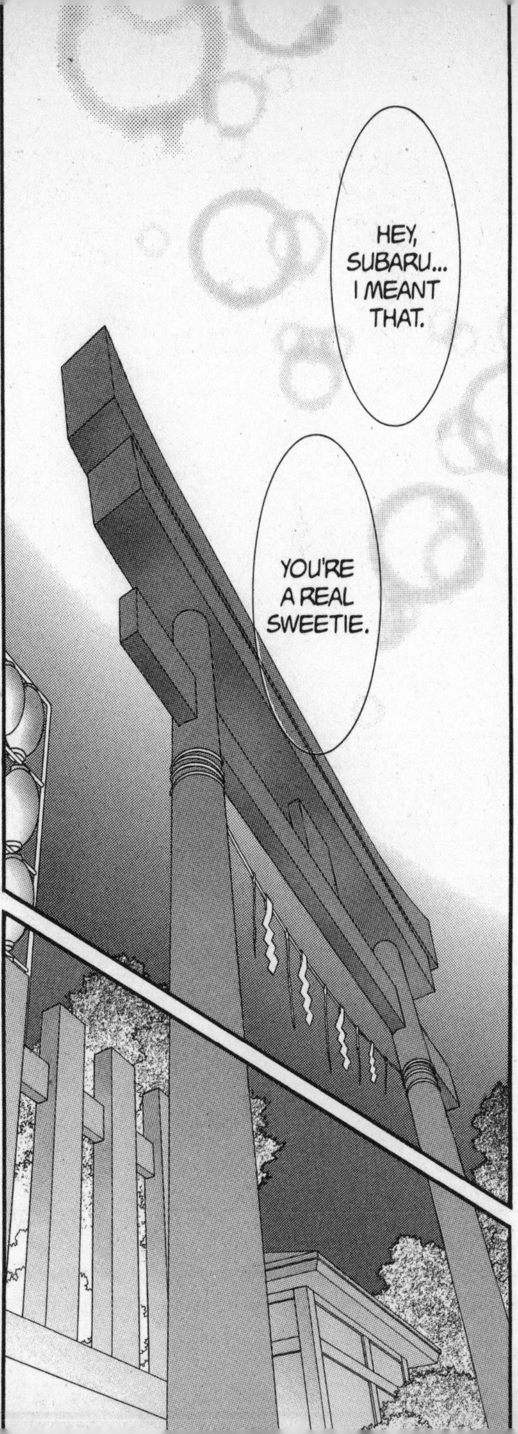
HEY, SUBARU... I MEANT THAT.
YOU'RE A REAL SWEETIE.

hot gimmick

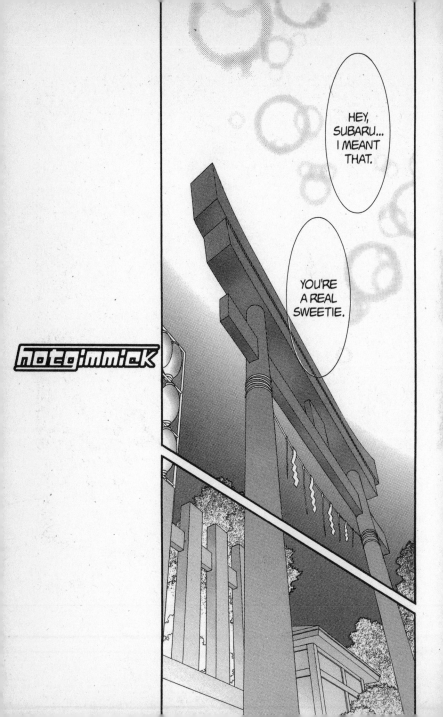

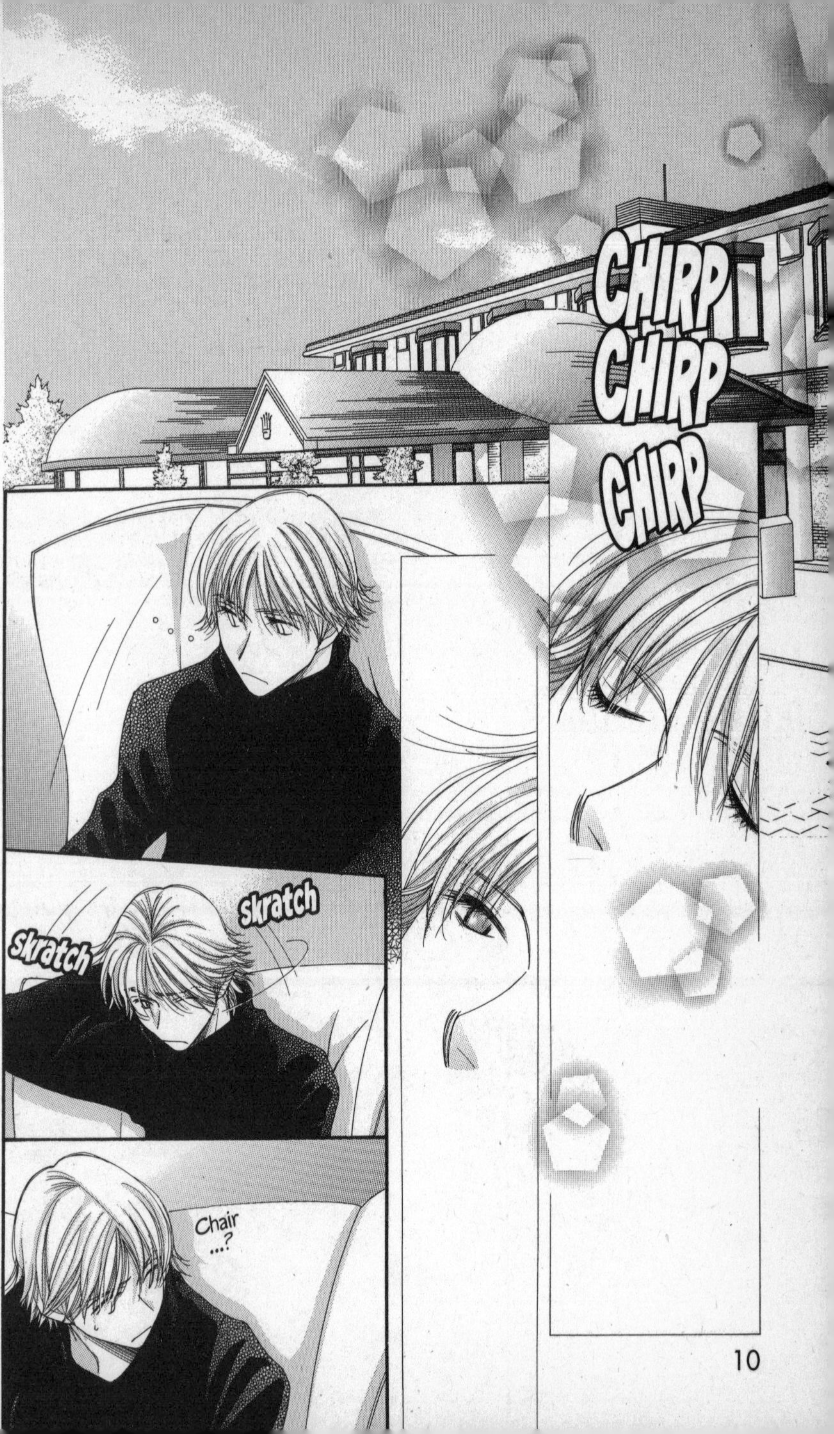
CHIRP
CHIRP
CHIRP
skratch
skratch
Chair ...?

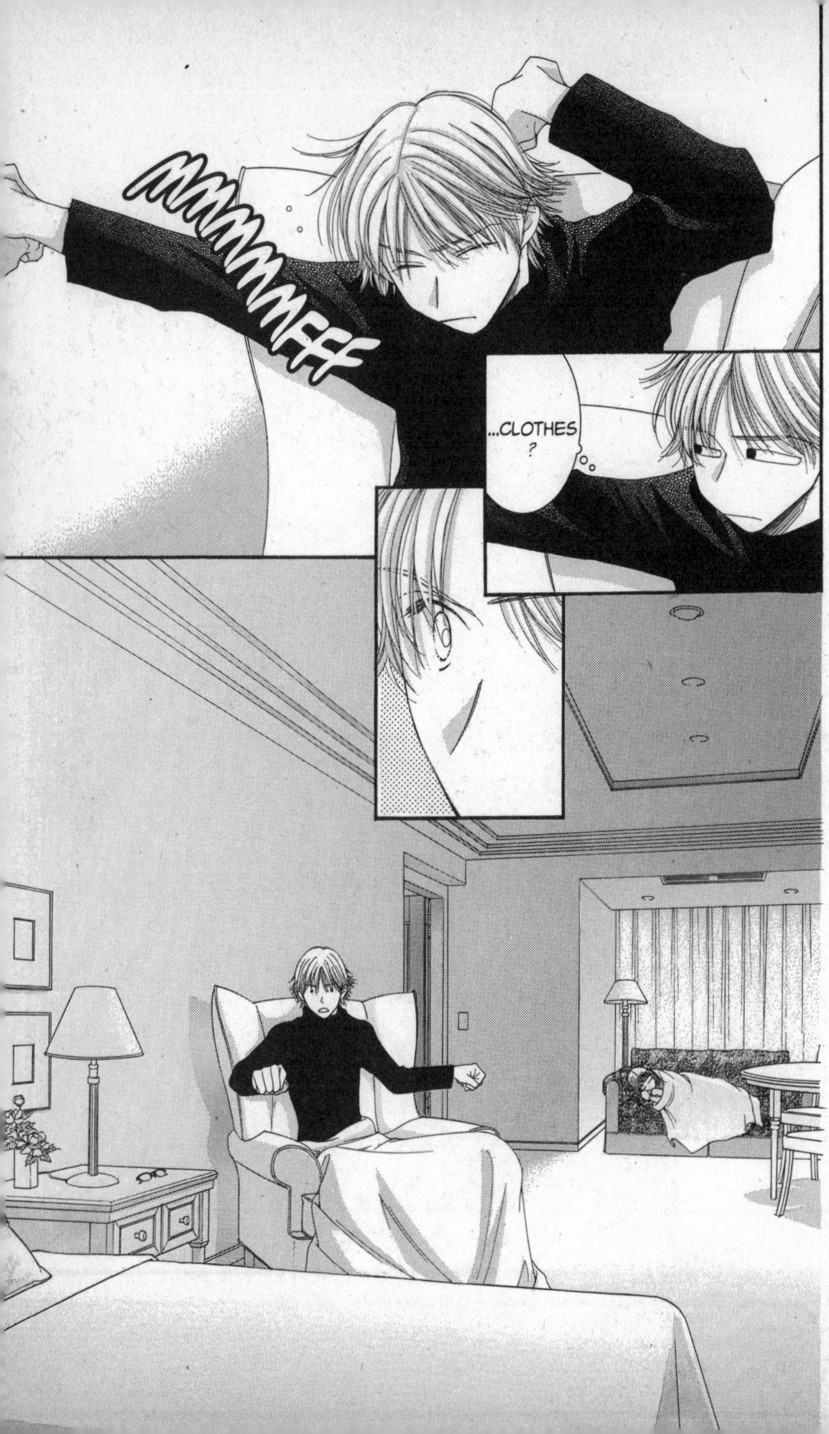
MMMMMFFF
...CLOTHES ?

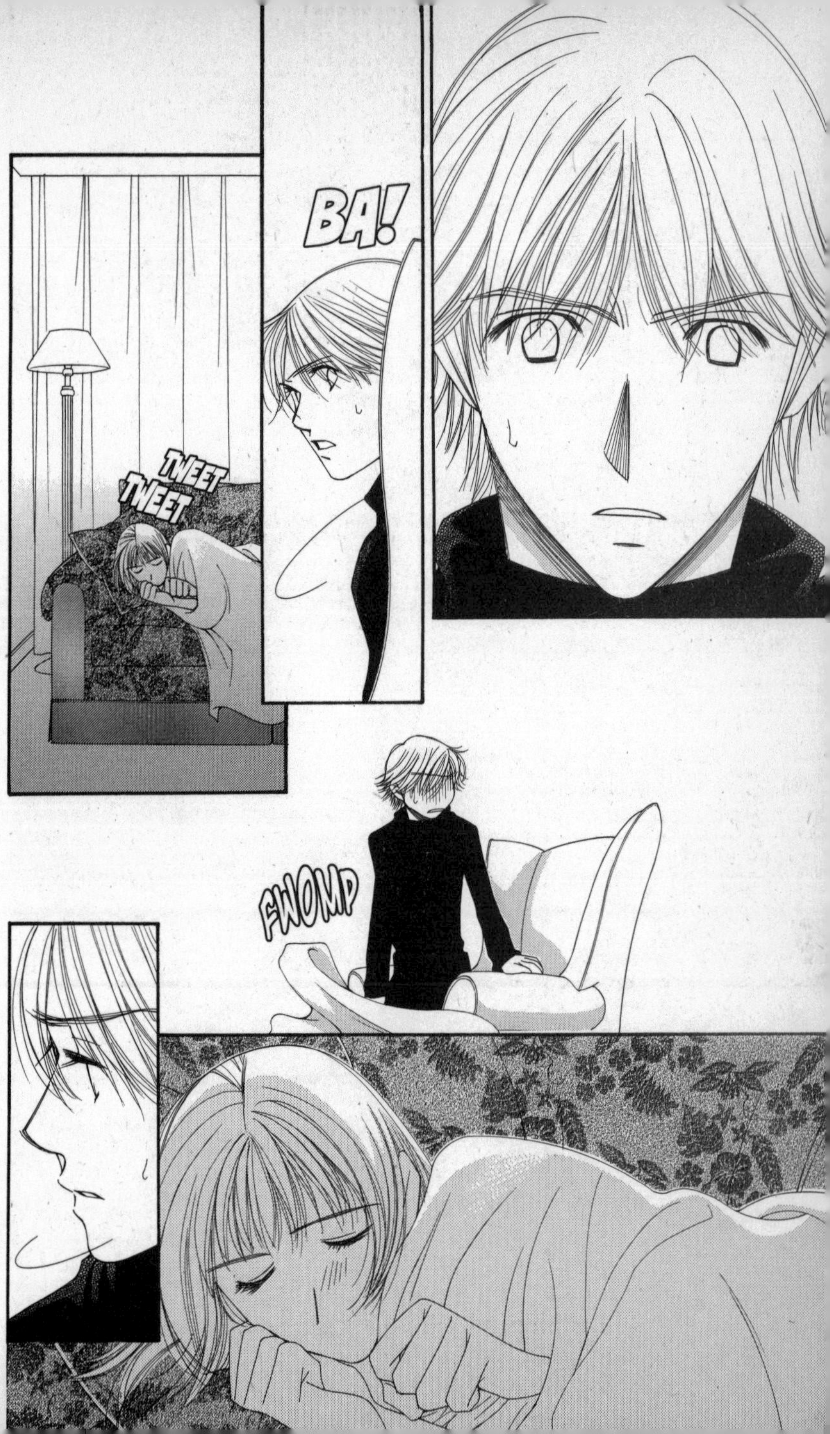
BA!
TWEET
TWEET
FWOMP

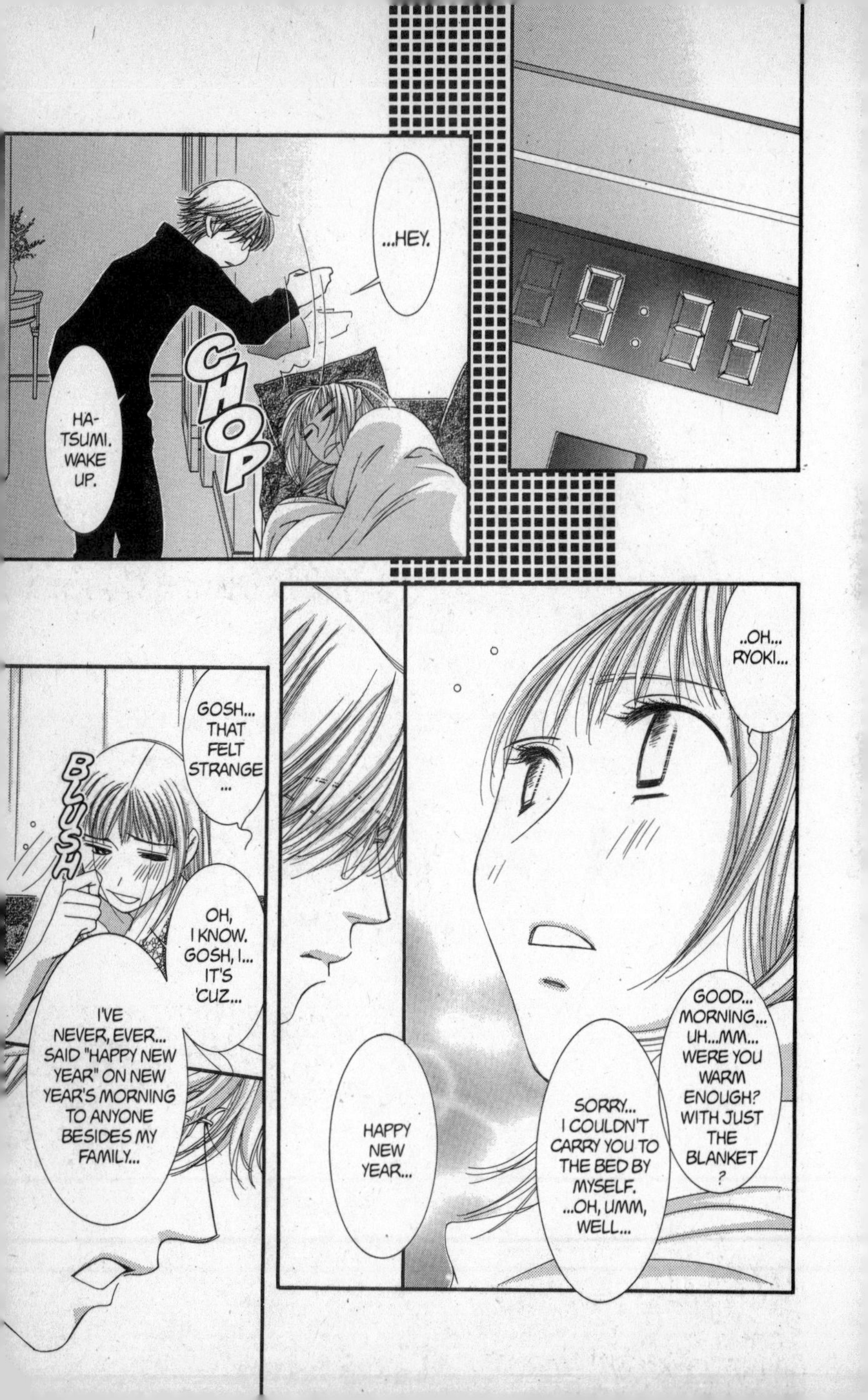
...HEY.
CHOP
HA-TSUMI. WAKE UP.
..OH... RYOKI...
GOOD... MORNING... UH...MM... WERE YOU WARM ENOUGH? WITH JUST THE BLANKET ?
SORRY... I COULDN'T CARRY YOU TO THE BED BY MYSELF. ...OH, UMM, WELL...
HAPPY NEW YEAR...
GOSH... THAT FELT STRANGE ...
BLUSH
OH, I KNOW. GOSH, I... IT'S 'CUZ...
I'VE NEVER, EVER... SAID "HAPPY NEW YEAR" ON NEW YEAR'S MORNING TO ANYONE BESIDES MY FAMILY...

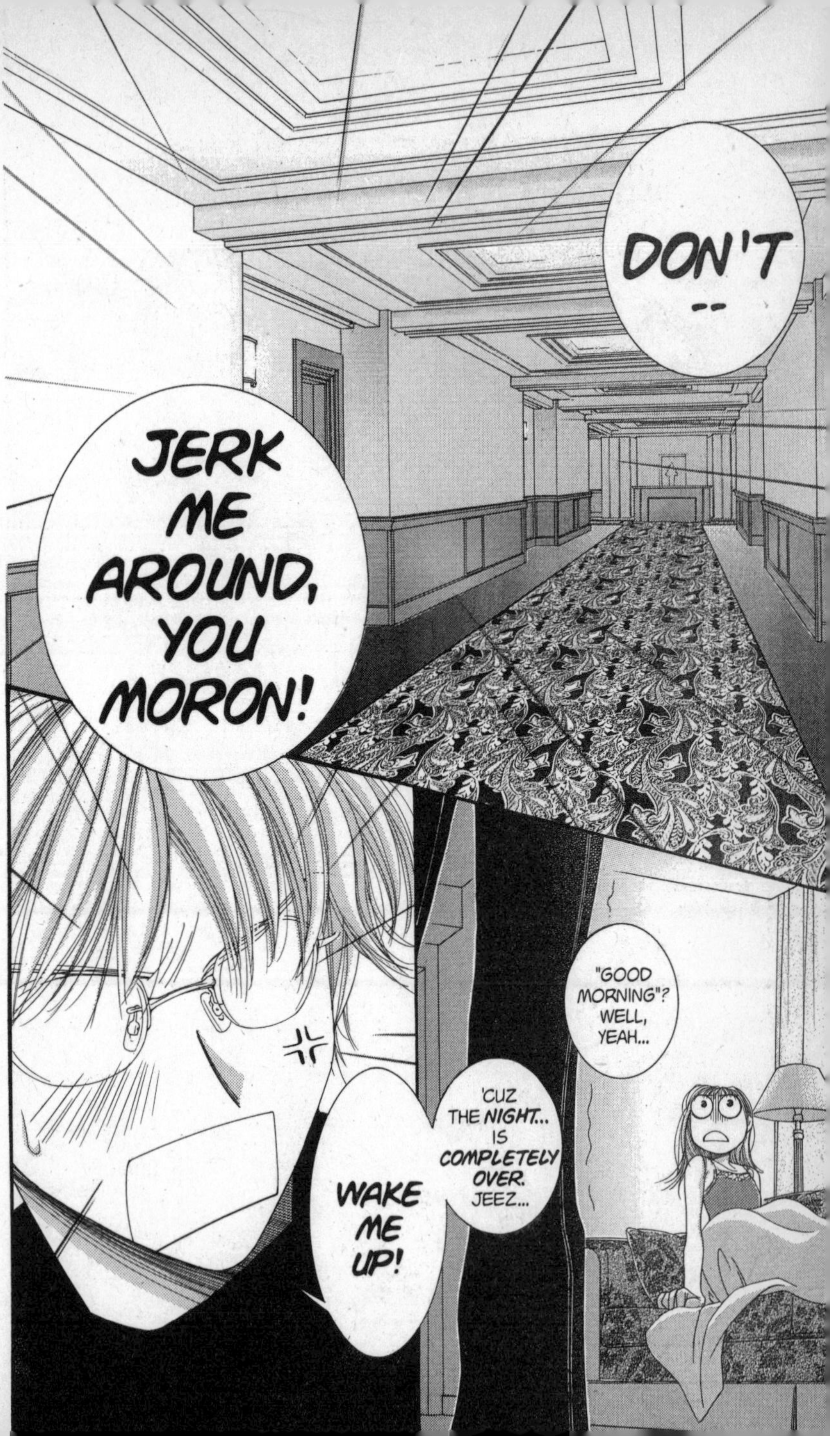
DON'T --
JERK ME AROUND, YOU MORON!
"GOOD MORNING"? WELL, YEAH...
'CUZ THE NIGHT... IS COMPLETELY OVER. JEEZ...
WAKE ME UP!

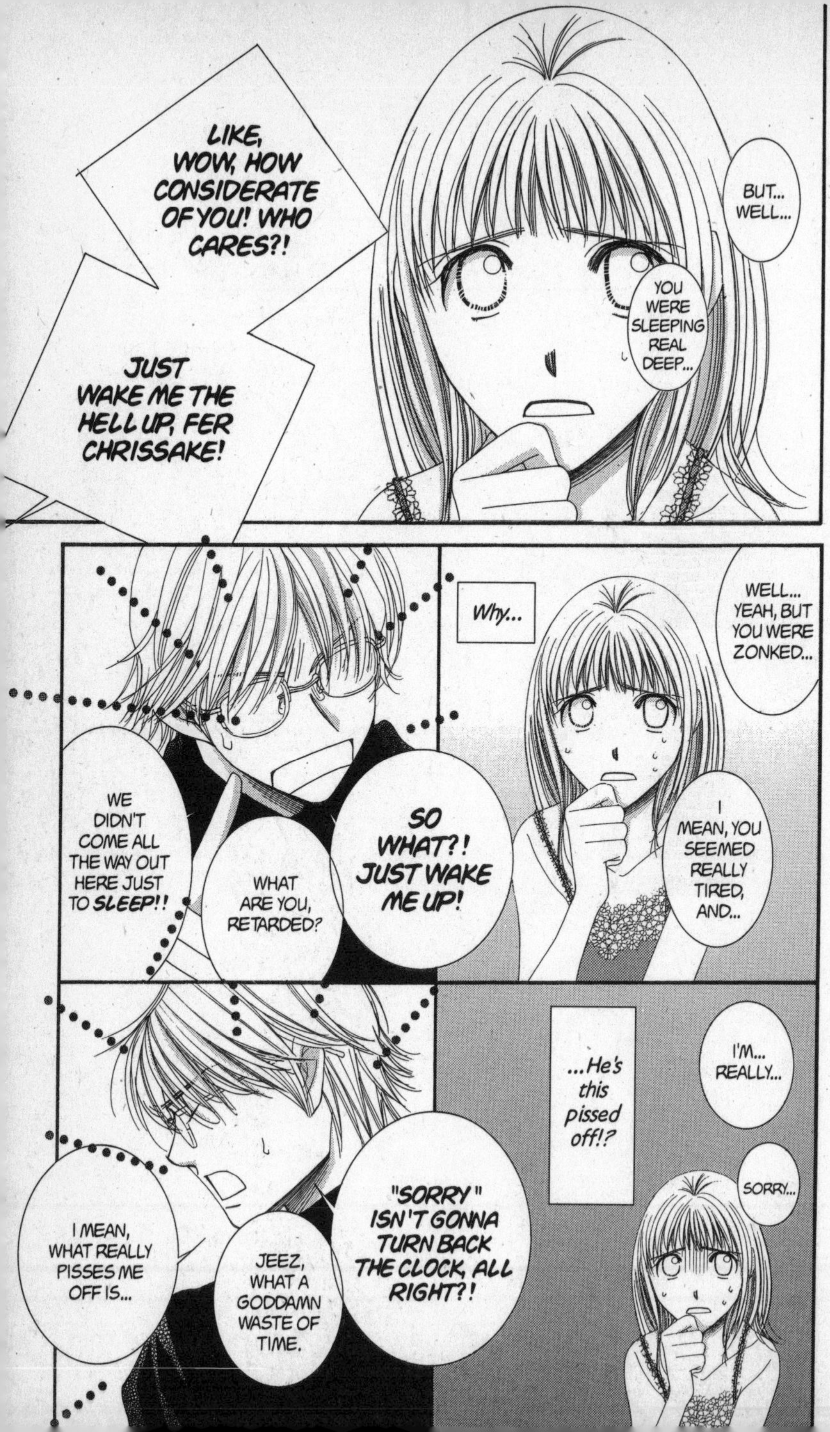
BUT... WELL...
YOU WERE SLEEPING REAL DEEP...
LIKE, WOW, HOW CONSIDERATE OF YOU! WHO CARES?!
JUST WAKE ME THE HELL UP, FER CHRISSAKE!
WELL... YEAH, BUT YOU WERE ZONKED...
Why...
I MEAN, YOU SEEMED REALLY TIRED, AND...
SO WHAT?! JUST WAKE ME UP!
WHAT ARE YOU, RETARDED?
WE DIDN'T COME ALL THE WAY OUT HERE JUST TO SLEEP!!
I'M... REALLY...
...He's this pissed off!?
SORRY...
"SORRY" ISN'T GONNA TURN BACK THE CLOCK, ALL RIGHT?!
JEEZ, WHAT A GODDAMN WASTE OF TIME.
I MEAN, WHAT REALLY PISSES ME OFF IS...

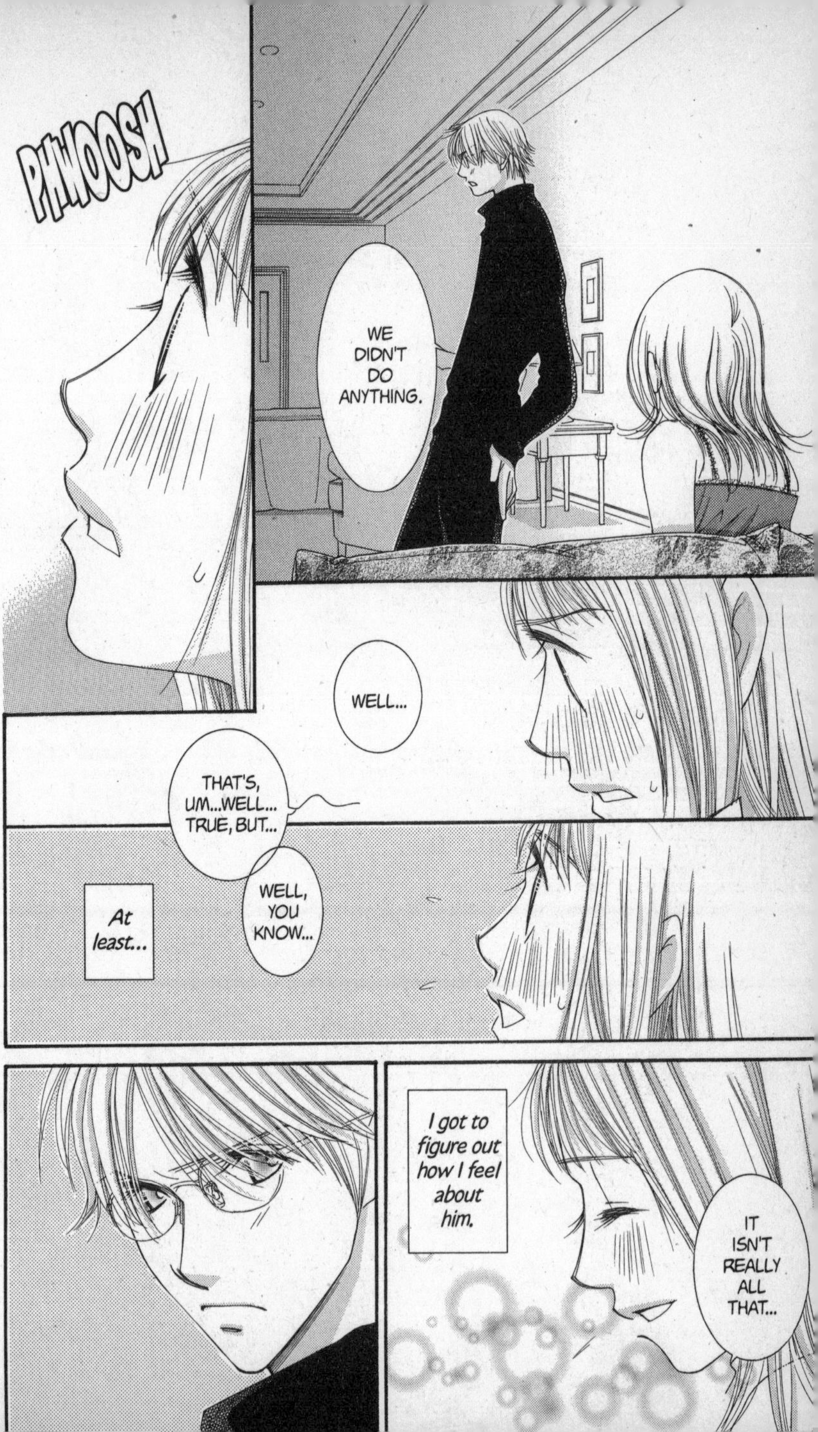
WE DIDN'T DO ANYTHING.
PHWOOSH
WELL...
THAT'S, UM...WELL... TRUE, BUT...
WELL, YOU KNOW...
At least...
I got to figure out how I feel about him.
IT ISN'T REALLY ALL THAT...

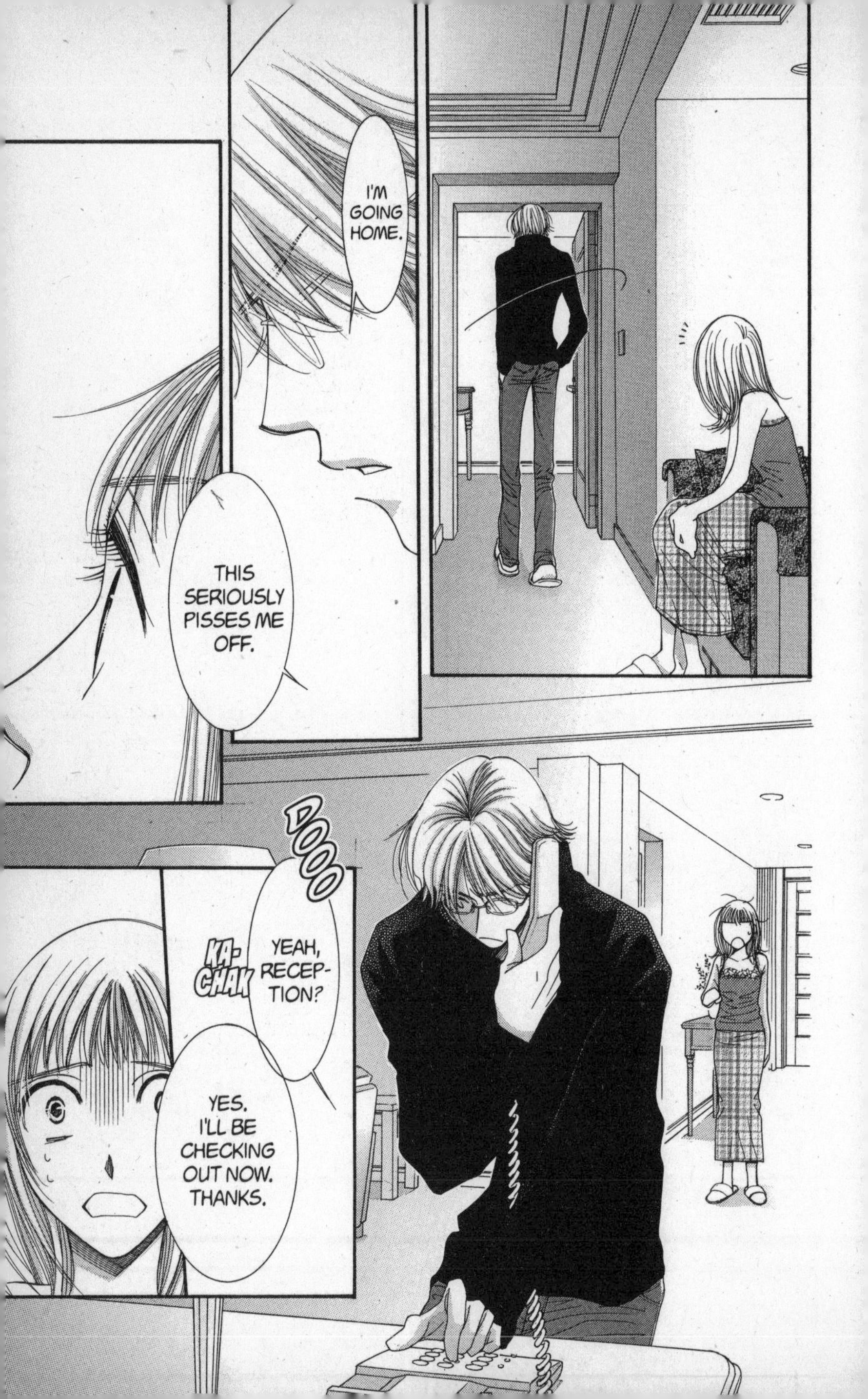
I'M GOING HOME.
THIS SERIOUSLY PISSES ME OFF.
DOOO
KA-CHAK
YEAH, RECEPTION?
YES. I'LL BE CHECKING OUT NOW. THANKS.

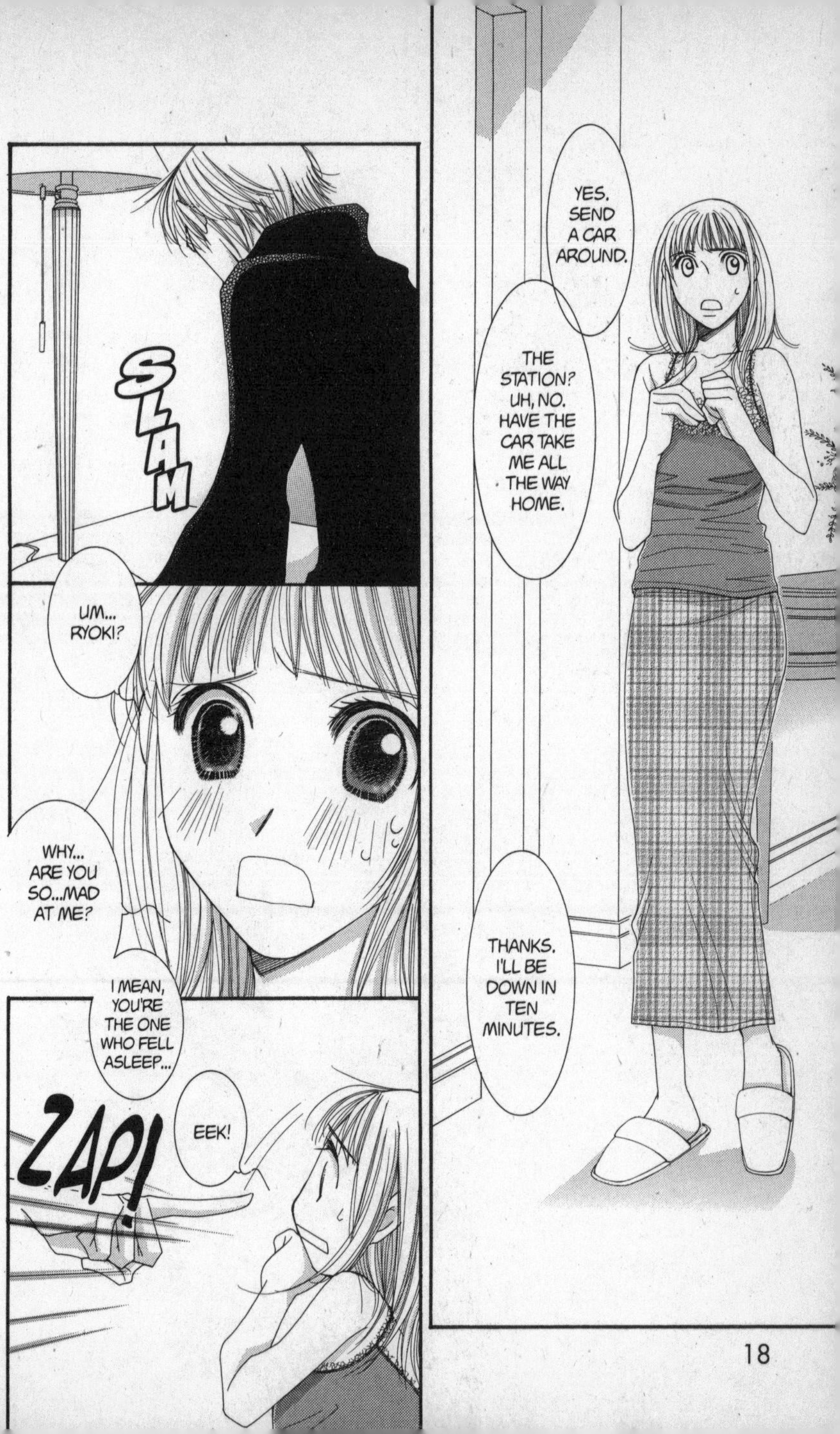
YES. SEND A CAR AROUND.
THE STATION? UH, NO. HAVE THE CAR TAKE ME ALL THE WAY HOME.
THANKS. I'LL BE DOWN IN TEN MINUTES.
SLAM
UM... RYOKI?
WHY... ARE YOU SO...MAD AT ME?
I MEAN, YOU'RE THE ONE WHO FELL ASLEEP...
EEK!
ZAP!

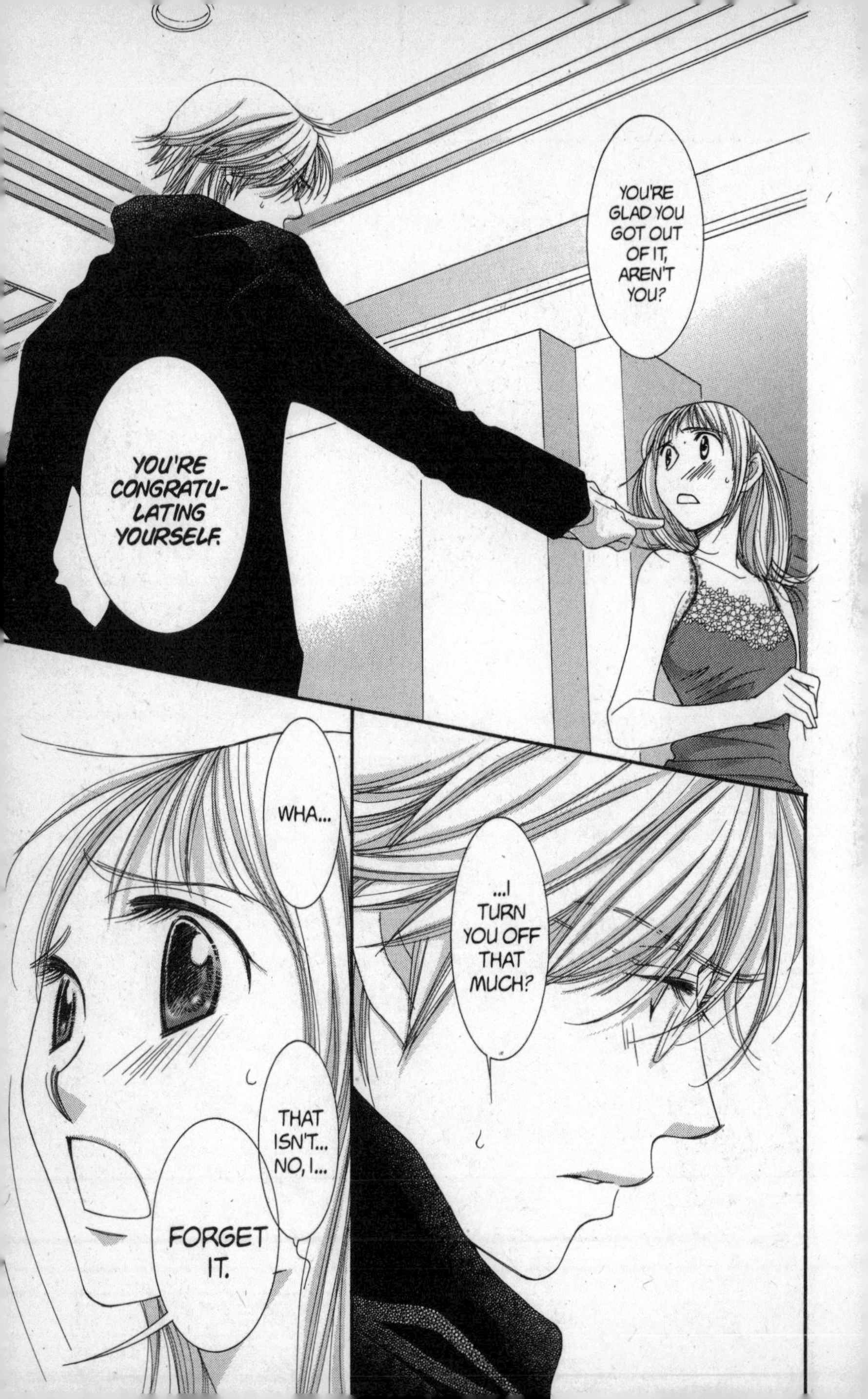
YOU'RE GLAD YOU GOT OUT OF IT, AREN'T YOU?
YOU'RE CONGRATU-LATING YOURSELF.
...I TURN YOU OFF THAT MUCH?
WHA...
THAT ISN'T... NO, I...
FORGET IT.

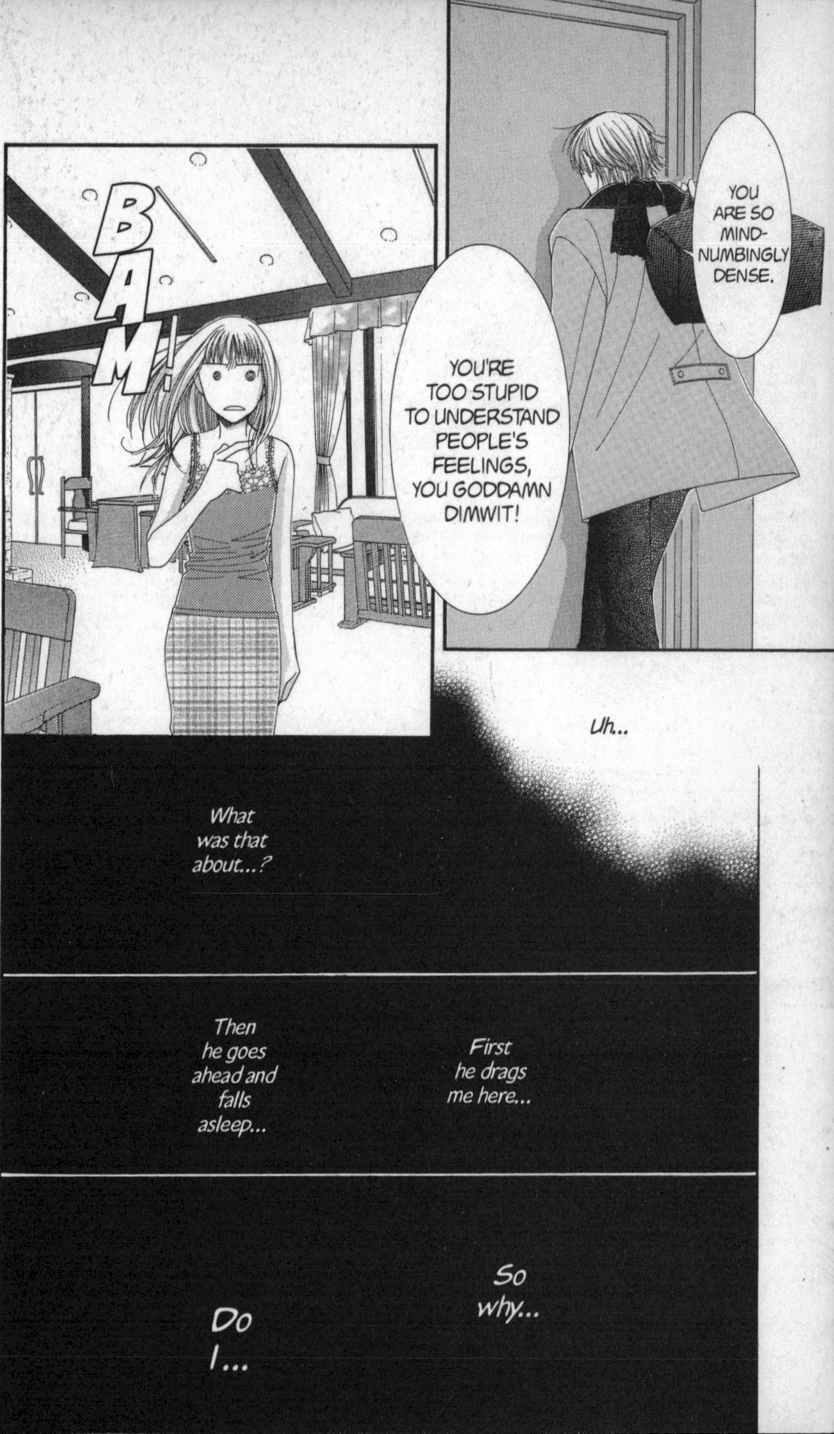
YOU ARE SO MIND-NUMBINGLY DENSE.
YOU'RE TOO STUPID TO UNDERSTAND PEOPLE'S FEELINGS, YOU GODDAMN DIMWIT!
BAM!
Uh...
What was that about...?
First he drags me here...
Then he goes ahead and falls asleep...
So why...
Do I...

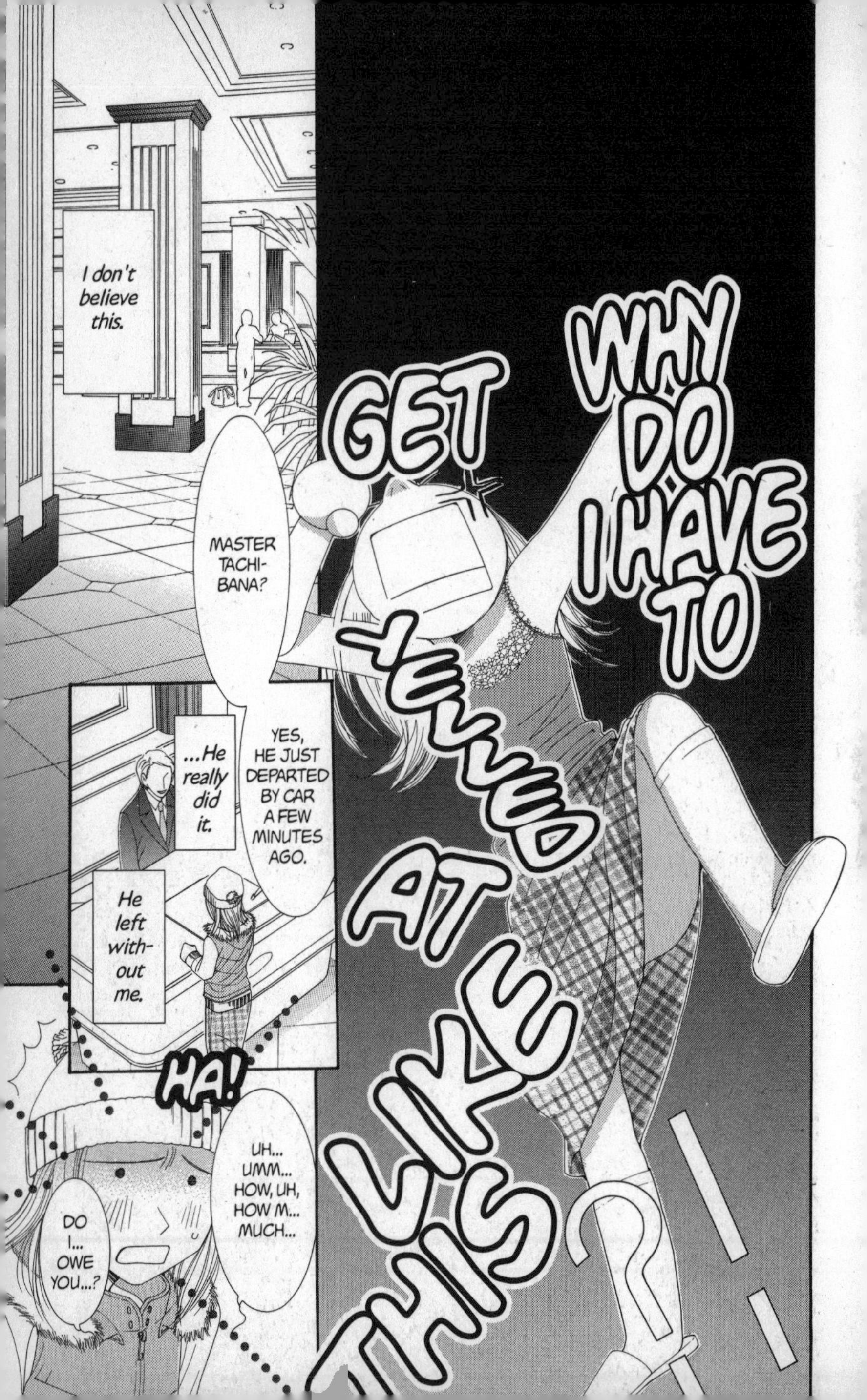
WHY DO I HAVE TO GET YELLED AT LIKE THIS?
I don't believe this.
MASTER TACHI-BANA?
YES, HE JUST DEPARTED BY CAR A FEW MINUTES AGO.
...He really did it.
He left with-out me.
HA!
UH... UMM... HOW, UH, HOW M... MUCH...
DO I... OWE YOU...?

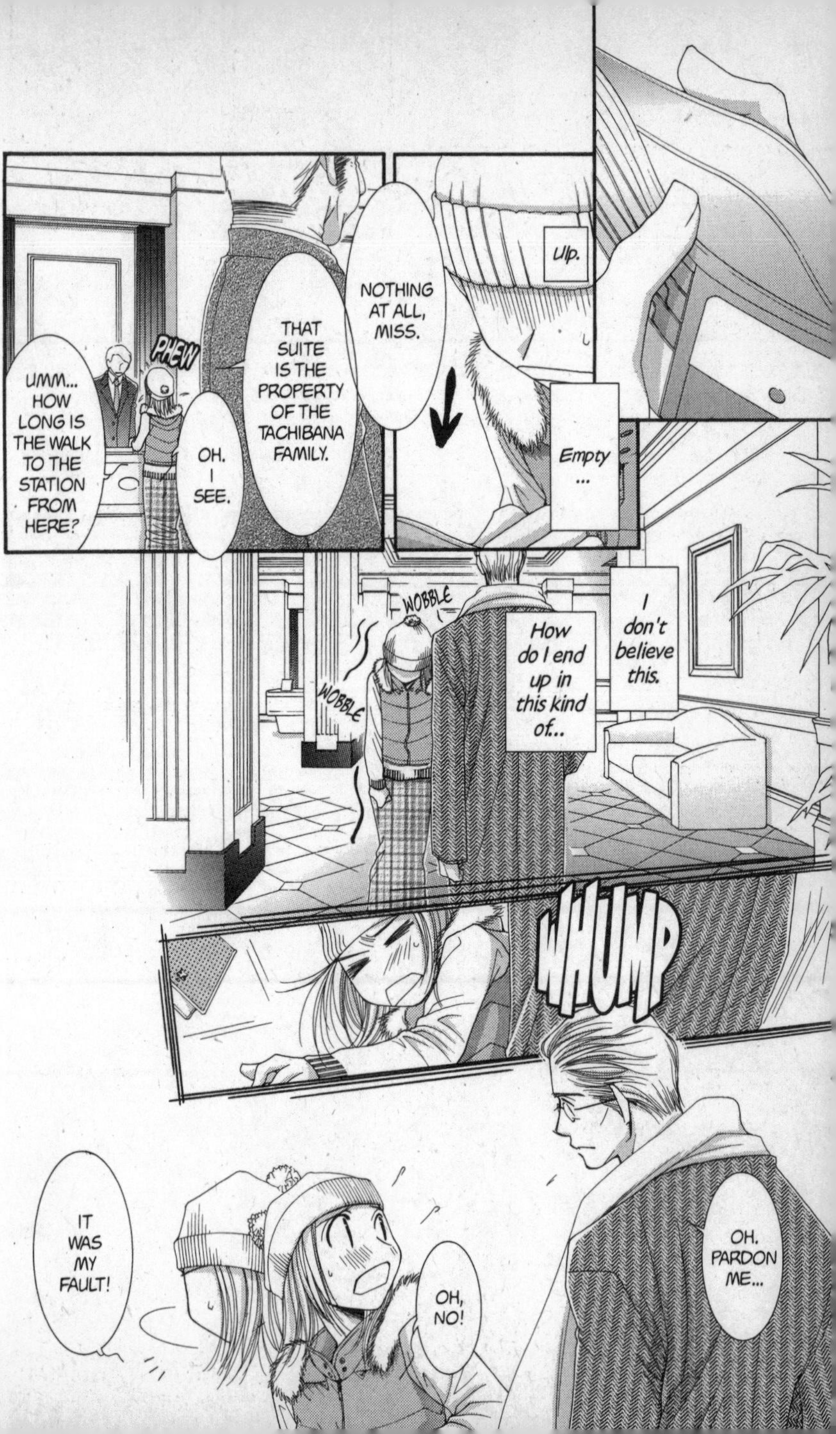
Ulp.
NOTHING AT ALL, MISS.
THAT SUITE IS THE PROPERTY OF THE TACHIBANA FAMILY.
OH. I SEE.
PHEW
UMM... HOW LONG IS THE WALK TO THE STATION FROM HERE?
Empty...
I don't believe this.
How do I end up in this kind of...
WOBBLE
WOBBLE
WHUMP
OH. PARDON ME...
OH, NO!
IT WAS MY FAULT!

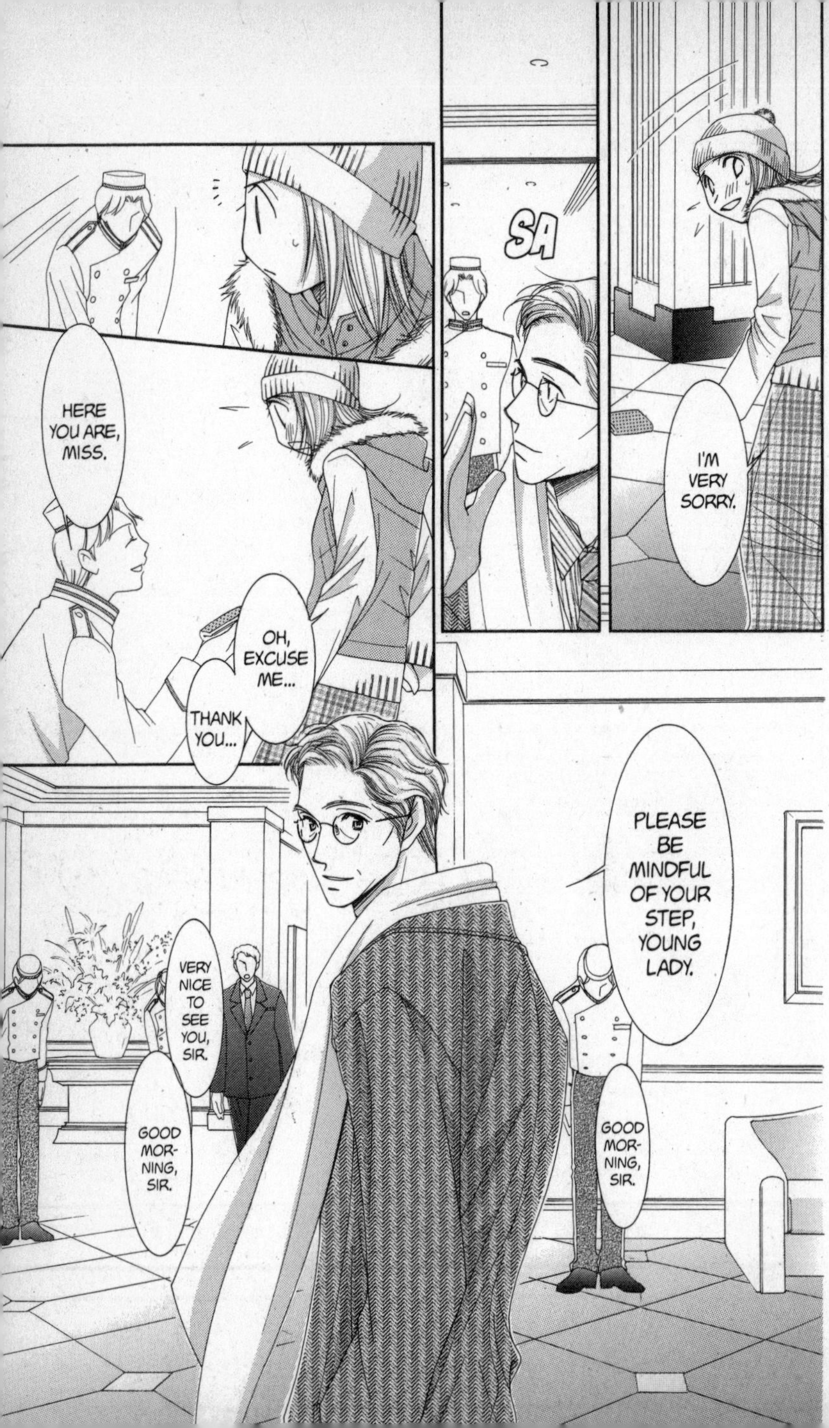
I'M VERY SORRY.
SA
HERE YOU ARE, MISS.
OH, EXCUSE ME...
THANK YOU...
PLEASE BE MINDFUL OF YOUR STEP, YOUNG LADY.
GOOD MORNING, SIR.
VERY NICE TO SEE YOU, SIR.
GOOD MORNING, SIR.

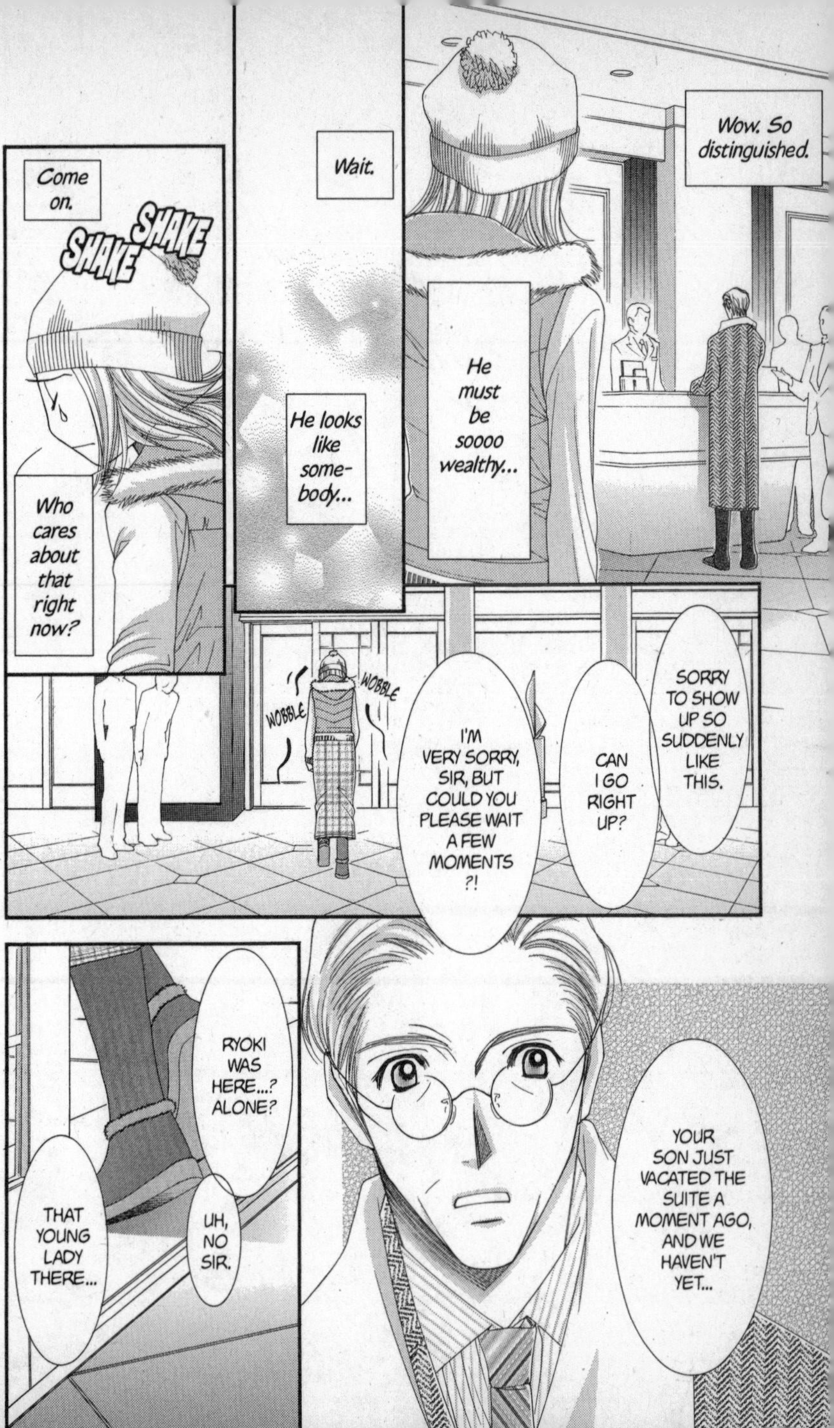
Wow. So distinguished.
He must be soooo wealthy...
Wait.
He looks like somebody...
Come on.
SHAKE SHAKE
Who cares about that right now?
SORRY TO SHOW UP SO SUDDENLY LIKE THIS.
CAN I GO RIGHT UP?
I'M VERY SORRY, SIR, BUT COULD YOU PLEASE WAIT A FEW MOMENTS?!
WOBBLE
WOBBLE
YOUR SON JUST VACATED THE SUITE A MOMENT AGO, AND WE HAVEN'T YET...
RYOKI WAS HERE...? ALONE?
UH, NO SIR.
THAT YOUNG LADY THERE...

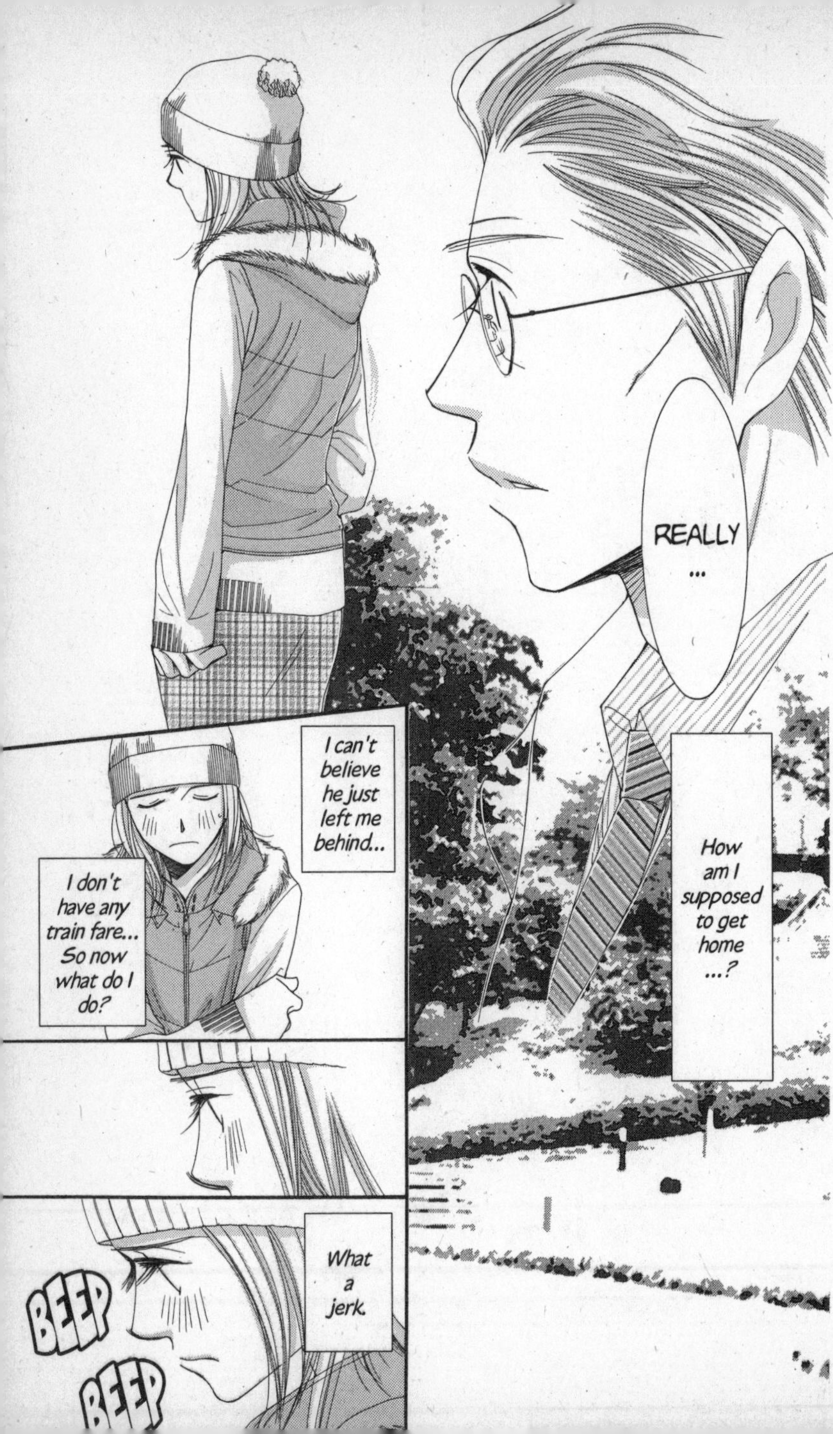
REALLY ...
How am I supposed to get home ...?
I can't believe he just left me behind...
I don't have any train fare... So now what do I do?
What a jerk.
BEEP
BEEP

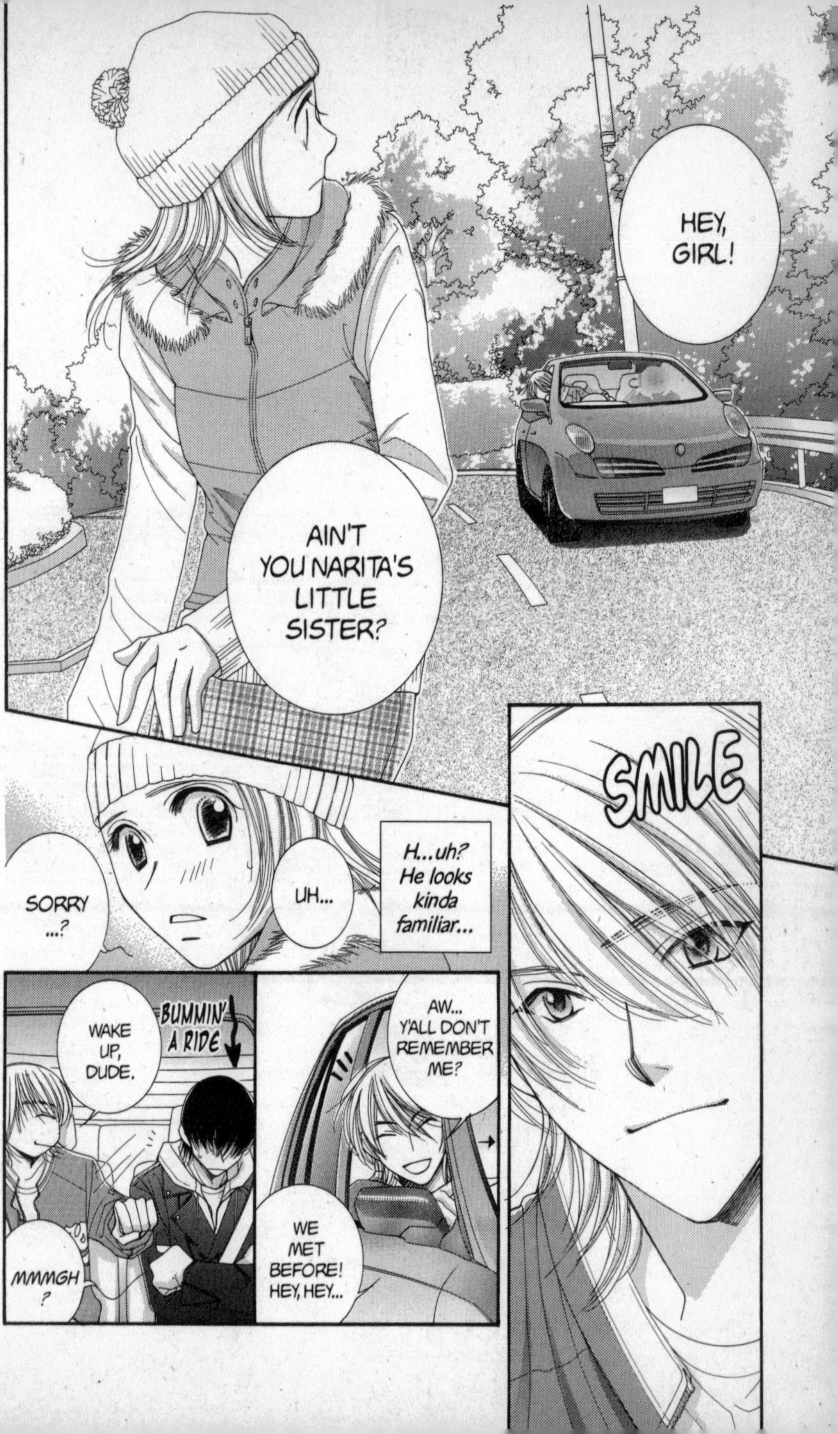
HEY, GIRL!
AIN'T YOU NARITA'S LITTLE SISTER?
SMILE
H...uh? He looks kinda familiar...
UH...
SORRY ...?
AW... Y'ALL DON'T REMEMBER ME?
WE MET BEFORE! HEY, HEY...
BUMMIN' A RIDE
WAKE UP, DUDE.
MMMGH ?

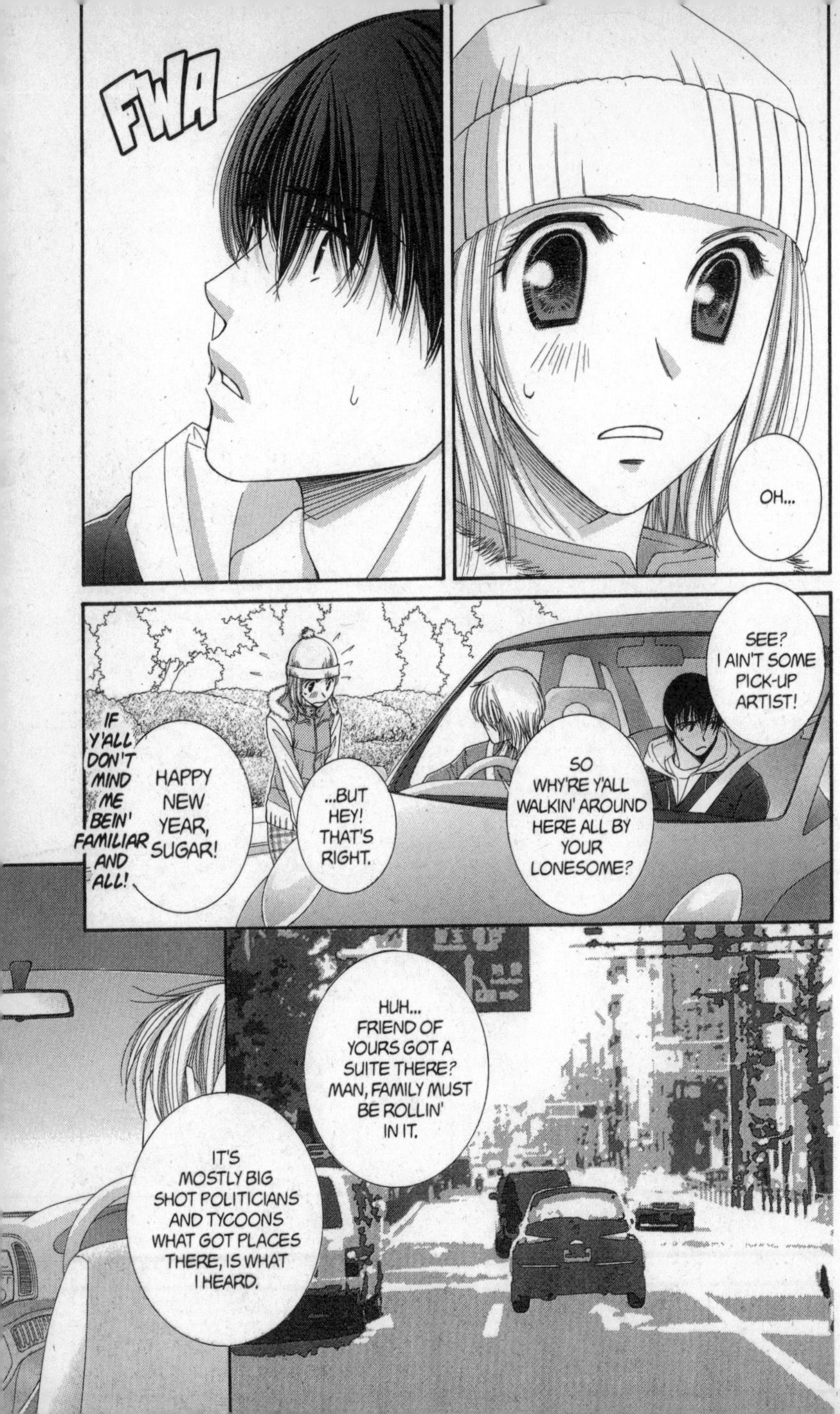
OH...
FWA
SEE? I AIN'T SOME PICK-UP ARTIST!
SO WHY'RE Y'ALL WALKIN' AROUND HERE ALL BY YOUR LONESOME?
...BUT HEY! THAT'S RIGHT.
HAPPY NEW YEAR, SUGAR!
IF Y'ALL DON'T MIND ME BEIN' FAMILIAR AND ALL!
HUH... FRIEND OF YOURS GOT A SUITE THERE? MAN, FAMILY MUST BE ROLLIN' IN IT.
IT'S MOSTLY BIG SHOT POLITICIANS AND TYCOONS WHAT GOT PLACES THERE, IS WHAT I HEARD.

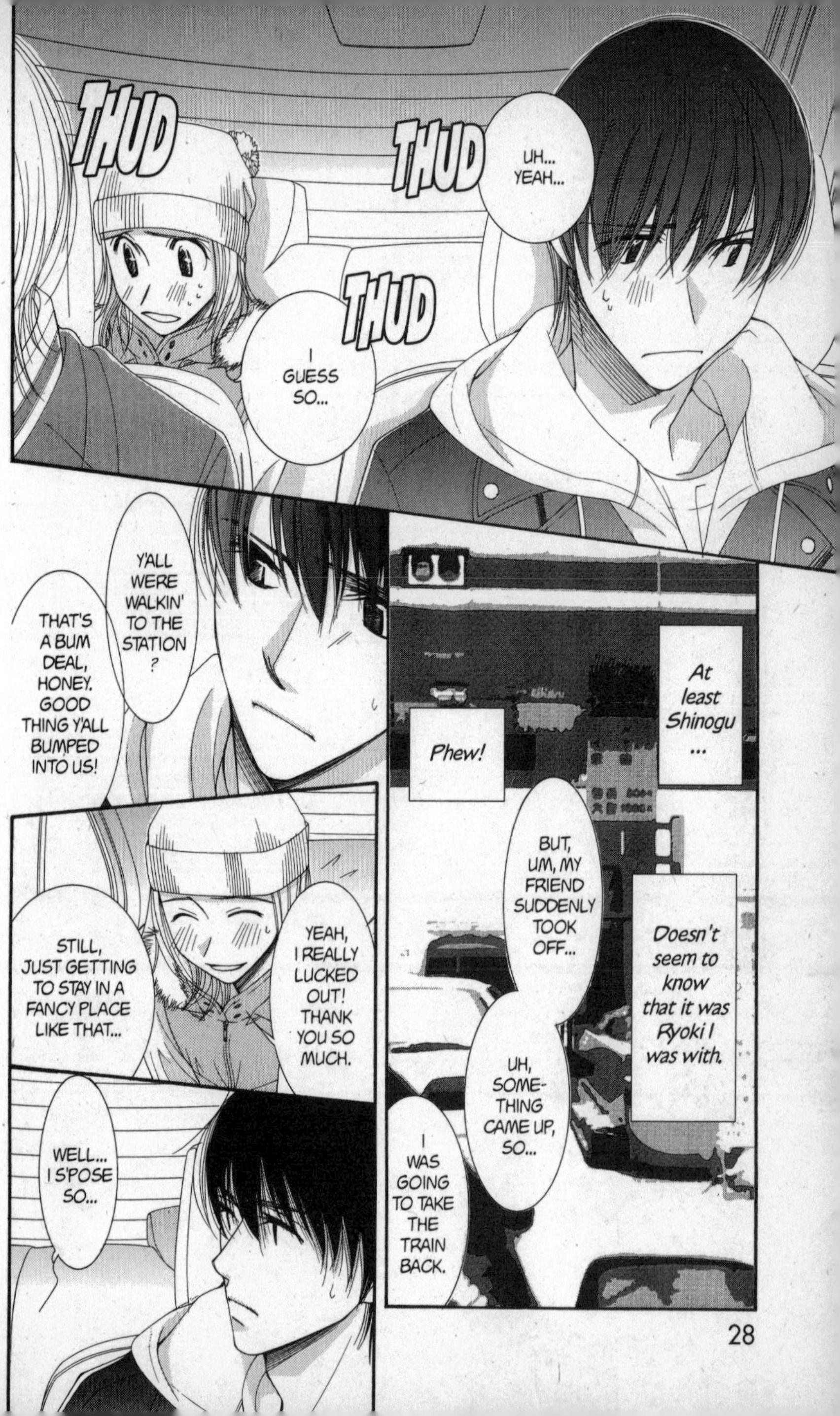
THUD
UH... YEAH...
THUD
THUD
I GUESS SO...
At least Shinogu...
Phew!
BUT, UM, MY FRIEND SUDDENLY TOOK OFF...
Doesn't seem to know that it was Ryoki I was with.
UH, SOME-THING CAME UP, SO...
I WAS GOING TO TAKE THE TRAIN BACK.
Y'ALL WERE WALKIN' TO THE STATION?
THAT'S A BUM DEAL, HONEY. GOOD THING Y'ALL BUMPED INTO US!
YEAH, I REALLY LUCKED OUT! THANK YOU SO MUCH.
STILL, JUST GETTING TO STAY IN A FANCY PLACE LIKE THAT...
WELL... I S'POSE SO...

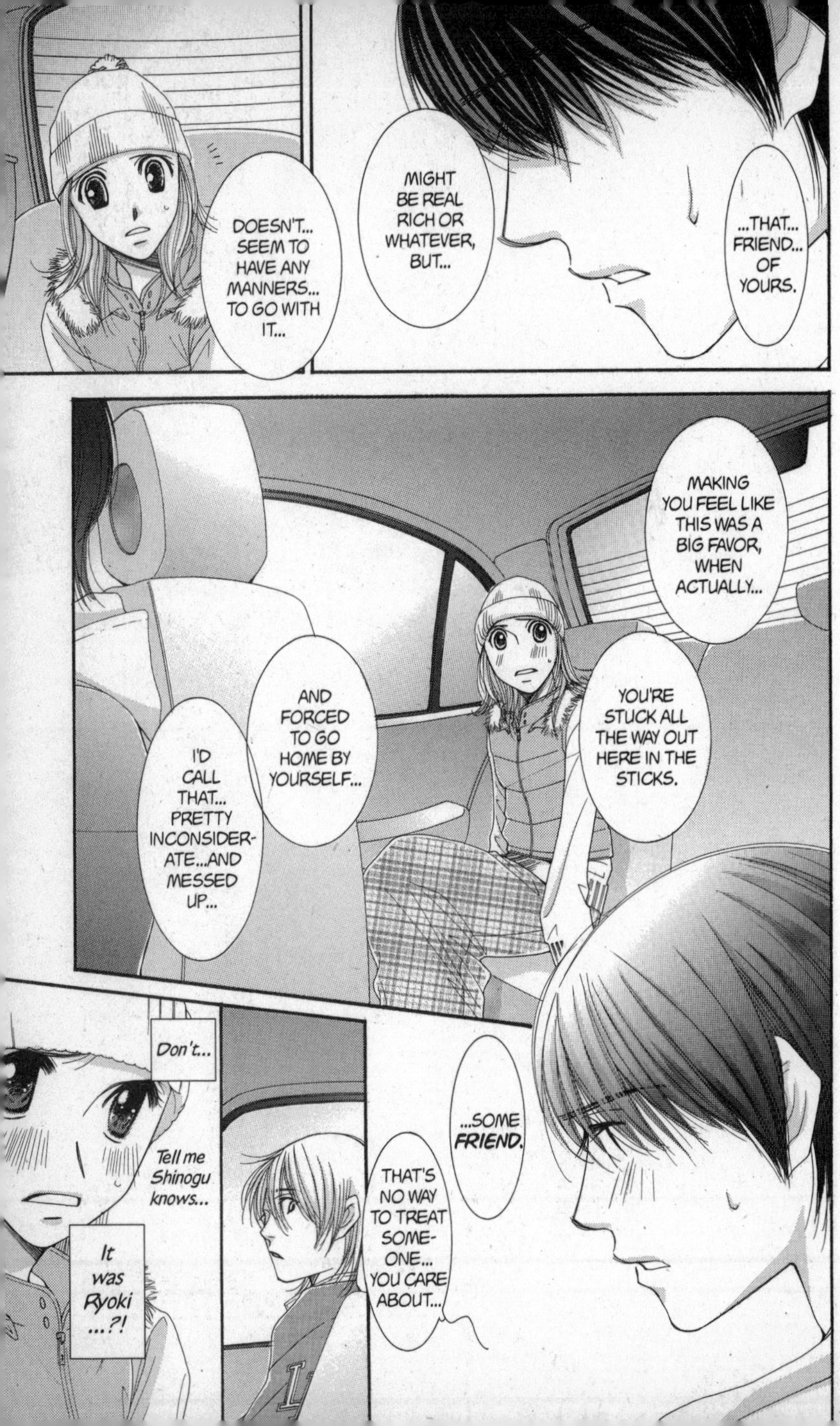
...THAT... FRIEND... OF YOURS.
MIGHT BE REAL RICH OR WHATEVER, BUT...
DOESN'T... SEEM TO HAVE ANY MANNERS... TO GO WITH IT...
MAKING YOU FEEL LIKE THIS WAS A BIG FAVOR, WHEN ACTUALLY...
YOU'RE STUCK ALL THE WAY OUT HERE IN THE STICKS.
AND FORCED TO GO HOME BY YOURSELF...
I'D CALL THAT... PRETTY INCONSIDER-ATE...AND MESSED UP...
...SOME FRIEND.
THAT'S NO WAY TO TREAT SOME-ONE... YOU CARE ABOUT...
Don't...
Tell me Shinogu knows...
It was Ryoki ...?!

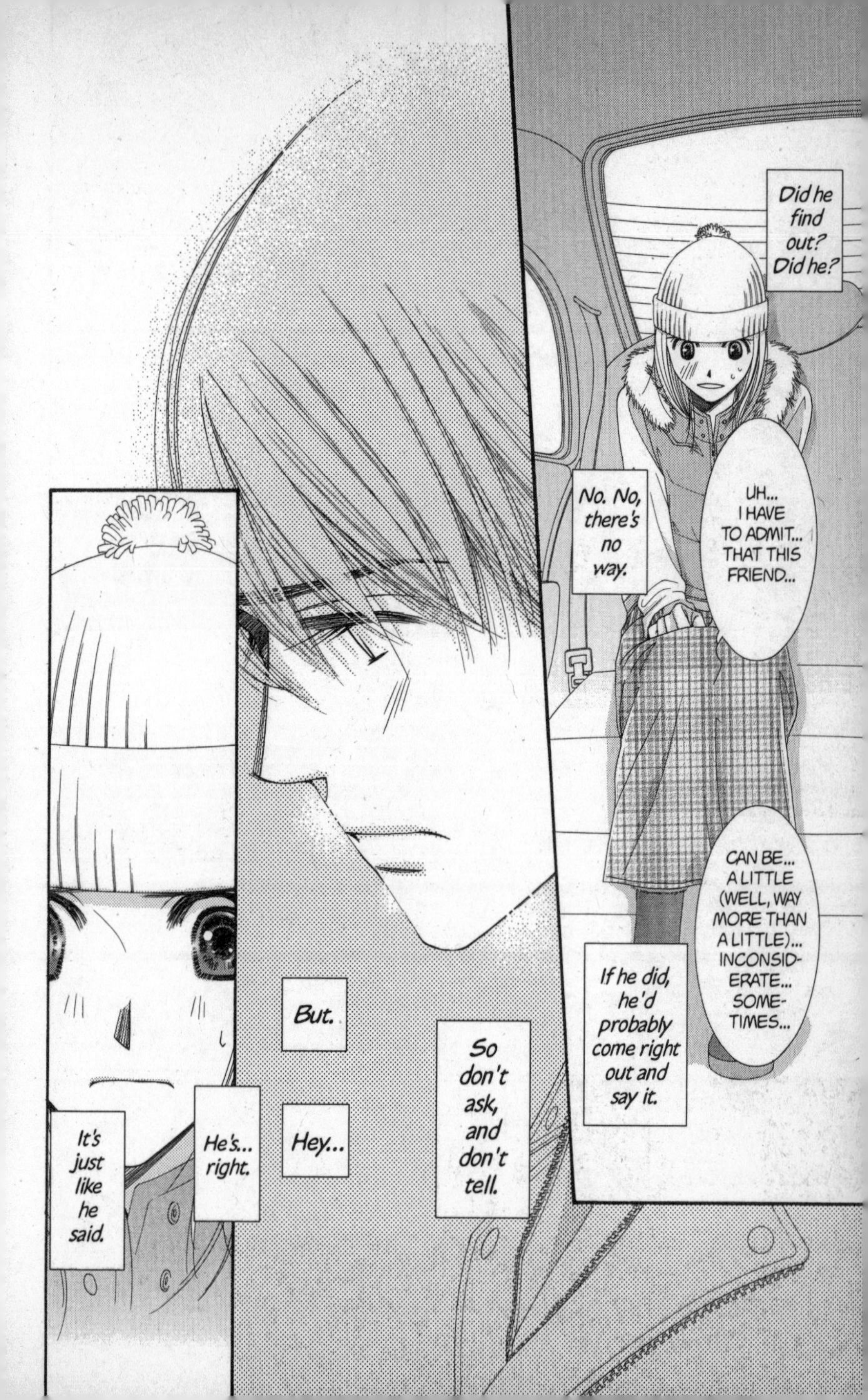
Did he find out? Did he?
UH... I HAVE TO ADMIT... THAT THIS FRIEND...
No. No, there's no way.
CAN BE... A LITTLE (WELL, WAY MORE THAN A LITTLE)... INCONSID-ERATE... SOME-TIMES...
If he did, he'd probably come right out and say it.
So don't ask, and don't tell.
But.
Hey...
He's... right.
It's just like he said.

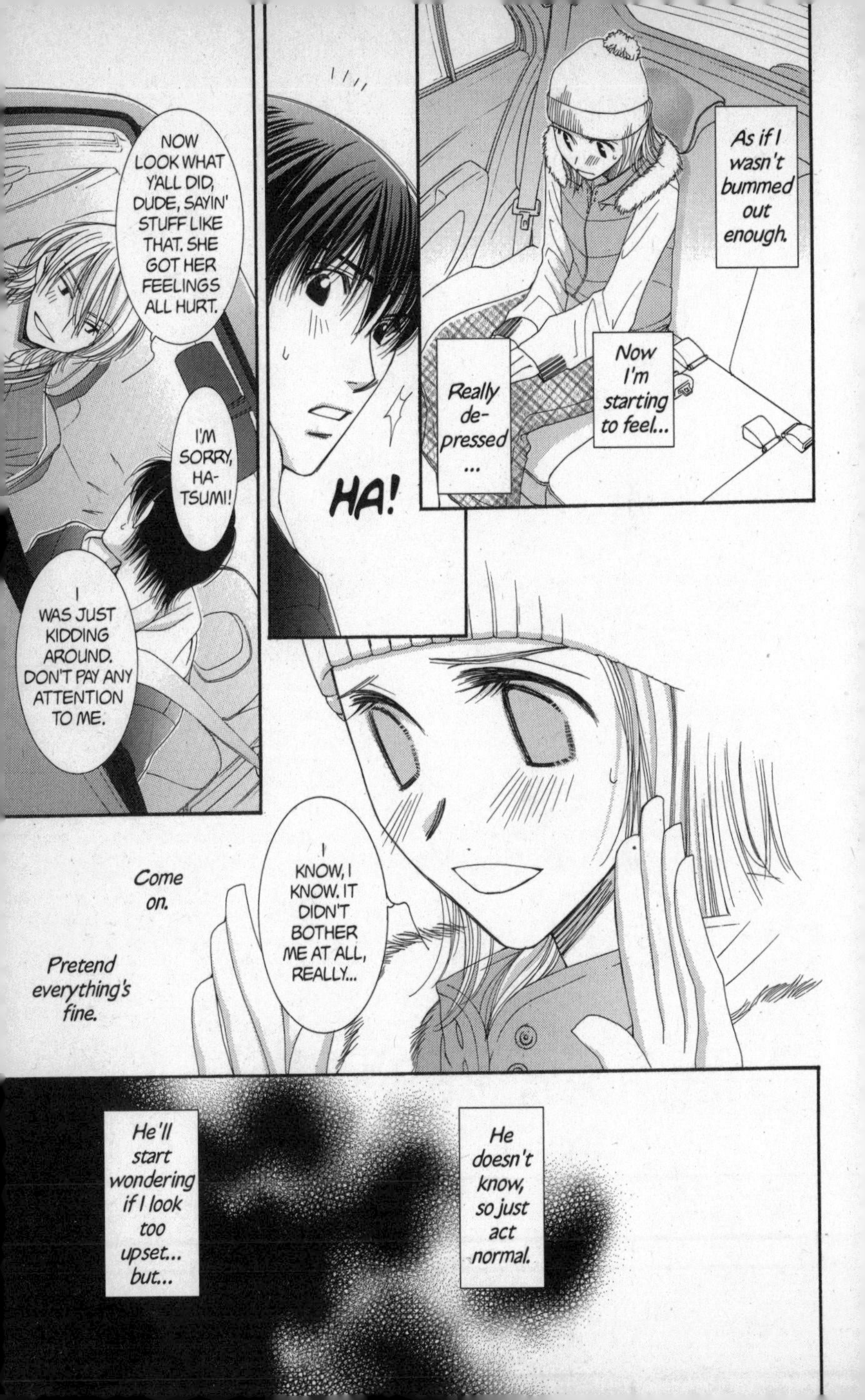
As if I wasn't bummed out enough.
Now I'm starting to feel...
Really de-pressed ...
HA!
NOW LOOK WHAT Y'ALL DID, DUDE, SAYIN' STUFF LIKE THAT. SHE GOT HER FEELINGS ALL HURT.
I'M SORRY, HA-TSUMI!
I WAS JUST KIDDING AROUND. DON'T PAY ANY ATTENTION TO ME.
I KNOW, I KNOW. IT DIDN'T BOTHER ME AT ALL, REALLY...
Come on.
Pretend everything's fine.
He doesn't know, so just act normal.
He'll start wondering if I look too upset... but...

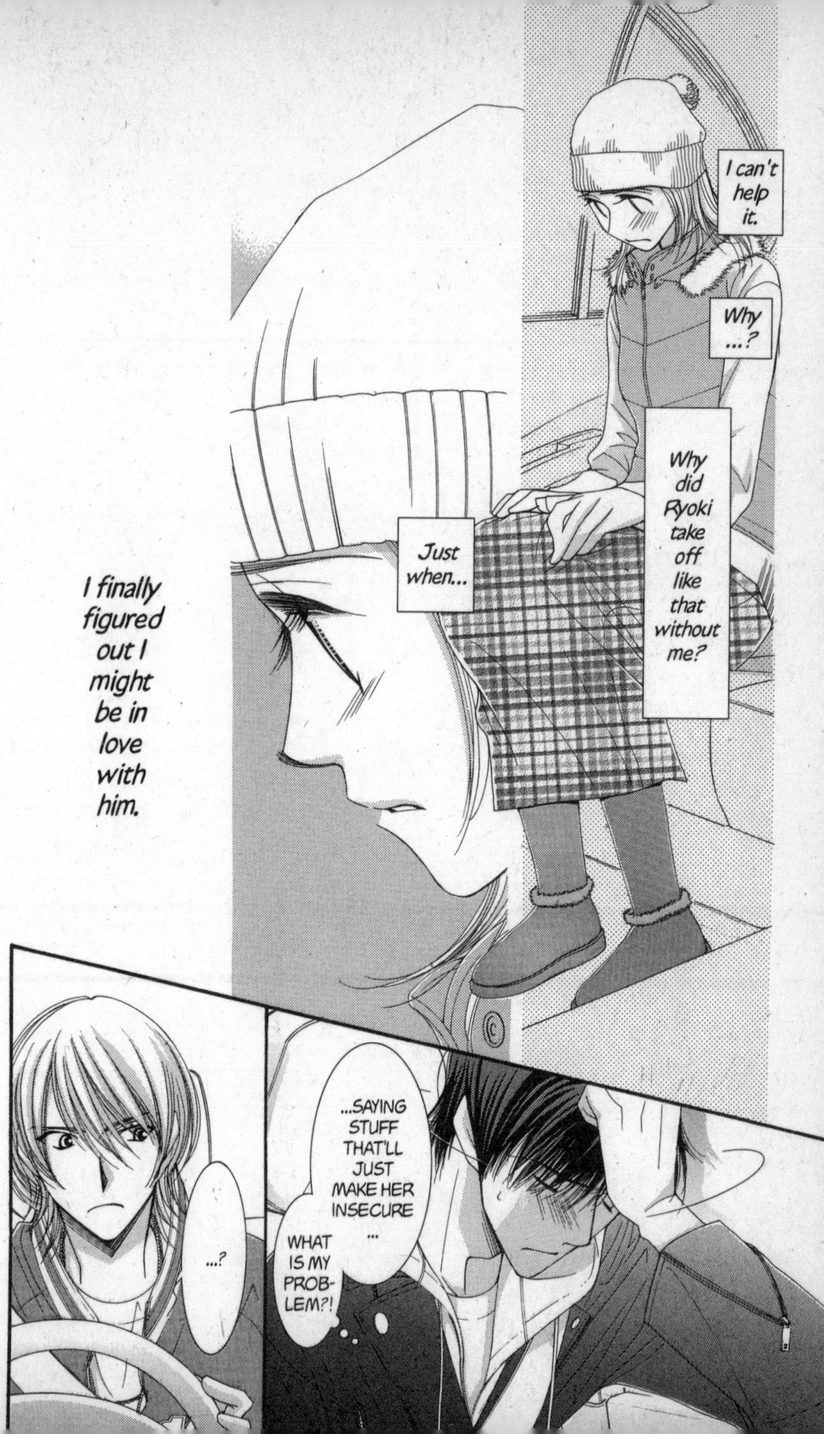
I can't help it.
Why ...?
Why did Ryoki take off like that without me?
Just when...
I finally figured out I might be in love with him.
...SAYING STUFF THAT'LL JUST MAKE HER INSECURE ...
WHAT IS MY PROB-LEM?!
...?

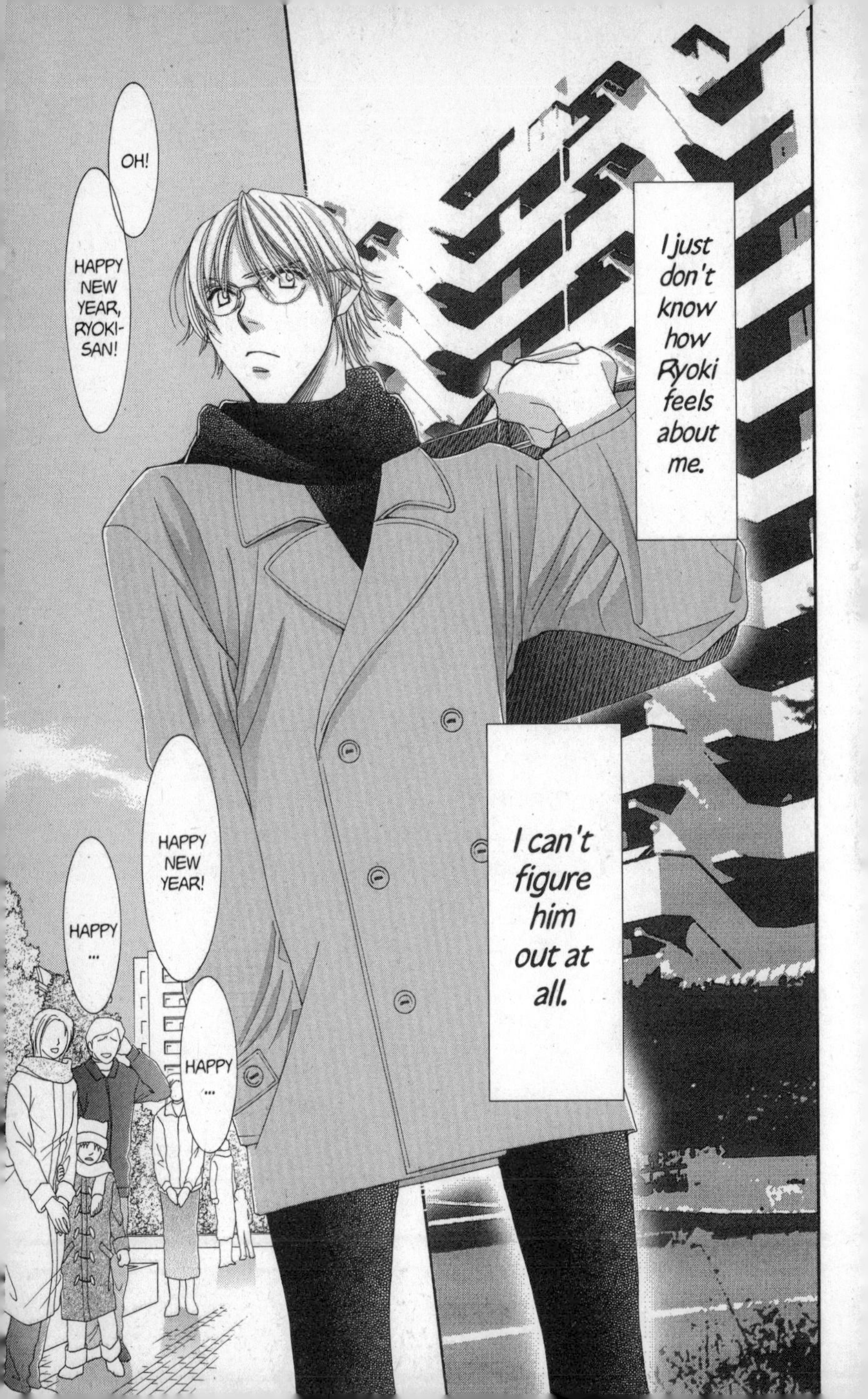

I just don't know how Ryoki feels about me.
OH!
HAPPY NEW YEAR, RYOKI-SAN!
I can't figure him out at all.
HAPPY NEW YEAR!
HAPPY ...
HAPPY ...

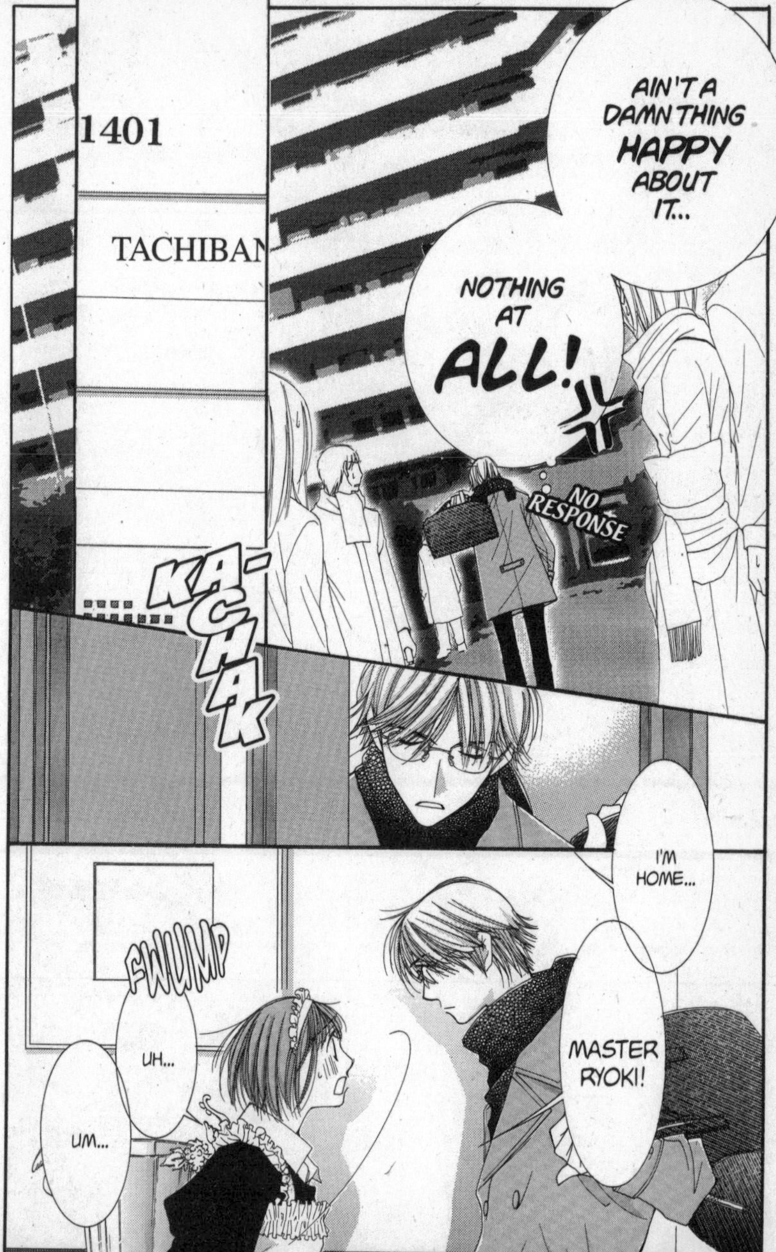
1401
TACHIBAN
AIN'T A DAMN THING HAPPY ABOUT IT...
NOTHING AT ALL!
NO RESPONSE
KA-CHAK
I'M HOME...
MASTER RYOKI!
FWUMP
UH...
UM...

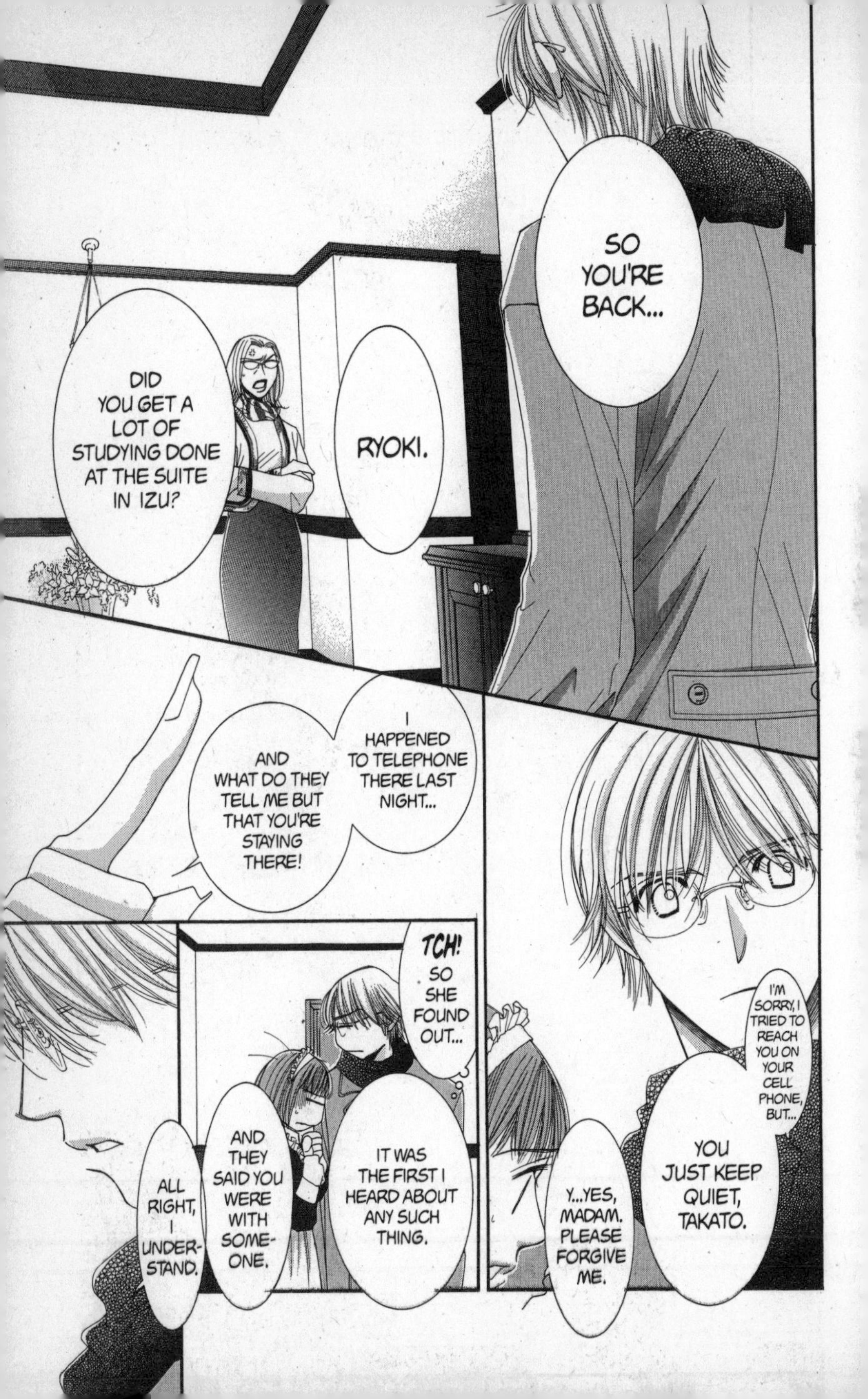
SO YOU'RE BACK...
RYOKI.
DID YOU GET A LOT OF STUDYING DONE AT THE SUITE IN IZU?
I'M SORRY, I TRIED TO REACH YOU ON YOUR CELL PHONE, BUT...
YOU JUST KEEP QUIET, TAKATO.
Y...YES, MADAM. PLEASE FORGIVE ME.
I HAPPENED TO TELEPHONE THERE LAST NIGHT...
AND WHAT DO THEY TELL ME BUT THAT YOU'RE STAYING THERE!
TCH! SO SHE FOUND OUT...
IT WAS THE FIRST I HEARD ABOUT ANY SUCH THING.
AND THEY SAID YOU WERE WITH SOMEONE.
ALL RIGHT, I UNDERSTAND.

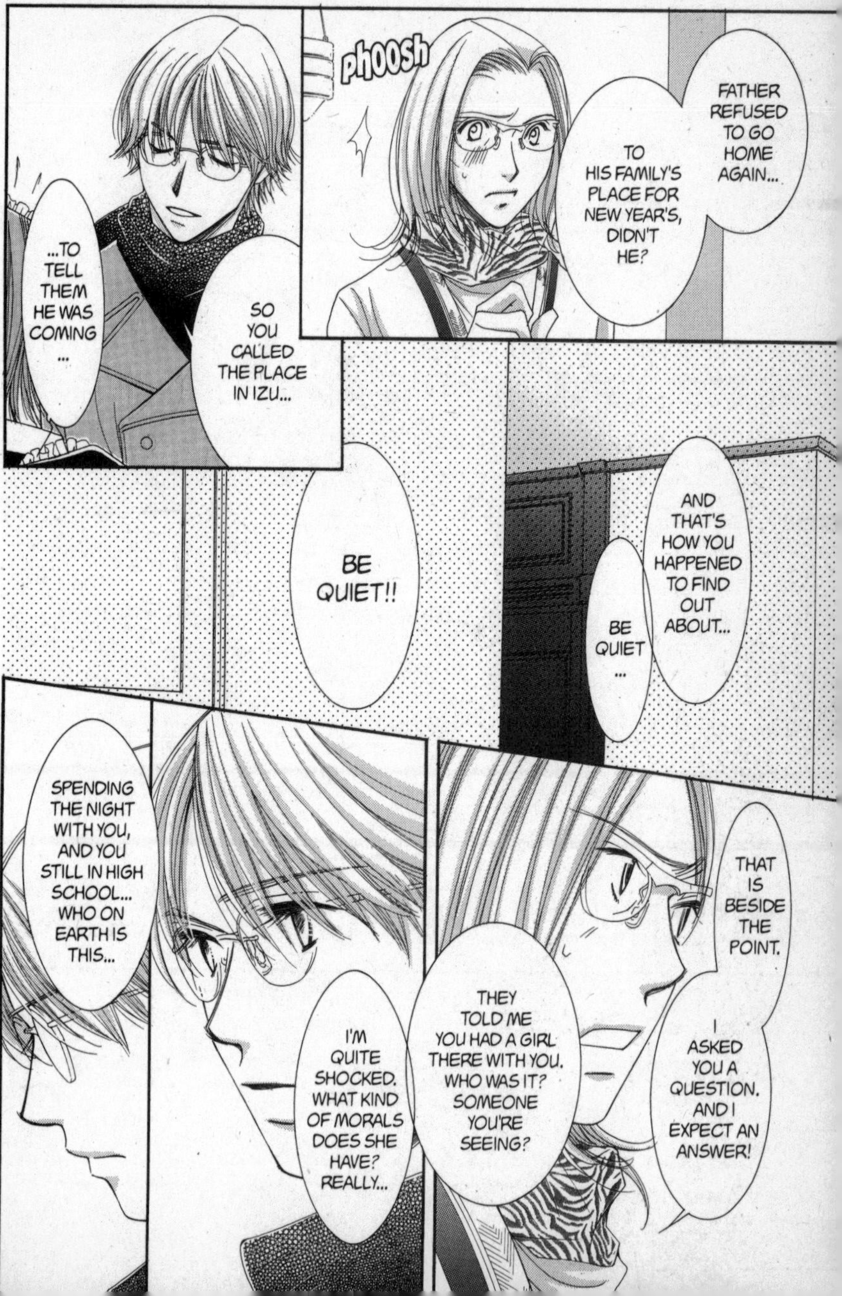
phoosh
FATHER REFUSED TO GO HOME AGAIN...
TO HIS FAMILY'S PLACE FOR NEW YEAR'S, DIDN'T HE?
SO YOU CALLED THE PLACE IN IZU...
...TO TELL THEM HE WAS COMING ...
AND THAT'S HOW YOU HAPPENED TO FIND OUT ABOUT...
BE QUIET ...
BE QUIET!!
THAT IS BESIDE THE POINT.
I ASKED YOU A QUESTION. AND I EXPECT AN ANSWER!
THEY TOLD ME YOU HAD A GIRL THERE WITH YOU. WHO WAS IT? SOMEONE YOU'RE SEEING?
I'M QUITE SHOCKED. WHAT KIND OF MORALS DOES SHE HAVE? REALLY...
SPENDING THE NIGHT WITH YOU, AND YOU STILL IN HIGH SCHOOL... WHO ON EARTH IS THIS...

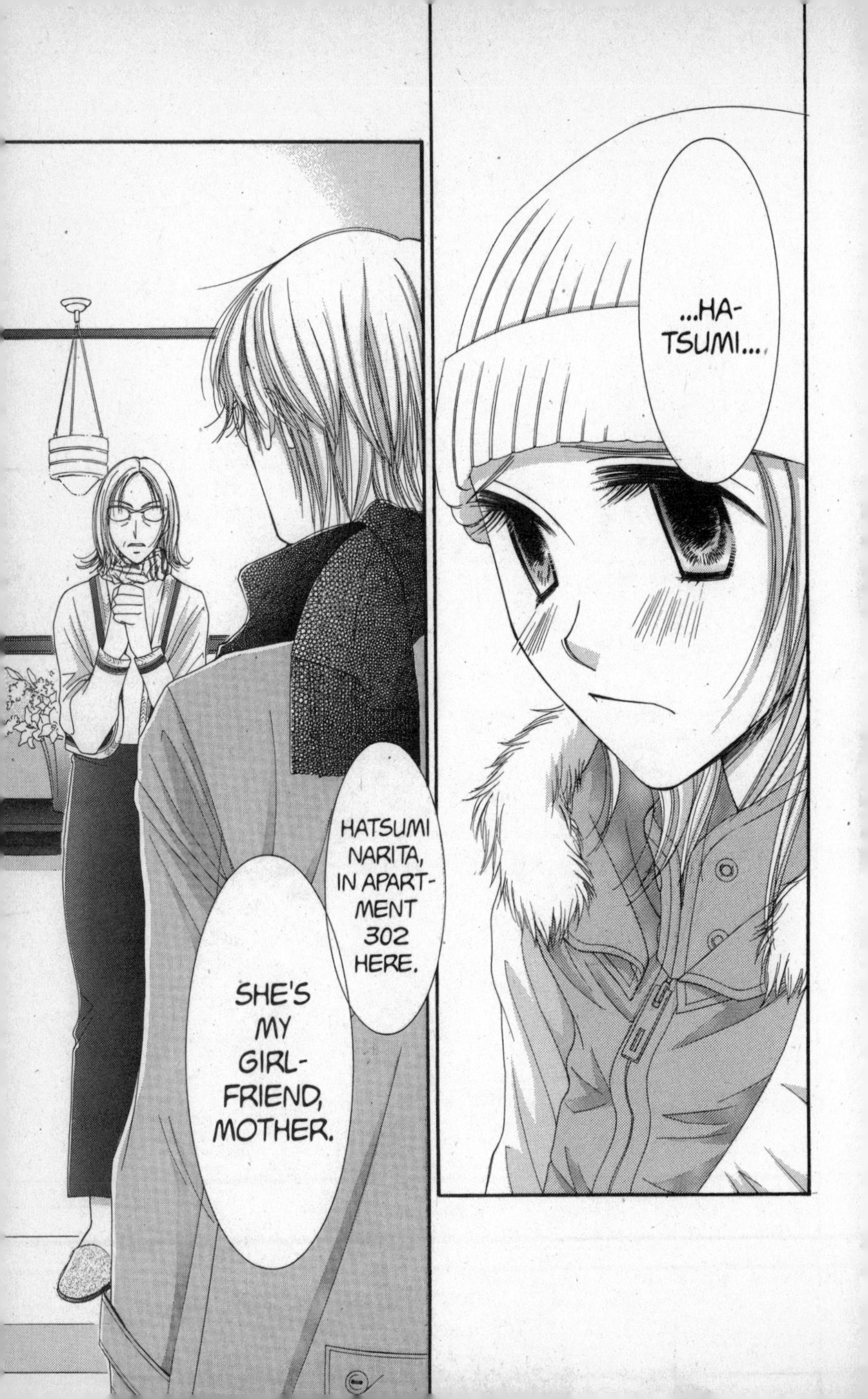
...HA-TSUMI...
HATSUMI NARITA, IN APARTMENT 302 HERE.
SHE'S MY GIRLFRIEND, MOTHER.

Egad! He told her...

What the maid saw...
Part 2

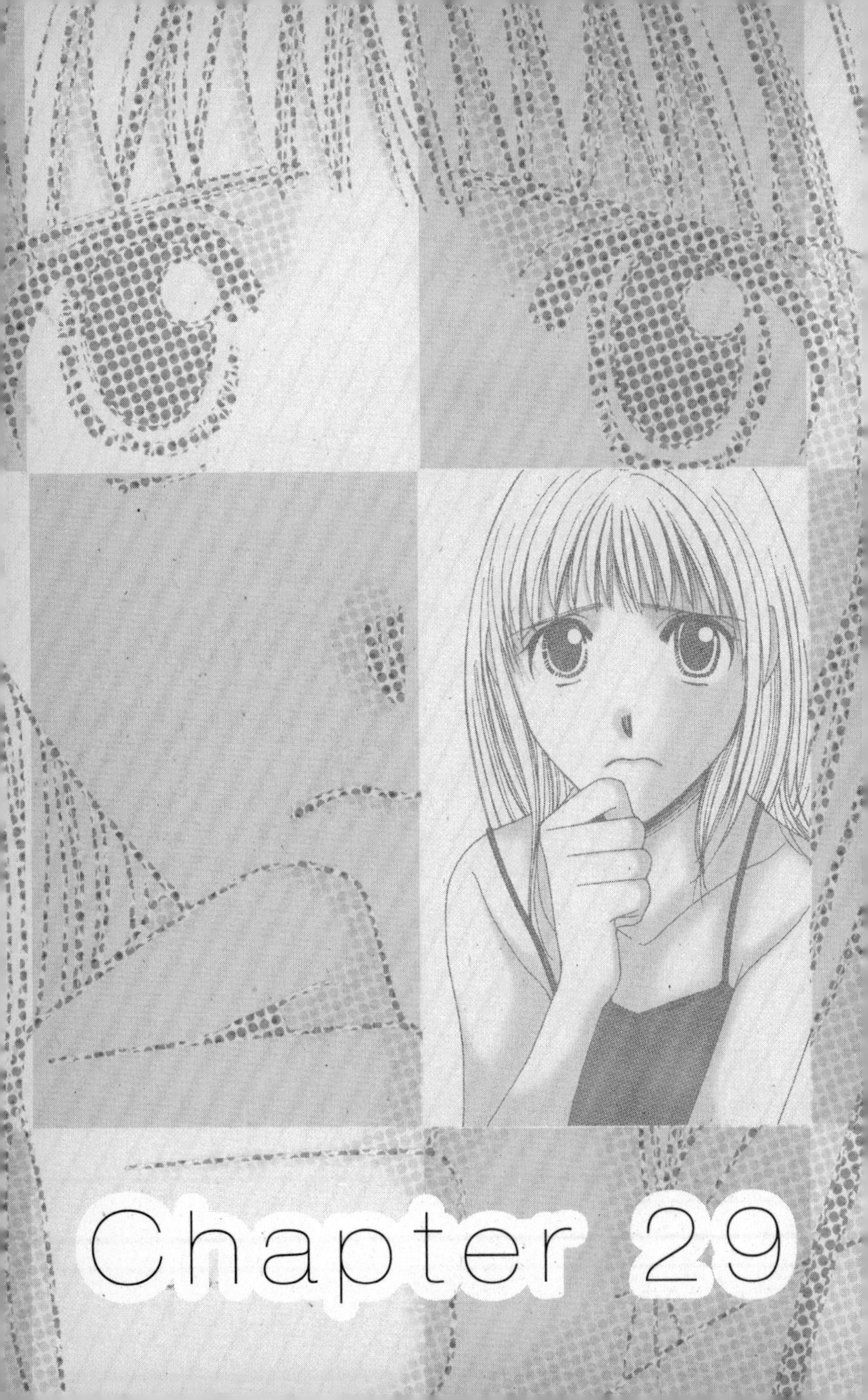
Chapter 29

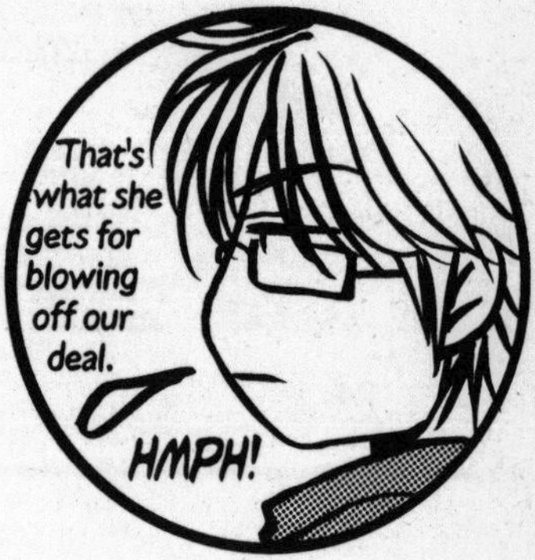
That's what she gets for blowing off our deal.
HMPH!

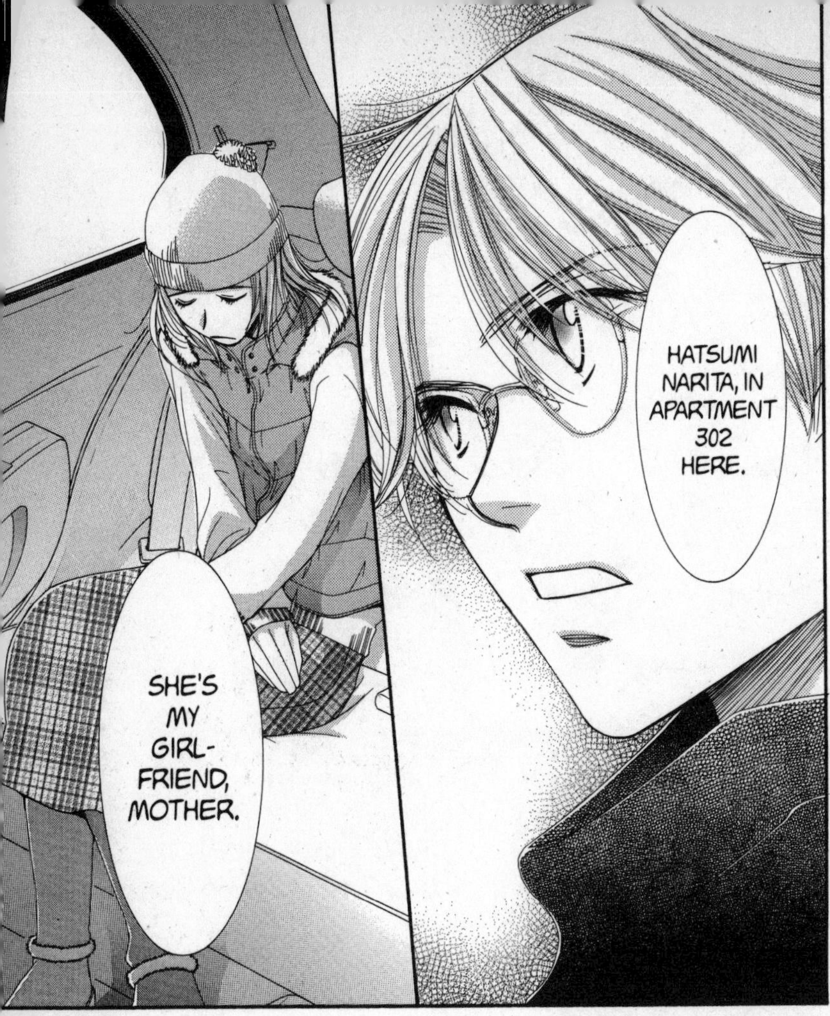
HATSUMI NARITA, IN APARTMENT 302 HERE.
SHE'S MY GIRL-FRIEND, MOTHER.

hot gimmick

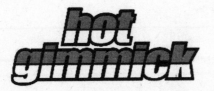

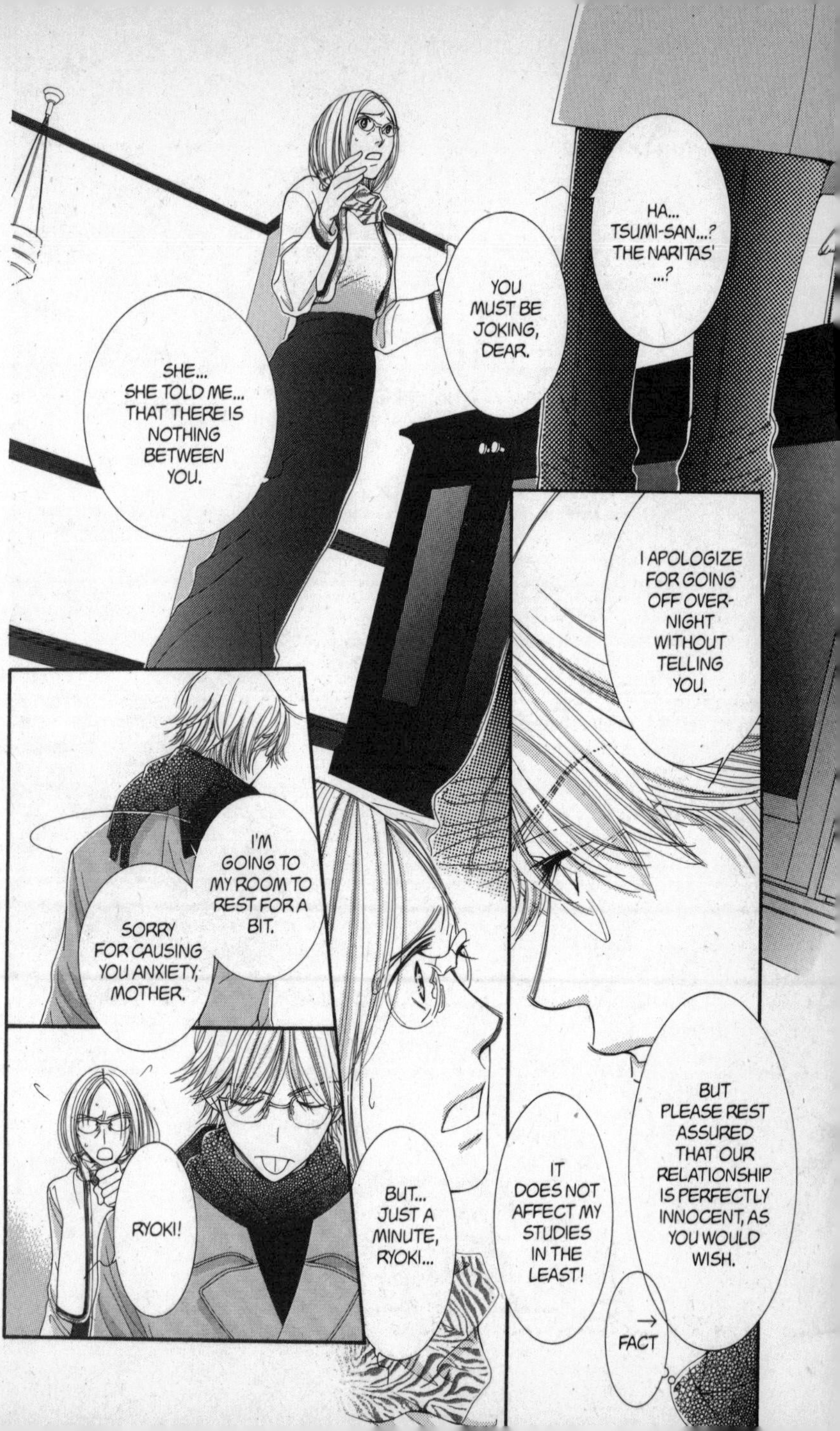
HA... TSUMI-SAN...? THE NARITAS' ...?
YOU MUST BE JOKING, DEAR.
SHE... SHE TOLD ME... THAT THERE IS NOTHING BETWEEN YOU.
I APOLOGIZE FOR GOING OFF OVER-NIGHT WITHOUT TELLING YOU.
BUT PLEASE REST ASSURED THAT OUR RELATIONSHIP IS PERFECTLY INNOCENT, AS YOU WOULD WISH.
→ FACT
IT DOES NOT AFFECT MY STUDIES IN THE LEAST!
BUT... JUST A MINUTE, RYOKI...
I'M GOING TO MY ROOM TO REST FOR A BIT.
SORRY FOR CAUSING YOU ANXIETY, MOTHER.
RYOKI!

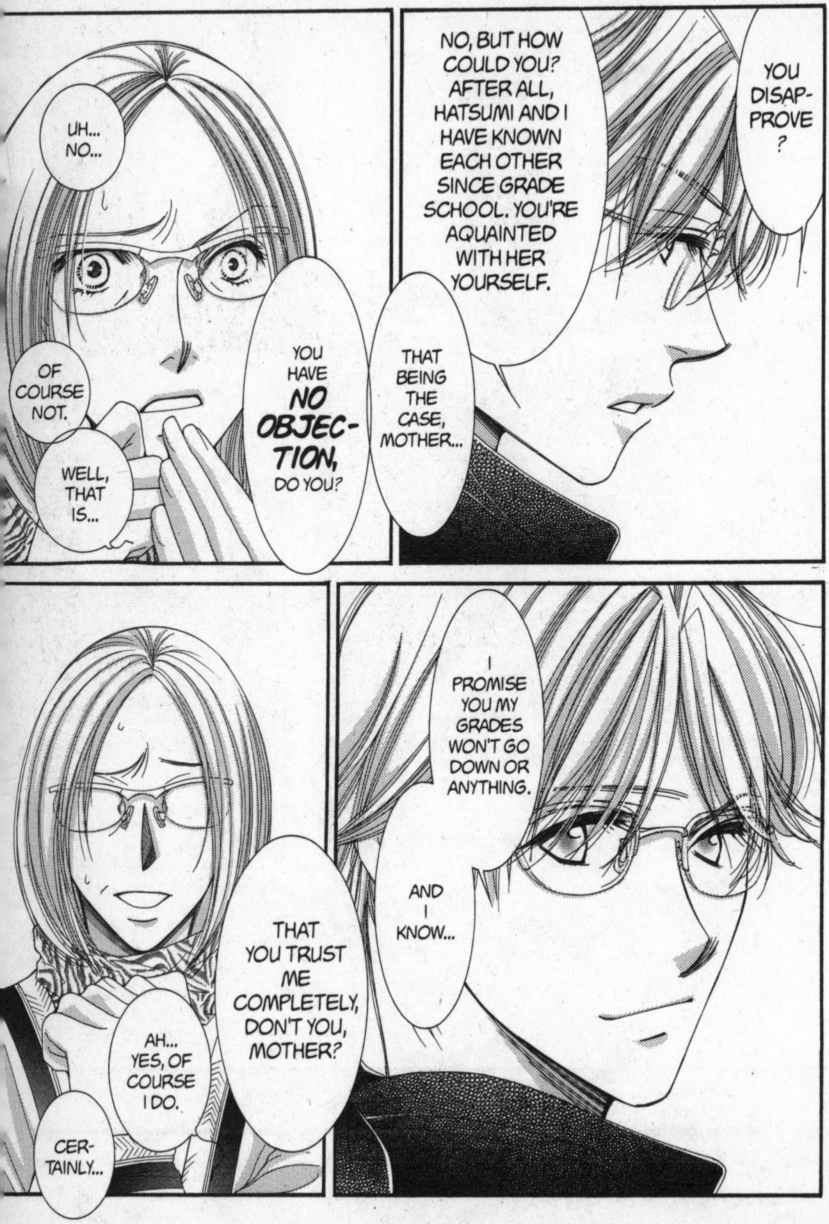
YOU DISAP-PROVE?
NO, BUT HOW COULD YOU? AFTER ALL, HATSUMI AND I HAVE KNOWN EACH OTHER SINCE GRADE SCHOOL. YOU'RE AQUAINTED WITH HER YOURSELF.
THAT BEING THE CASE, MOTHER...
YOU HAVE **NO OBJEC-TION,** DO YOU?
UH... NO...
OF COURSE NOT.
WELL, THAT IS...
I PROMISE YOU MY GRADES WON'T GO DOWN OR ANYTHING.
AND I KNOW...
THAT YOU TRUST ME COMPLETELY, DON'T YOU, MOTHER?
AH... YES, OF COURSE I DO.
CER-TAINLY...

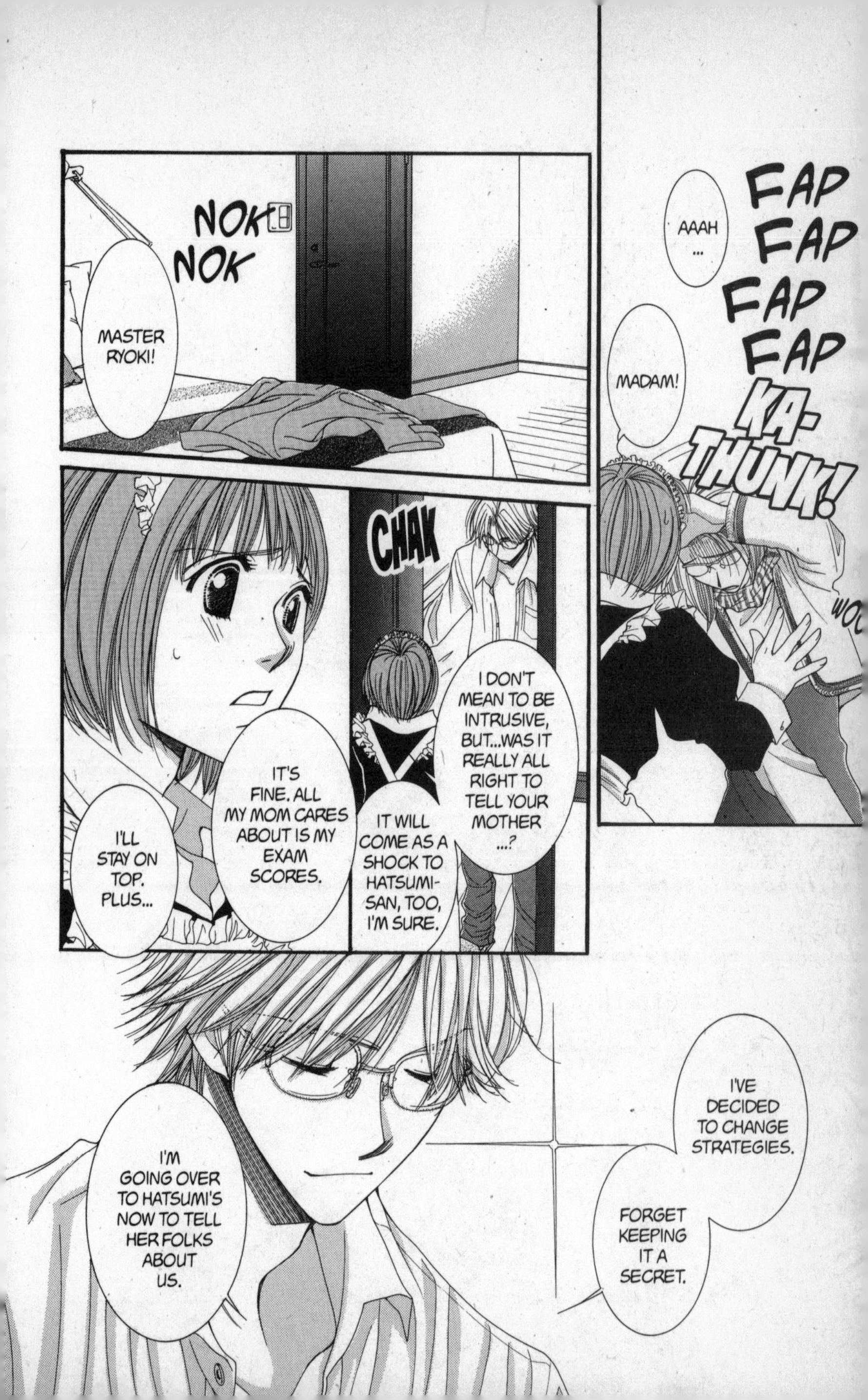
AAAH ...
MADAM!
FAP FAP FAP FAP
KA-THUNK!
NOK NOK
MASTER RYOKI!
CHAK
I DON'T MEAN TO BE INTRUSIVE, BUT...WAS IT REALLY ALL RIGHT TO TELL YOUR MOTHER ...?
IT WILL COME AS A SHOCK TO HATSUMI-SAN, TOO, I'M SURE.
IT'S FINE. ALL MY MOM CARES ABOUT IS MY EXAM SCORES.
I'LL STAY ON TOP. PLUS...
I'VE DECIDED TO CHANGE STRATEGIES.
FORGET KEEPING IT A SECRET.
I'M GOING OVER TO HATSUMI'S NOW TO TELL HER FOLKS ABOUT US.

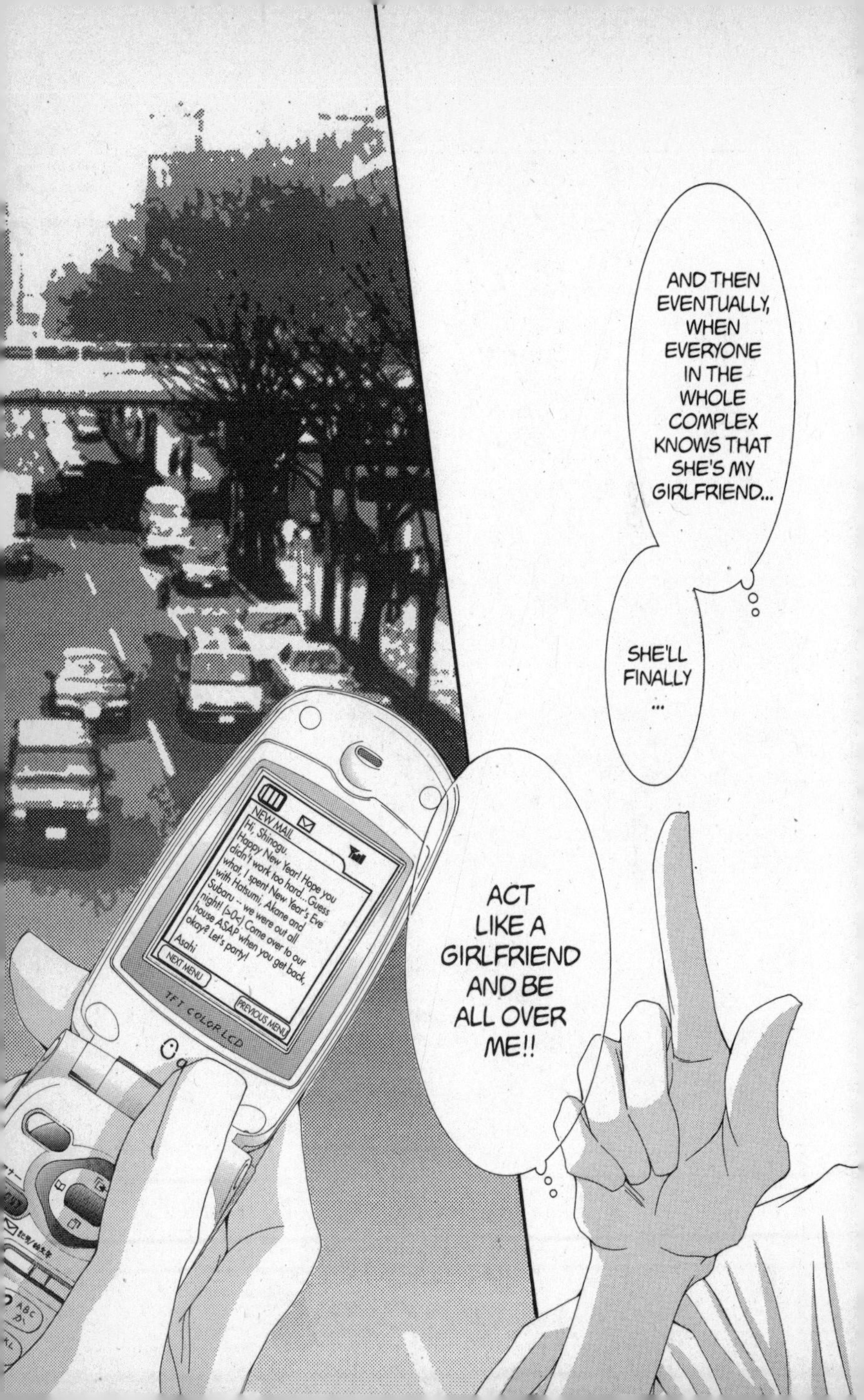
AND THEN EVENTUALLY, WHEN EVERYONE IN THE WHOLE COMPLEX KNOWS THAT SHE'S MY GIRLFRIEND...
SHE'LL FINALLY ...
ACT LIKE A GIRLFRIEND AND BE ALL OVER ME!!
NEW MAIL
Hi, Shinogu. Happy New Year! Hope you didn't work too hard...Guess what, I spent New Year's Eve with Hatsumi, Akane and Subaru -- we were out all night! [>0<] Come over to our house ASAP when you get back, okay? Let's party!
Asahi
NEXT MENU
PREVIOUS MENU
TFT COLOR LCD

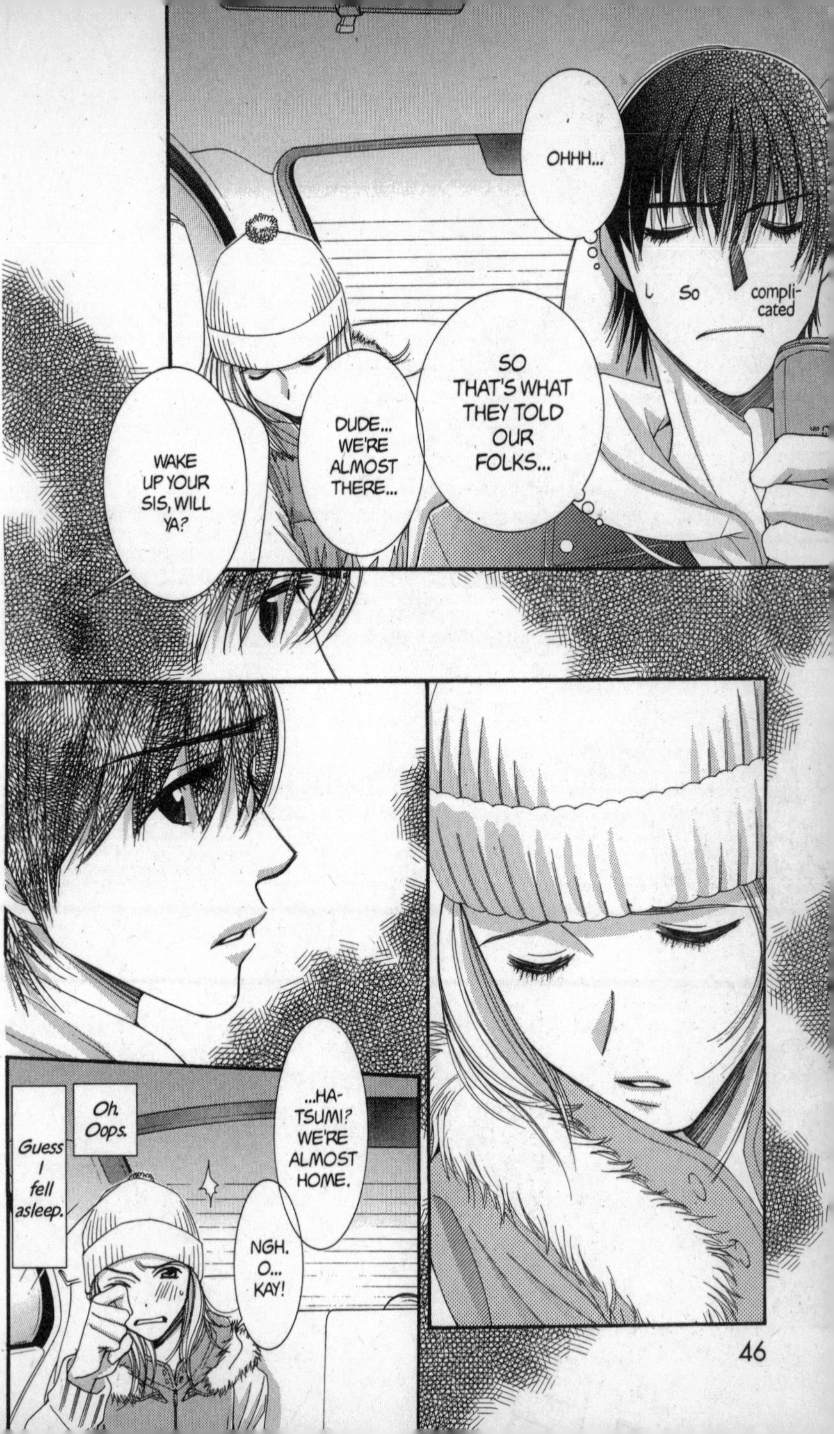
OHHH...
So complicated
SO THAT'S WHAT THEY TOLD OUR FOLKS...
DUDE... WE'RE ALMOST THERE...
WAKE UP YOUR SIS, WILL YA?
...HA-TSUMI? WE'RE ALMOST HOME.
NGH. O... KAY!
Oh. Oops.
Guess I fell asleep.

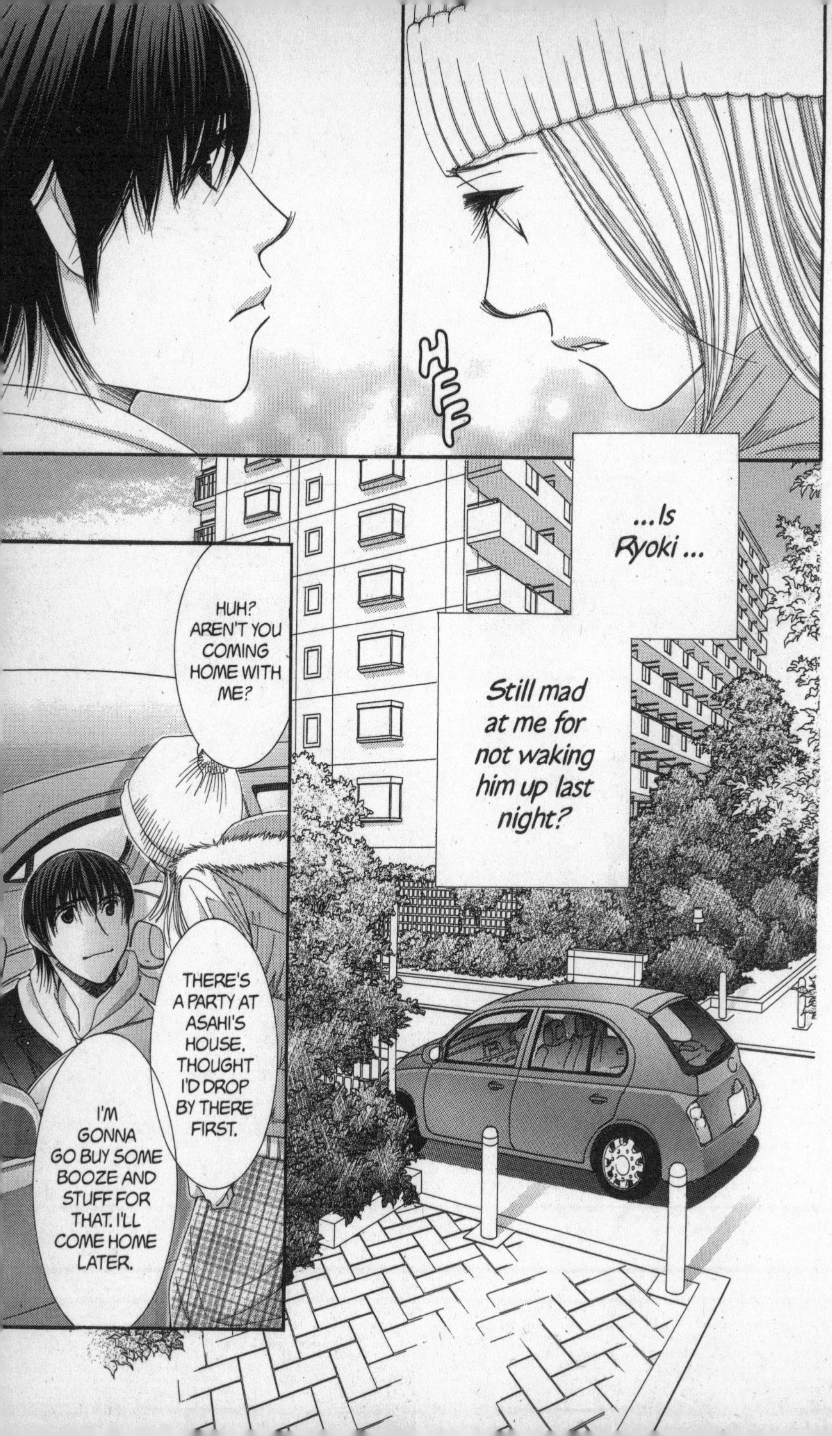
HEFF
...Is Ryoki ...
Still mad at me for not waking him up last night?
HUH? AREN'T YOU COMING HOME WITH ME?
THERE'S A PARTY AT ASAHI'S HOUSE. THOUGHT I'D DROP BY THERE FIRST.
I'M GONNA GO BUY SOME BOOZE AND STUFF FOR THAT. I'LL COME HOME LATER.

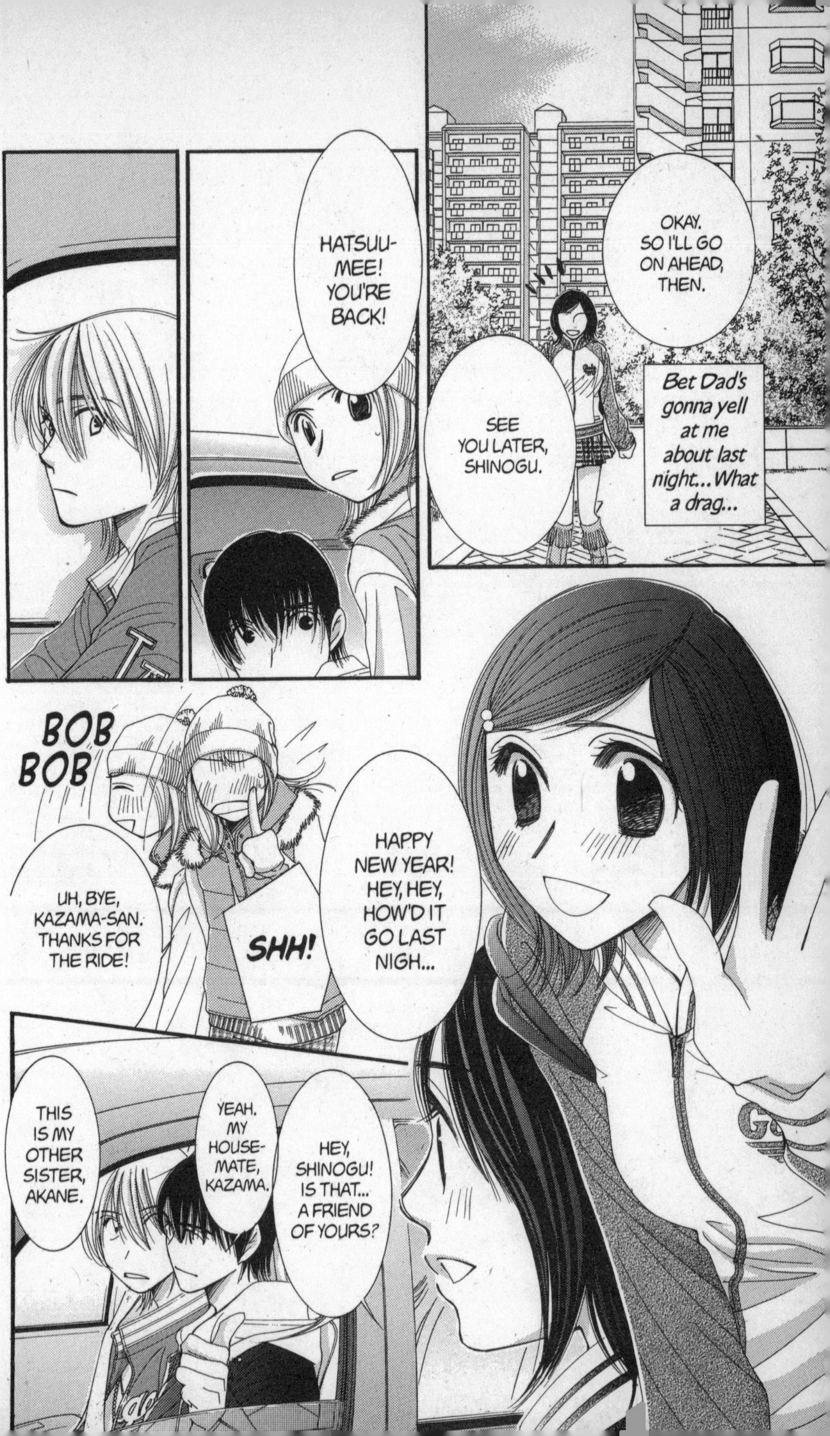
OKAY. SO I'LL GO ON AHEAD, THEN.
Bet Dad's gonna yell at me about last night...What a drag...
SEE YOU LATER, SHINOGU.
HATSUU-MEE! YOU'RE BACK!
HAPPY NEW YEAR! HEY, HEY, HOW'D IT GO LAST NIGH...
SHH!
BOB BOB
UH, BYE, KAZAMA-SAN. THANKS FOR THE RIDE!
HEY, SHINOGU! IS THAT... A FRIEND OF YOURS?
YEAH. MY HOUSE-MATE, KAZAMA.
THIS IS MY OTHER SISTER, AKANE.

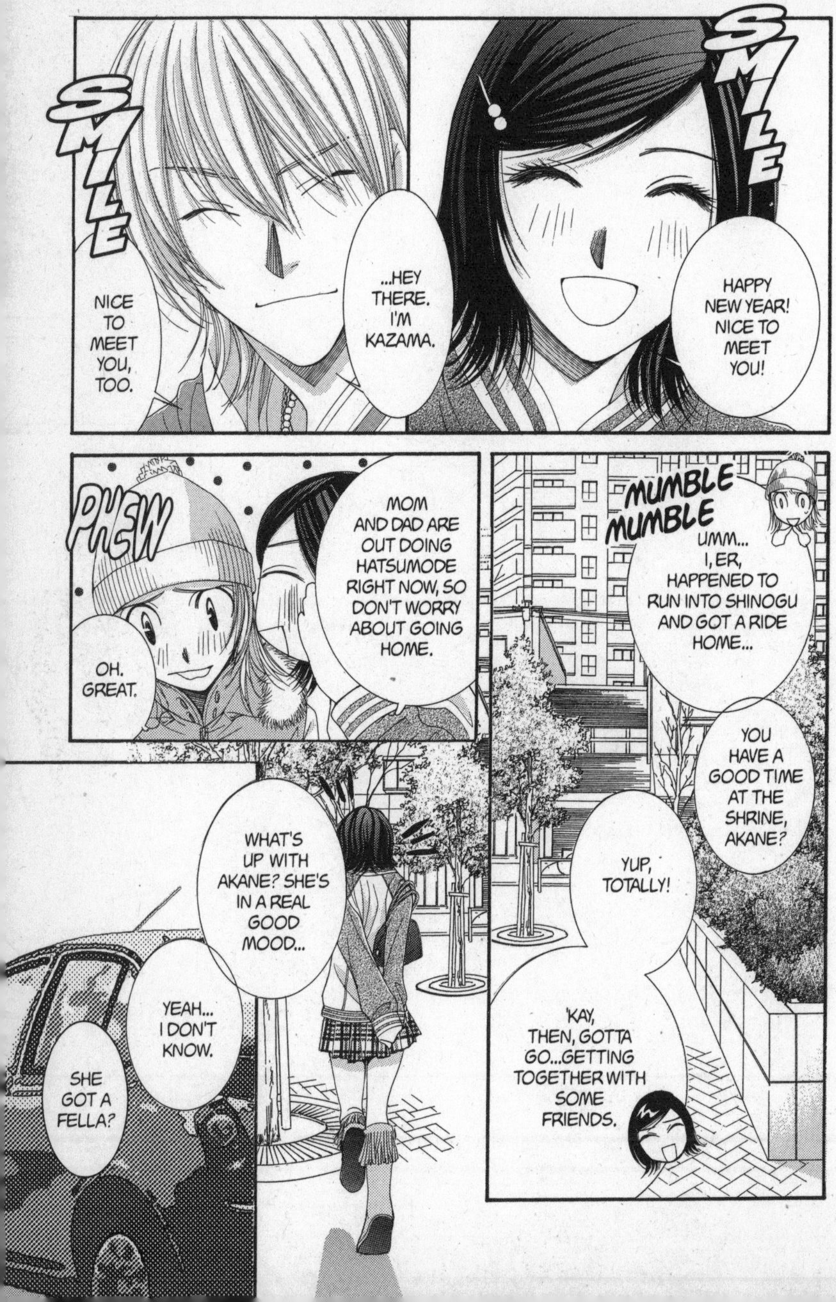
SMILE
HAPPY NEW YEAR! NICE TO MEET YOU!
SMILE
...HEY THERE. I'M KAZAMA.
NICE TO MEET YOU, TOO.
MUMBLE MUMBLE
UMM... I, ER, HAPPENED TO RUN INTO SHINOGU AND GOT A RIDE HOME...
YOU HAVE A GOOD TIME AT THE SHRINE, AKANE?
YUP, TOTALLY!
'KAY, THEN, GOTTA GO...GETTING TOGETHER WITH SOME FRIENDS.
MOM AND DAD ARE OUT DOING HATSUMODE RIGHT NOW, SO DON'T WORRY ABOUT GOING HOME.
PHEW
OH. GREAT.
WHAT'S UP WITH AKANE? SHE'S IN A REAL GOOD MOOD...
YEAH... I DON'T KNOW.
SHE GOT A FELLA?

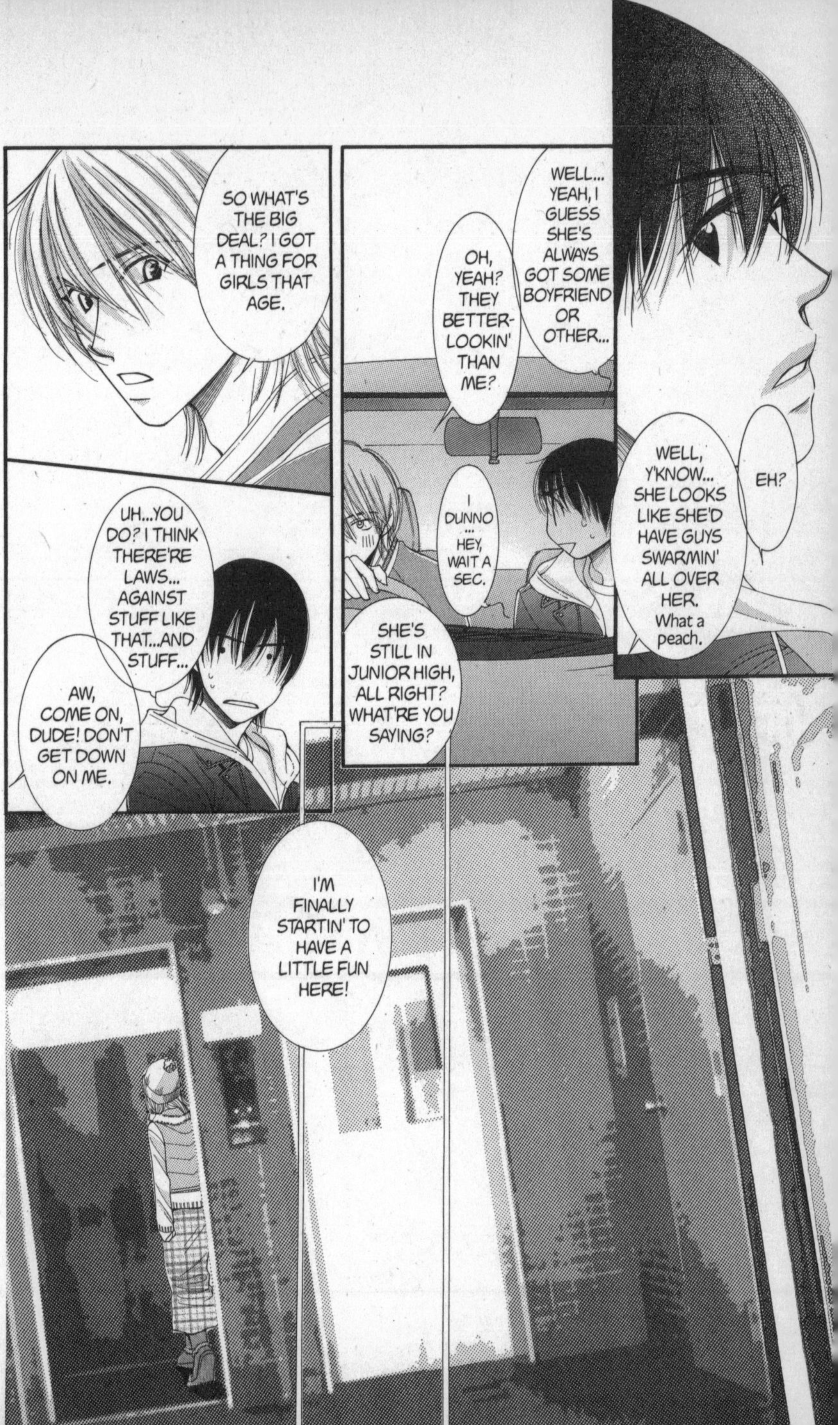

EH?
WELL, Y'KNOW... SHE LOOKS LIKE SHE'D HAVE GUYS SWARMIN' ALL OVER HER. What a peach.
WELL... YEAH, I GUESS SHE'S ALWAYS GOT SOME BOYFRIEND OR OTHER...
OH, YEAH? THEY BETTER-LOOKIN' THAN ME?
I DUNNO... HEY, WAIT A SEC.
SHE'S STILL IN JUNIOR HIGH, ALL RIGHT? WHAT'RE YOU SAYING?
SO WHAT'S THE BIG DEAL? I GOT A THING FOR GIRLS THAT AGE.
UH...YOU DO? I THINK THERE'RE LAWS... AGAINST STUFF LIKE THAT...AND STUFF...
AW, COME ON, DUDE! DON'T GET DOWN ON ME.
I'M FINALLY STARTIN' TO HAVE A LITTLE FUN HERE!

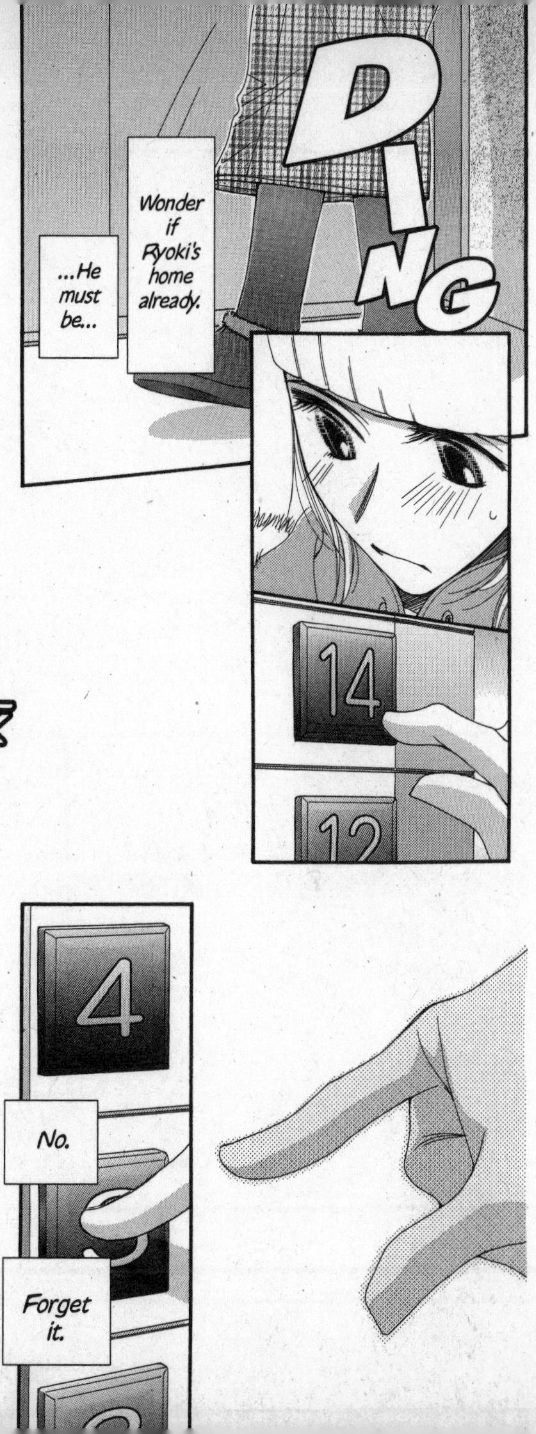
DING
Wonder if Ryoki's home already.
...He must be...
14
12
4
No.
Forget it.

hotgimmick

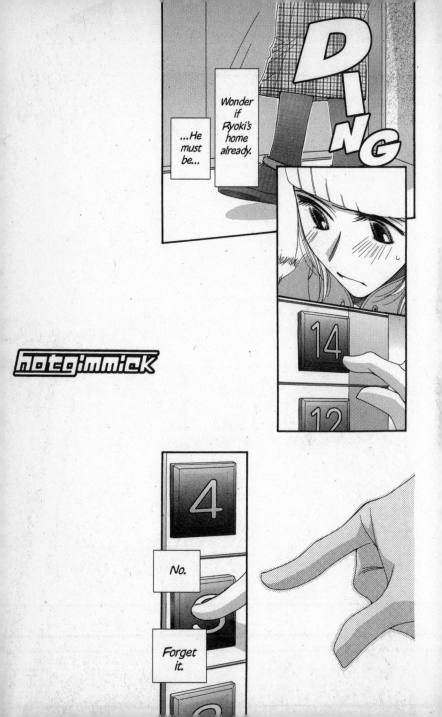

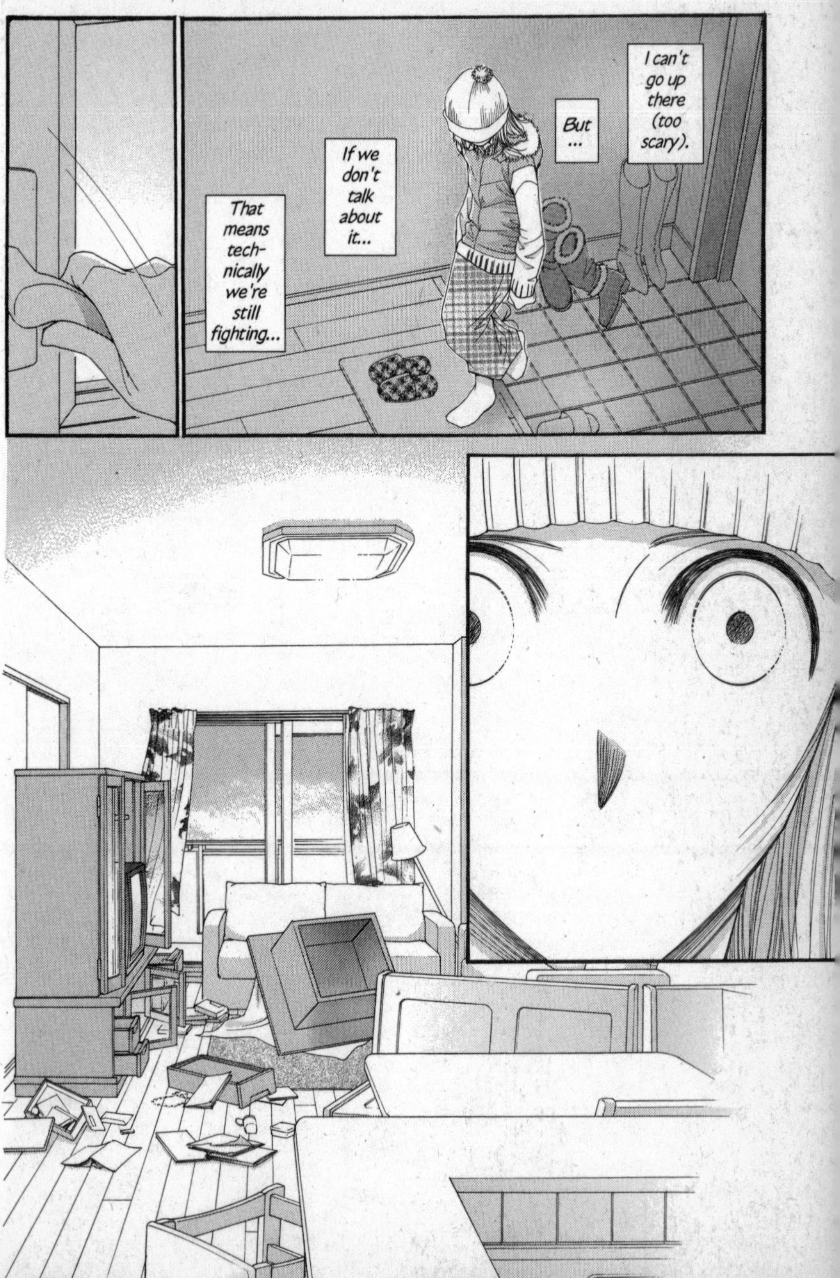
I can't go up there (too scary).
But ...
If we don't talk about it...
That means tech-nically we're still fighting...

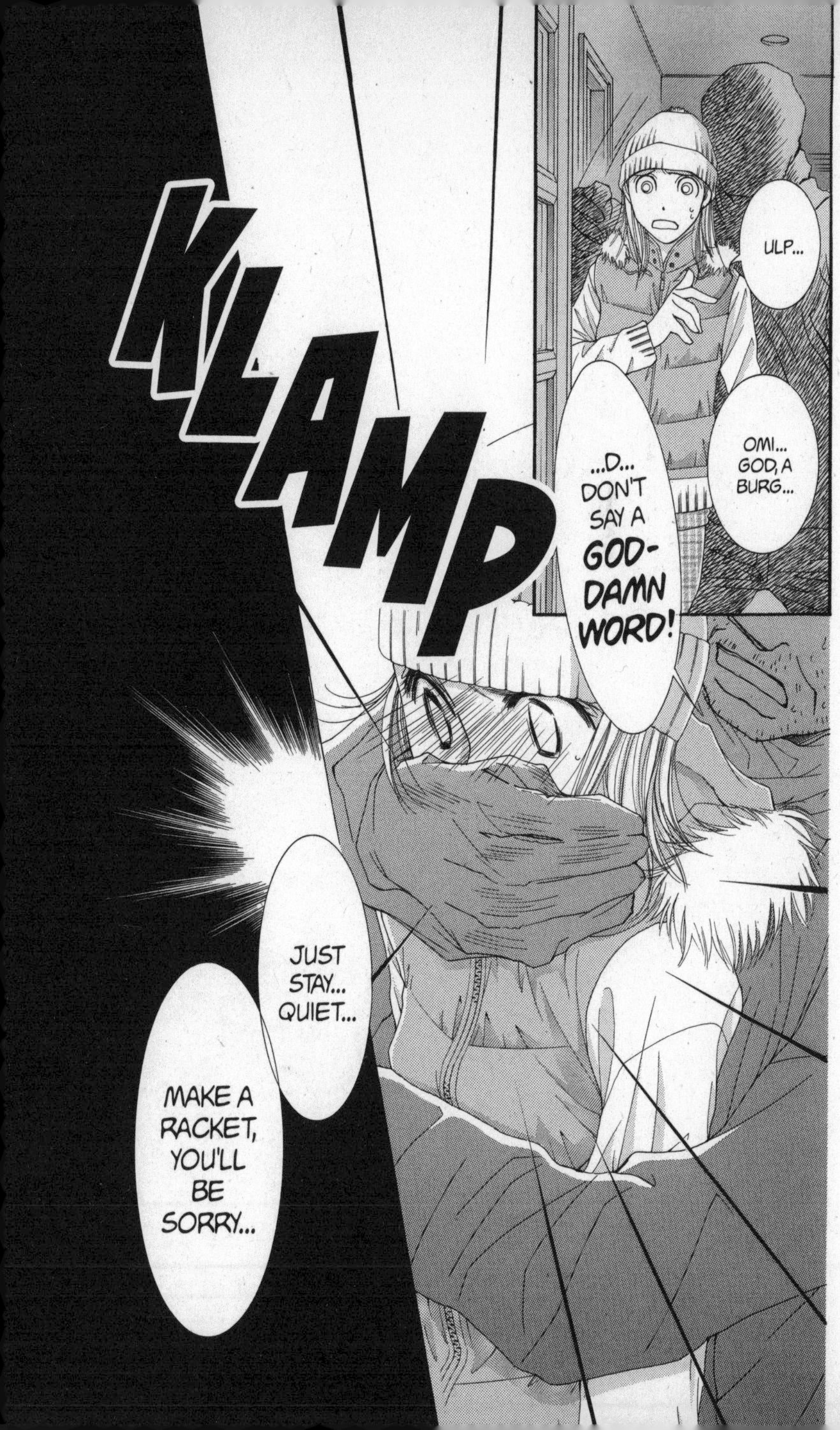
ULP...
OMI... GOD, A BURG...
...D... DON'T SAY A GOD-DAMN WORD!
KLAMP
JUST STAY... QUIET...
MAKE A RACKET, YOU'LL BE SORRY...

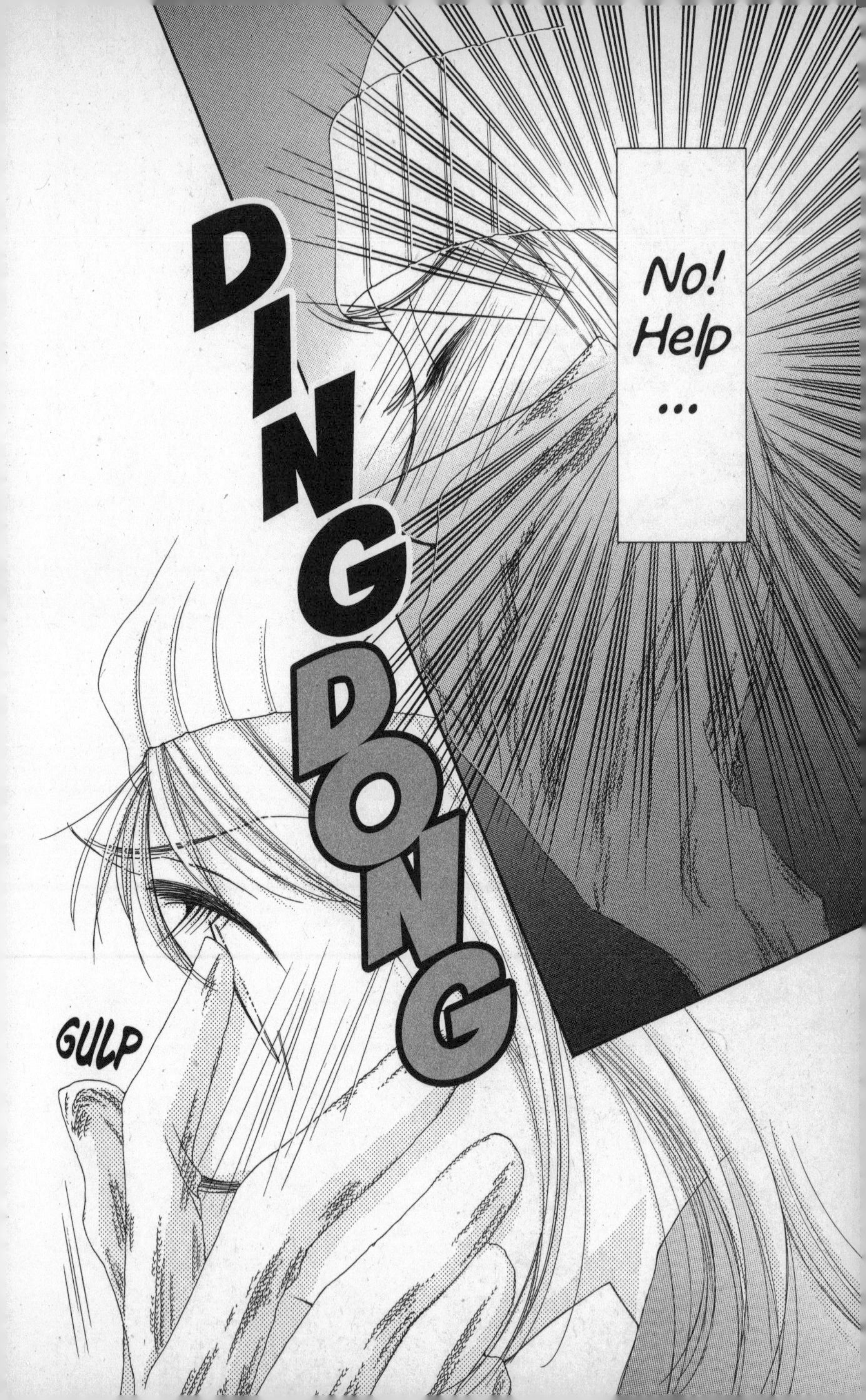
No! Help ...
DING DONG
GULP

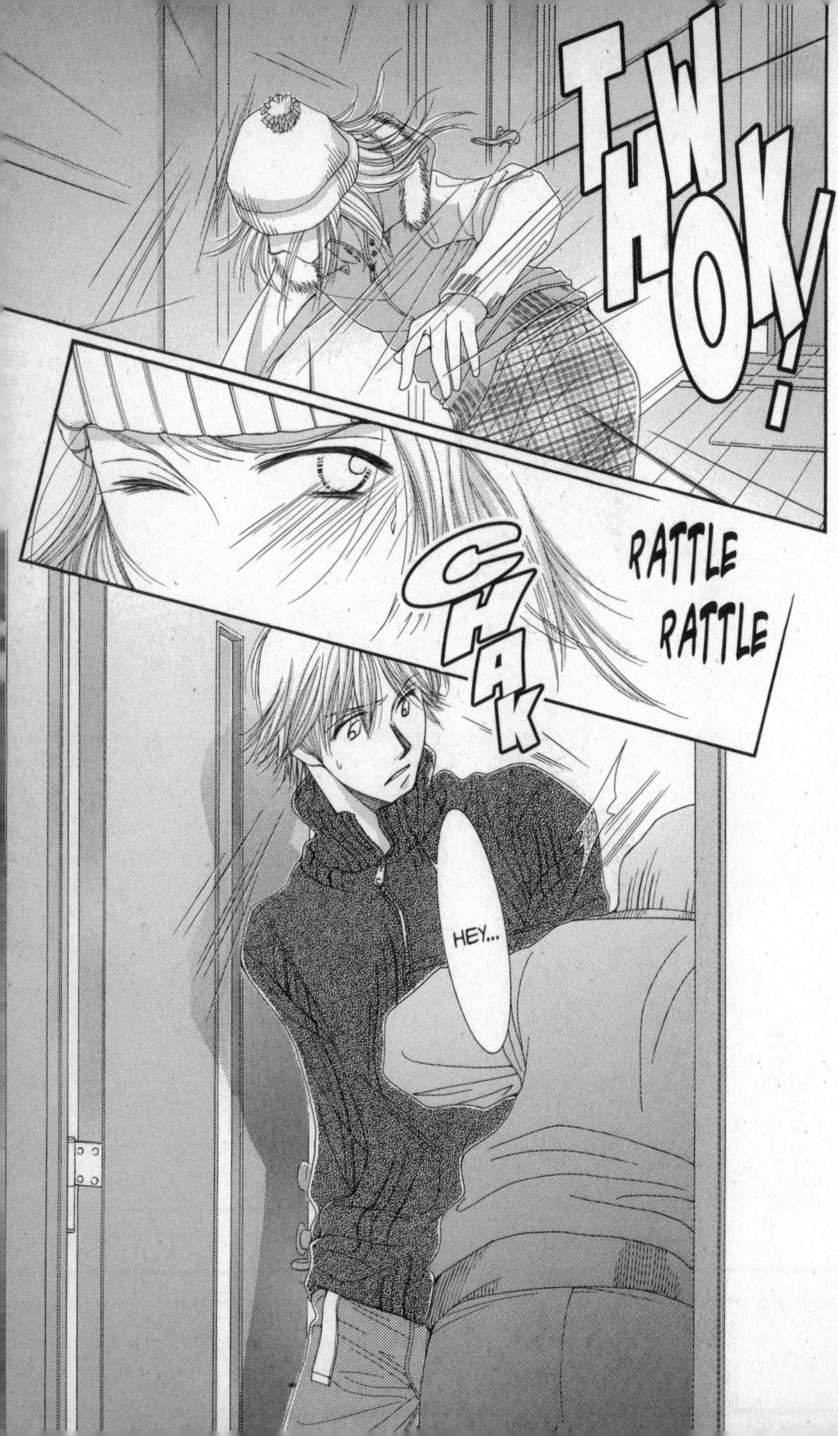
THWONK!
RATTLE RATTLE
CHAK
HEY...

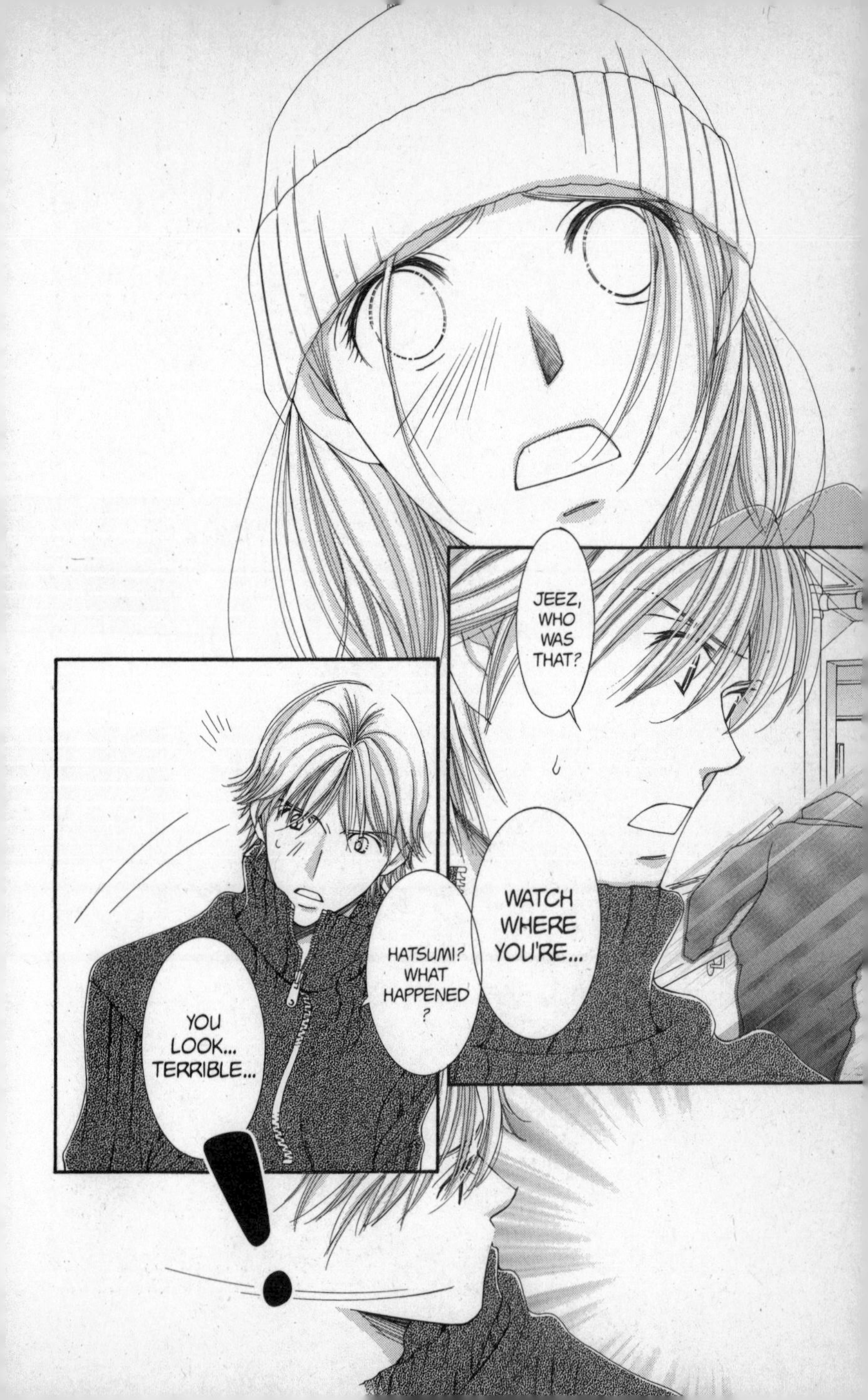
JEEZ, WHO WAS THAT?
WATCH WHERE YOU'RE...
HATSUMI? WHAT HAPPENED?
YOU LOOK... TERRIBLE...
!

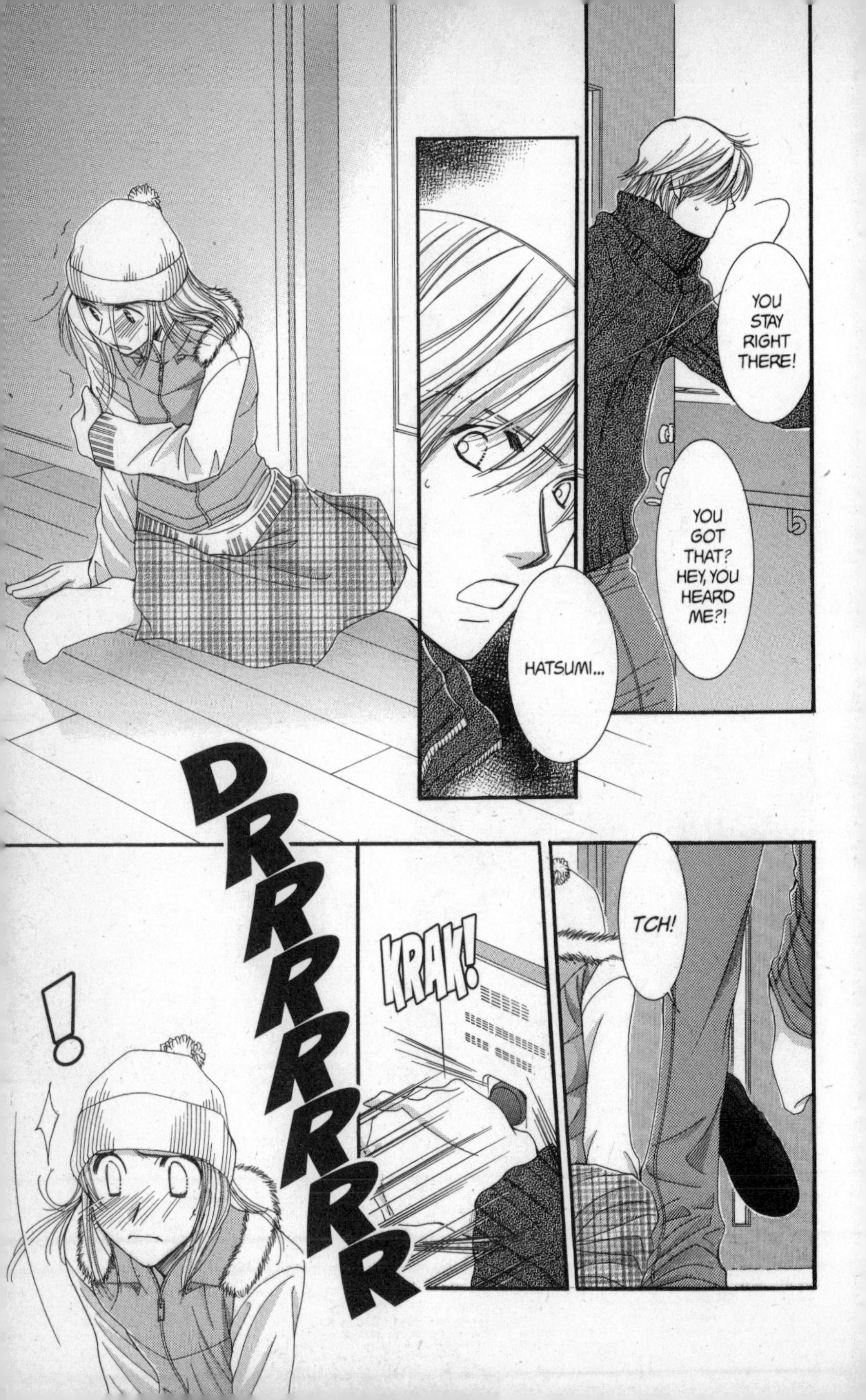
YOU STAY RIGHT THERE!
YOU GOT THAT? HEY, YOU HEARD ME?!
HATSUMI...
TCH!
KRAK!
DRRRRRRR
!

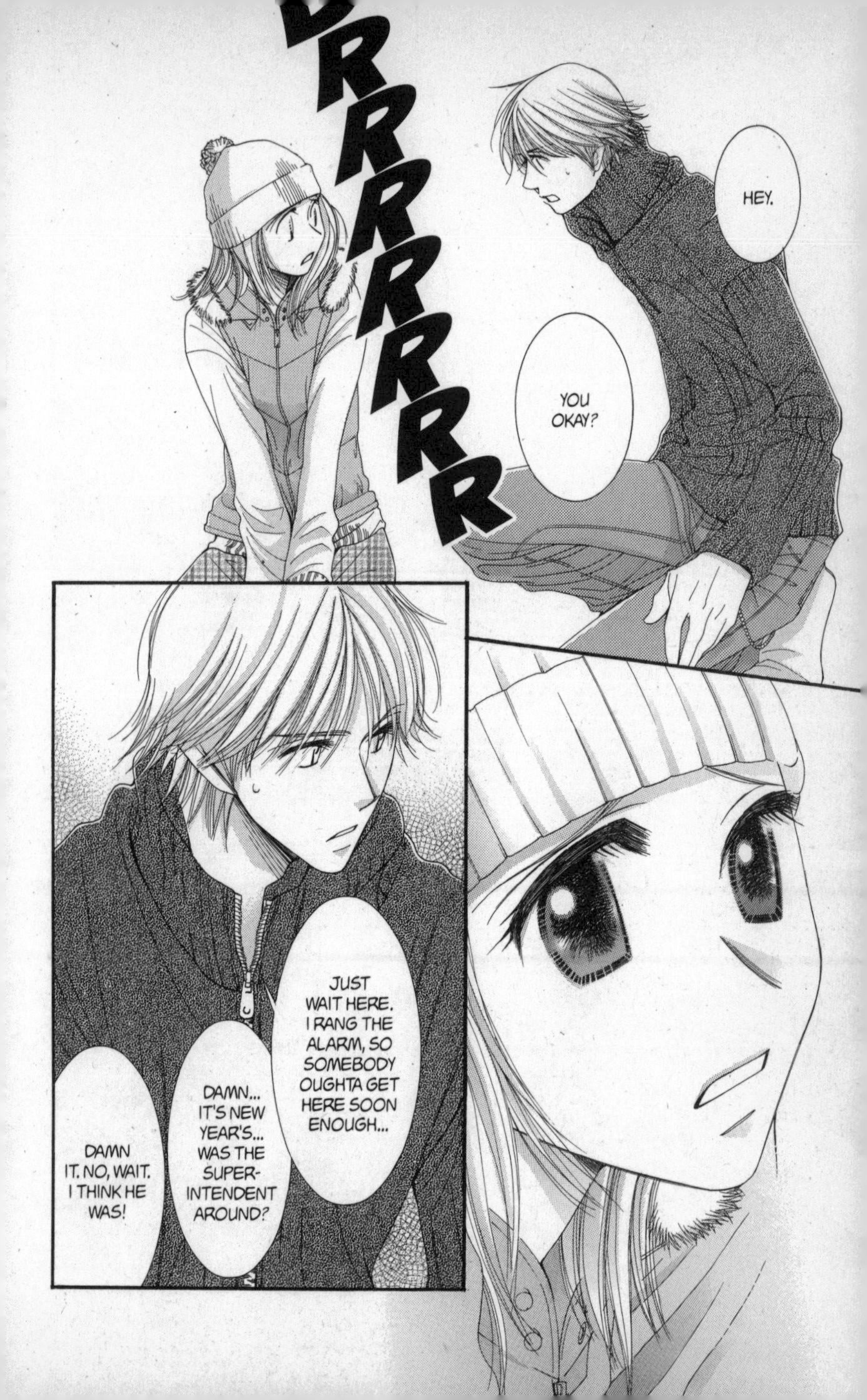
VRRRRRR
HEY.
YOU OKAY?
JUST WAIT HERE. I RANG THE ALARM, SO SOMEBODY OUGHTA GET HERE SOON ENOUGH...
DAMN... IT'S NEW YEAR'S... WAS THE SUPER-INTENDENT AROUND?
DAMN IT. NO, WAIT. I THINK HE WAS!

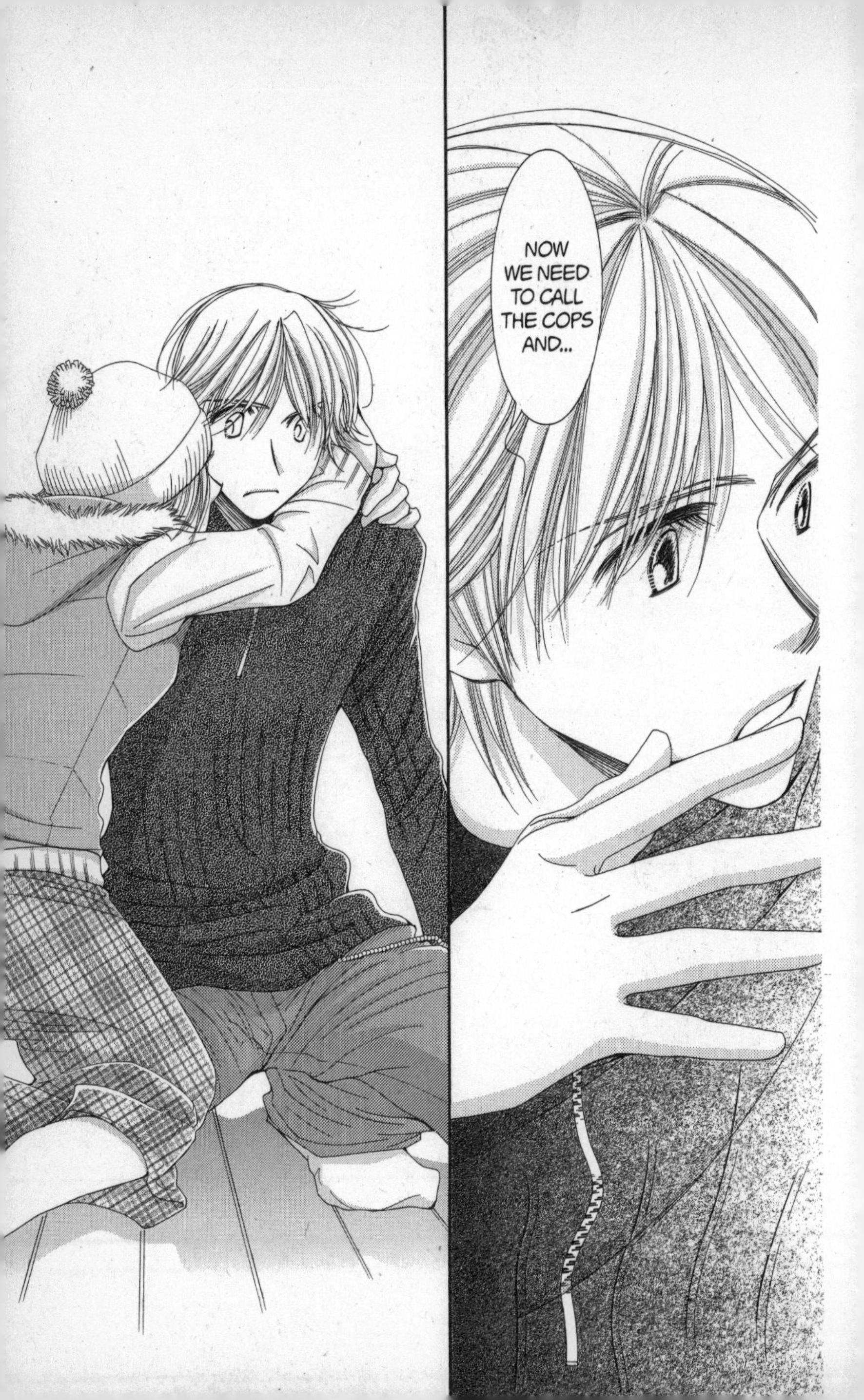
NOW WE NEED TO CALL THE COPS AND...

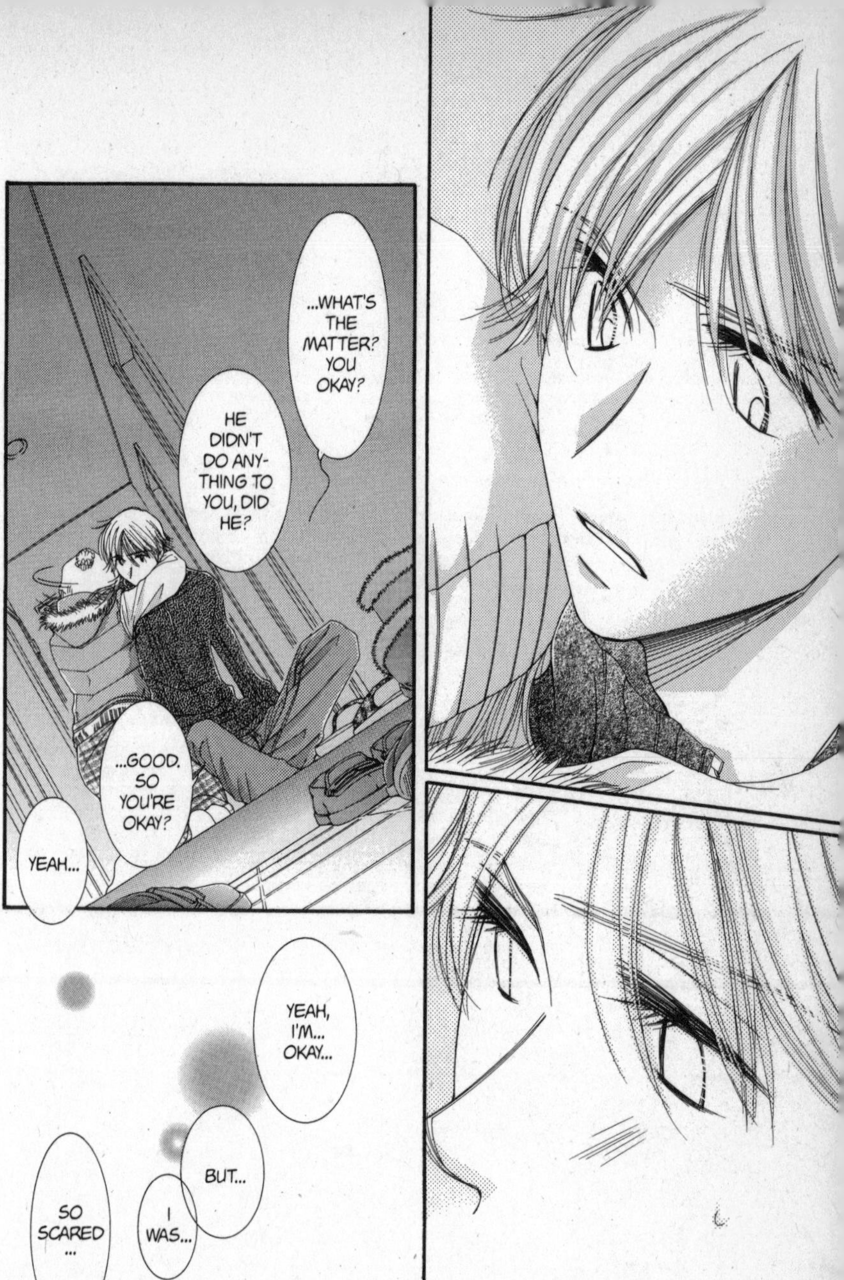
...WHAT'S THE MATTER? YOU OKAY?
HE DIDN'T DO ANY-THING TO YOU, DID HE?
...GOOD. SO YOU'RE OKAY?
YEAH...
YEAH, I'M... OKAY...
BUT...
I WAS...
SO SCARED ...

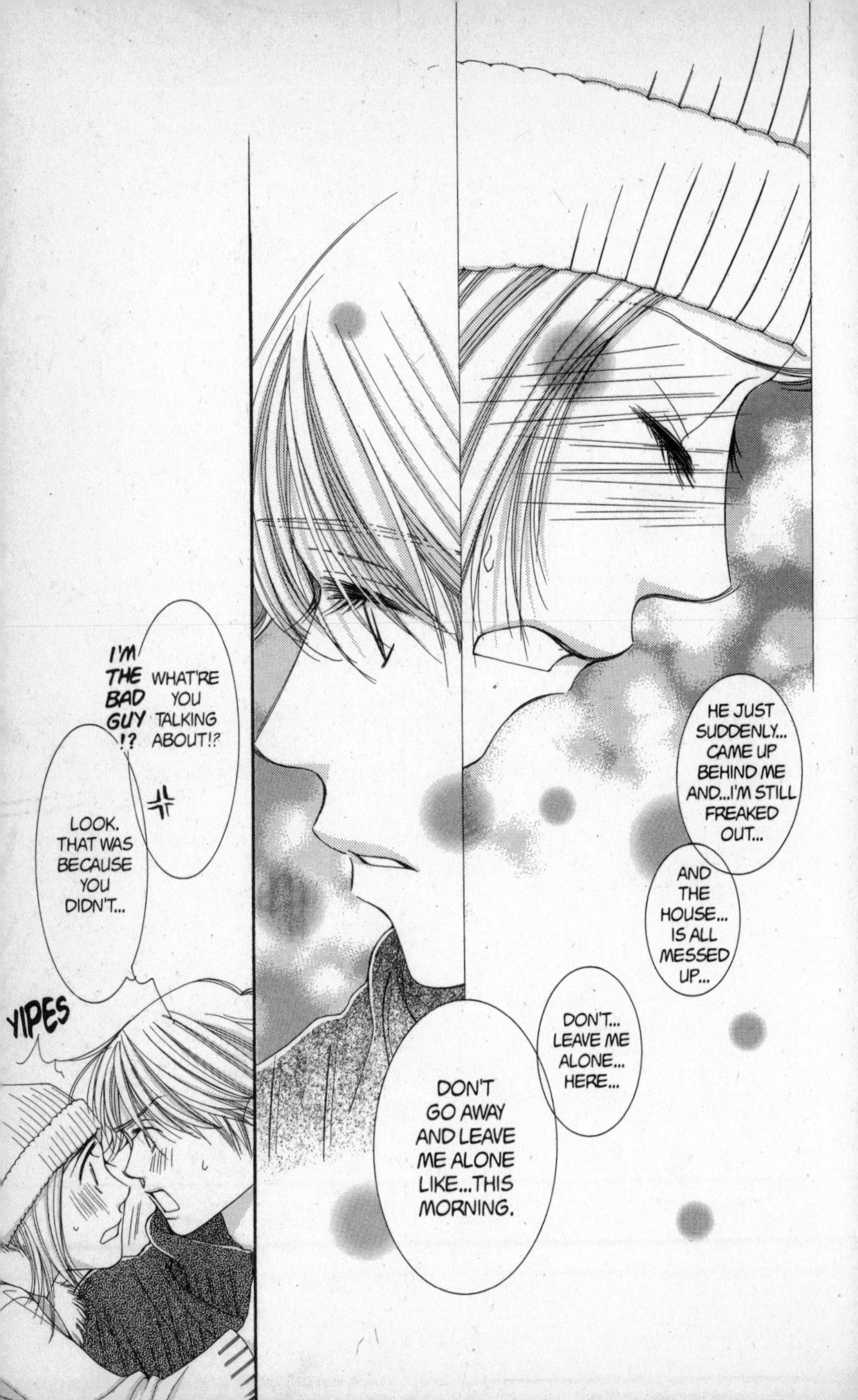
HE JUST SUDDENLY... CAME UP BEHIND ME AND...I'M STILL FREAKED OUT...
AND THE HOUSE... IS ALL MESSED UP...
DON'T... LEAVE ME ALONE... HERE...
DON'T GO AWAY AND LEAVE ME ALONE LIKE...THIS MORNING.
WHAT'RE YOU TALKING ABOUT!?
I'M THE BAD GUY !?
LOOK. THAT WAS BECAUSE YOU DIDN'T...
YIPES

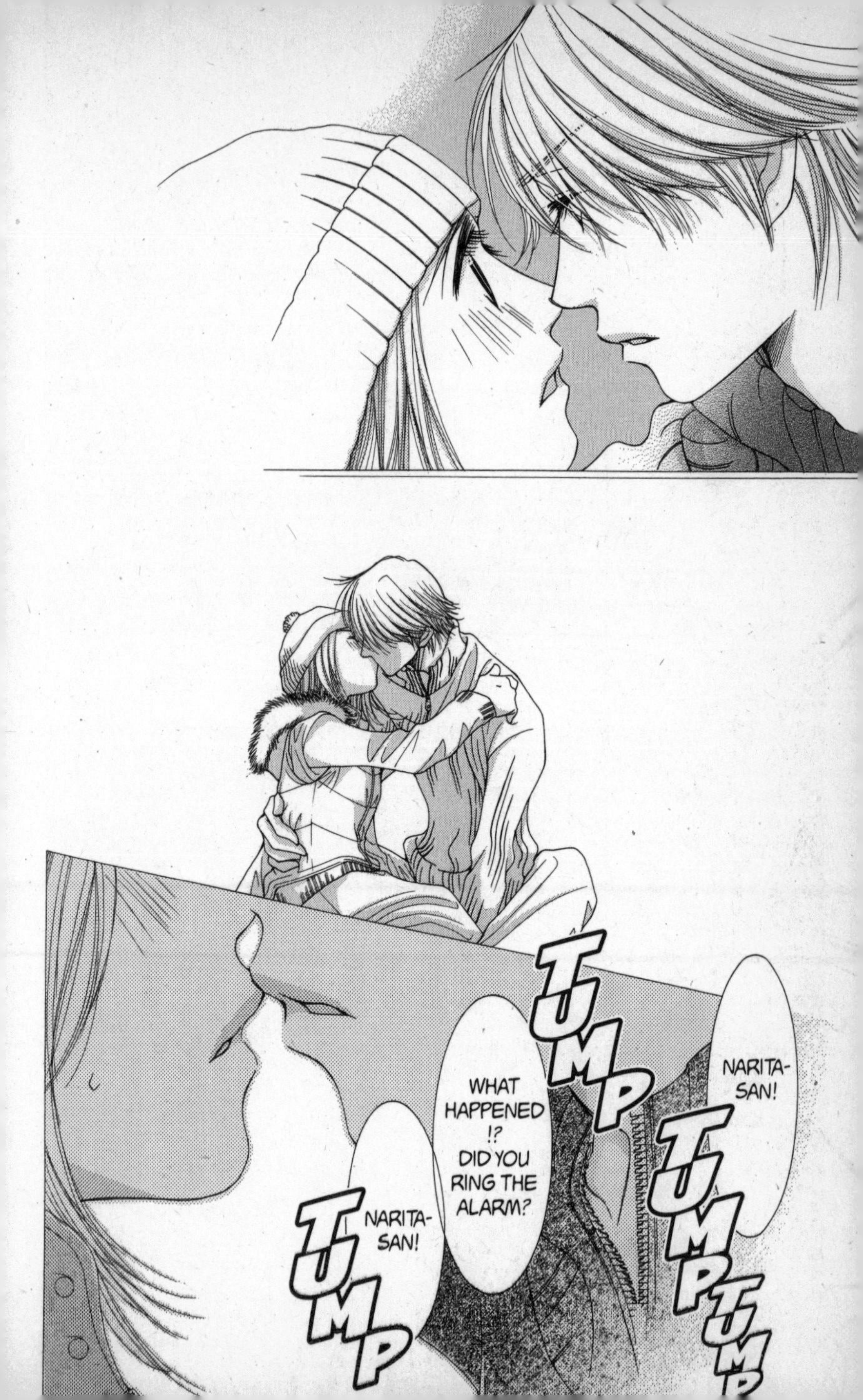
NARITA-SAN!
TUMP
TUMP
TUMP
WHAT HAPPENED !? DID YOU RING THE ALARM?
NARITA-SAN!
TUMP

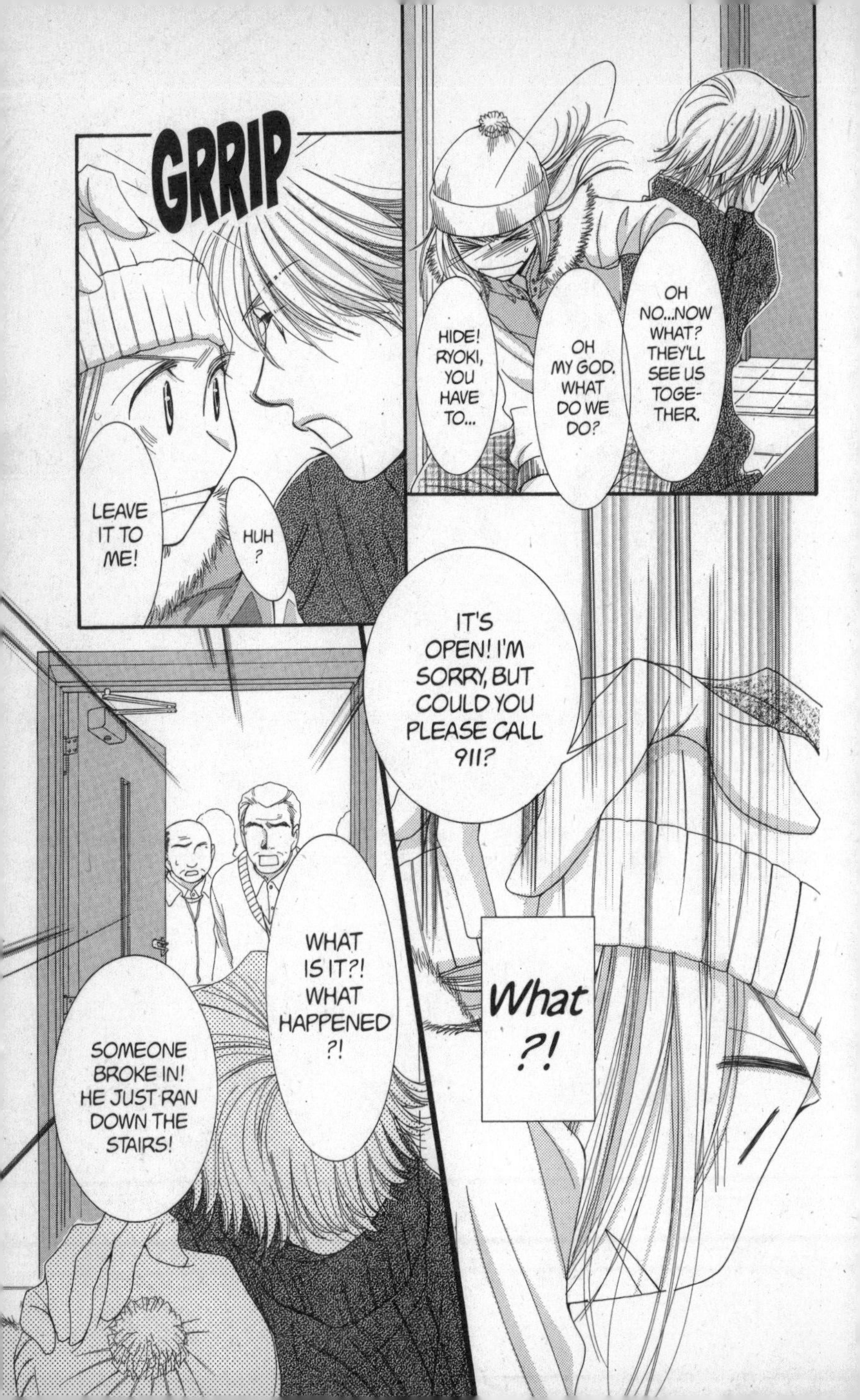
OH NO...NOW WHAT? THEY'LL SEE US TOGE-THER.
OH MY GOD. WHAT DO WE DO?
HIDE! RYOKI, YOU HAVE TO...
GRRIP
HUH?
LEAVE IT TO ME!
IT'S OPEN! I'M SORRY, BUT COULD YOU PLEASE CALL 911?
What?!
WHAT IS IT?! WHAT HAPPENED?!
SOMEONE BROKE IN! HE JUST RAN DOWN THE STAIRS!

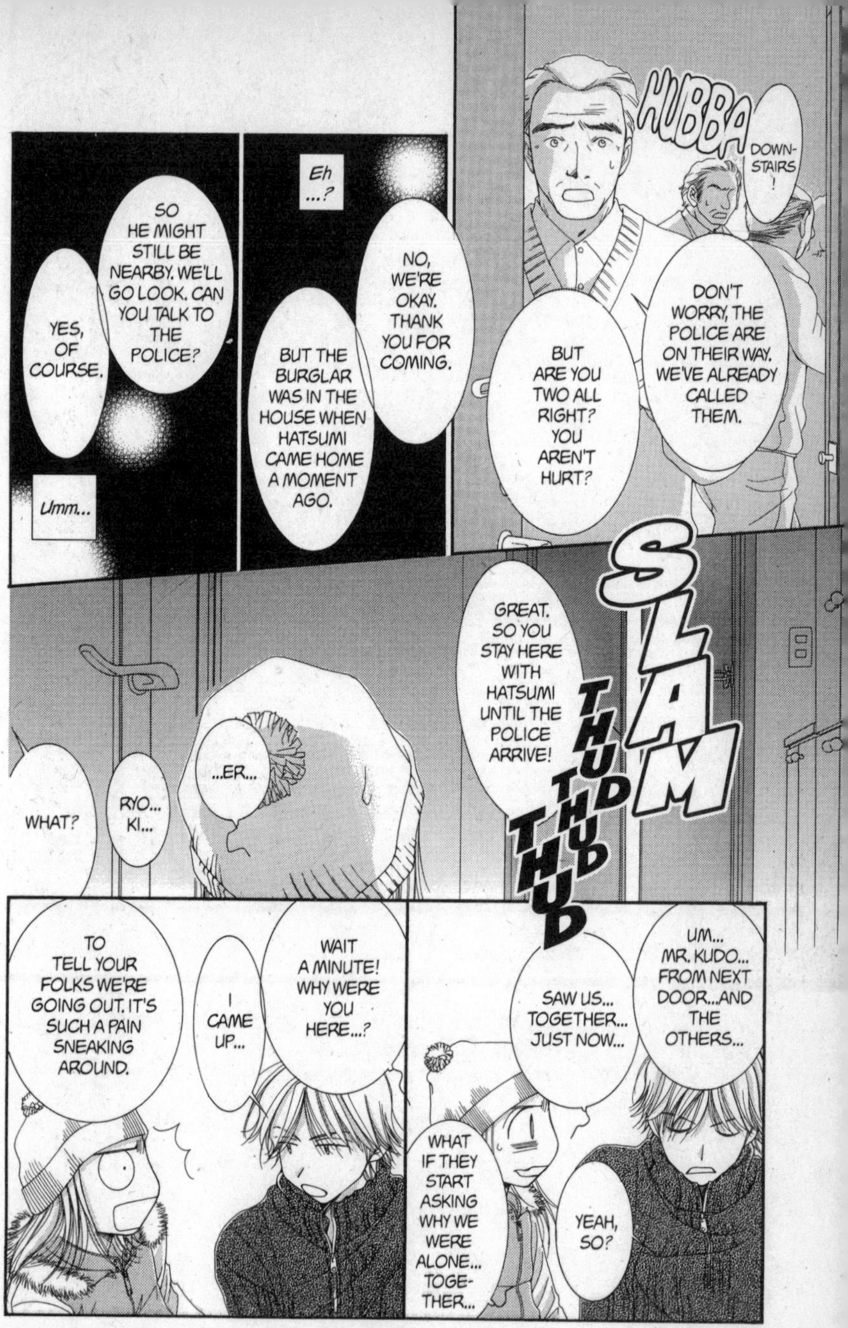
HUBBA
DOWN-STAIRS!
DON'T WORRY, THE POLICE ARE ON THEIR WAY. WE'VE ALREADY CALLED THEM.
BUT ARE YOU TWO ALL RIGHT? YOU AREN'T HURT?
Eh ...?
NO, WE'RE OKAY. THANK YOU FOR COMING.
BUT THE BURGLAR WAS IN THE HOUSE WHEN HATSUMI CAME HOME A MOMENT AGO.
SO HE MIGHT STILL BE NEARBY. WE'LL GO LOOK. CAN YOU TALK TO THE POLICE?
YES, OF COURSE.
Umm...
SLAM
THUD THUD THUD
GREAT. SO YOU STAY HERE WITH HATSUMI UNTIL THE POLICE ARRIVE!
...ER...
RYO... KI...
WHAT?
UM... MR. KUDO... FROM NEXT DOOR...AND THE OTHERS...
SAW US... TOGETHER... JUST NOW...
YEAH, SO?
WHAT IF THEY START ASKING WHY WE WERE ALONE... TOGE-THER...
WAIT A MINUTE! WHY WERE YOU HERE...?
I CAME UP...
TO TELL YOUR FOLKS WE'RE GOING OUT. IT'S SUCH A PAIN SNEAKING AROUND.

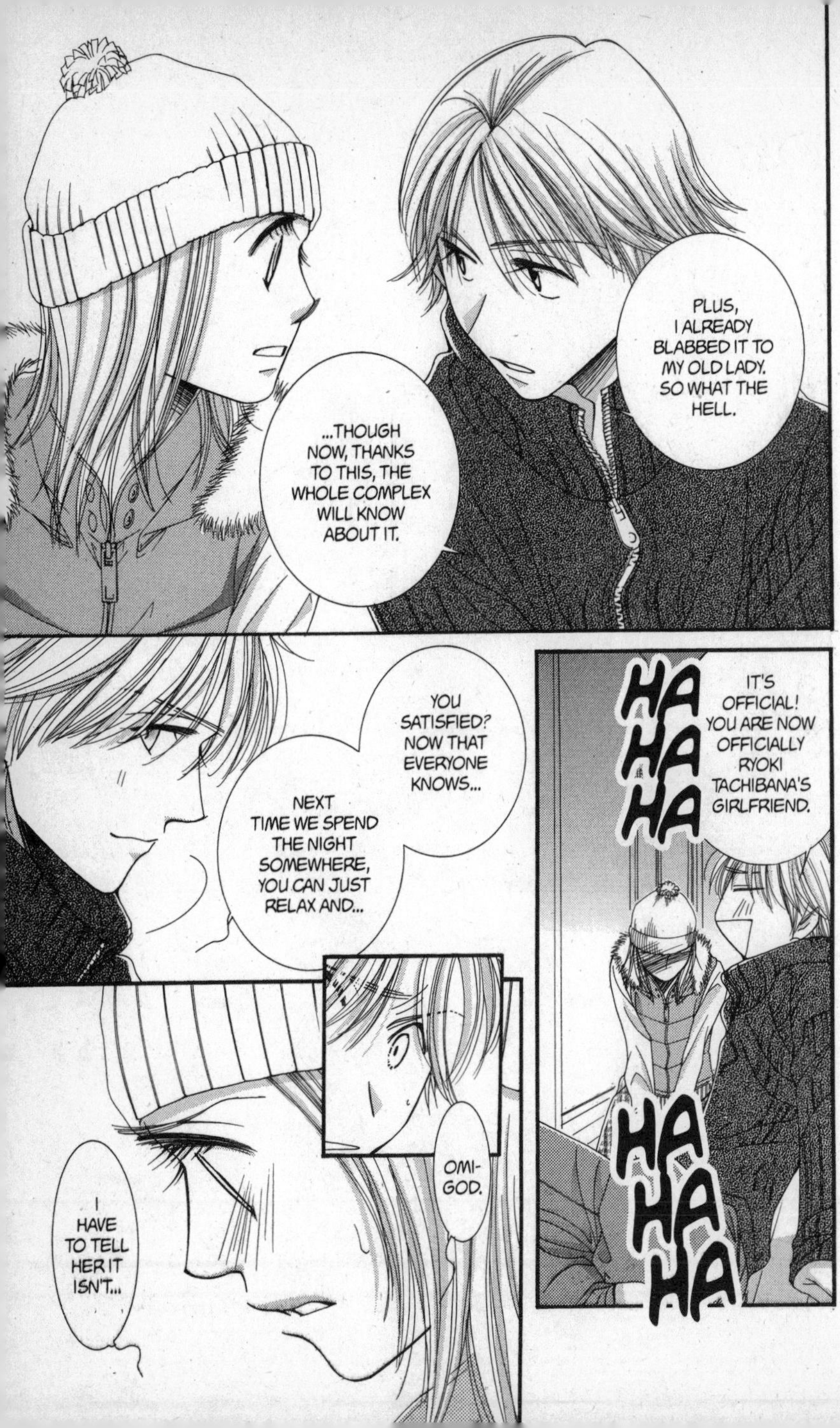
PLUS, I ALREADY BLABBED IT TO MY OLD LADY. SO WHAT THE HELL.
...THOUGH NOW, THANKS TO THIS, THE WHOLE COMPLEX WILL KNOW ABOUT IT.
HA HA HA
IT'S OFFICIAL! YOU ARE NOW OFFICIALLY RYOKI TACHIBANA'S GIRLFRIEND.
HA HA HA HA
YOU SATISFIED? NOW THAT EVERYONE KNOWS...
NEXT TIME WE SPEND THE NIGHT SOMEWHERE, YOU CAN JUST RELAX AND...
OMI-GOD.
I HAVE TO TELL HER IT ISN'T...

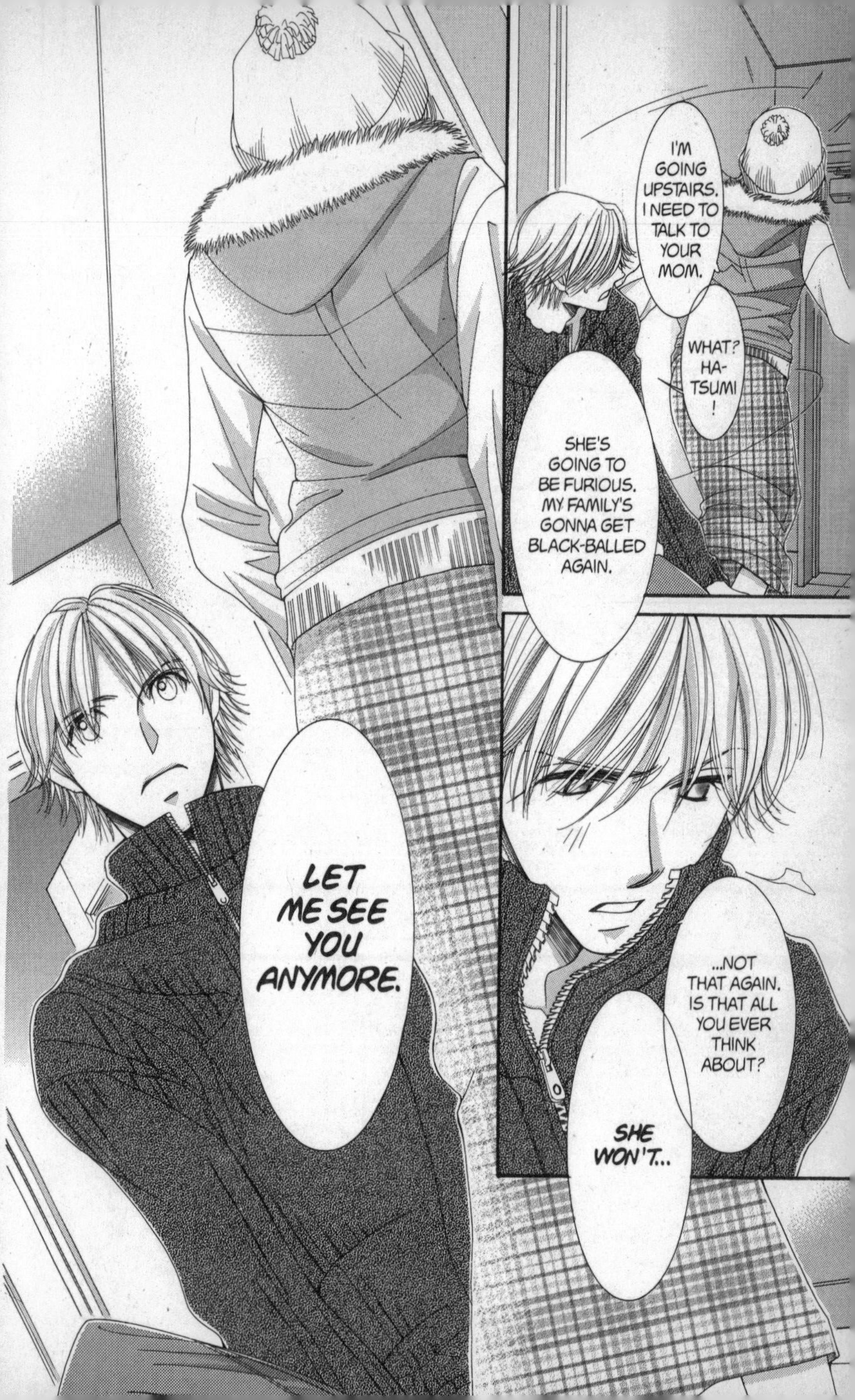
I'M GOING UPSTAIRS. I NEED TO TALK TO YOUR MOM.
WHAT? HA-TSUMI!
SHE'S GOING TO BE FURIOUS. MY FAMILY'S GONNA GET BLACK-BALLED AGAIN.
...NOT THAT AGAIN. IS THAT ALL YOU EVER THINK ABOUT?
SHE WON'T...
LET ME SEE YOU ANYMORE.

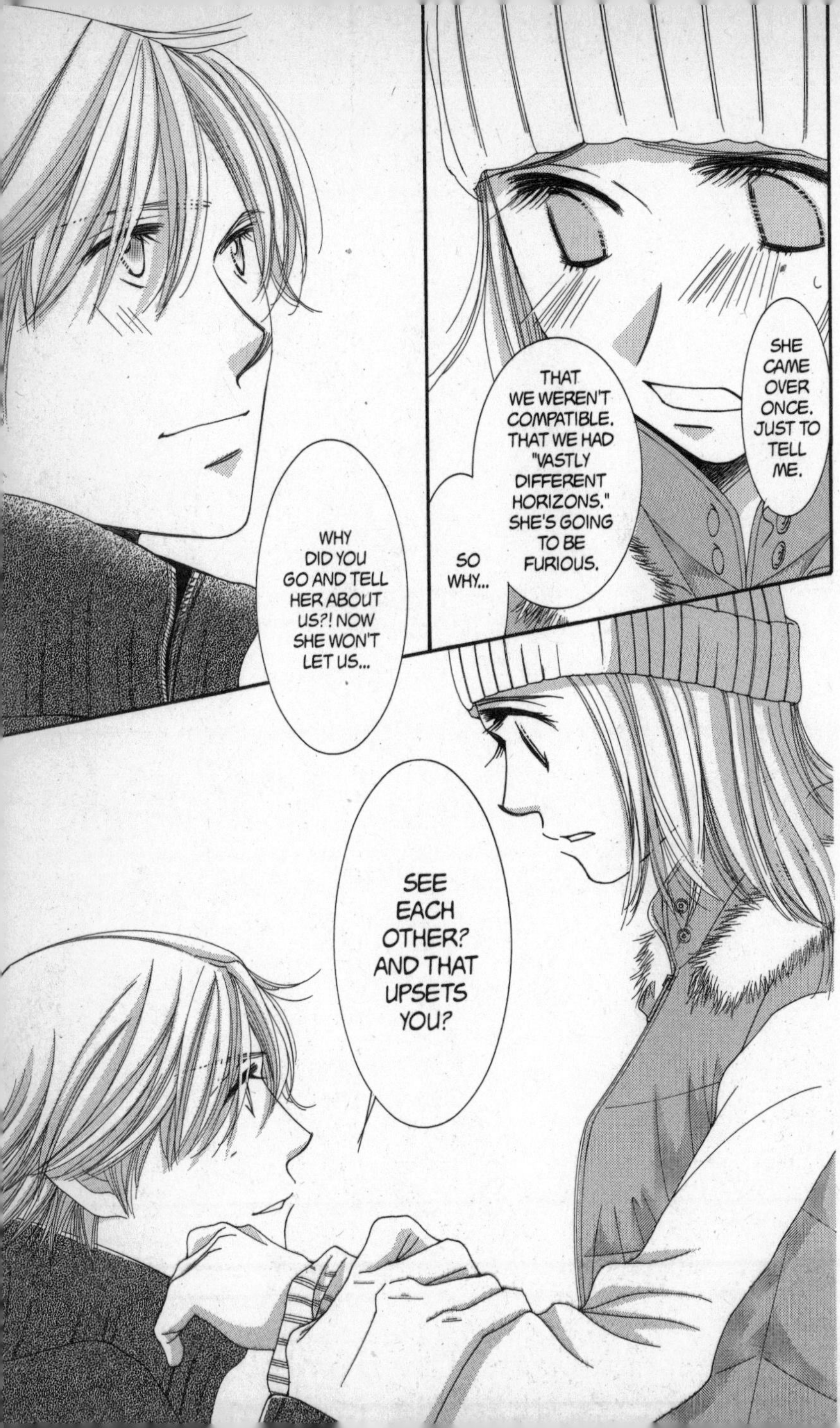
SHE CAME OVER ONCE. JUST TO TELL ME.
THAT WE WEREN'T COMPATIBLE. THAT WE HAD "VASTLY DIFFERENT HORIZONS." SHE'S GOING TO BE FURIOUS.
SO WHY...
WHY DID YOU GO AND TELL HER ABOUT US?! NOW SHE WON'T LET US...
SEE EACH OTHER? AND THAT UPSETS YOU?

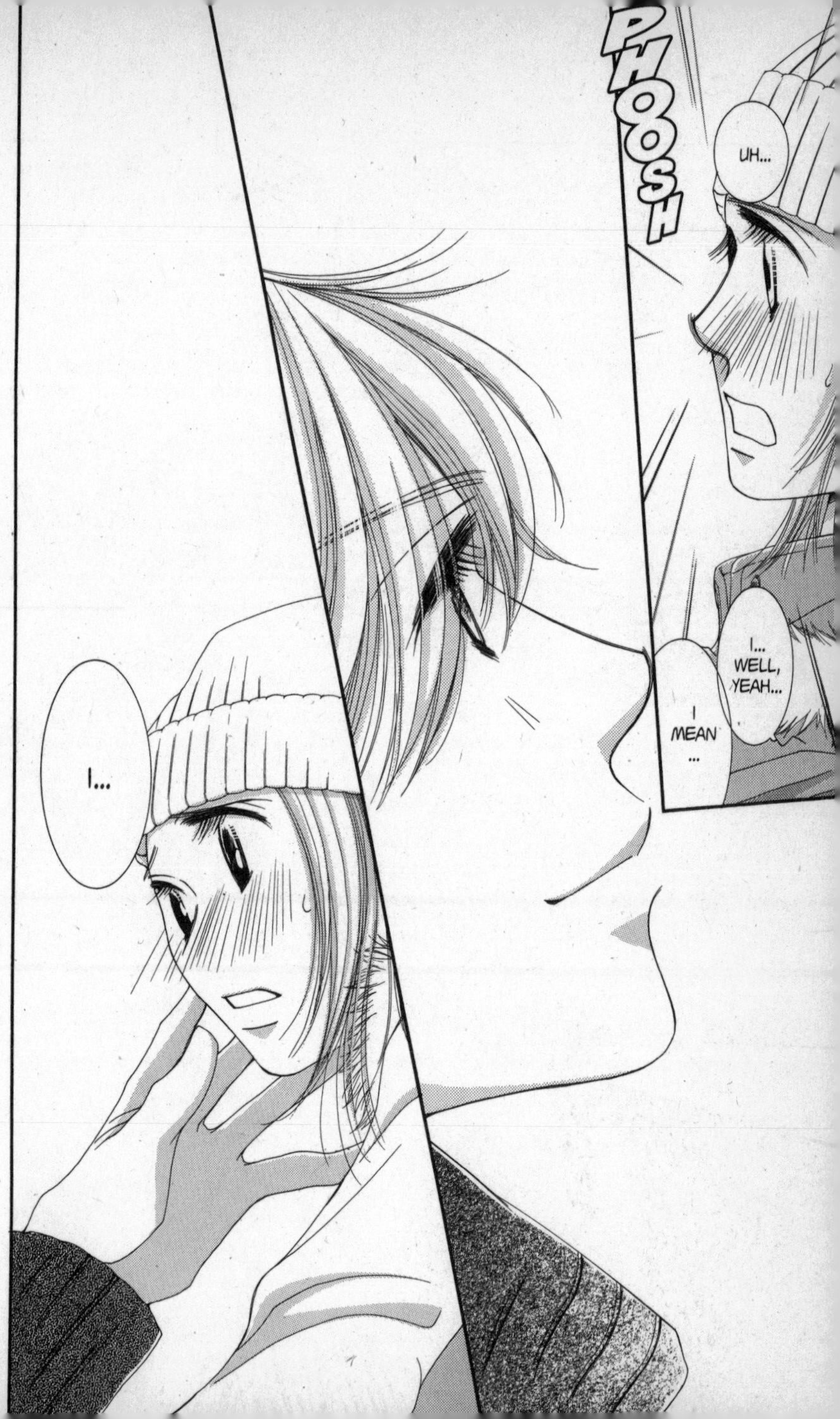
PHOOSH
UH...
I... WELL, YEAH...
I MEAN ...
I...

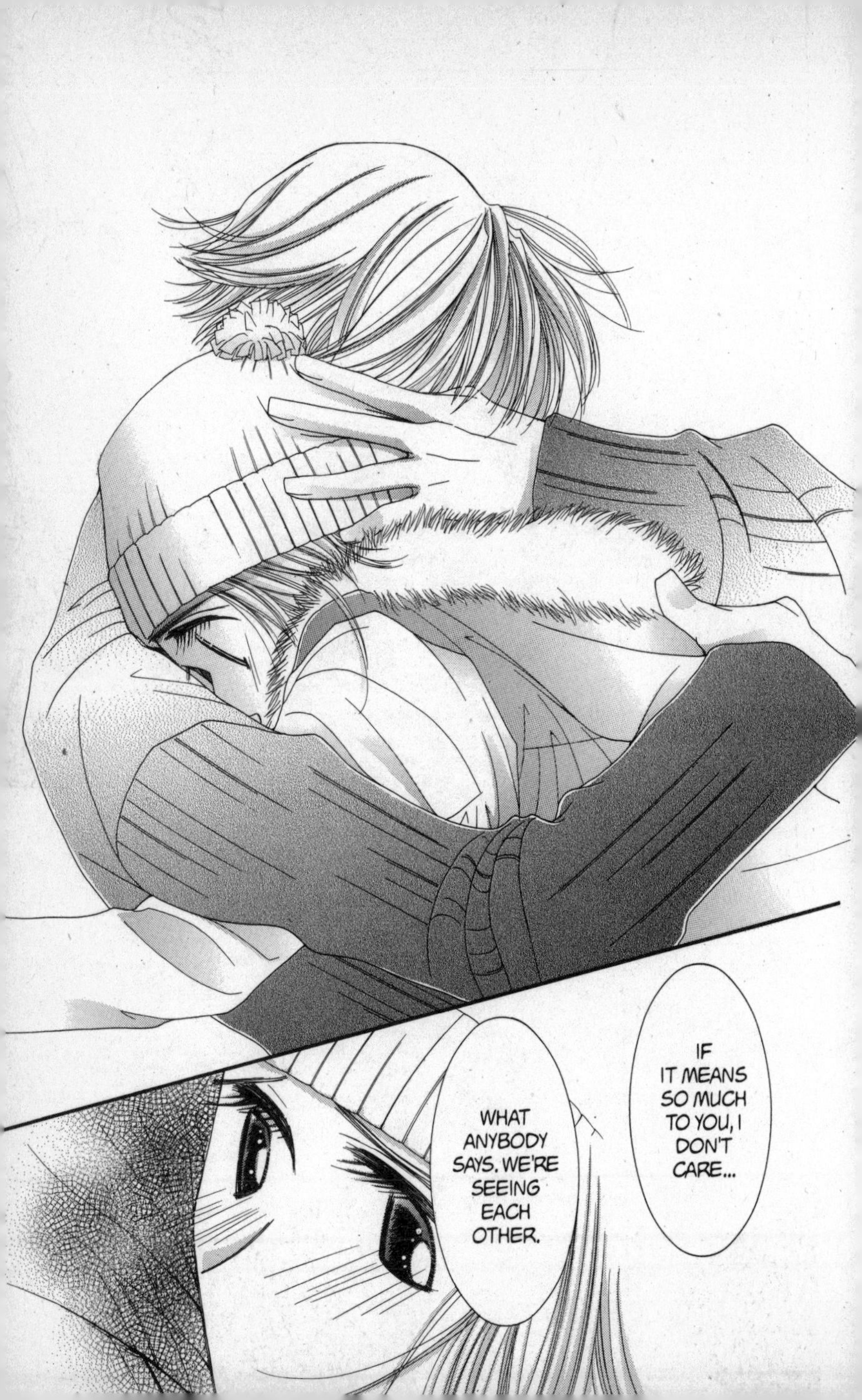
IF IT MEANS SO MUCH TO YOU, I DON'T CARE...
WHAT ANYBODY SAYS. WE'RE SEEING EACH OTHER.

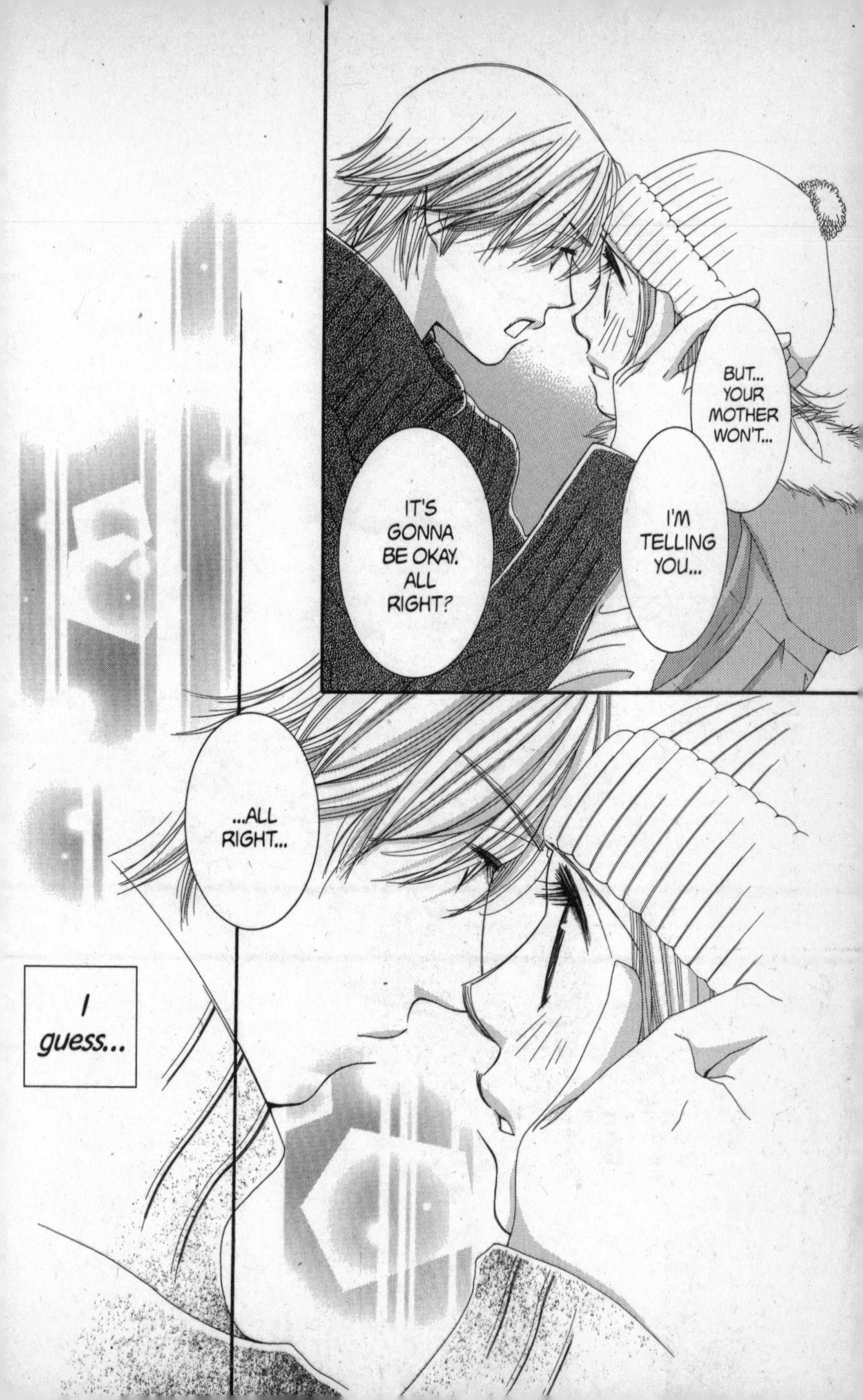
BUT... YOUR MOTHER WON'T...
I'M TELLING YOU...
IT'S GONNA BE OKAY. ALL RIGHT?
...ALL RIGHT...
I guess...

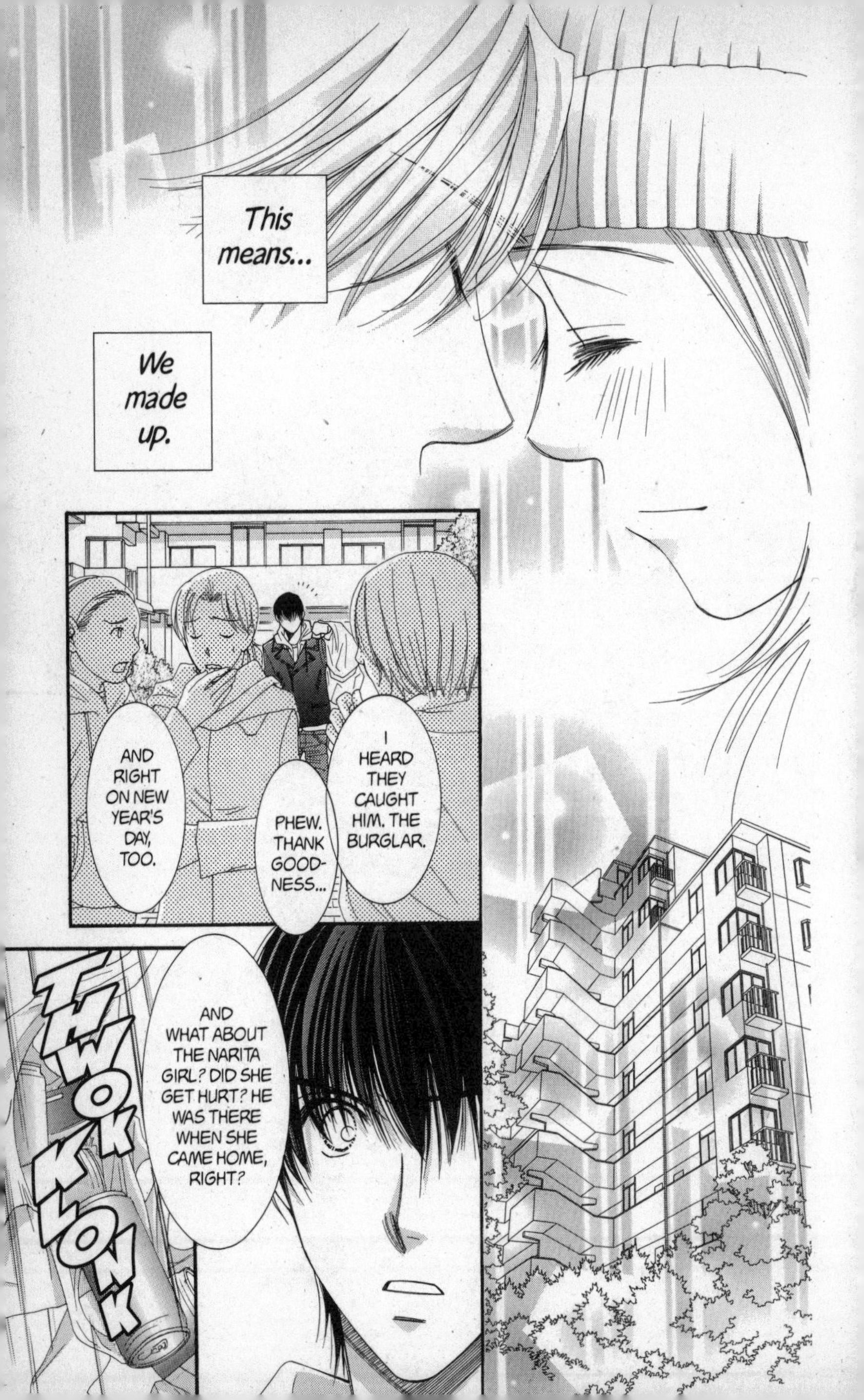
This means...
We made up.
I HEARD THEY CAUGHT HIM. THE BURGLAR.
PHEW. THANK GOODNESS...
AND RIGHT ON NEW YEAR'S DAY, TOO.
AND WHAT ABOUT THE NARITA GIRL? DID SHE GET HURT? HE WAS THERE WHEN SHE CAME HOME, RIGHT?
THWOK
KLONK

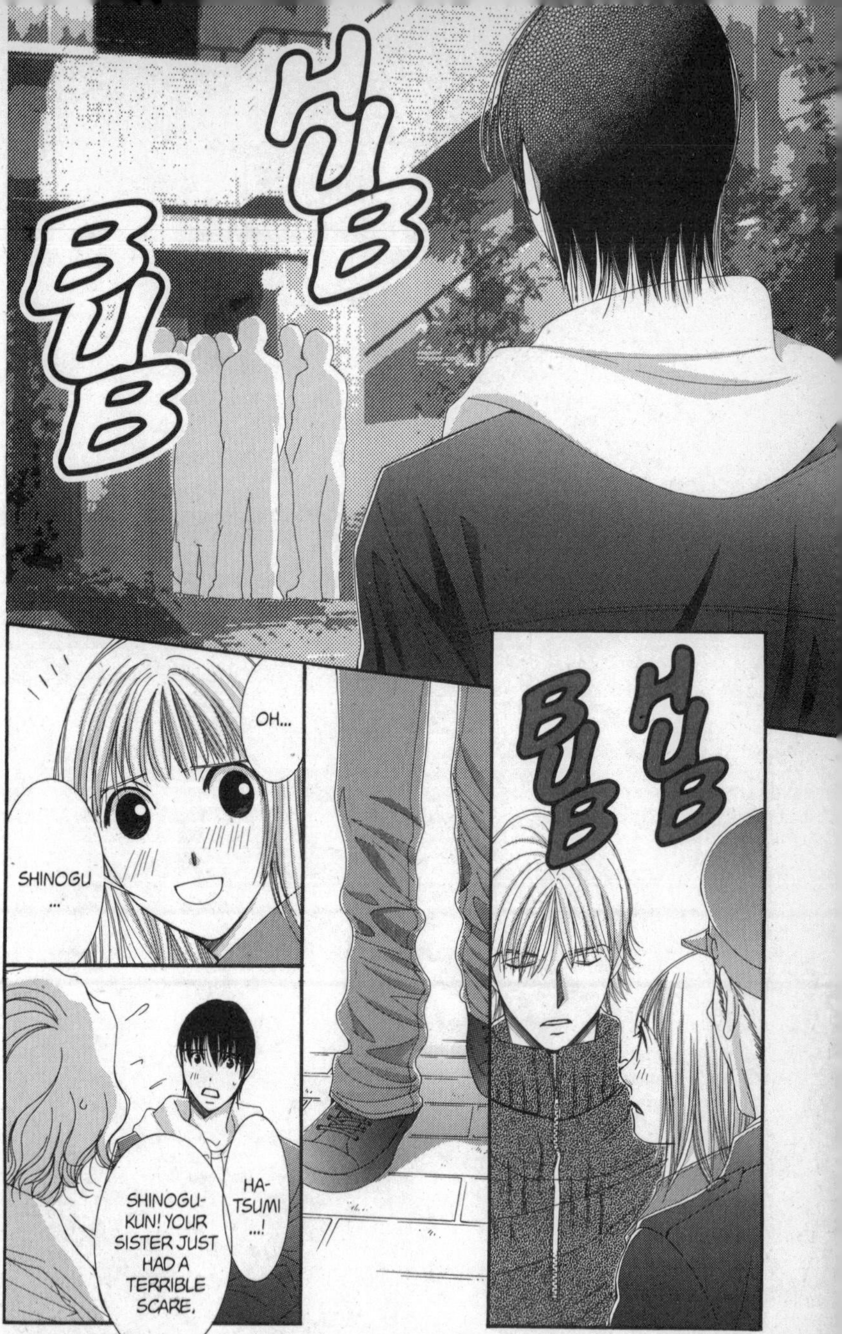
BUB
BUB
BUB
BUB
OH...
SHINOGU...
HA-TSUMI...!
SHINOGU-KUN! YOUR SISTER JUST HAD A TERRIBLE SCARE.

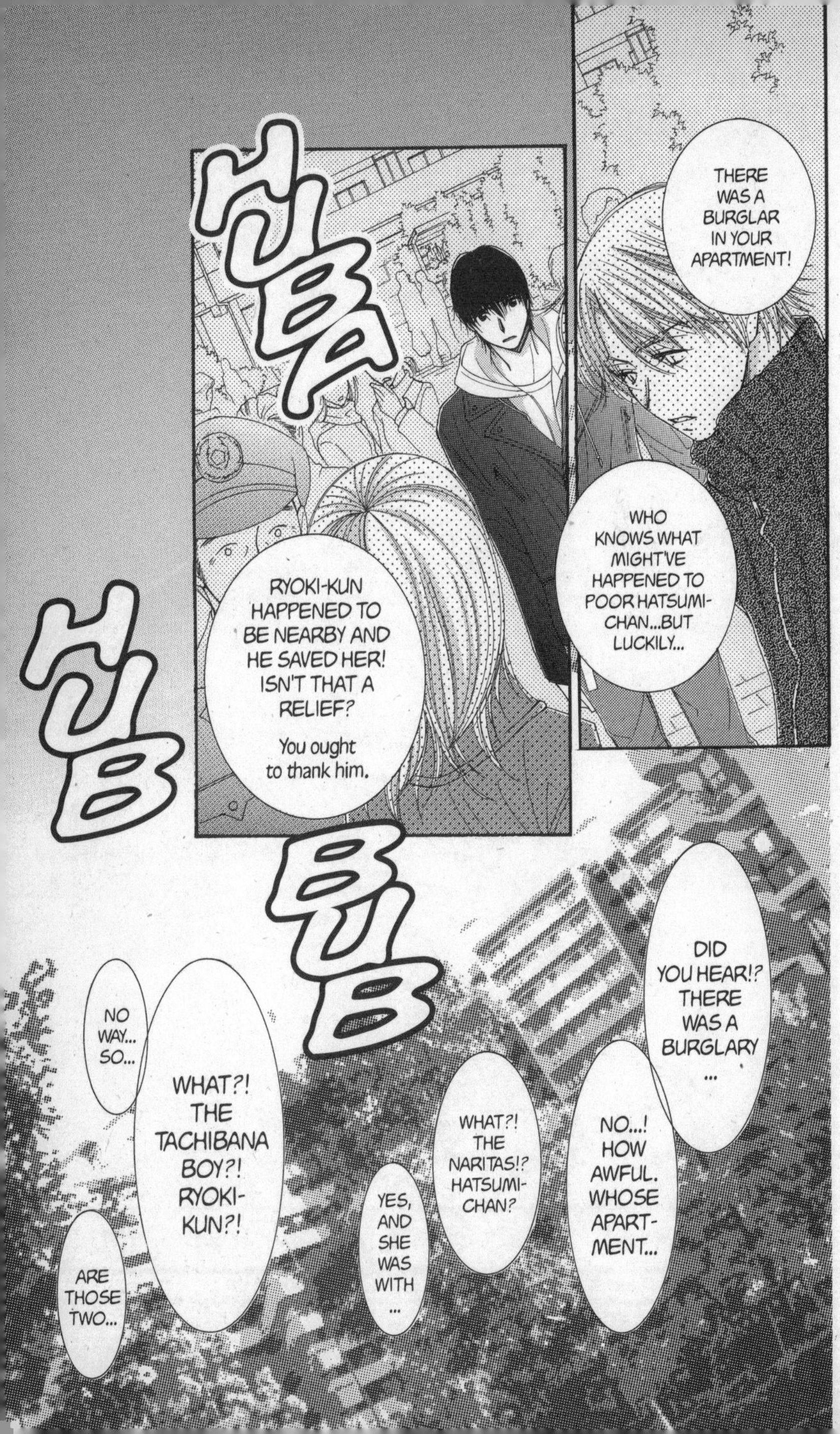

THERE WAS A BURGLAR IN YOUR APARTMENT!
WHO KNOWS WHAT MIGHT'VE HAPPENED TO POOR HATSUMI-CHAN...BUT LUCKILY...
RYOKI-KUN HAPPENED TO BE NEARBY AND HE SAVED HER! ISN'T THAT A RELIEF?
You ought to thank him.
DID YOU HEAR!? THERE WAS A BURGLARY ...
NO...! HOW AWFUL. WHOSE APART-MENT...
WHAT?! THE NARITAS!? HATSUMI-CHAN?
YES, AND SHE WAS WITH ...
WHAT?! THE TACHIBANA BOY?! RYOKI-KUN?!
NO WAY... SO...
ARE THOSE TWO...

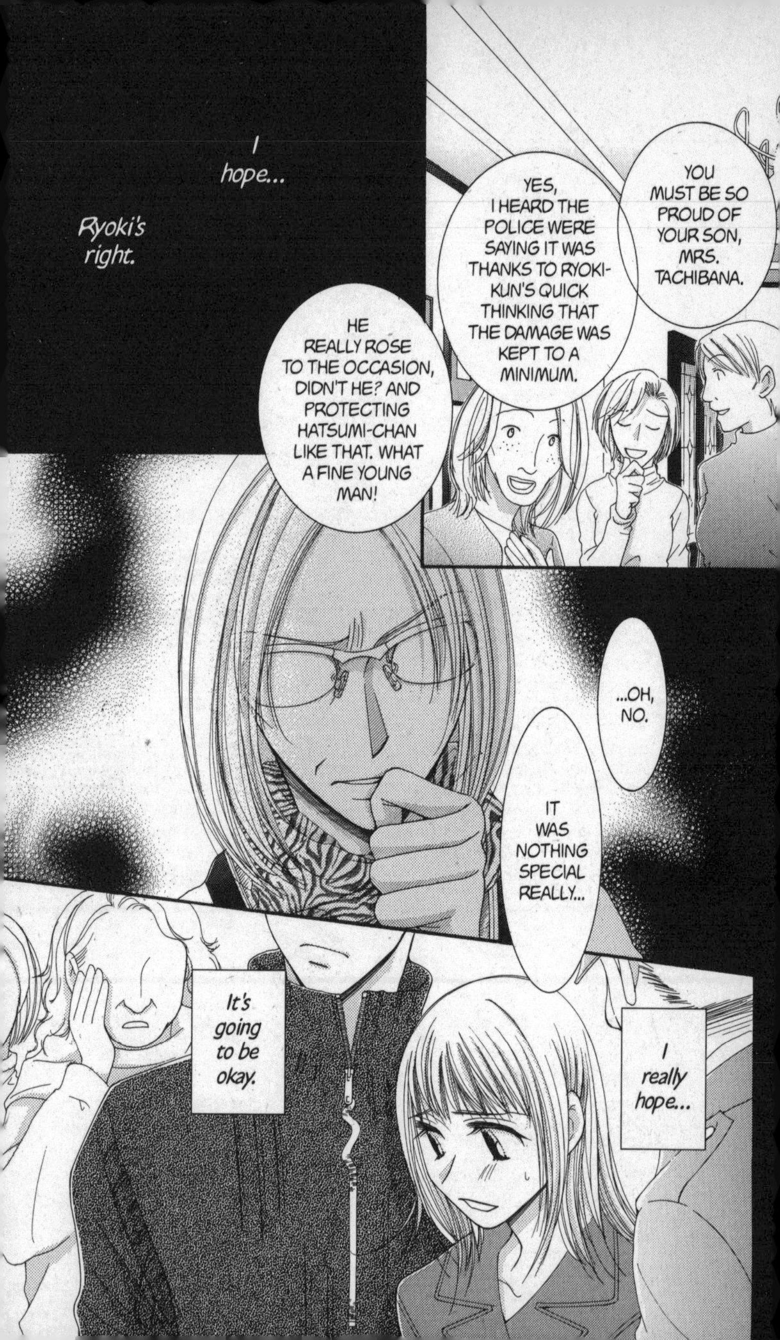
YOU MUST BE SO PROUD OF YOUR SON, MRS. TACHIBANA.
YES, I HEARD THE POLICE WERE SAYING IT WAS THANKS TO RYOKI-KUN'S QUICK THINKING THAT THE DAMAGE WAS KEPT TO A MINIMUM.
HE REALLY ROSE TO THE OCCASION, DIDN'T HE? AND PROTECTING HATSUMI-CHAN LIKE THAT. WHAT A FINE YOUNG MAN!
I hope...
Ryoki's right.
...OH, NO.
IT WAS NOTHING SPECIAL REALLY...
I really hope...
It's going to be okay.

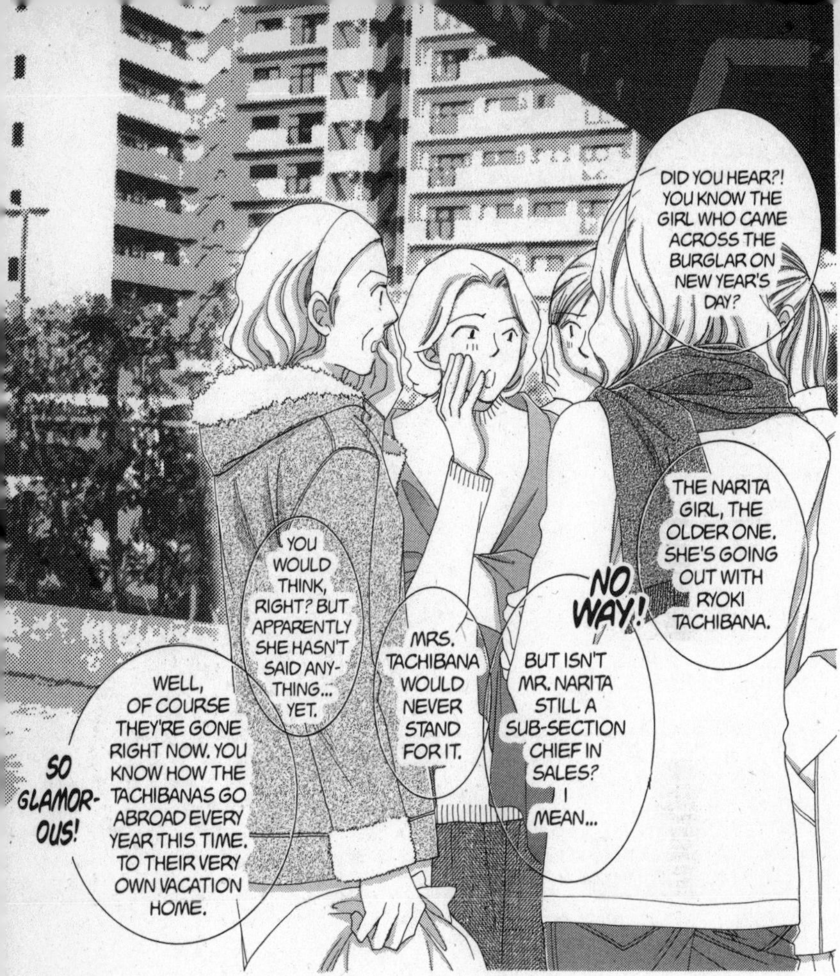
DID YOU HEAR?! YOU KNOW THE GIRL WHO CAME ACROSS THE BURGLAR ON NEW YEAR'S DAY?
THE NARITA GIRL, THE OLDER ONE. SHE'S GOING OUT WITH RYOKI TACHIBANA.
NO WAY!
BUT ISN'T MR. NARITA STILL A SUB-SECTION CHIEF IN SALES? I MEAN...
MRS. TACHIBANA WOULD NEVER STAND FOR IT.
YOU WOULD THINK, RIGHT? BUT APPARENTLY SHE HASN'T SAID ANY-THING... YET.
WELL, OF COURSE THEY'RE GONE RIGHT NOW. YOU KNOW HOW THE TACHIBANAS GO ABROAD EVERY YEAR THIS TIME. TO THEIR VERY OWN VACATION HOME.
SO GLAMOR-OUS!

hot gimmick

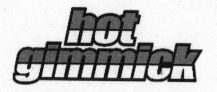

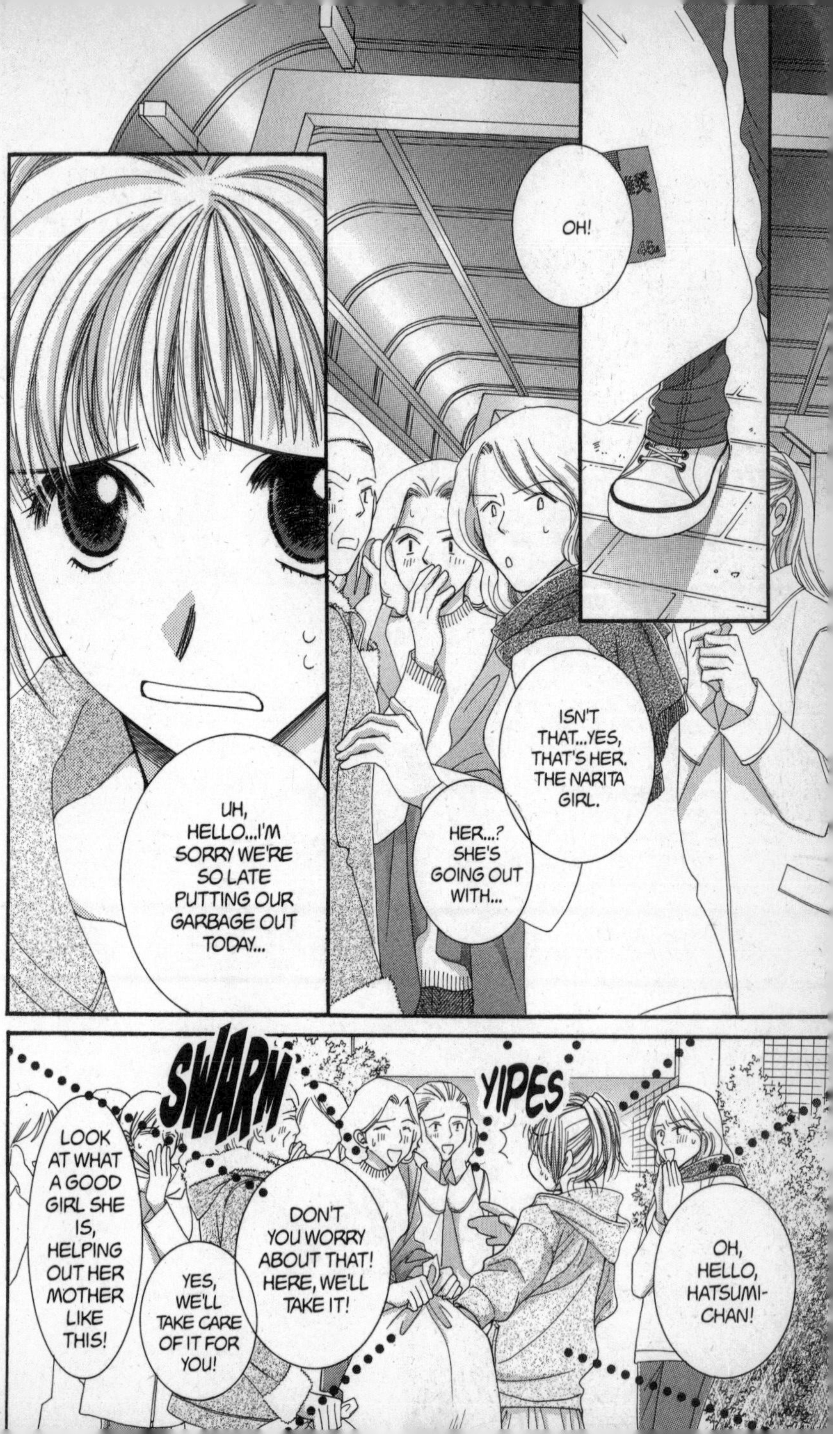
OH!
ISN'T THAT...YES, THAT'S HER. THE NARITA GIRL.
HER...? SHE'S GOING OUT WITH...
UH, HELLO...I'M SORRY WE'RE SO LATE PUTTING OUR GARBAGE OUT TODAY...
OH, HELLO, HATSUMI-CHAN!
YIPES
DON'T YOU WORRY ABOUT THAT! HERE, WE'LL TAKE IT!
YES, WE'LL TAKE CARE OF IT FOR YOU!
SWARM
LOOK AT WHAT A GOOD GIRL SHE IS, HELPING OUT HER MOTHER LIKE THIS!

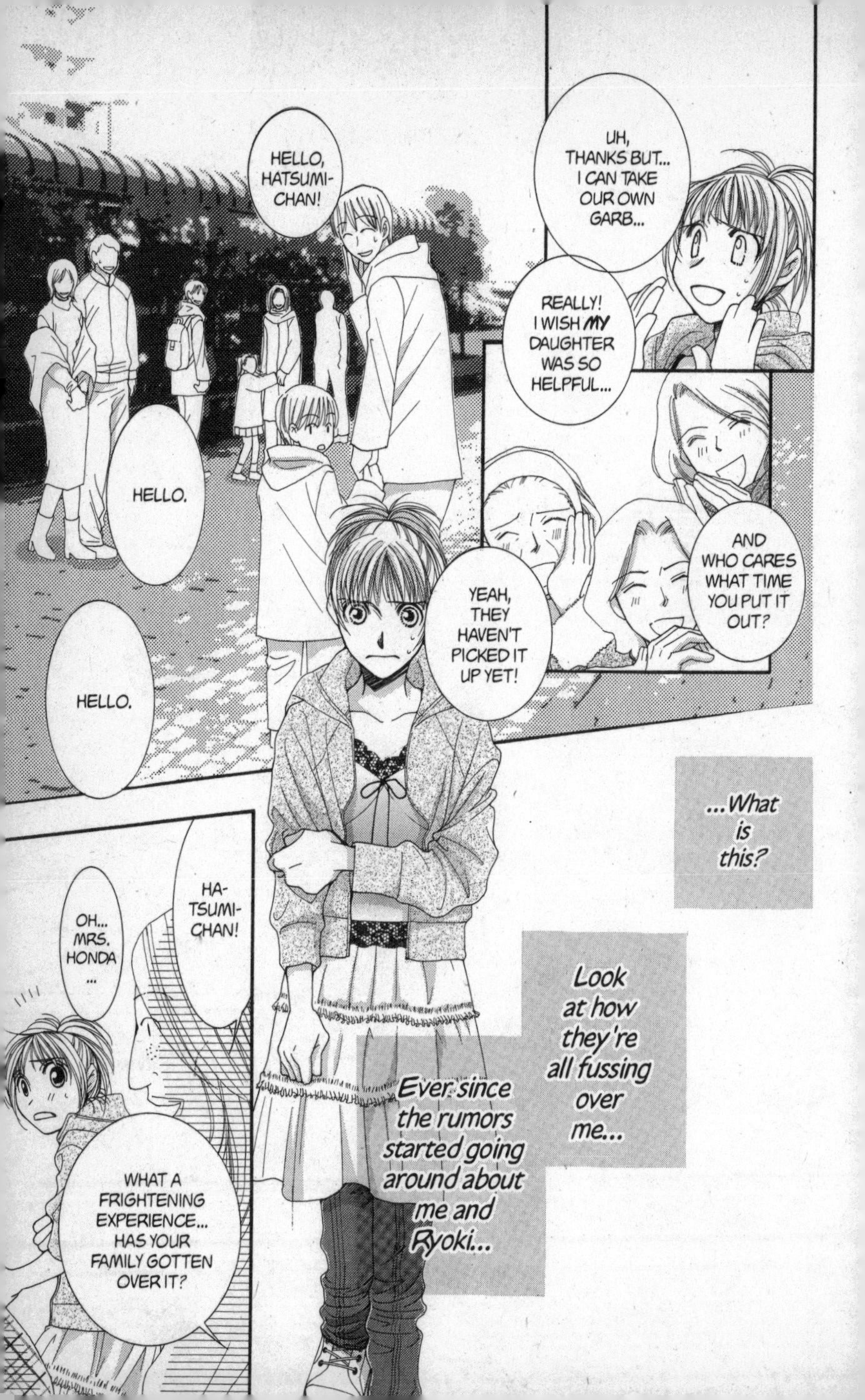
UH, THANKS BUT... I CAN TAKE OUR OWN GARB...
REALLY! I WISH MY DAUGHTER WAS SO HELPFUL...
AND WHO CARES WHAT TIME YOU PUT IT OUT?
YEAH, THEY HAVEN'T PICKED IT UP YET!
HELLO, HATSUMI-CHAN!
HELLO.
HELLO.
...What is this?
Look at how they're all fussing over me...
Ever since the rumors started going around about me and Ryoki...
HA-TSUMI-CHAN!
OH... MRS. HONDA ...
WHAT A FRIGHTENING EXPERIENCE... HAS YOUR FAMILY GOTTEN OVER IT?

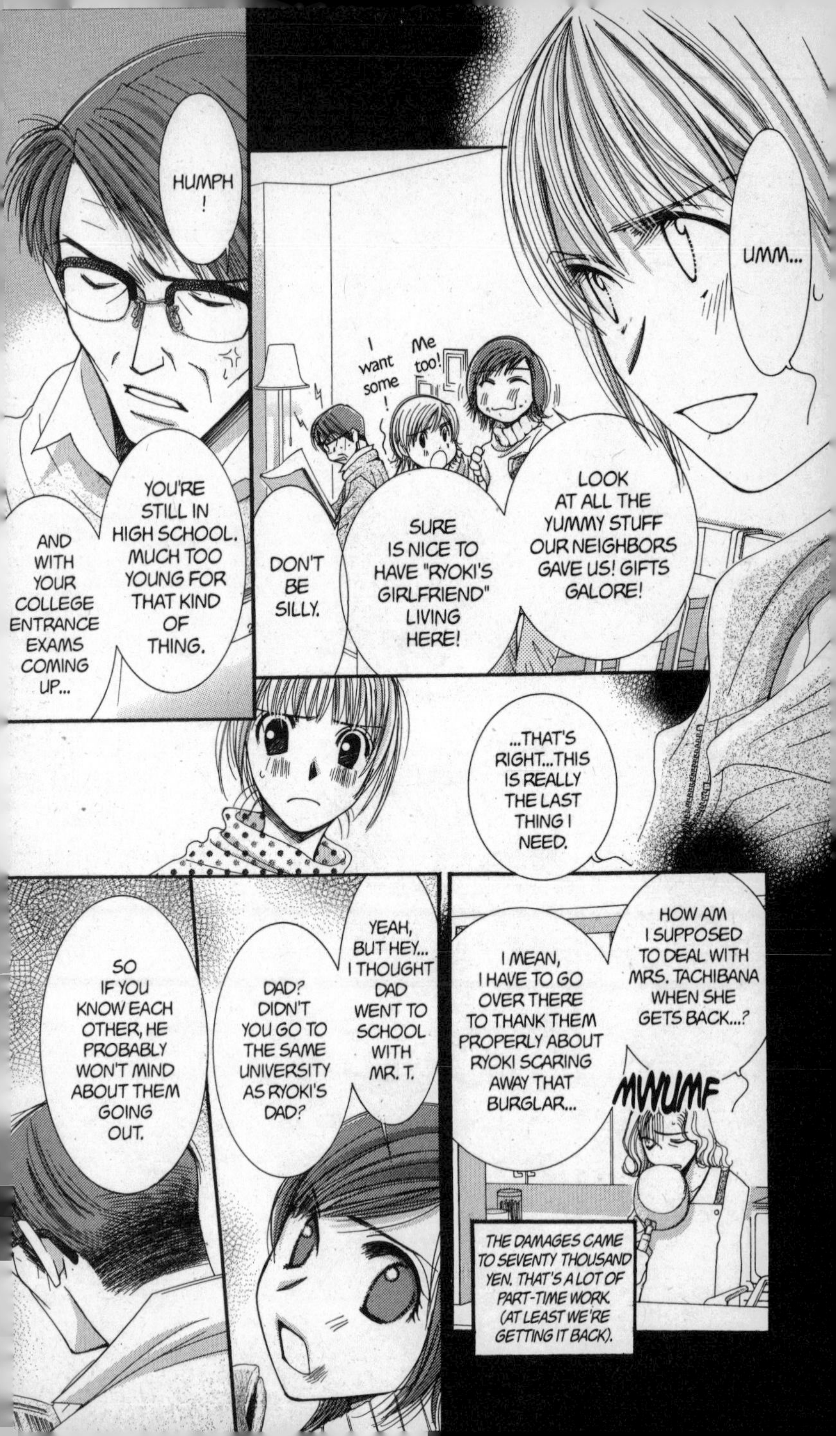
UMM...
Me too!
I want some!
LOOK AT ALL THE YUMMY STUFF OUR NEIGHBORS GAVE US! GIFTS GALORE!
SURE IS NICE TO HAVE "RYOKI'S GIRLFRIEND" LIVING HERE!
DON'T BE SILLY.
HUMPH!
YOU'RE STILL IN HIGH SCHOOL. MUCH TOO YOUNG FOR THAT KIND OF THING.
AND WITH YOUR COLLEGE ENTRANCE EXAMS COMING UP...
...THAT'S RIGHT...THIS IS REALLY THE LAST THING I NEED.
HOW AM I SUPPOSED TO DEAL WITH MRS. TACHIBANA WHEN SHE GETS BACK...?
I MEAN, I HAVE TO GO OVER THERE TO THANK THEM PROPERLY ABOUT RYOKI SCARING AWAY THAT BURGLAR...
MWUMF
THE DAMAGES CAME TO SEVENTY THOUSAND YEN. THAT'S A LOT OF PART-TIME WORK. (AT LEAST WE'RE GETTING IT BACK).
YEAH, BUT HEY... I THOUGHT DAD WENT TO SCHOOL WITH MR. T.
DAD? DIDN'T YOU GO TO THE SAME UNIVERSITY AS RYOKI'S DAD?
SO IF YOU KNOW EACH OTHER, HE PROBABLY WON'T MIND ABOUT THEM GOING OUT.

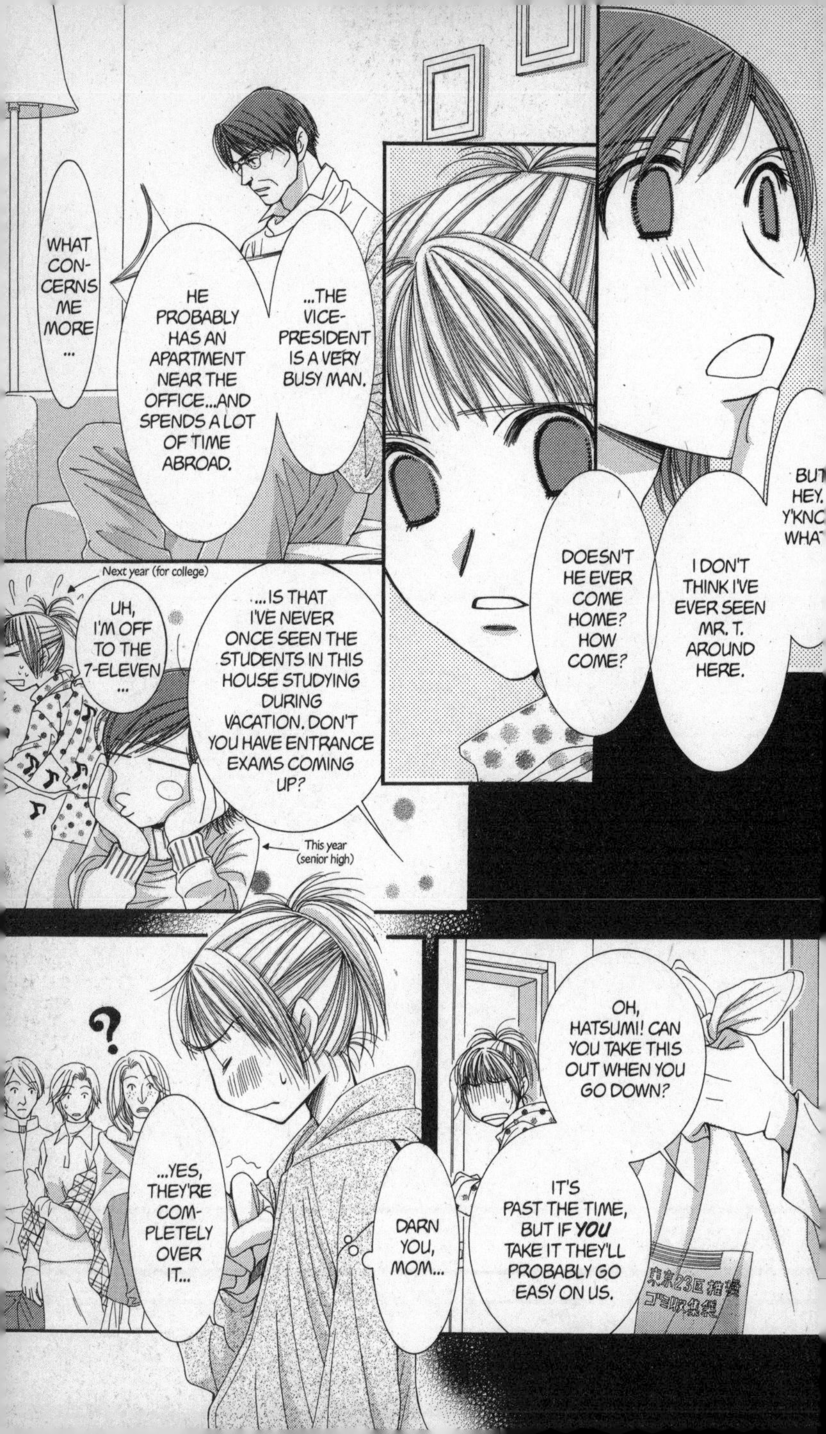
BUT HEY. Y'KNO WHAT
I DON'T THINK I'VE EVER SEEN MR. T. AROUND HERE.
DOESN'T HE EVER COME HOME? HOW COME?
...THE VICE-PRESIDENT IS A VERY BUSY MAN.
HE PROBABLY HAS AN APARTMENT NEAR THE OFFICE...AND SPENDS A LOT OF TIME ABROAD.
WHAT CON-CERNS ME MORE...
...IS THAT I'VE NEVER ONCE SEEN THE STUDENTS IN THIS HOUSE STUDYING DURING VACATION. DON'T YOU HAVE ENTRANCE EXAMS COMING UP?
UH, I'M OFF TO THE 7-ELEVEN...
Next year (for college)
This year (senior high)
OH, HATSUMI! CAN YOU TAKE THIS OUT WHEN YOU GO DOWN?
IT'S PAST THE TIME, BUT IF *YOU* TAKE IT THEY'LL PROBABLY GO EASY ON US.
東京23区推奨
ゴミ収集袋
DARN YOU, MOM...
...YES, THEY'RE COM-PLETELY OVER IT...

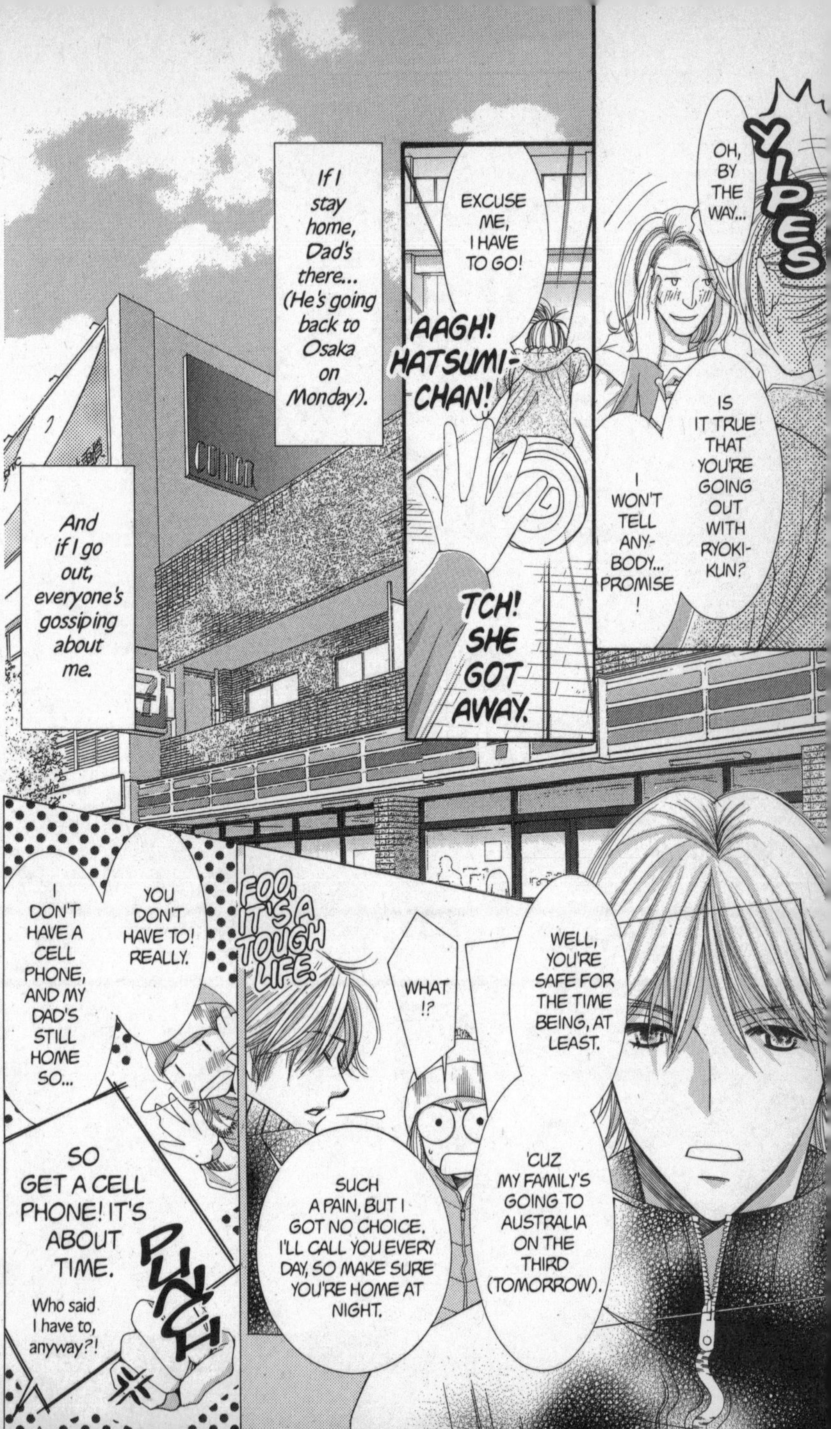
YIPES
OH, BY THE WAY...
IS IT TRUE THAT YOU'RE GOING OUT WITH RYOKI-KUN?
I WON'T TELL ANYBODY... PROMISE!
EXCUSE ME, I HAVE TO GO!
AAGH! HATSUMI-CHAN!
TCH! SHE GOT AWAY.
If I stay home, Dad's there... (He's going back to Osaka on Monday).
And if I go out, everyone's gossiping about me.
WELL, YOU'RE SAFE FOR THE TIME BEING, AT LEAST.
'CUZ MY FAMILY'S GOING TO AUSTRALIA ON THE THIRD (TOMORROW).
WHAT!?
FOO, IT'S A TOUGH LIFE.
SUCH A PAIN, BUT I GOT NO CHOICE. I'LL CALL YOU EVERY DAY, SO MAKE SURE YOU'RE HOME AT NIGHT.
YOU DON'T HAVE TO! REALLY.
I DON'T HAVE A CELL PHONE, AND MY DAD'S STILL HOME SO...
SO GET A CELL PHONE! IT'S ABOUT TIME.
PUNCH
Who said I have to, anyway?!

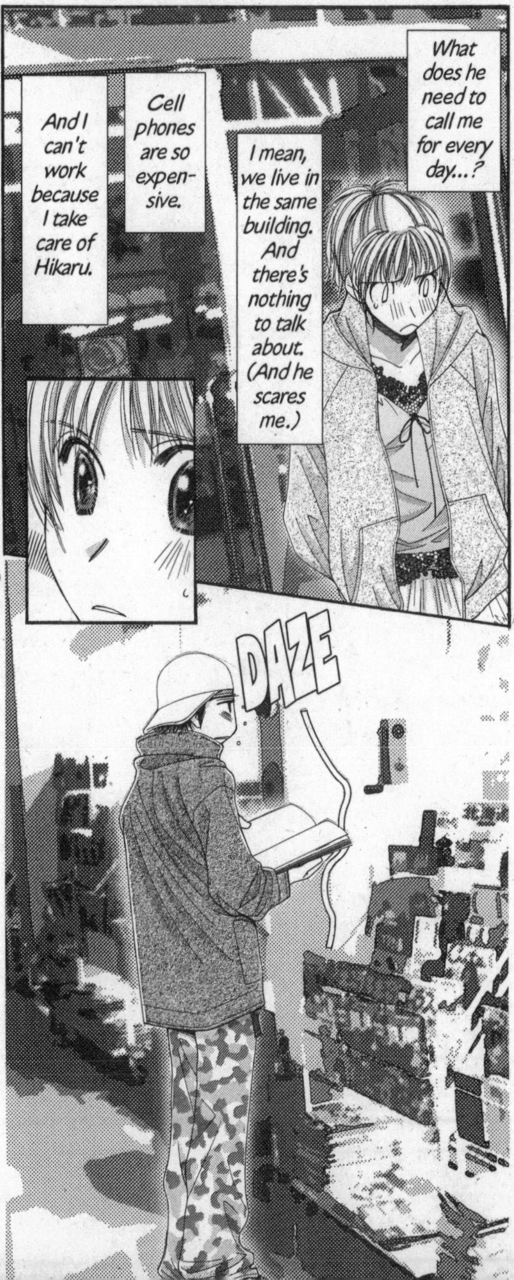
What does he need to call me for every day...?
I mean, we live in the same building. And there's nothing to talk about. (And he scares me.)
Cell phones are so expensive.
And I can't work because I take care of Hikaru.
DAZE

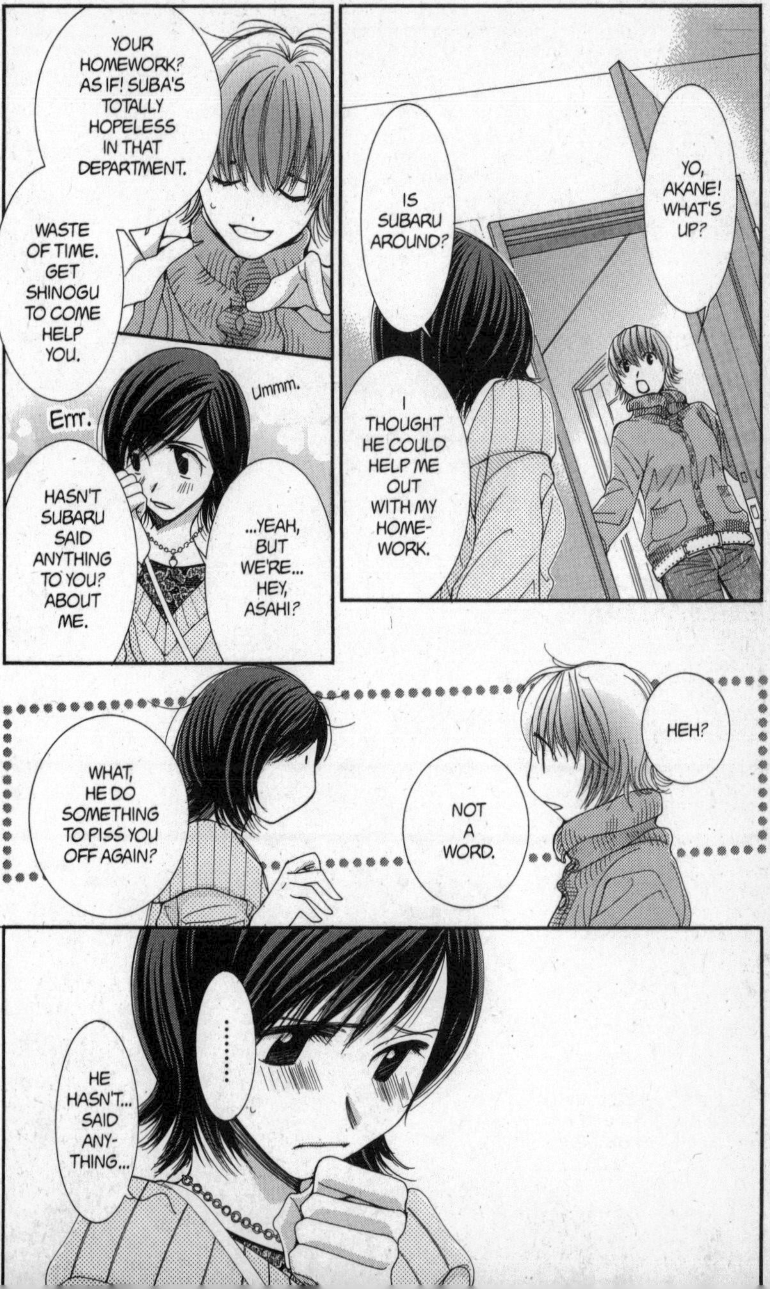
YO, AKANE! WHAT'S UP?
IS SUBARU AROUND?
I THOUGHT HE COULD HELP ME OUT WITH MY HOME-WORK.
YOUR HOMEWORK? AS IF! SUBA'S TOTALLY HOPELESS IN THAT DEPARTMENT.
WASTE OF TIME. GET SHINOGU TO COME HELP YOU.
Ummm.
Errr.
...YEAH, BUT WE'RE... HEY, ASAHI?
HASN'T SUBARU SAID ANYTHING TO YOU? ABOUT ME.
HEH?
NOT A WORD.
WHAT, HE DO SOMETHING TO PISS YOU OFF AGAIN?
......
HE HASN'T... SAID ANY-THING...

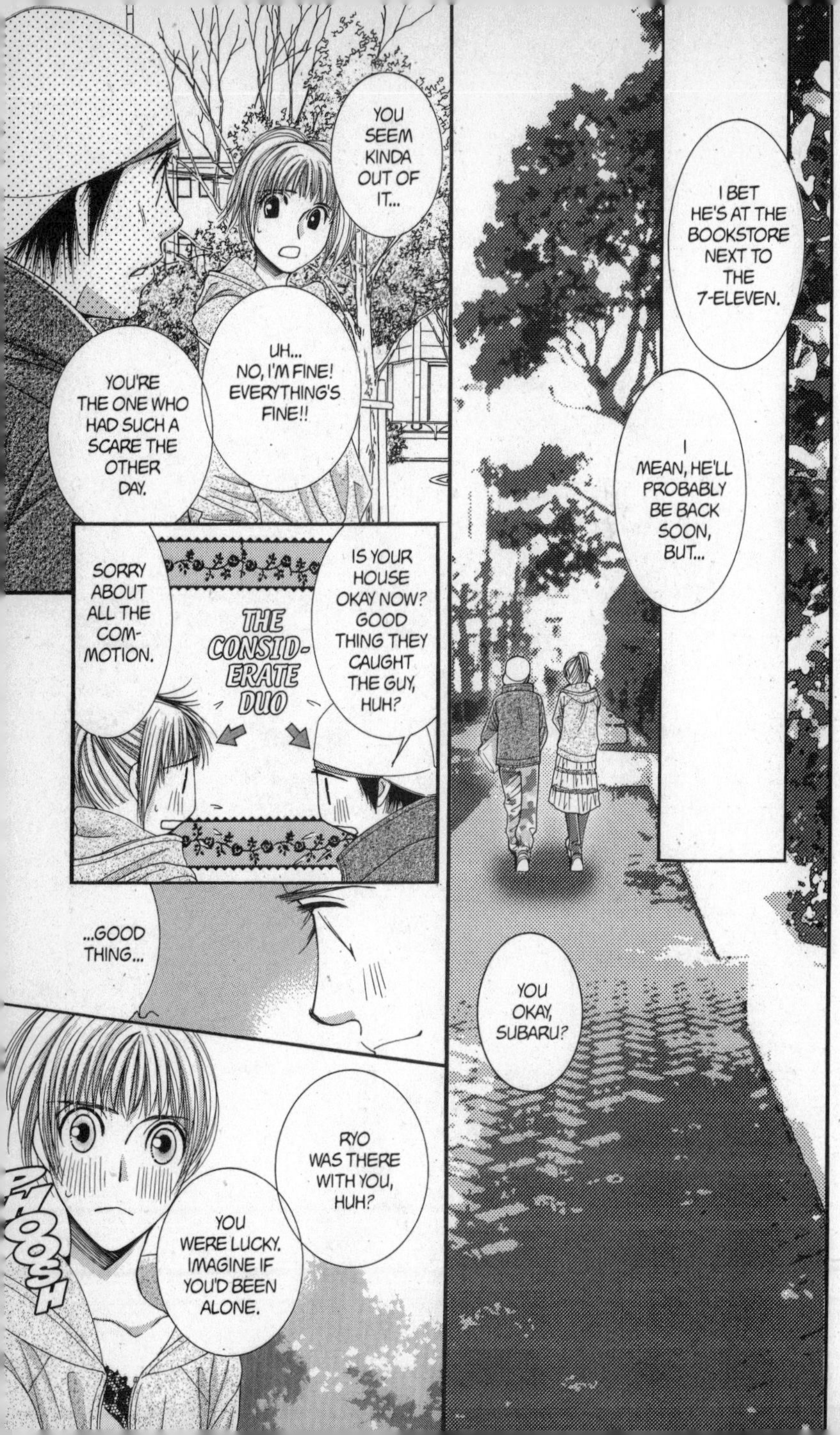
I BET HE'S AT THE BOOKSTORE NEXT TO THE 7-ELEVEN.
I MEAN, HE'LL PROBABLY BE BACK SOON, BUT...
YOU OKAY, SUBARU?
YOU SEEM KINDA OUT OF IT...
UH... NO, I'M FINE! EVERYTHING'S FINE!!
YOU'RE THE ONE WHO HAD SUCH A SCARE THE OTHER DAY.
IS YOUR HOUSE OKAY NOW? GOOD THING THEY CAUGHT THE GUY, HUH?
THE CONSID-ERATE DUO
SORRY ABOUT ALL THE COM-MOTION.
...GOOD THING...
RYO WAS THERE WITH YOU, HUH?
YOU WERE LUCKY. IMAGINE IF YOU'D BEEN ALONE.

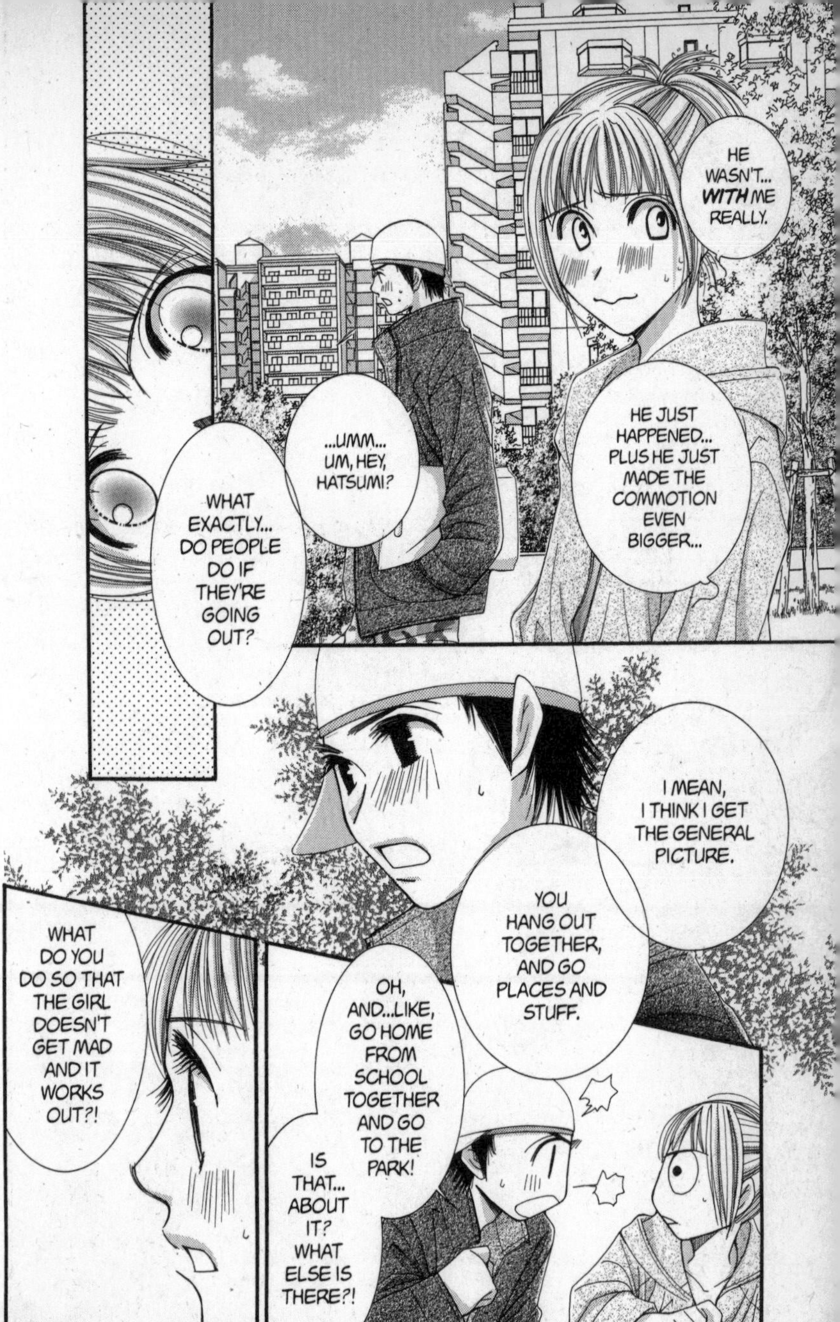
HE WASN'T... WITH ME REALLY.
HE JUST HAPPENED... PLUS HE JUST MADE THE COMMOTION EVEN BIGGER...
...UMM... UM, HEY, HATSUMI?
WHAT EXACTLY... DO PEOPLE DO IF THEY'RE GOING OUT?
I MEAN, I THINK I GET THE GENERAL PICTURE.
YOU HANG OUT TOGETHER, AND GO PLACES AND STUFF.
OH, AND...LIKE, GO HOME FROM SCHOOL TOGETHER AND GO TO THE PARK!
IS THAT... ABOUT IT? WHAT ELSE IS THERE?!
WHAT DO YOU DO SO THAT THE GIRL DOESN'T GET MAD AND IT WORKS OUT?!

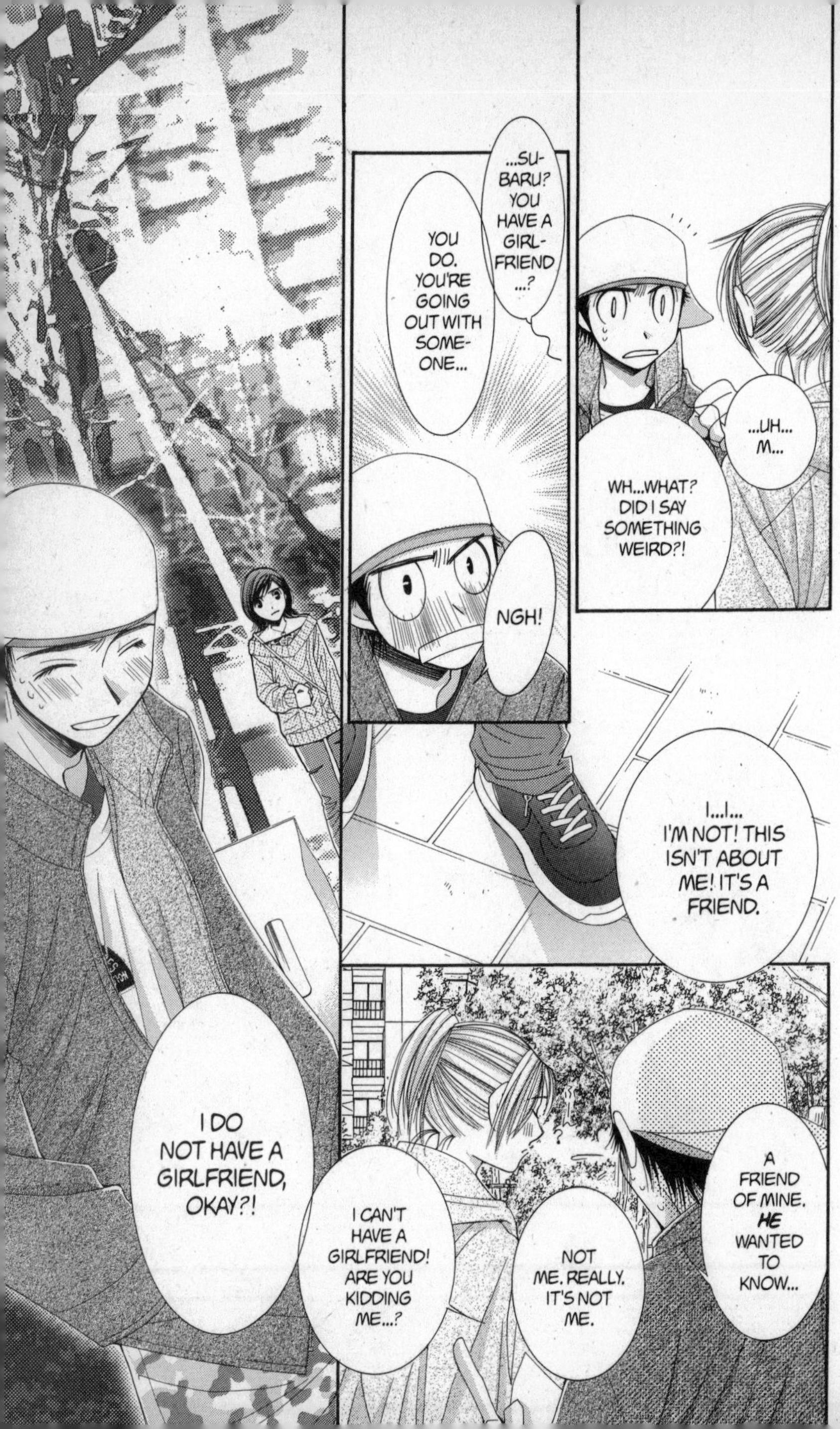
...UH... M...
WH...WHAT? DID I SAY SOMETHING WEIRD?!
...SU-BARU? YOU HAVE A GIRL-FRIEND ...?
YOU DO. YOU'RE GOING OUT WITH SOME-ONE...
NGH!
I...I... I'M NOT! THIS ISN'T ABOUT ME! IT'S A FRIEND.
A FRIEND OF MINE. HE WANTED TO KNOW...
NOT ME. REALLY. IT'S NOT ME.
I CAN'T HAVE A GIRLFRIEND! ARE YOU KIDDING ME...?
I DO NOT HAVE A GIRLFRIEND, OKAY?!

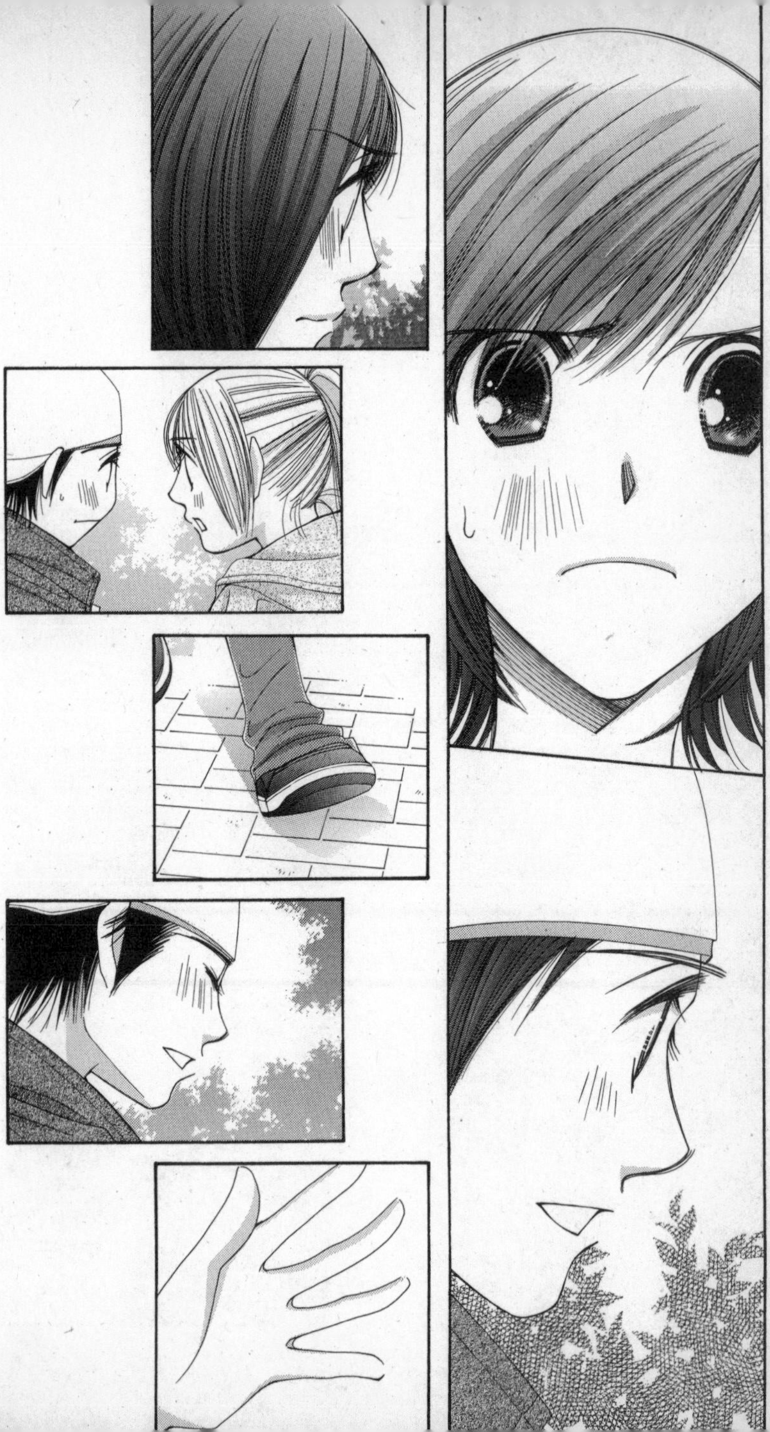

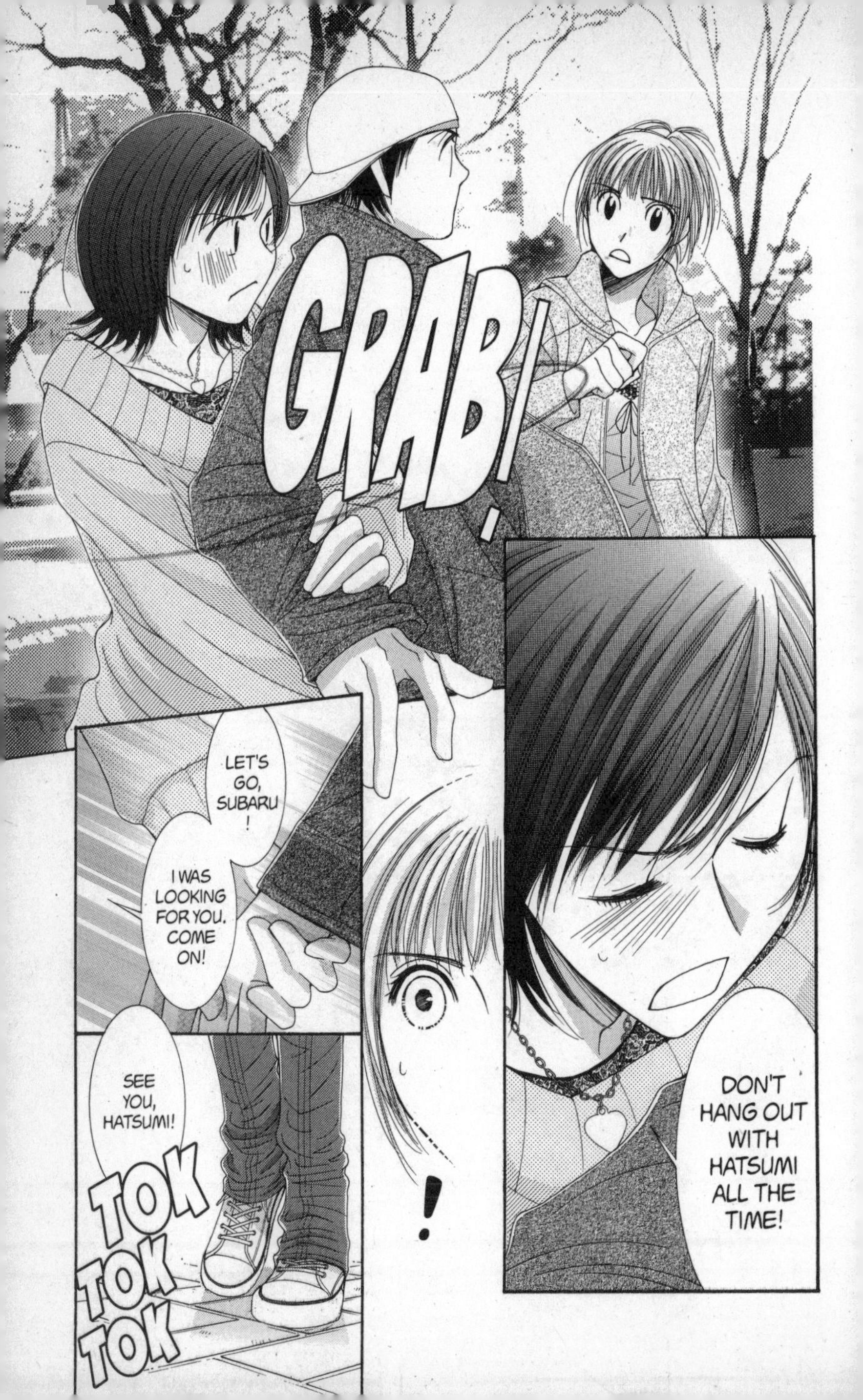
GRAB!
DON'T HANG OUT WITH HATSUMI ALL THE TIME!
!
LET'S GO, SUBARU!
I WAS LOOKING FOR YOU. COME ON!
SEE YOU, HATSUMI!
TOK TOK TOK

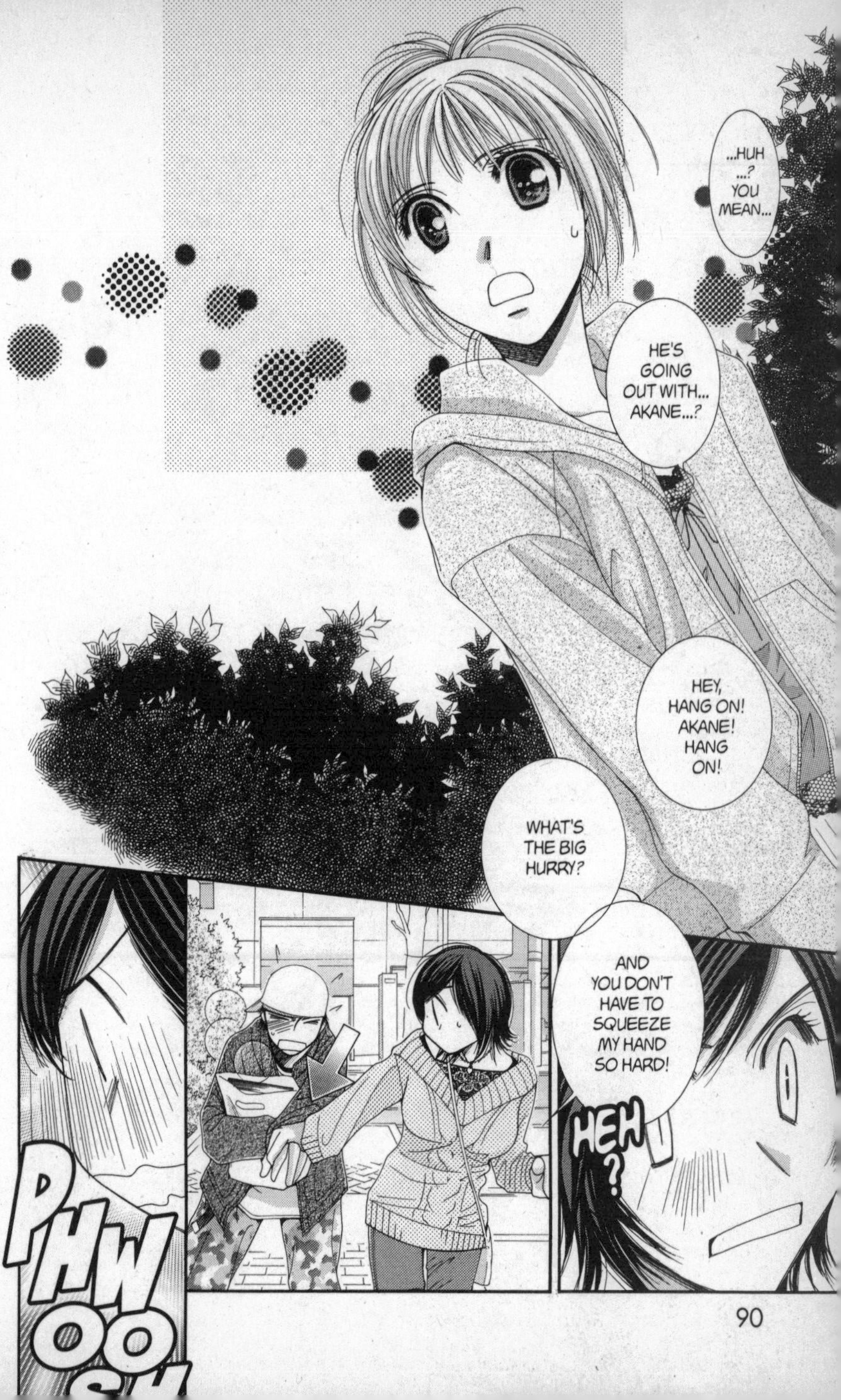
...HUH ...? YOU MEAN...
HE'S GOING OUT WITH... AKANE...?
HEY, HANG ON! AKANE! HANG ON!
WHAT'S THE BIG HURRY?
AND YOU DON'T HAVE TO SQUEEZE MY HAND SO HARD!
HEH ?
PHWOO

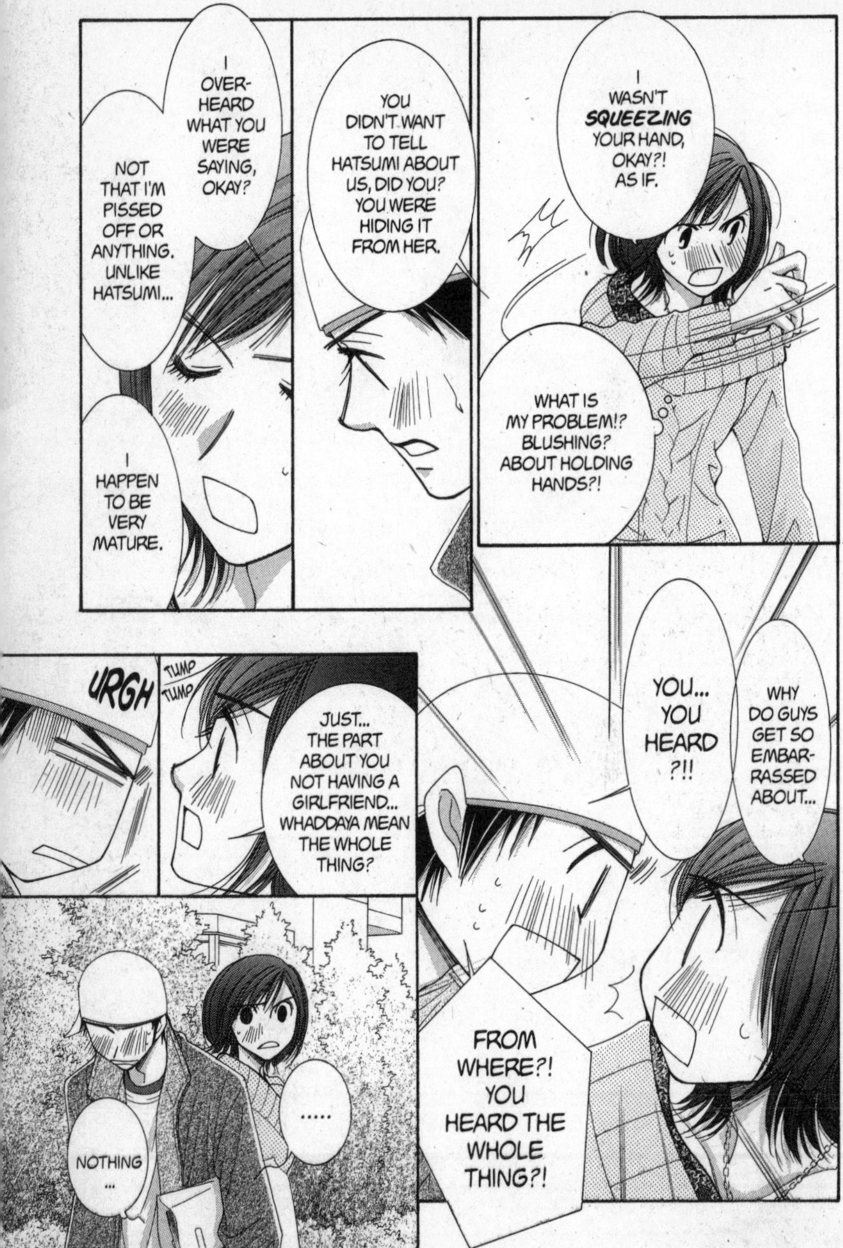
I WASN'T **SQUEEZING** YOUR HAND, OKAY?! AS IF.
WHAT IS MY PROBLEM!? BLUSHING? ABOUT HOLDING HANDS?!
YOU DIDN'T WANT TO TELL HATSUMI ABOUT US, DID YOU? YOU WERE HIDING IT FROM HER.
I OVER-HEARD WHAT YOU WERE SAYING, OKAY?
NOT THAT I'M PISSED OFF OR ANYTHING. UNLIKE HATSUMI...
I HAPPEN TO BE VERY MATURE.
WHY DO GUYS GET SO EMBAR-RASSED ABOUT...
YOU... YOU HEARD ?!!
FROM WHERE?! YOU HEARD THE WHOLE THING?!
TUMP TUMP
JUST... THE PART ABOUT YOU NOT HAVING A GIRLFRIEND... WHADDAYA MEAN THE WHOLE THING?
URGH
.....
NOTHING ...

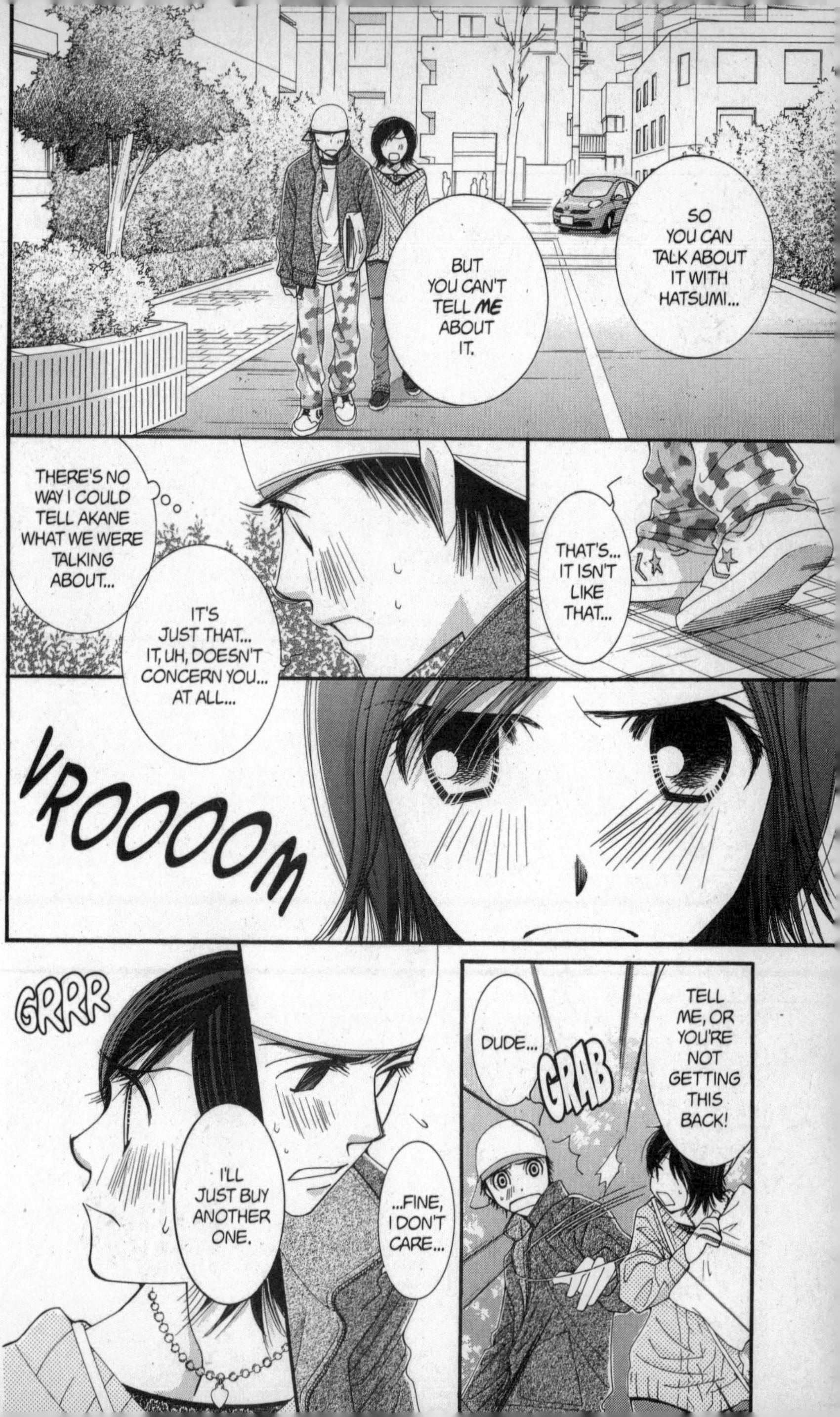
SO YOU CAN TALK ABOUT IT WITH HATSUMI...
BUT YOU CAN'T TELL *ME* ABOUT IT.
THAT'S... IT ISN'T LIKE THAT...
THERE'S NO WAY I COULD TELL AKANE WHAT WE WERE TALKING ABOUT...
IT'S JUST THAT... IT, UH, DOESN'T CONCERN YOU... AT ALL...
VROOOOM
TELL ME, OR YOU'RE NOT GETTING THIS BACK!
GRAB
DUDE...
GRRR
...FINE, I DON'T CARE...
I'LL JUST BUY ANOTHER ONE.

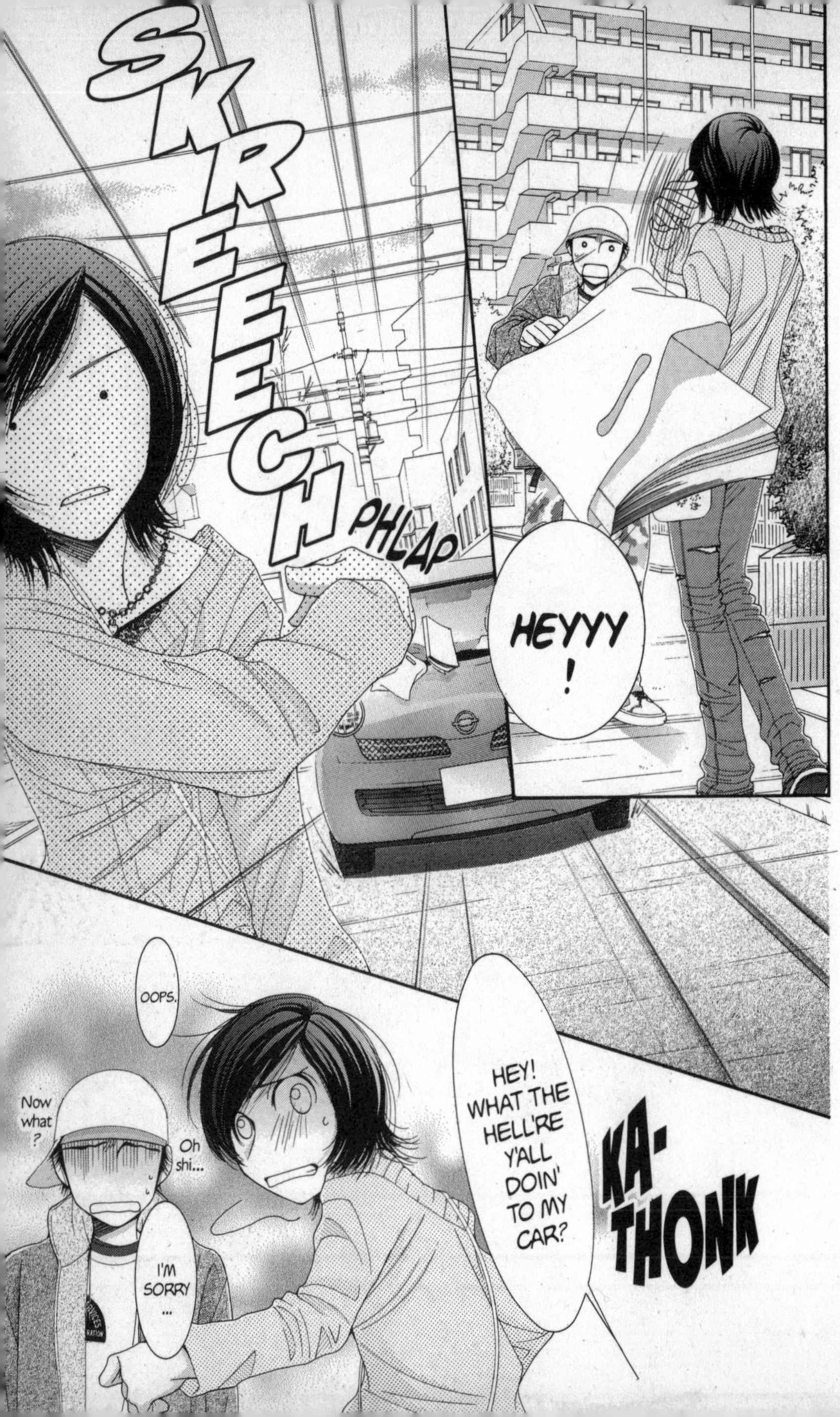
HEYYY!
SKREECH
PHLAP
KA-THONK
HEY! WHAT THE HELL'RE Y'ALL DOIN' TO MY CAR?
OOPS.
Oh shi...
Now what?
I'M SORRY...

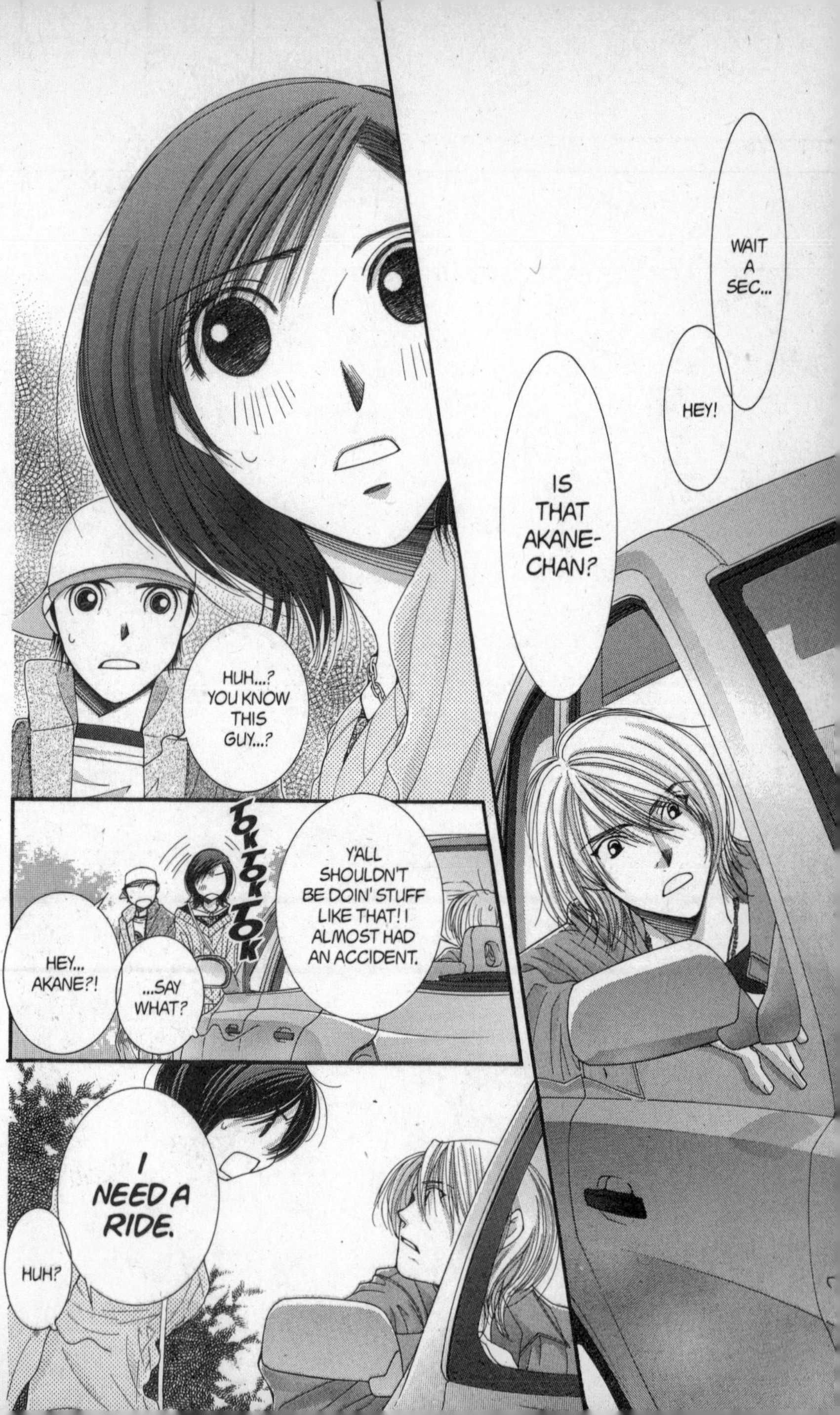
WAIT A SEC...
HEY!
IS THAT AKANE-CHAN?
HUH...? YOU KNOW THIS GUY...?
TOK TOK TOK
Y'ALL SHOULDN'T BE DOIN' STUFF LIKE THAT!! ALMOST HAD AN ACCIDENT.
...SAY WHAT?
HEY... AKANE?!
I NEED A RIDE.
HUH?

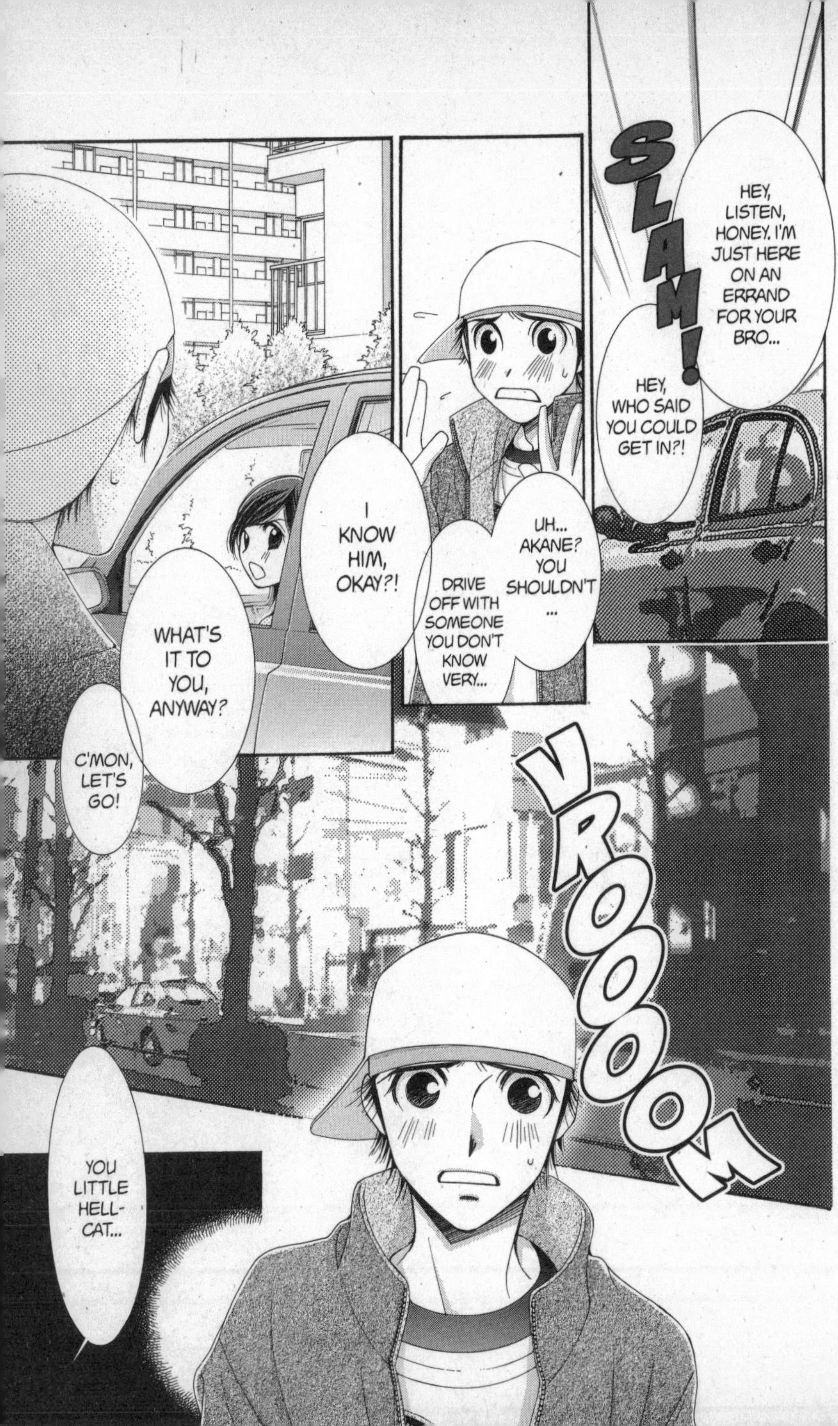
SLAM!
HEY, LISTEN, HONEY. I'M JUST HERE ON AN ERRAND FOR YOUR BRO...
HEY, WHO SAID YOU COULD GET IN?!
UH... AKANE? YOU SHOULDN'T ...
DRIVE OFF WITH SOMEONE YOU DON'T KNOW VERY...
I KNOW HIM, OKAY?!
WHAT'S IT TO YOU, ANYWAY?
C'MON, LET'S GO!
VROOOOOM
YOU LITTLE HELL-CAT...

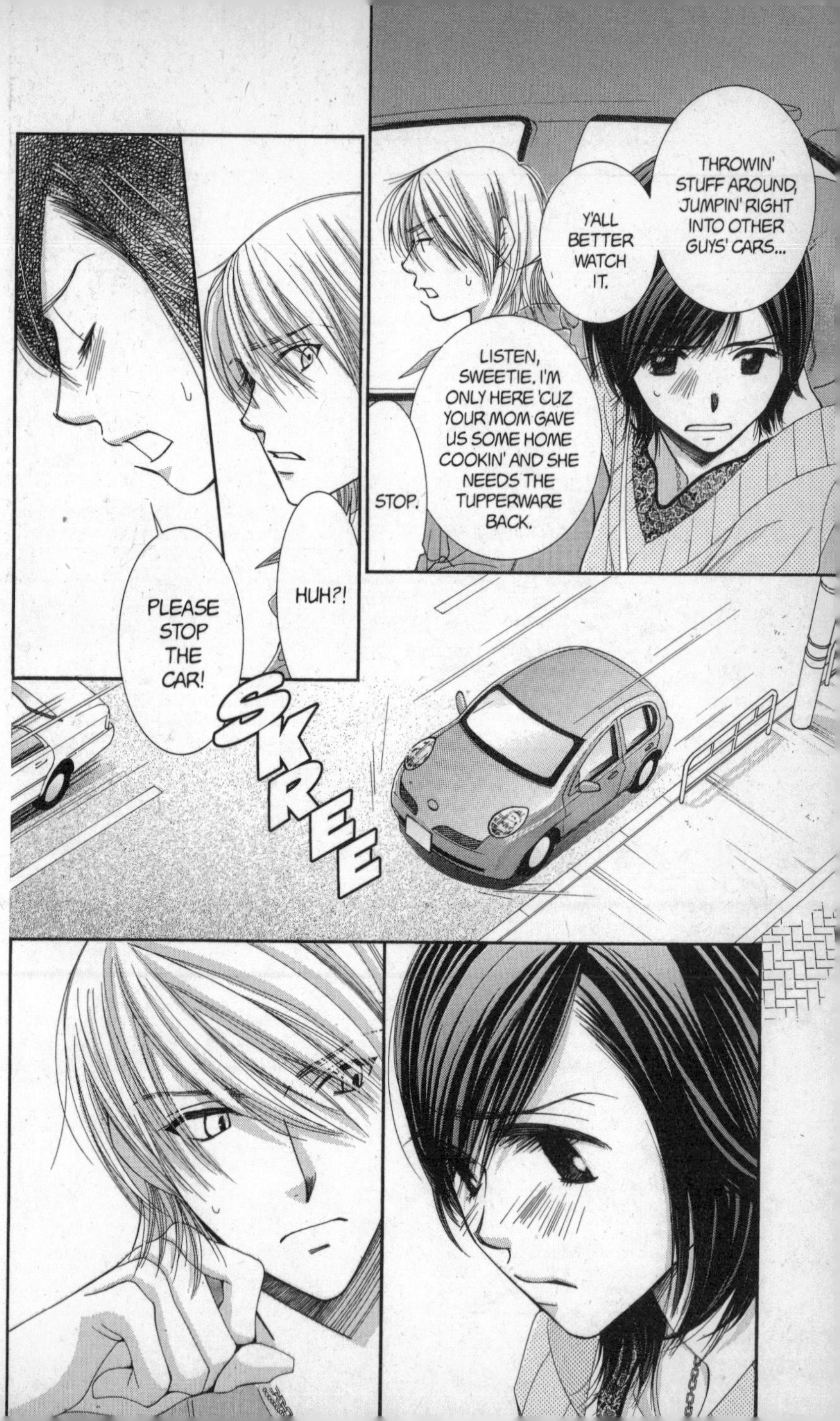
THROWIN' STUFF AROUND, JUMPIN' RIGHT INTO OTHER GUYS' CARS...
Y'ALL BETTER WATCH IT.
LISTEN, SWEETIE. I'M ONLY HERE 'CUZ YOUR MOM GAVE US SOME HOME COOKIN' AND SHE NEEDS THE TUPPERWARE BACK.
STOP.
HUH?!
PLEASE STOP THE CAR!
SKREE

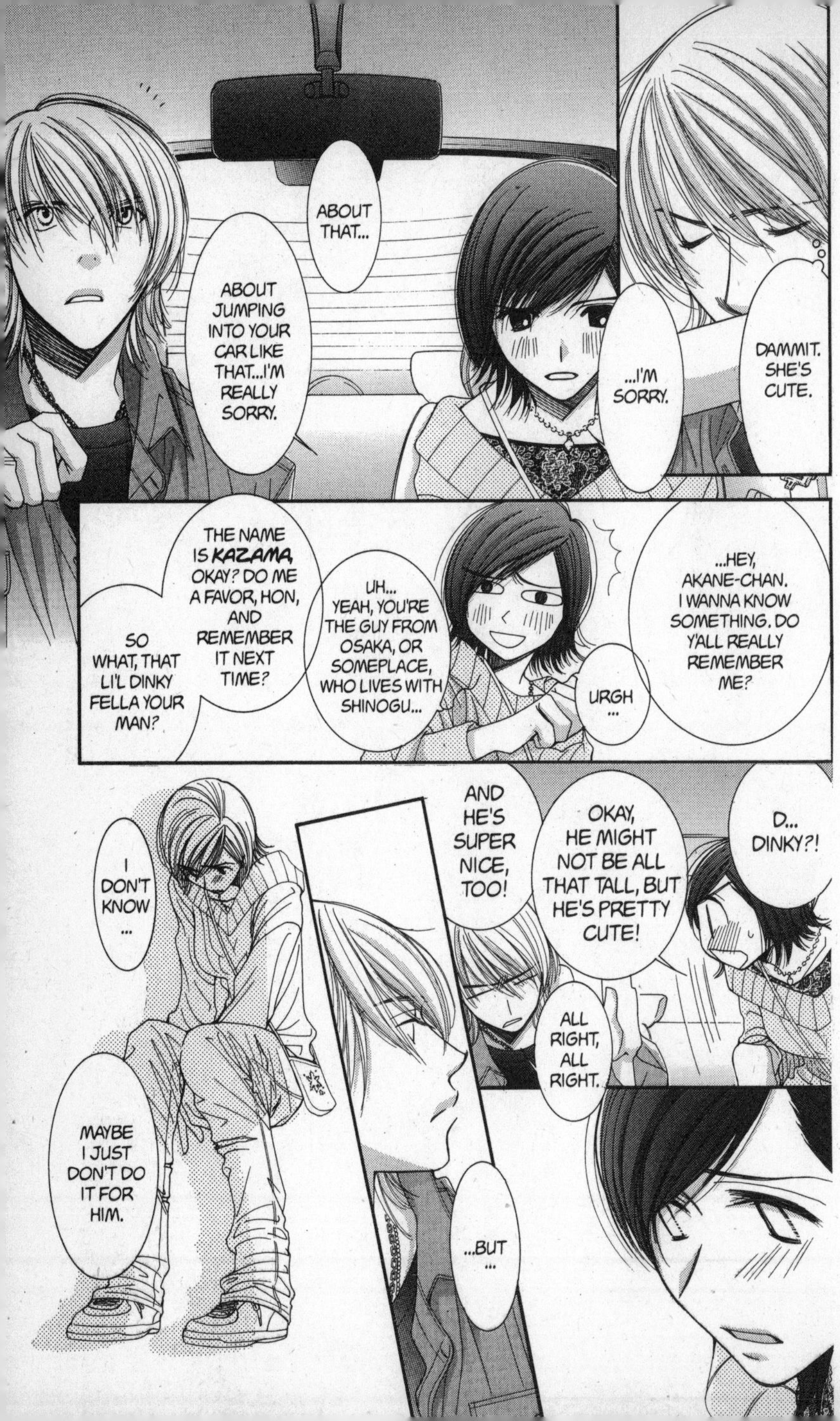
DAMMIT. SHE'S CUTE.
ABOUT THAT...
ABOUT JUMPING INTO YOUR CAR LIKE THAT...I'M REALLY SORRY.
...I'M SORRY.
...HEY, AKANE-CHAN. I WANNA KNOW SOMETHING. DO Y'ALL REALLY REMEMBER ME?
URGH...
UH... YEAH, YOU'RE THE GUY FROM OSAKA, OR SOMEPLACE, WHO LIVES WITH SHINOGU...
THE NAME IS **KAZAMA**, OKAY? DO ME A FAVOR, HON, AND REMEMBER IT NEXT TIME?
SO WHAT, THAT LI'L DINKY FELLA YOUR MAN?
D... DINKY?!
OKAY, HE MIGHT NOT BE ALL THAT TALL, BUT HE'S PRETTY CUTE!
AND HE'S SUPER NICE, TOO!
ALL RIGHT, ALL RIGHT.
...BUT...
I DON'T KNOW...
MAYBE I JUST DON'T DO IT FOR HIM.

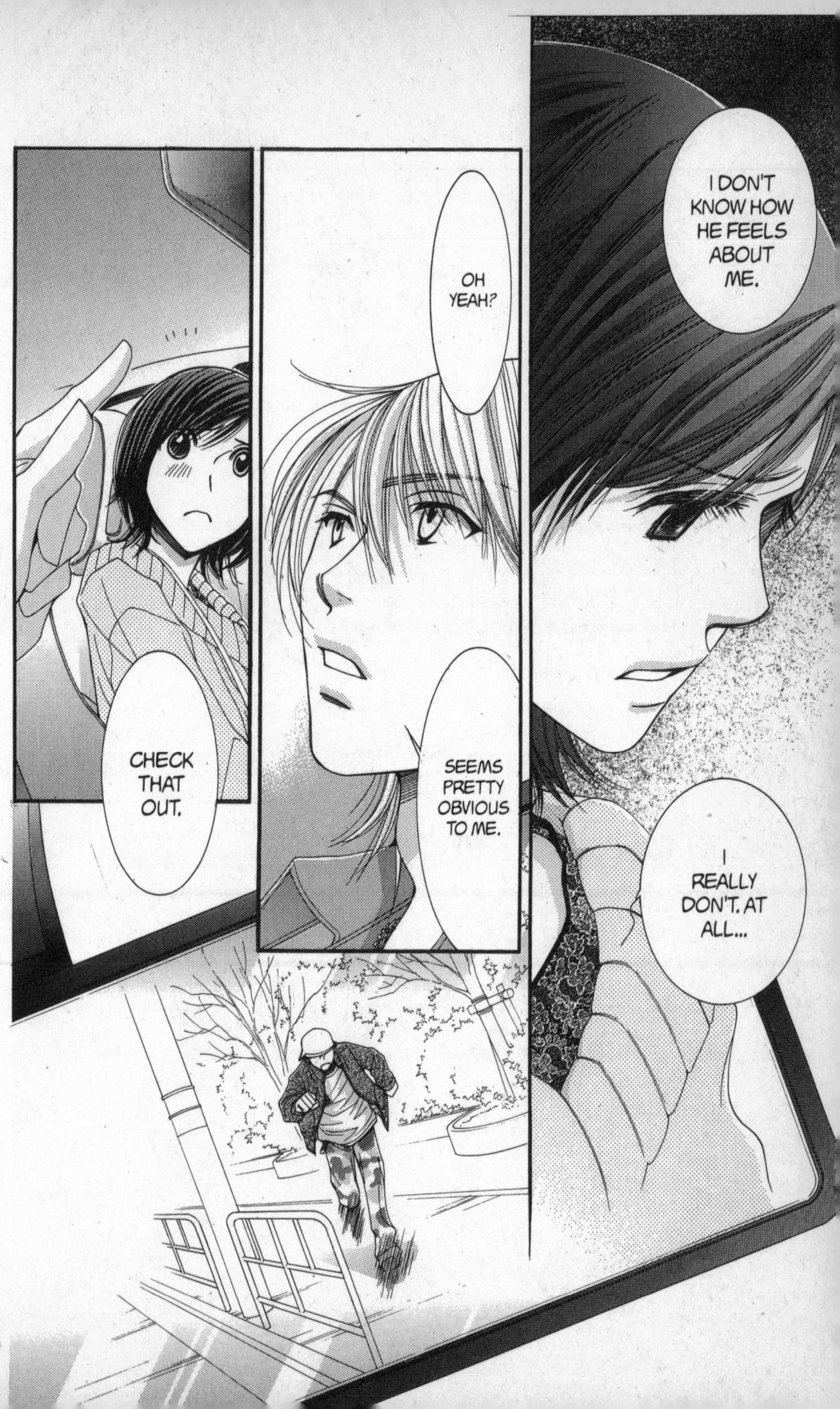

I DON'T KNOW HOW HE FEELS ABOUT ME.
OH YEAH?
SEEMS PRETTY OBVIOUS TO ME.
I REALLY DON'T. AT ALL...
CHECK THAT OUT.

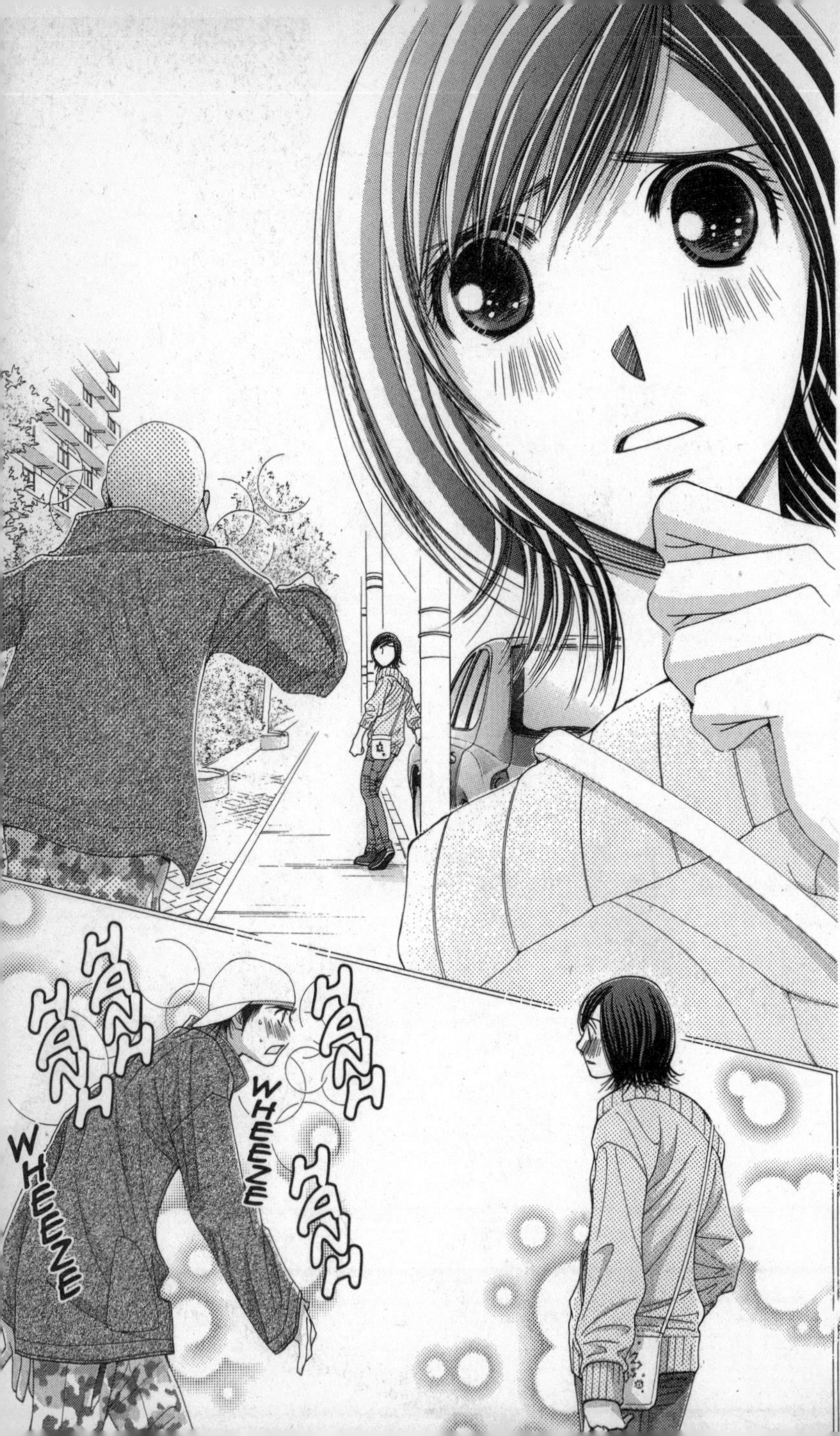
HAAH
HAAH
WHEEZE
HAAH
HAAH
WHEEZE

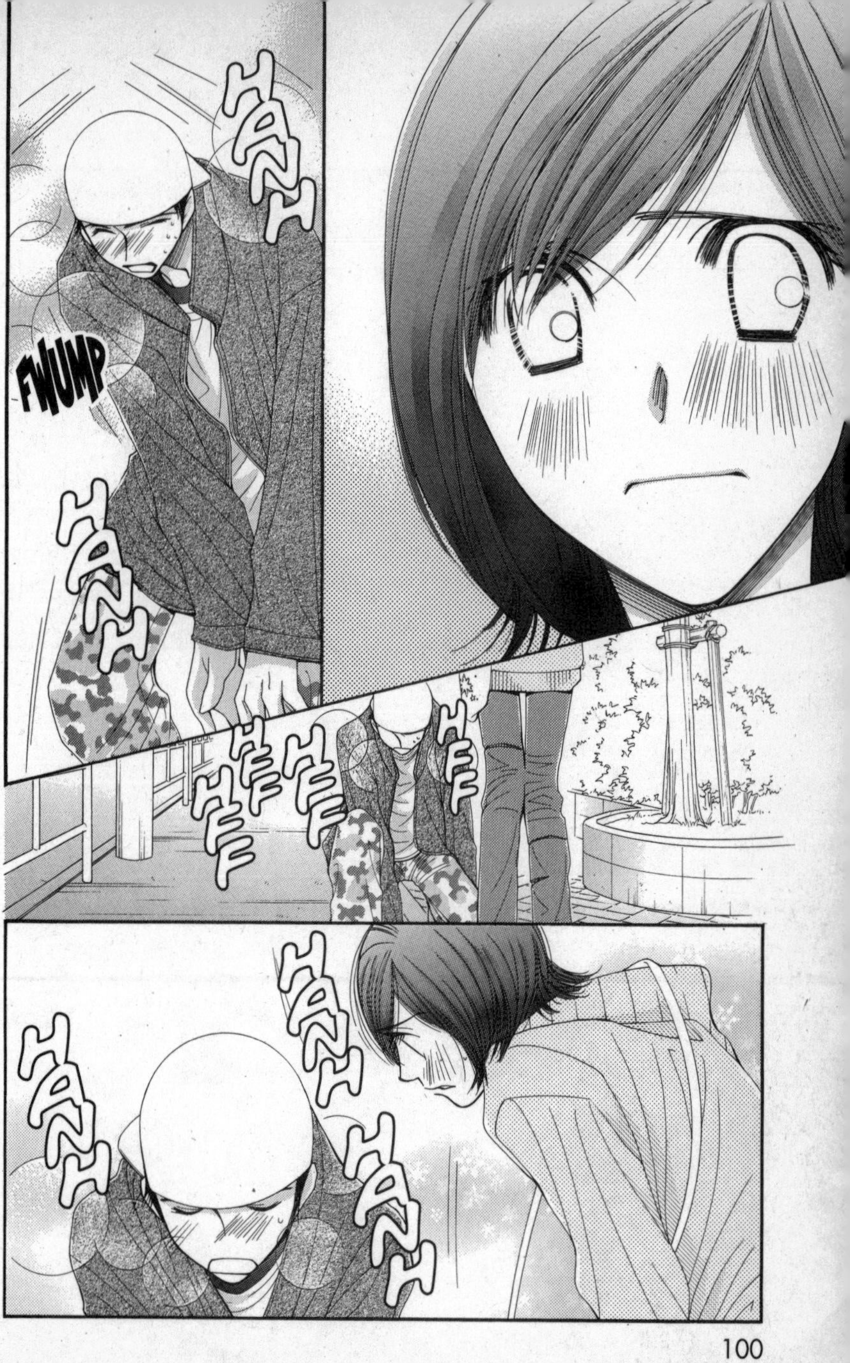
HAH
FWUMP
HAH
HEF
HEF
HEF
HEF
HAH
HAH
HAH

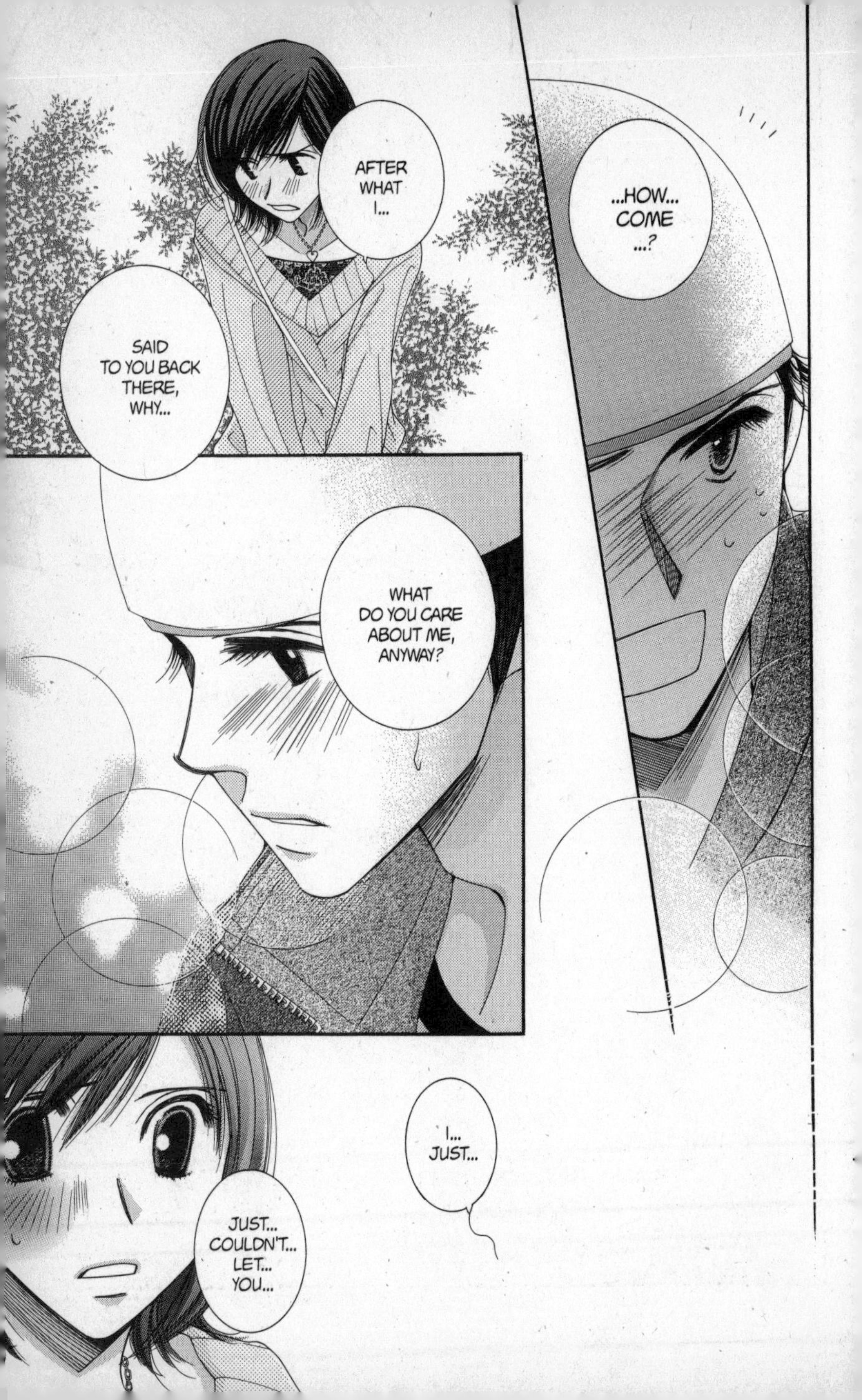
...HOW... COME ...?
AFTER WHAT I...
SAID TO YOU BACK THERE, WHY...
WHAT DO YOU CARE ABOUT ME, ANYWAY?
I... JUST...
JUST... COULDN'T... LET... YOU...

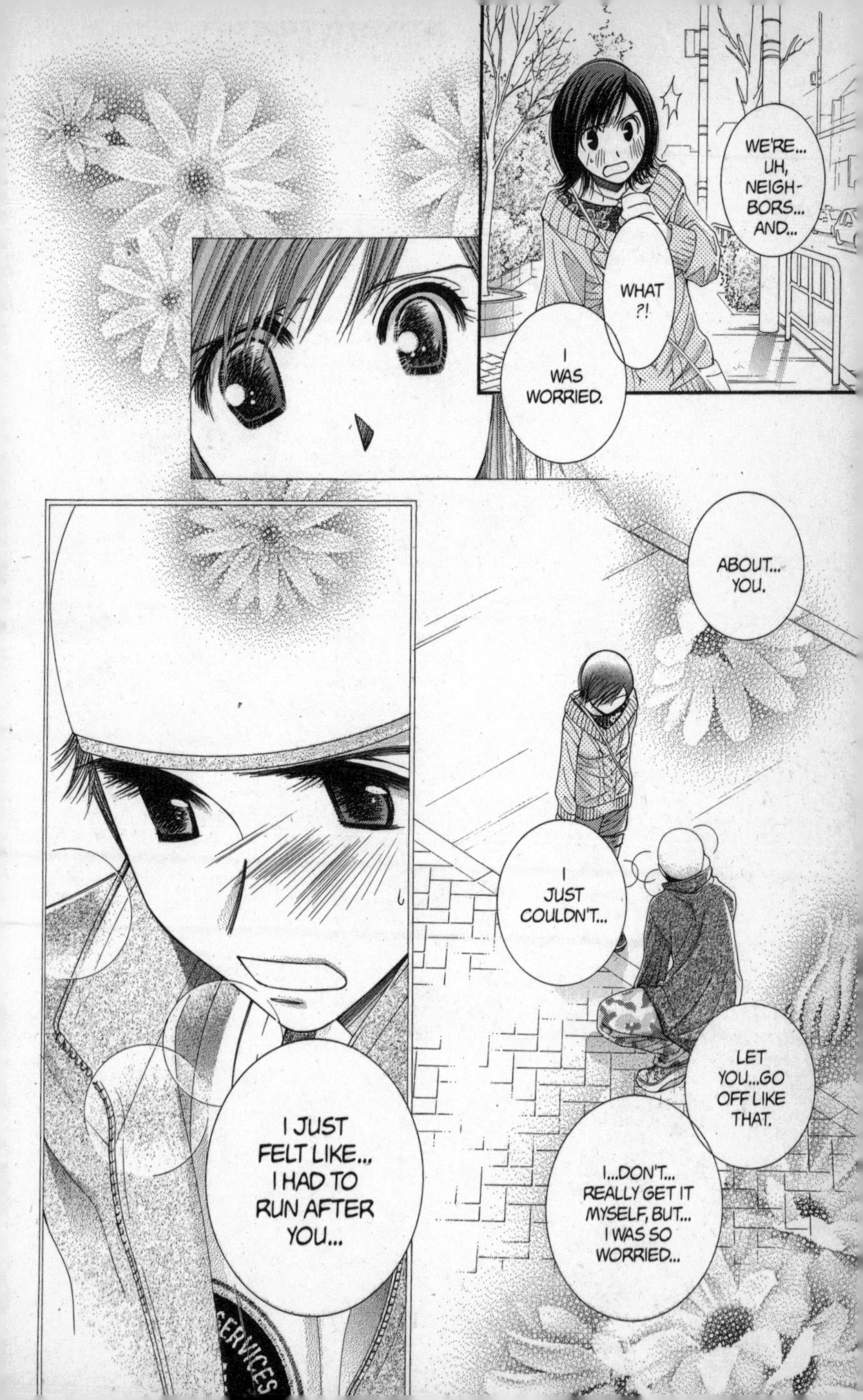
WE'RE... UH, NEIGHBORS... AND...
WHAT?!
I WAS WORRIED.
ABOUT... YOU.
I JUST COULDN'T...
LET YOU...GO OFF LIKE THAT.
I...DON'T... REALLY GET IT MYSELF, BUT... I WAS SO WORRIED...
I JUST FELT LIKE... I HAD TO RUN AFTER YOU...
SERVICES

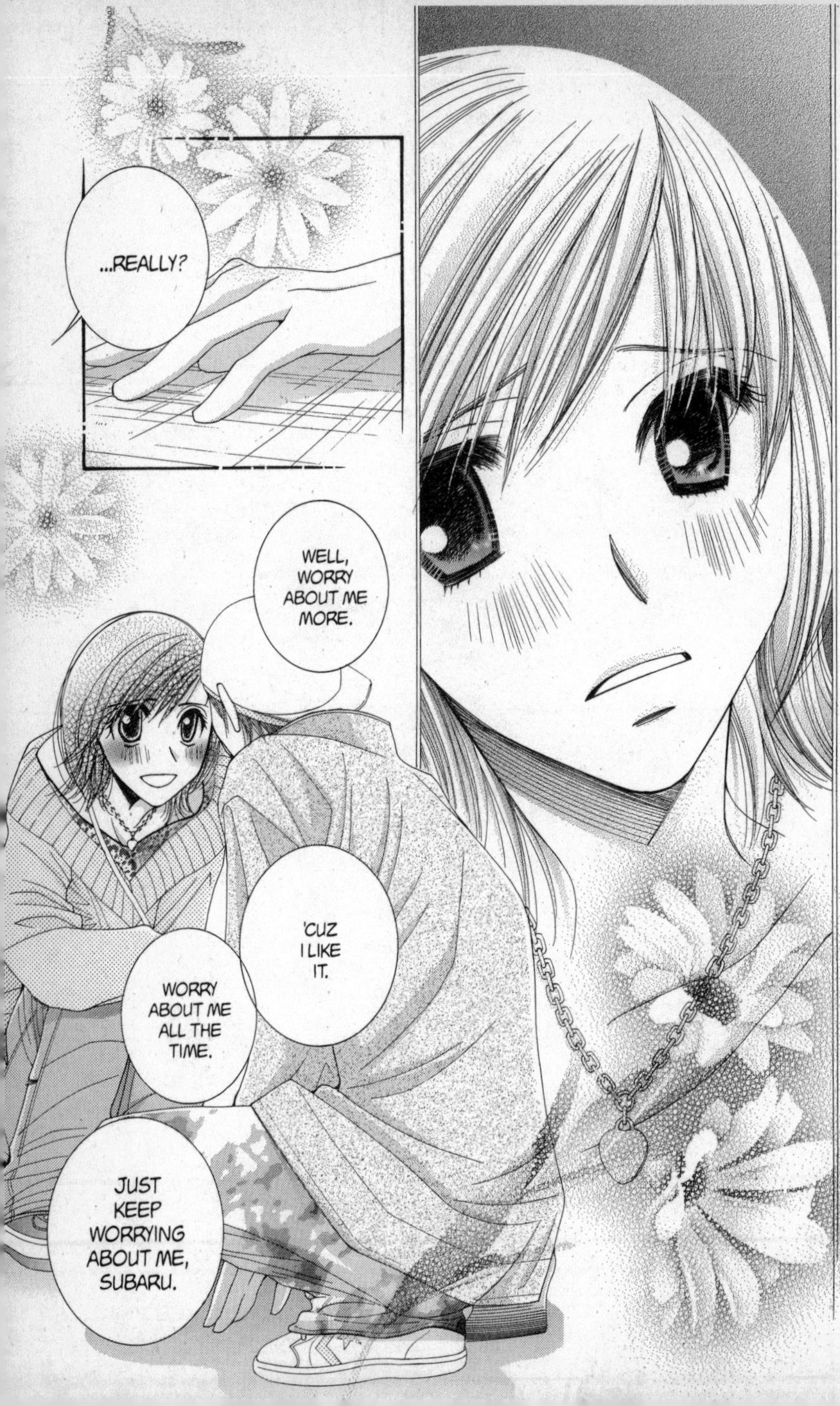
...REALLY?
WELL, WORRY ABOUT ME MORE.
'CUZ I LIKE IT.
WORRY ABOUT ME ALL THE TIME.
JUST KEEP WORRYING ABOUT ME, SUBARU.

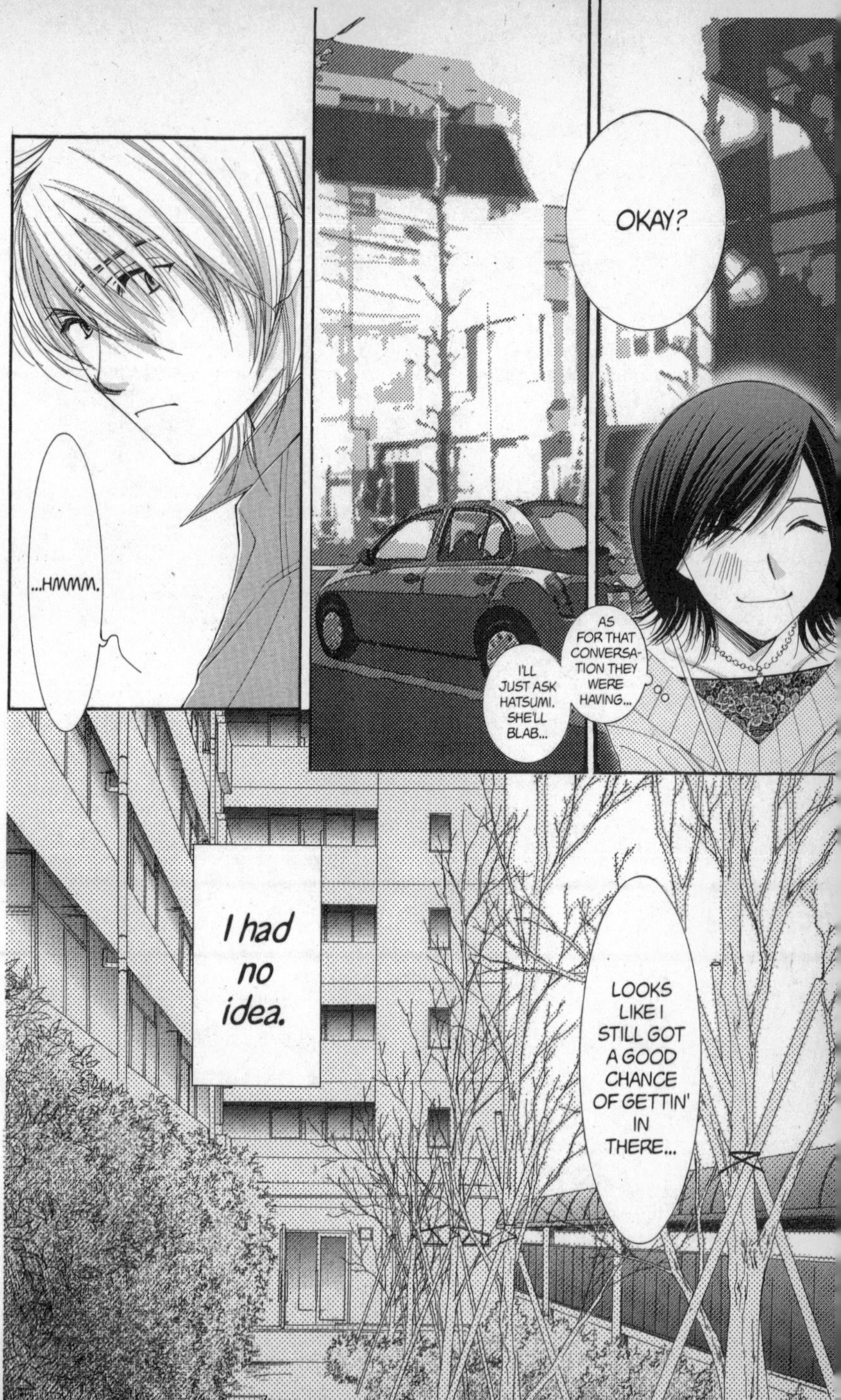
OKAY?
AS FOR THAT CONVERSATION THEY WERE HAVING...
I'LL JUST ASK HATSUMI. SHE'LL BLAB...
...HMMM.
LOOKS LIKE I STILL GOT A GOOD CHANCE OF GETTIN' IN THERE...
I had no idea.

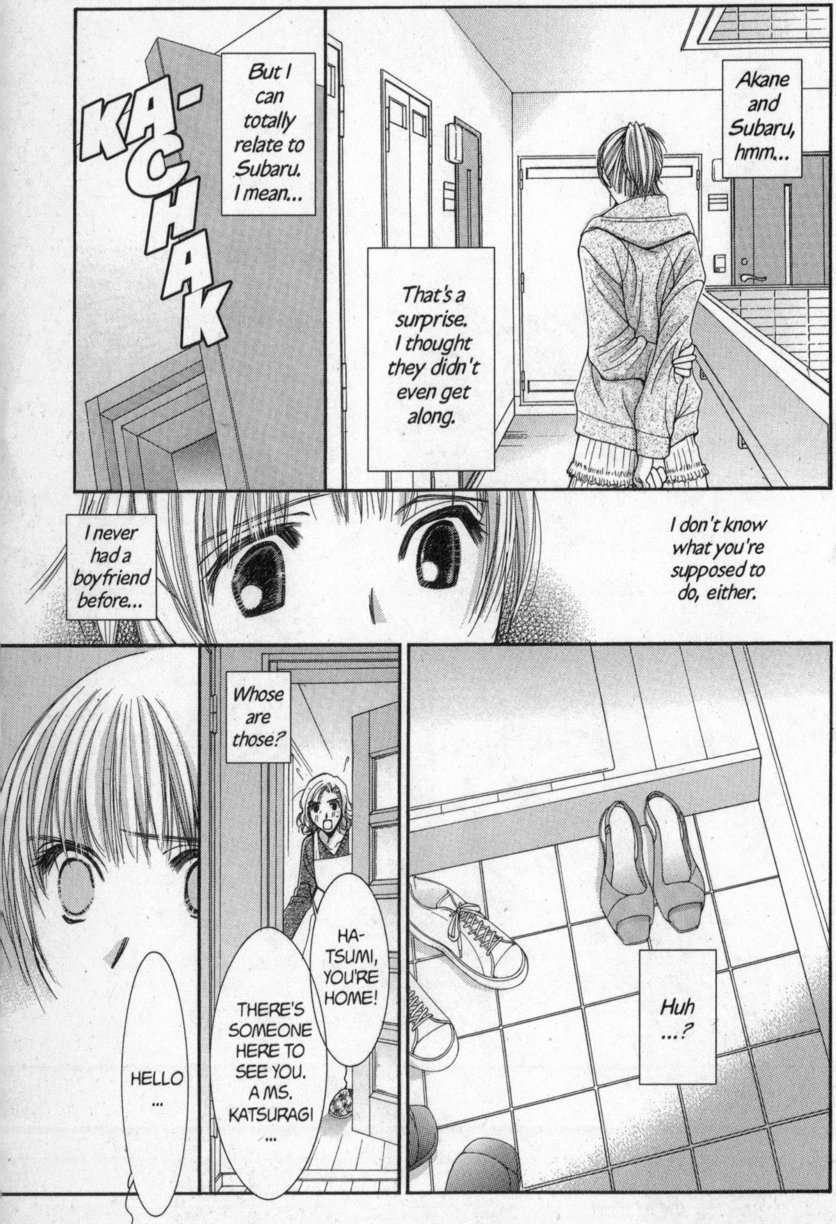
Akane and Subaru, hmm...
That's a surprise. I thought they didn't even get along.
But I can totally relate to Subaru. I mean...
KA-CHAK
I don't know what you're supposed to do, either.
I never had a boyfriend before...
Huh ...?
Whose are those?
HA-TSUMI, YOU'RE HOME!
THERE'S SOMEONE HERE TO SEE YOU. A MS. KATSURAGI ...
HELLO ...

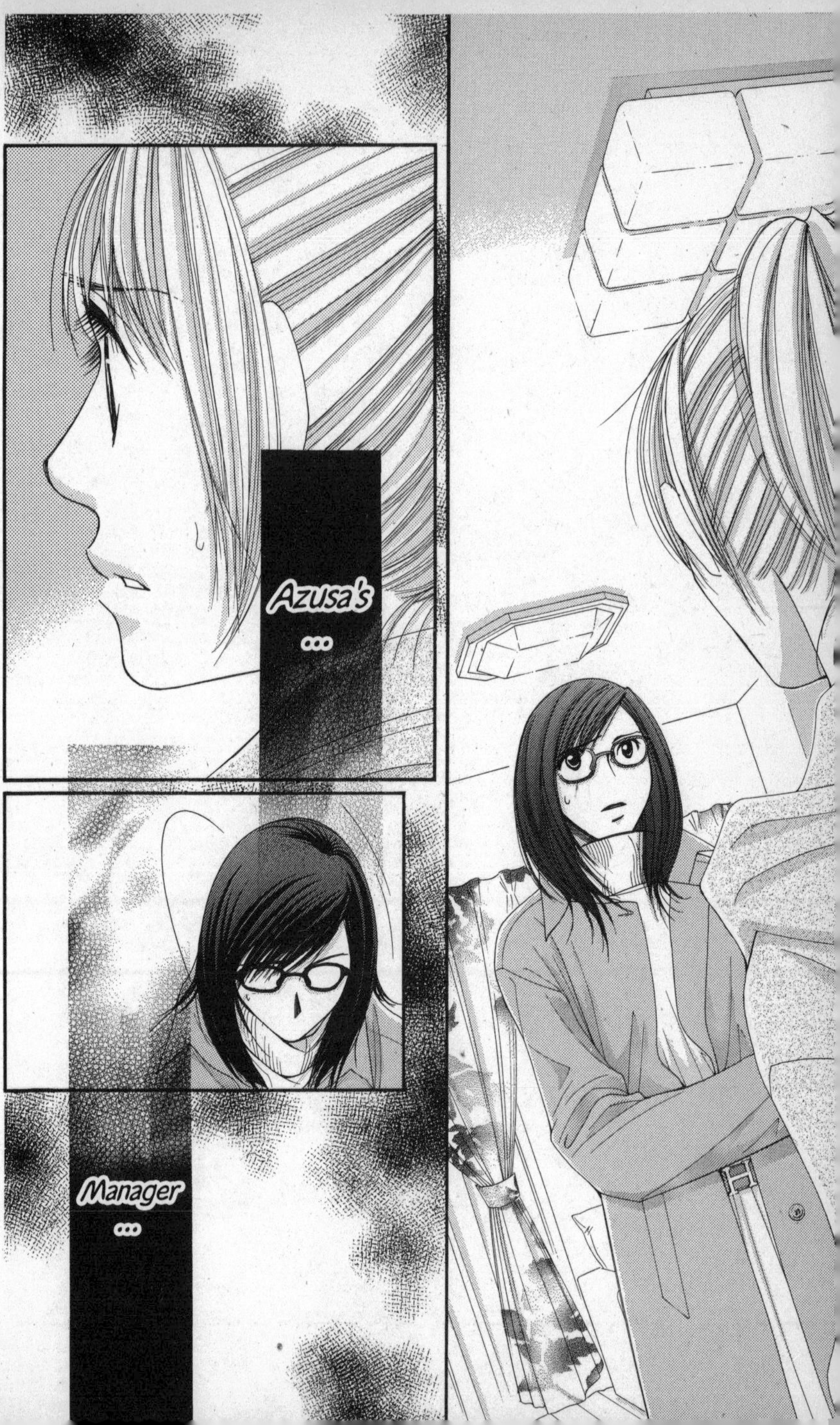
Azusa's ...
Manager ...

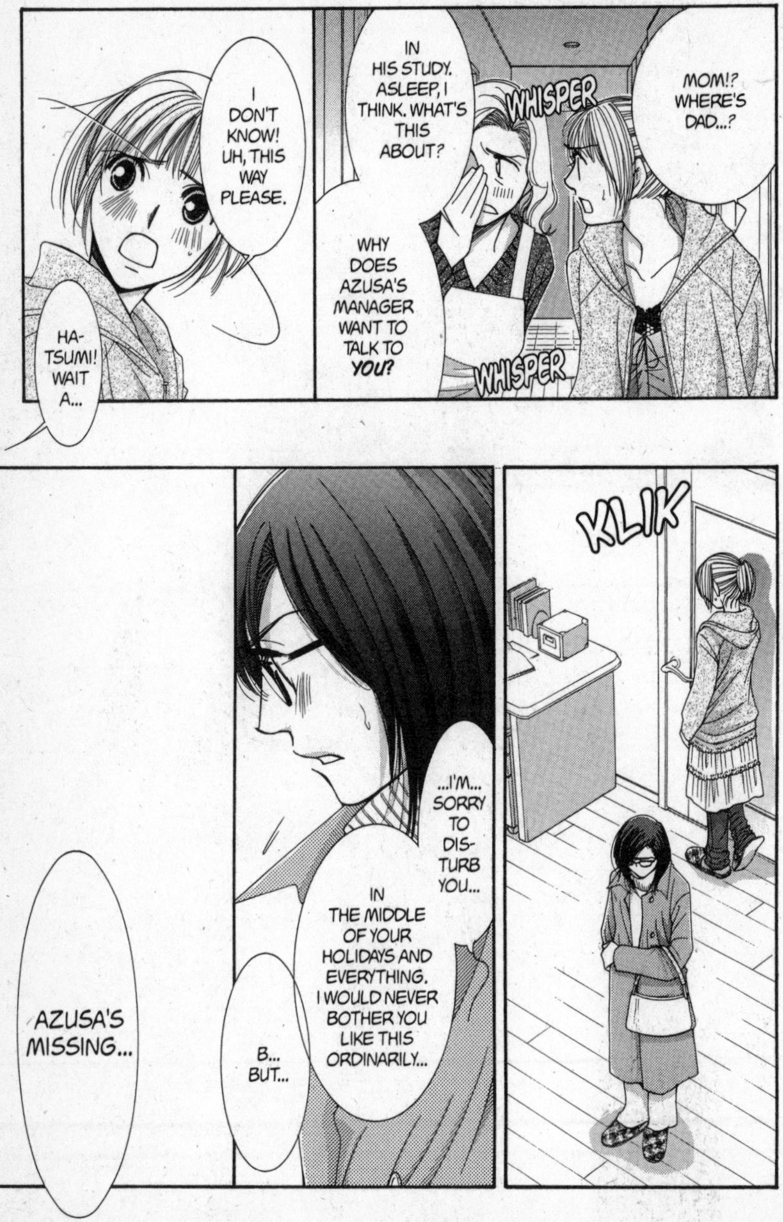
MOM!? WHERE'S DAD...?
IN HIS STUDY. ASLEEP, I THINK. WHAT'S THIS ABOUT?
WHISPER
WHY DOES AZUSA'S MANAGER WANT TO TALK TO *YOU?*
WHISPER
I DON'T KNOW! UH, THIS WAY PLEASE.
HA-TSUMI! WAIT A...
KLIK
...I'M... SORRY TO DISTURB YOU...
IN THE MIDDLE OF YOUR HOLIDAYS AND EVERYTHING. I WOULD NEVER BOTHER YOU LIKE THIS ORDINARILY...
B... BUT...
AZUSA'S MISSING...

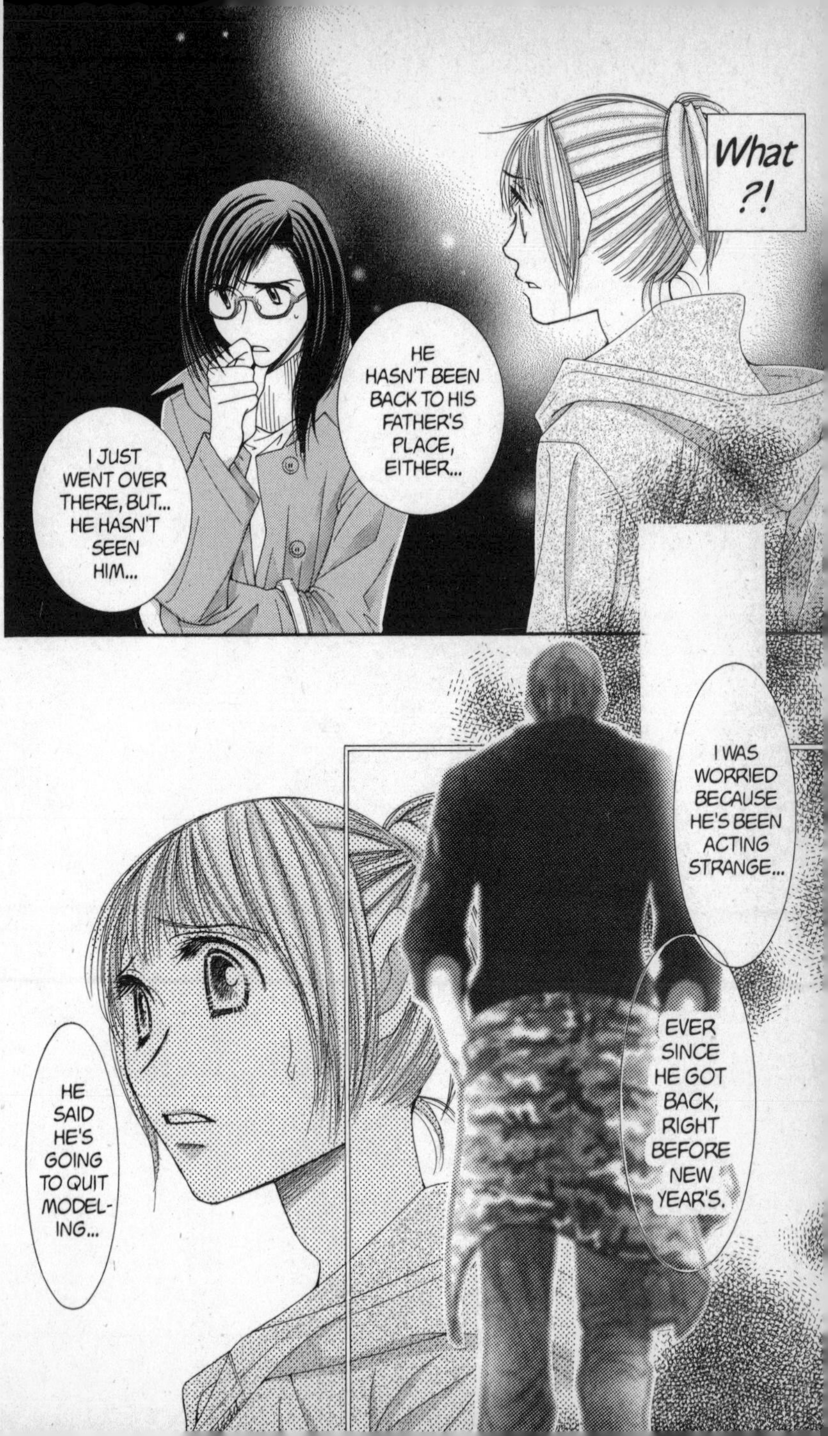
What?!
HE HASN'T BEEN BACK TO HIS FATHER'S PLACE, EITHER...
I JUST WENT OVER THERE, BUT... HE HASN'T SEEN HIM...
I WAS WORRIED BECAUSE HE'S BEEN ACTING STRANGE...
EVER SINCE HE GOT BACK, RIGHT BEFORE NEW YEAR'S.
HE SAID HE'S GOING TO QUIT MODEL-ING...

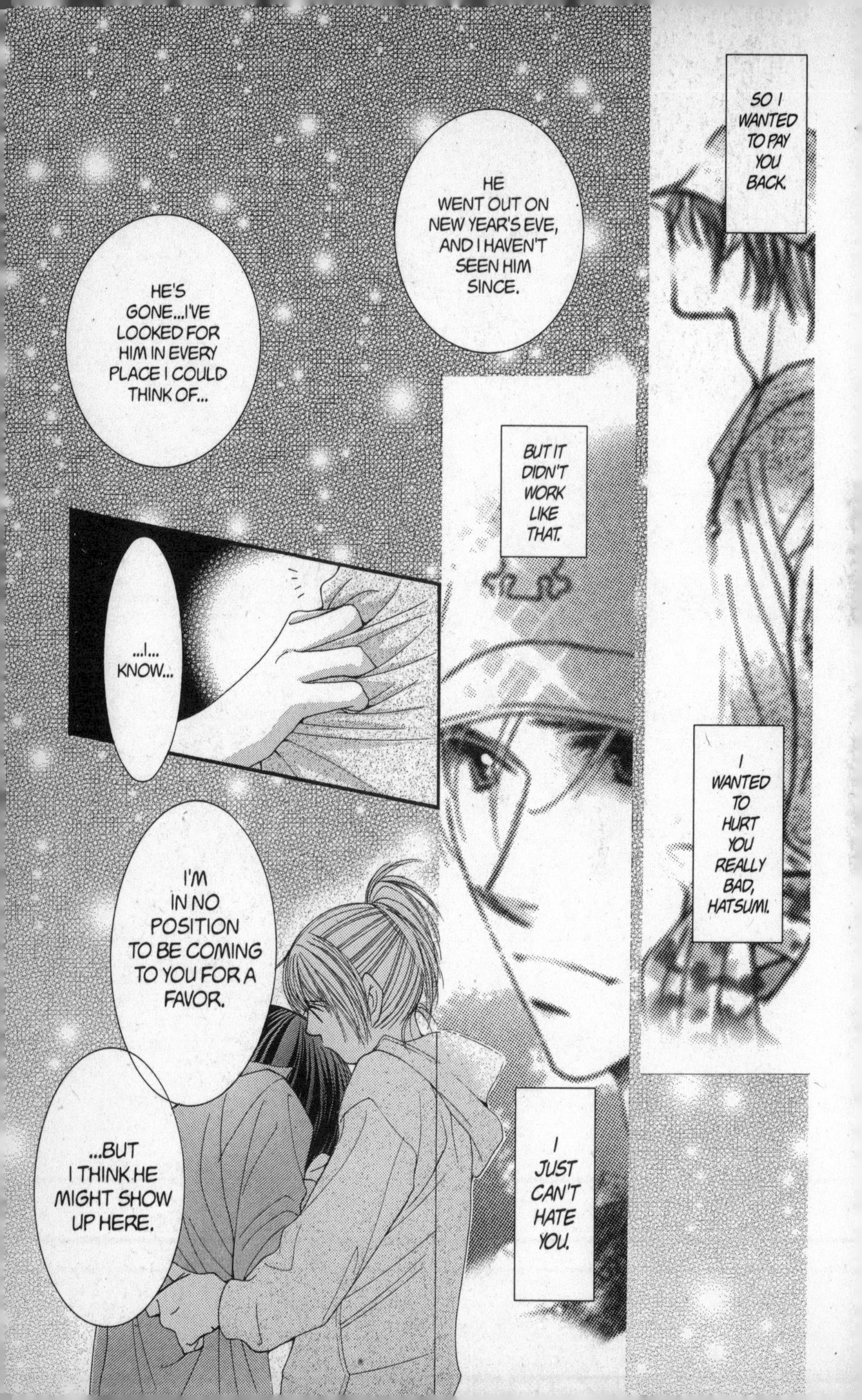
SO I WANTED TO PAY YOU BACK.
I WANTED TO HURT YOU REALLY BAD, HATSUMI.
HE WENT OUT ON NEW YEAR'S EVE, AND I HAVEN'T SEEN HIM SINCE.
HE'S GONE...I'VE LOOKED FOR HIM IN EVERY PLACE I COULD THINK OF...
BUT IT DIDN'T WORK LIKE THAT.
...I... KNOW...
I JUST CAN'T HATE YOU.
I'M IN NO POSITION TO BE COMING TO YOU FOR A FAVOR.
...BUT I THINK HE MIGHT SHOW UP HERE.

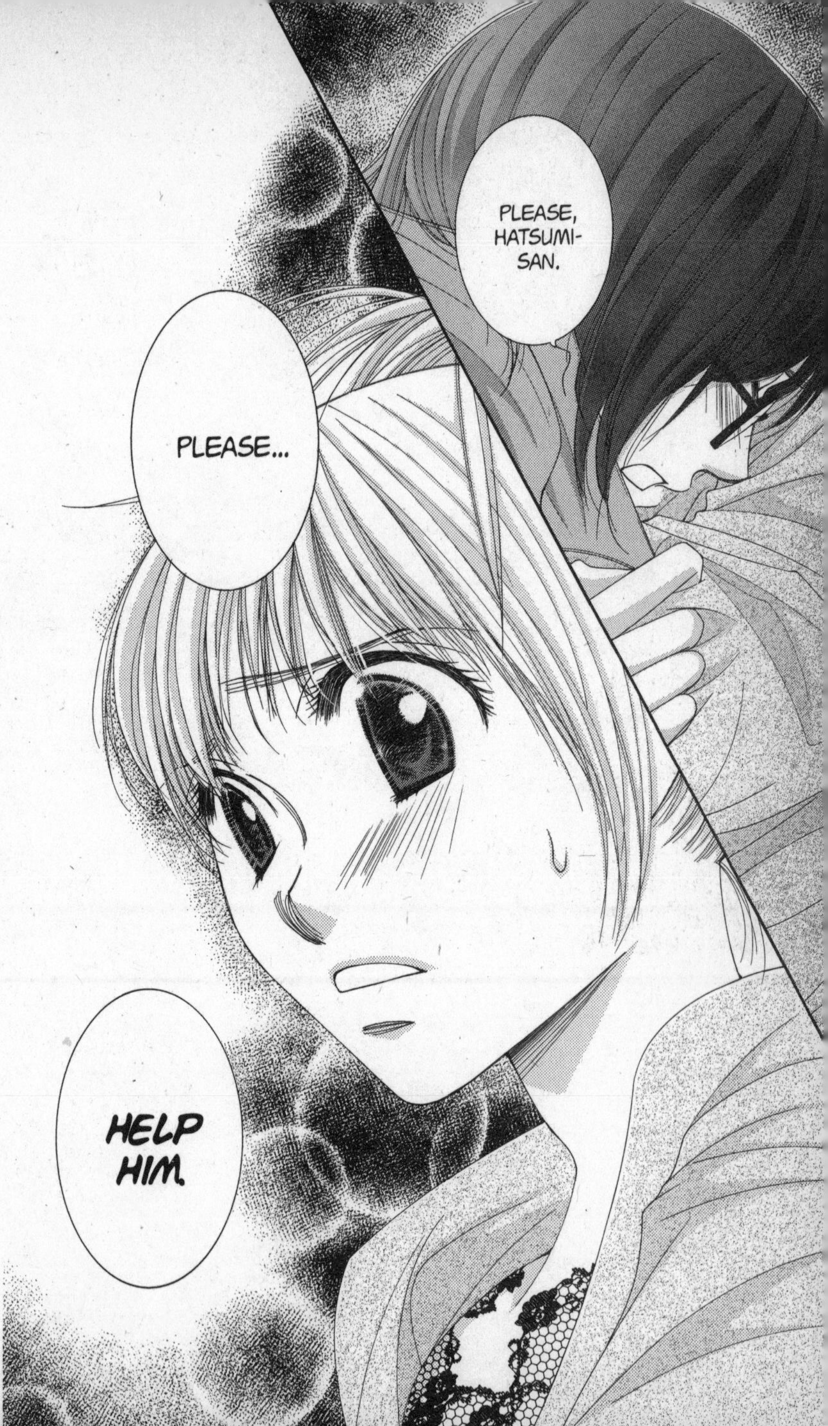
PLEASE, HATSUMI-SAN.
PLEASE...
HELP HIM.

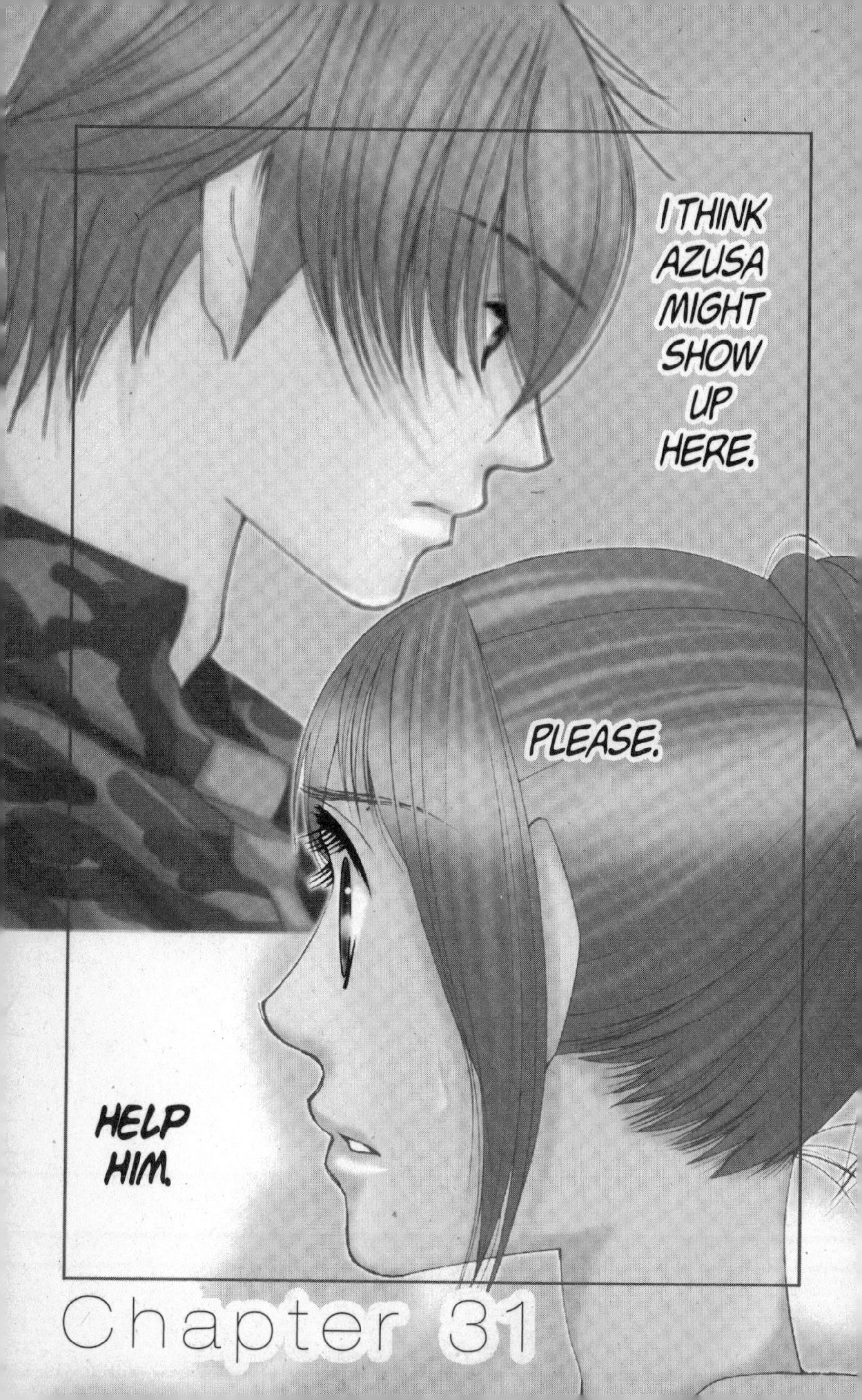
I THINK AZUSA MIGHT SHOW UP HERE.
PLEASE.
HELP HIM.

Chapter 31

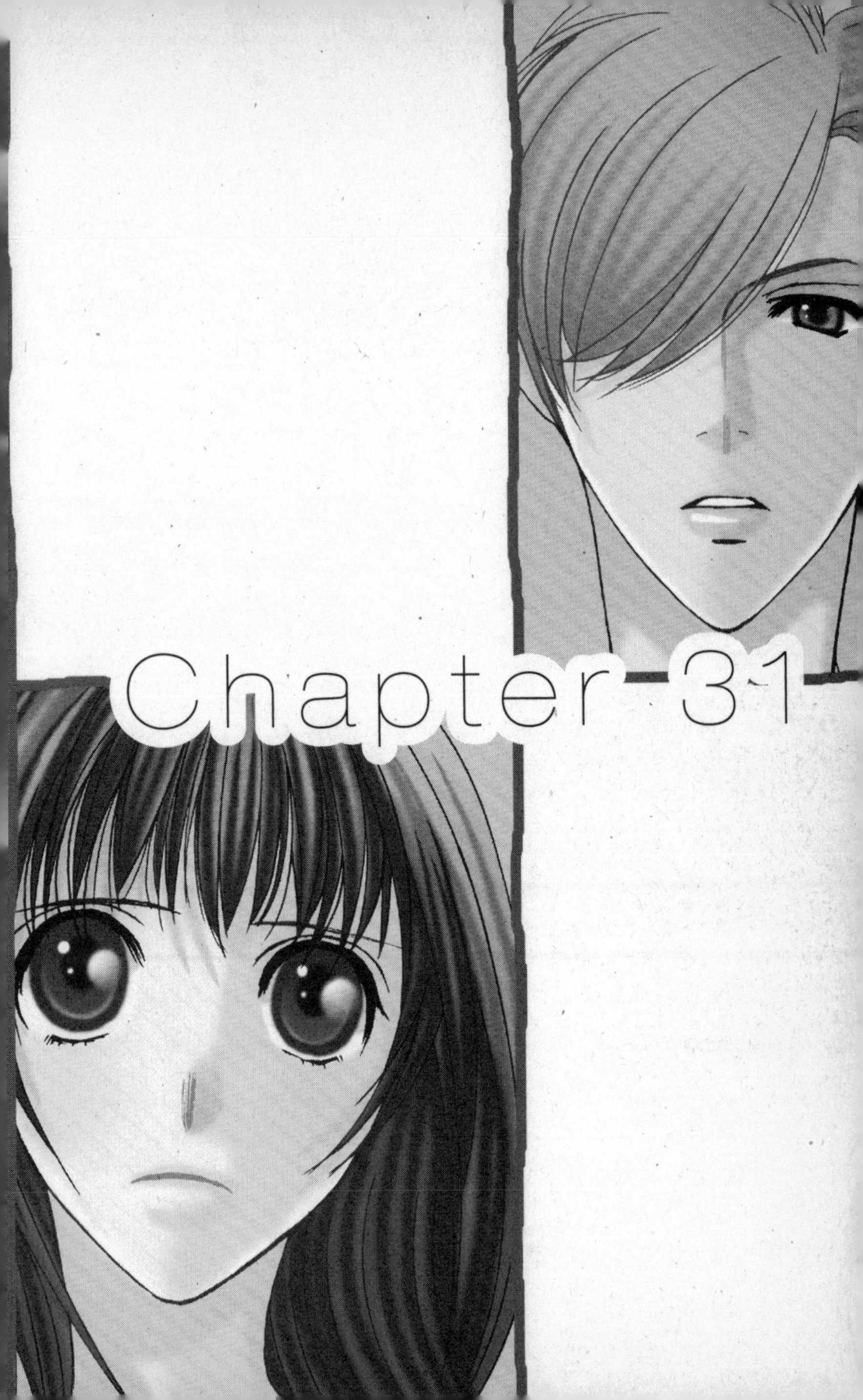
Chapter 31

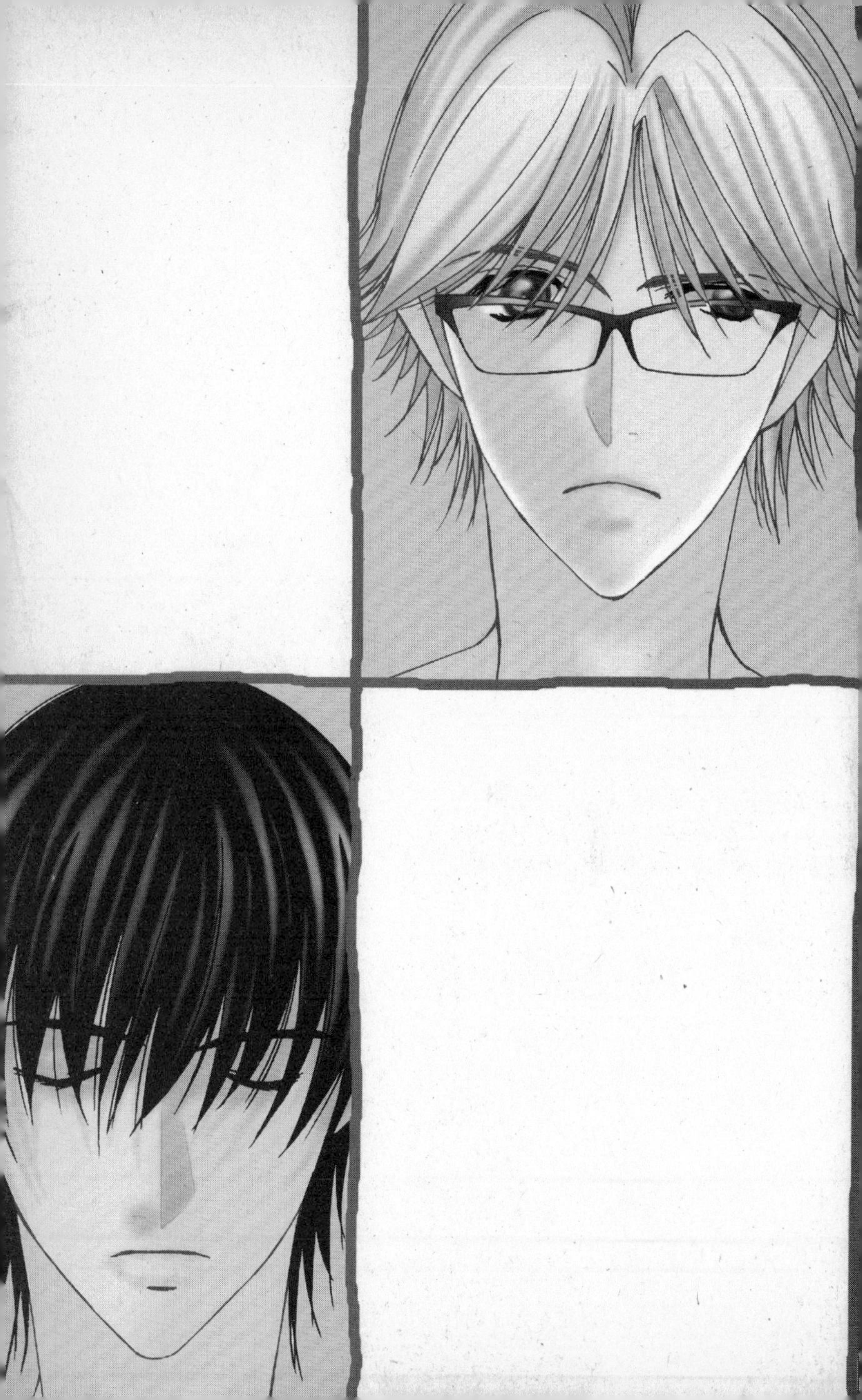

Let's see... Emi, Kaoru, Sayo, Yuri... All girls...

BIP! BIP!

Azusa's cell phone memory...

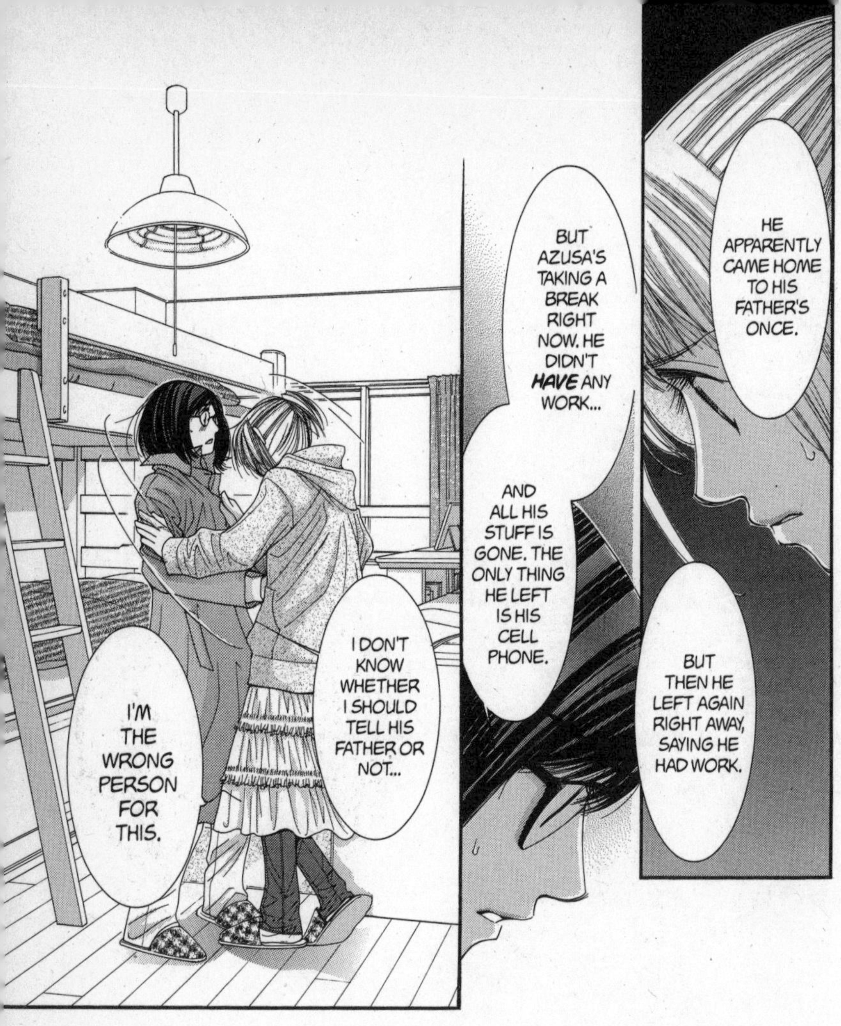
HE APPARENTLY CAME HOME TO HIS FATHER'S ONCE.
BUT THEN HE LEFT AGAIN RIGHT AWAY, SAYING HE HAD WORK.
BUT AZUSA'S TAKING A BREAK RIGHT NOW. HE DIDN'T *HAVE* ANY WORK...
AND ALL HIS STUFF IS GONE. THE ONLY THING HE LEFT IS HIS CELL PHONE.
I DON'T KNOW WHETHER I SHOULD TELL HIS FATHER OR NOT...
I'M THE WRONG PERSON FOR THIS.

hot gimmick

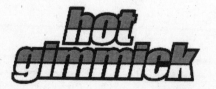

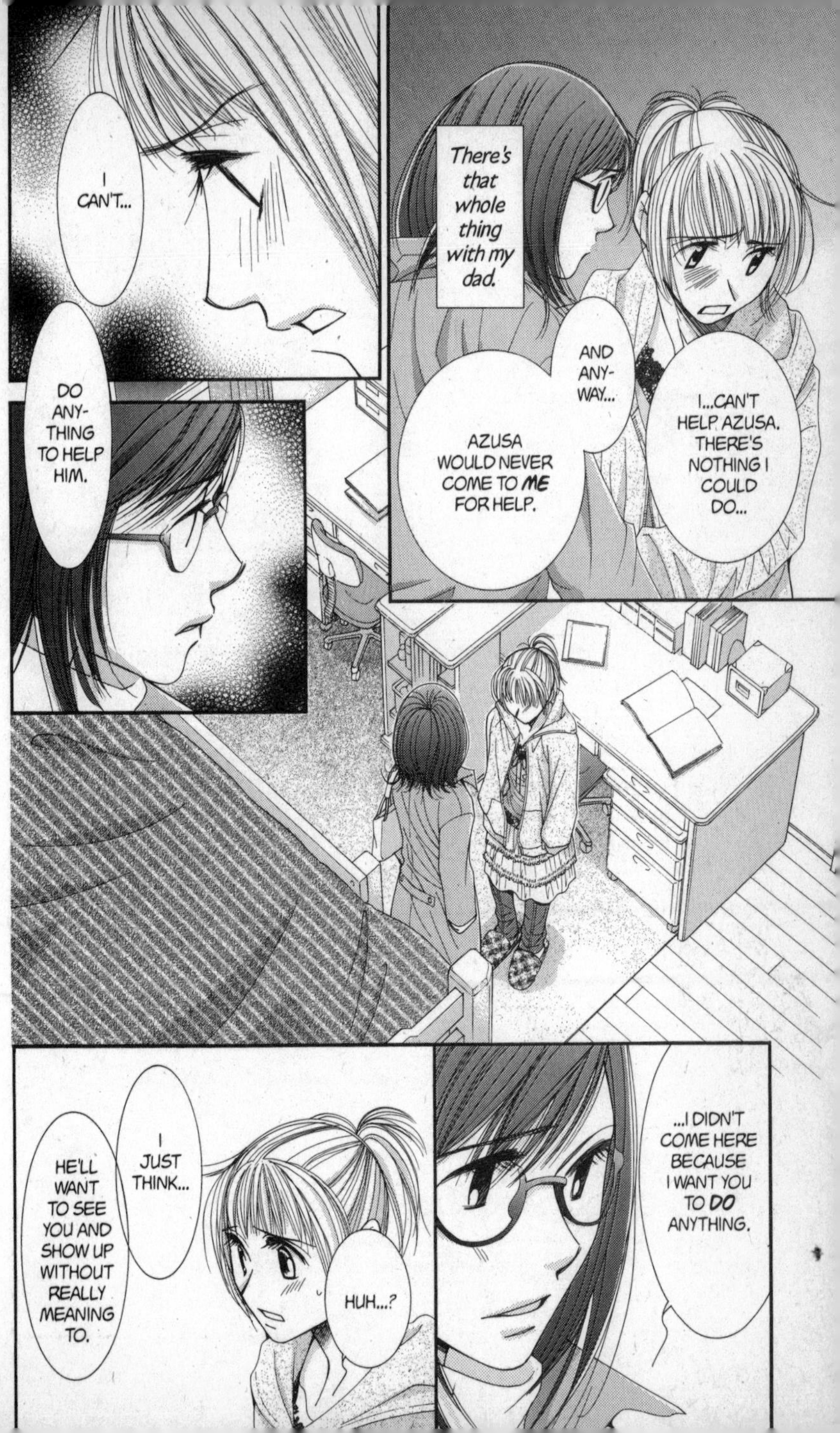
There's that whole thing with my dad.
I...CAN'T HELP AZUSA. THERE'S NOTHING I COULD DO...
AND ANYWAY...
AZUSA WOULD NEVER COME TO ME FOR HELP.
I CAN'T...
DO ANYTHING TO HELP HIM.
...I DIDN'T COME HERE BECAUSE I WANT YOU TO DO ANYTHING.
HUH...?
I JUST THINK...
HE'LL WANT TO SEE YOU AND SHOW UP WITHOUT REALLY MEANING TO.

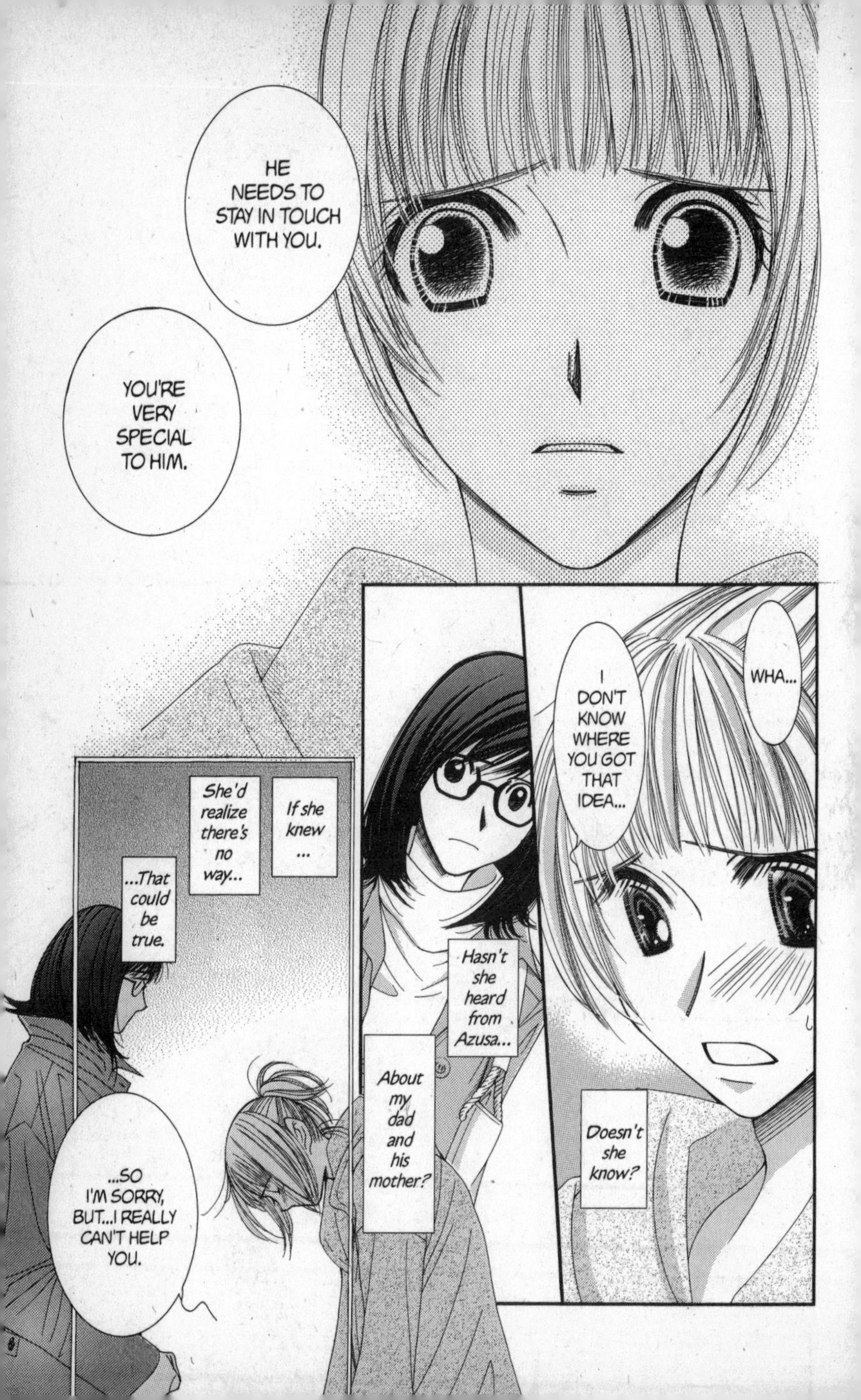
HE NEEDS TO STAY IN TOUCH WITH YOU.
YOU'RE VERY SPECIAL TO HIM.
WHA...
I DON'T KNOW WHERE YOU GOT THAT IDEA...
Doesn't she know?
Hasn't she heard from Azusa...
About my dad and his mother?
If she knew...
She'd realize there's no way...
...That could be true.
...SO I'M SORRY, BUT...I REALLY CAN'T HELP YOU.

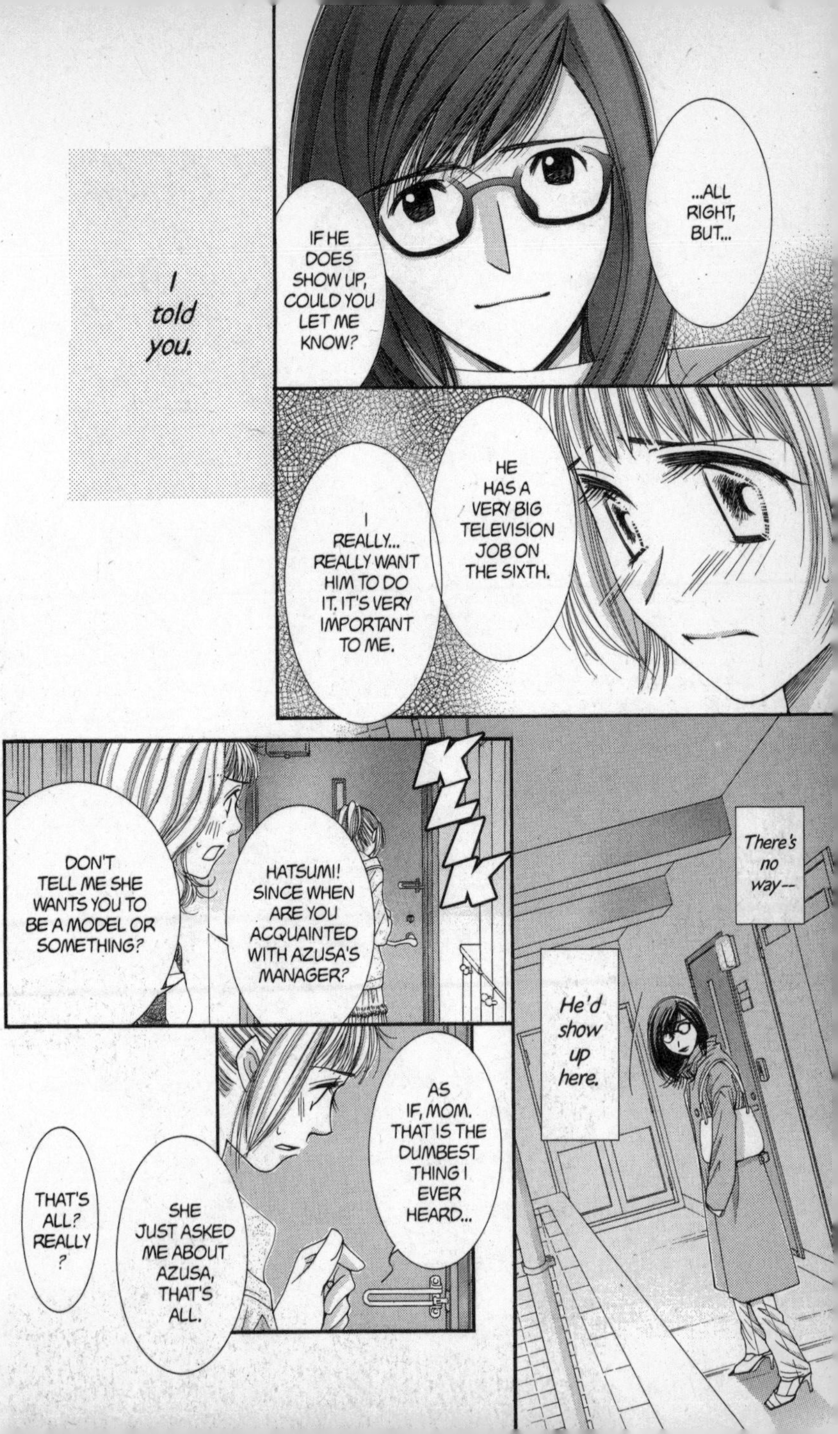
...ALL RIGHT, BUT...
IF HE DOES SHOW UP, COULD YOU LET ME KNOW?
HE HAS A VERY BIG TELEVISION JOB ON THE SIXTH.
I REALLY... REALLY WANT HIM TO DO IT. IT'S VERY IMPORTANT TO ME.
I told you.
There's no way--
He'd show up here.
KLIK
HATSUMI! SINCE WHEN ARE YOU ACQUAINTED WITH AZUSA'S MANAGER?
DON'T TELL ME SHE WANTS YOU TO BE A MODEL OR SOMETHING?
AS IF, MOM. THAT IS THE DUMBEST THING I EVER HEARD...
SHE JUST ASKED ME ABOUT AZUSA, THAT'S ALL.
THAT'S ALL? REALLY?

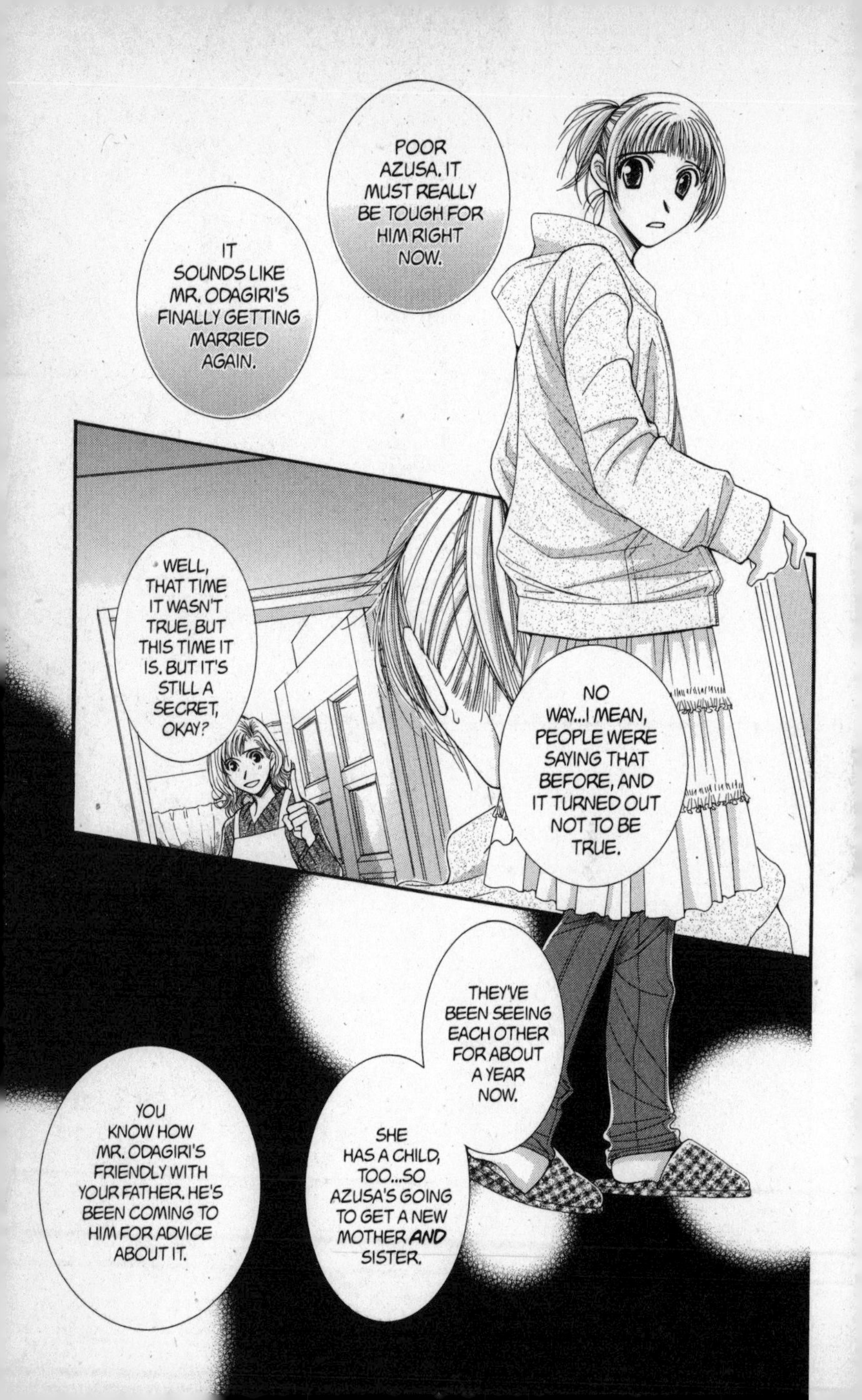
POOR AZUSA. IT MUST REALLY BE TOUGH FOR HIM RIGHT NOW.
IT SOUNDS LIKE MR. ODAGIRI'S FINALLY GETTING MARRIED AGAIN.
NO WAY...I MEAN, PEOPLE WERE SAYING THAT BEFORE, AND IT TURNED OUT NOT TO BE TRUE.
WELL, THAT TIME IT WASN'T TRUE, BUT THIS TIME IT IS. BUT IT'S STILL A SECRET, OKAY?
THEY'VE BEEN SEEING EACH OTHER FOR ABOUT A YEAR NOW.
SHE HAS A CHILD, TOO...SO AZUSA'S GOING TO GET A NEW MOTHER *AND* SISTER.
YOU KNOW HOW MR. ODAGIRI'S FRIENDLY WITH YOUR FATHER. HE'S BEEN COMING TO HIM FOR ADVICE ABOUT IT.

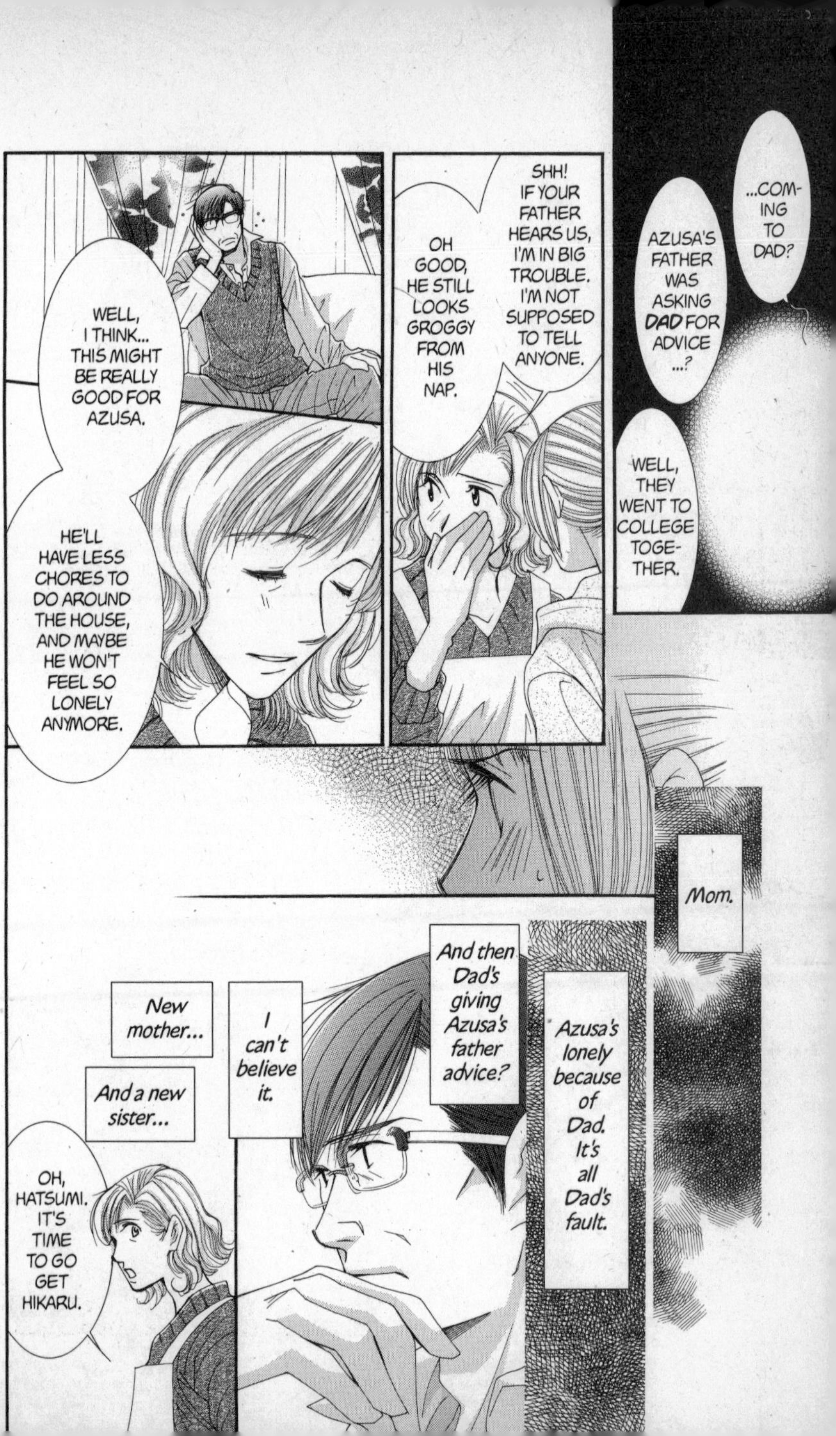
...COMING TO DAD?
AZUSA'S FATHER WAS ASKING **DAD** FOR ADVICE ...?
WELL, THEY WENT TO COLLEGE TOGETHER.
SHH! IF YOUR FATHER HEARS US, I'M IN BIG TROUBLE. I'M NOT SUPPOSED TO TELL ANYONE.
OH GOOD, HE STILL LOOKS GROGGY FROM HIS NAP.
WELL, I THINK... THIS MIGHT BE REALLY GOOD FOR AZUSA.
HE'LL HAVE LESS CHORES TO DO AROUND THE HOUSE, AND MAYBE HE WON'T FEEL SO LONELY ANYMORE.
Mom.
Azusa's lonely because of Dad. It's all Dad's fault.
And then Dad's giving Azusa's father advice?
I can't believe it.
New mother...
And a new sister...
OH, HATSUMI. IT'S TIME TO GO GET HIKARU.

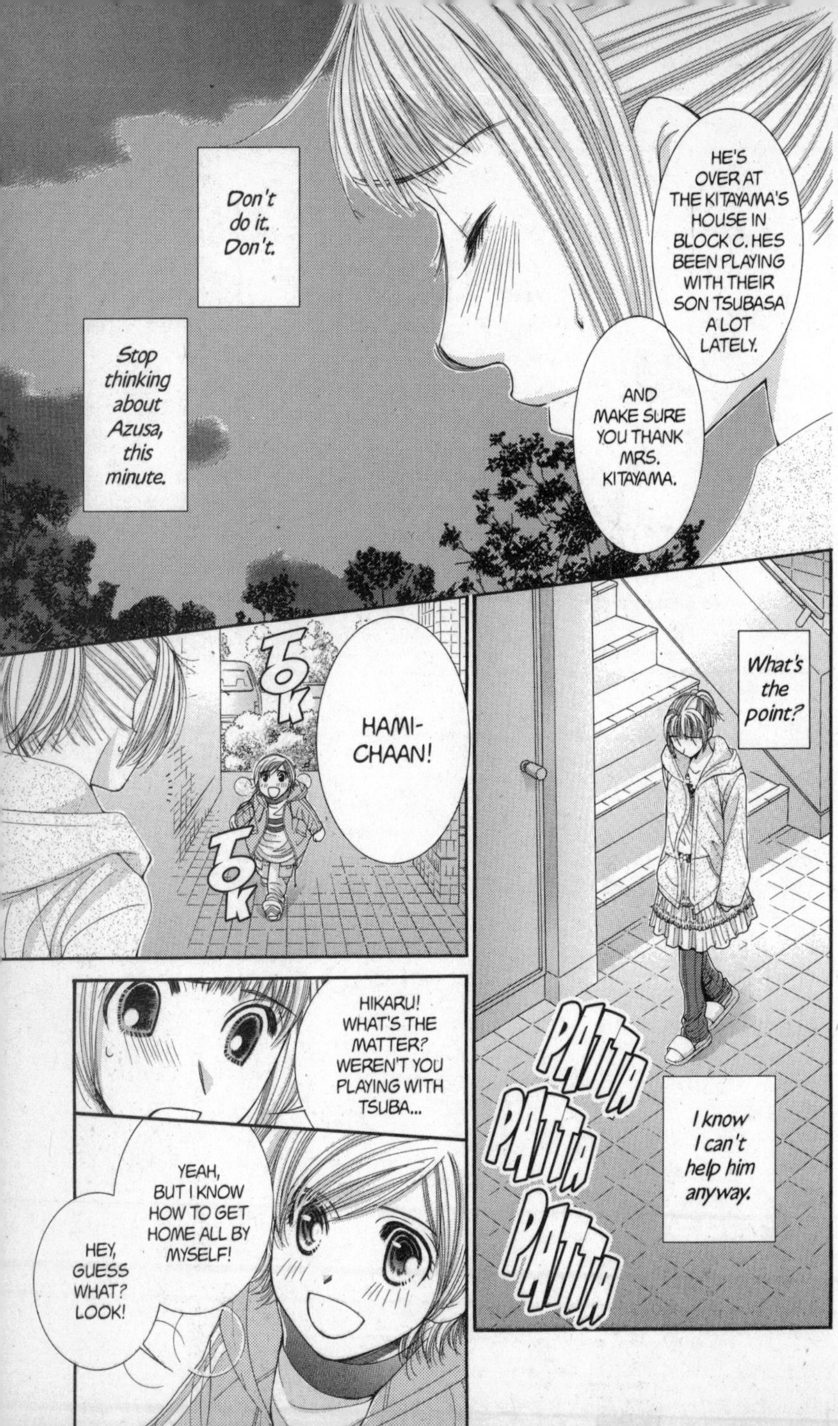
HE'S OVER AT THE KITAYAMA'S HOUSE IN BLOCK C. HES BEEN PLAYING WITH THEIR SON TSUBASA A LOT LATELY.
AND MAKE SURE YOU THANK MRS. KITAYAMA.
Don't do it. Don't.
Stop thinking about Azusa, this minute.
What's the point?
PATTA
PATTA
PATTA
I know I can't help him anyway.
TOK
TOK
HAMI-CHAAN!
HIKARU! WHAT'S THE MATTER? WEREN'T YOU PLAYING WITH TSUBA...
YEAH, BUT I KNOW HOW TO GET HOME ALL BY MYSELF!
HEY, GUESS WHAT? LOOK!

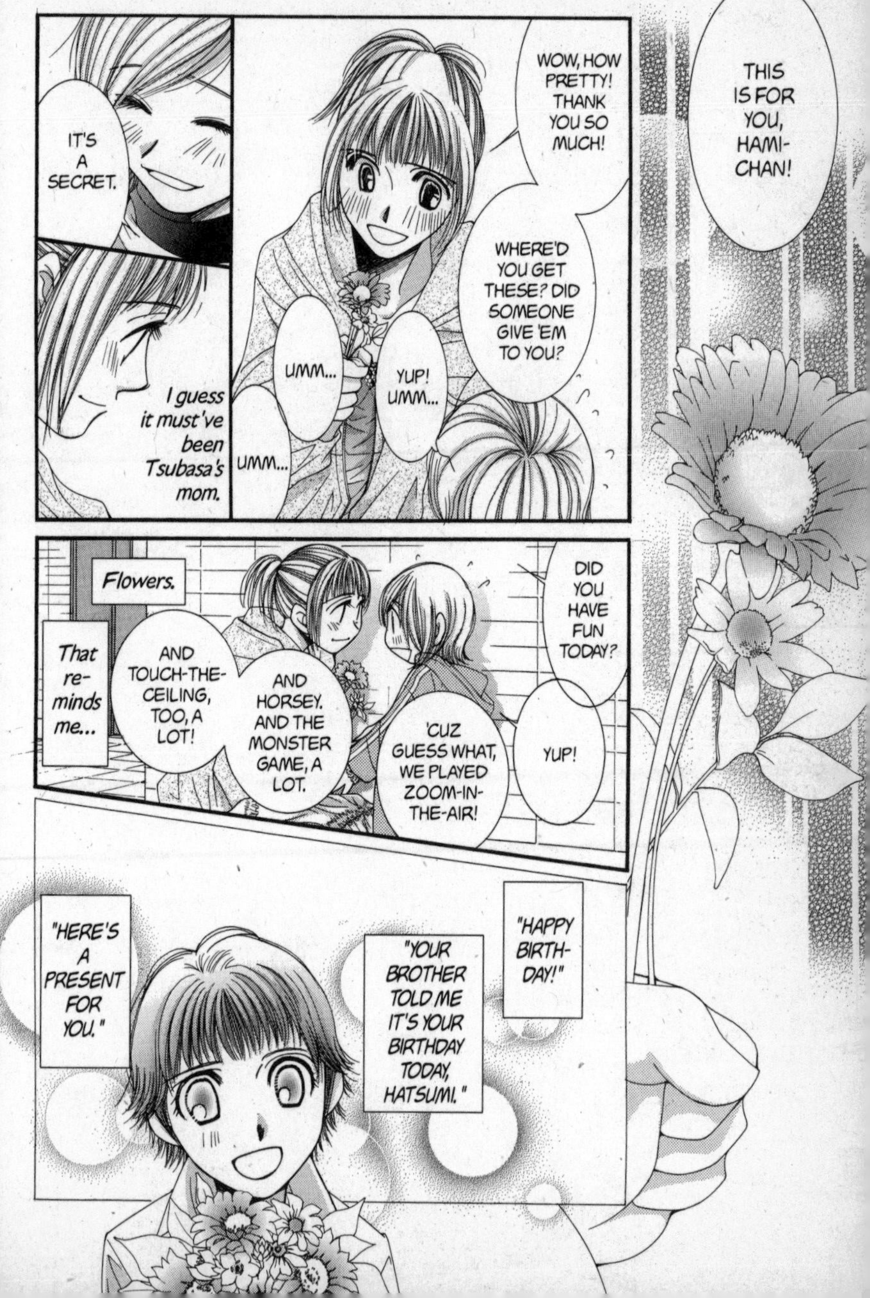
THIS IS FOR YOU, HAMI-CHAN!
WOW, HOW PRETTY! THANK YOU SO MUCH!
WHERE'D YOU GET THESE? DID SOMEONE GIVE 'EM TO YOU?
YUP! UMM...
UMM...
UMM...
IT'S A SECRET.
I guess it must've been Tsubasa's mom.
DID YOU HAVE FUN TODAY?
YUP!
'CUZ GUESS WHAT, WE PLAYED ZOOM-IN-THE-AIR!
AND HORSEY. AND THE MONSTER GAME, A LOT.
AND TOUCH-THE-CEILING, TOO, A LOT!
Flowers.
That reminds me...
"HAPPY BIRTHDAY!"
"YOUR BROTHER TOLD ME IT'S YOUR BIRTHDAY TODAY, HATSUMI."
"HERE'S A PRESENT FOR YOU."

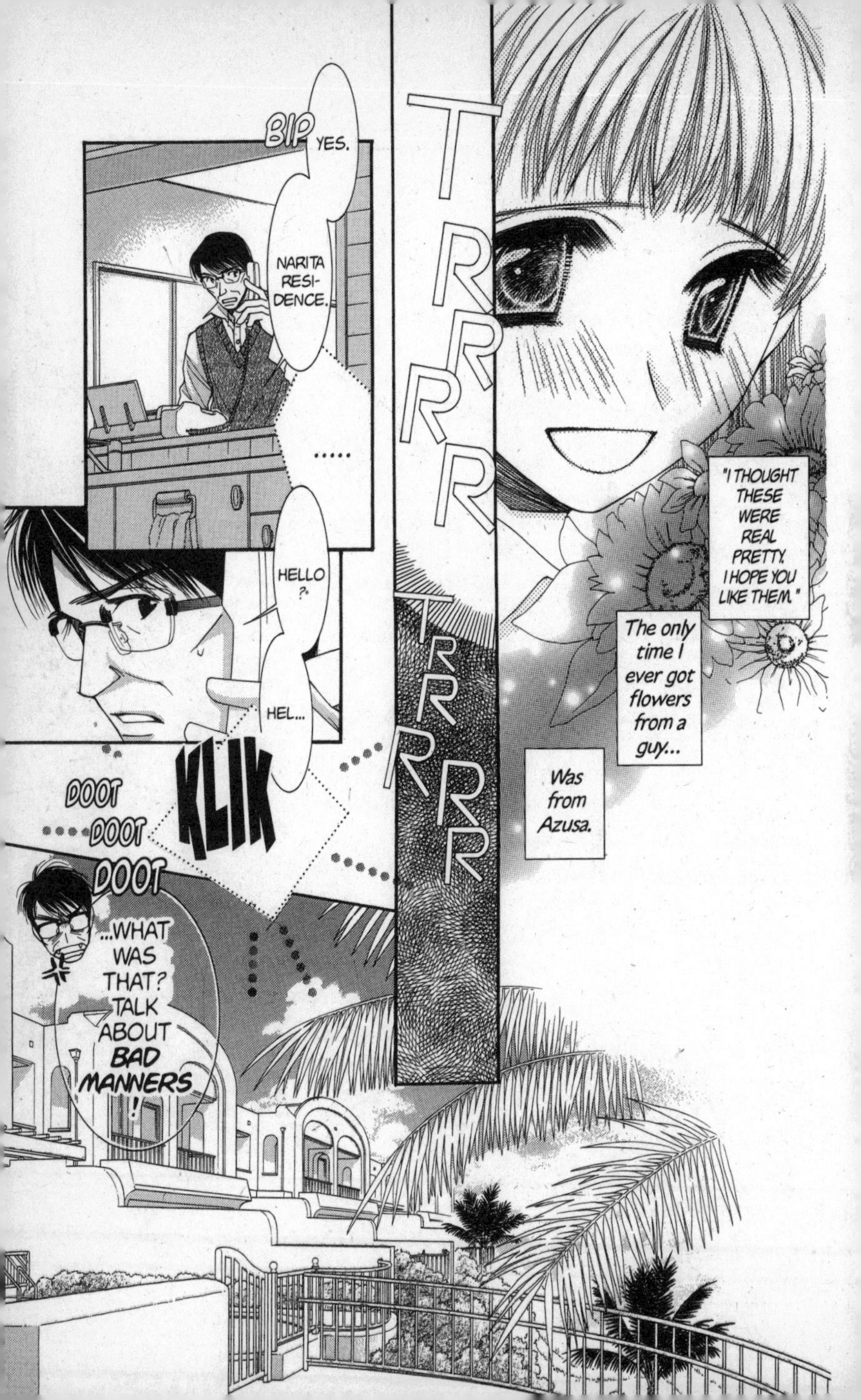
"I THOUGHT THESE WERE REAL PRETTY. I HOPE YOU LIKE THEM."
The only time I ever got flowers from a guy...
Was from Azusa.
TRRRR
TRRRR
BIP
YES.
NARITA RESIDENCE.
.....
HELLO?
HEL...
KLIK
DOOT DOOT DOOT
...WHAT WAS THAT? TALK ABOUT BAD MANNERS!

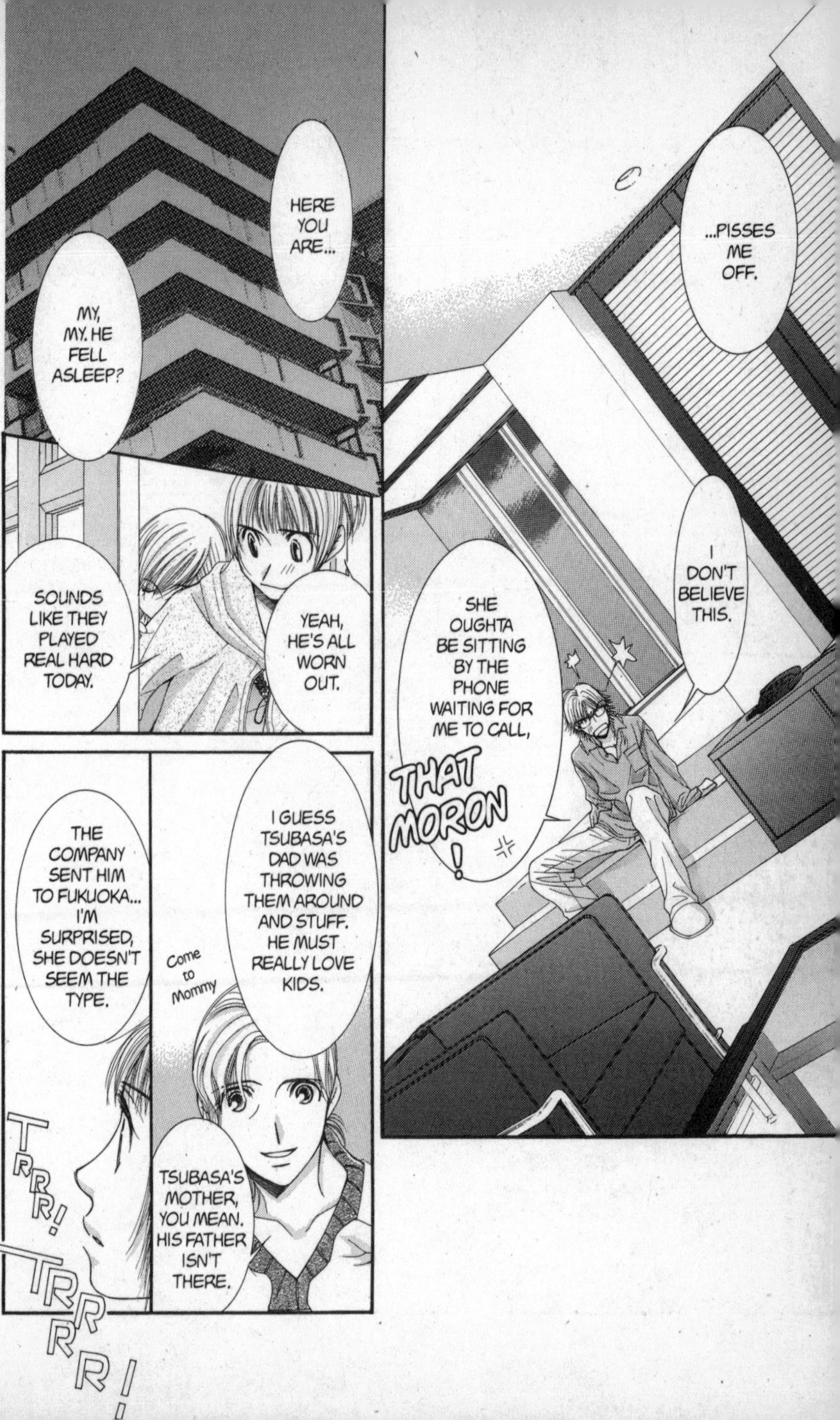
...PISSES ME OFF.
I DON'T BELIEVE THIS.
SHE OUGHTA BE SITTING BY THE PHONE WAITING FOR ME TO CALL,
THAT MORON!
HERE YOU ARE...
MY, MY. HE FELL ASLEEP?
YEAH, HE'S ALL WORN OUT.
SOUNDS LIKE THEY PLAYED REAL HARD TODAY.
I GUESS TSUBASA'S DAD WAS THROWING THEM AROUND AND STUFF. HE MUST REALLY LOVE KIDS.
Come to Mommy
TSUBASA'S MOTHER, YOU MEAN. HIS FATHER ISN'T THERE.
THE COMPANY SENT HIM TO FUKUOKA... I'M SURPRISED, SHE DOESN'T SEEM THE TYPE.
TRRR!
TRRRRRR!

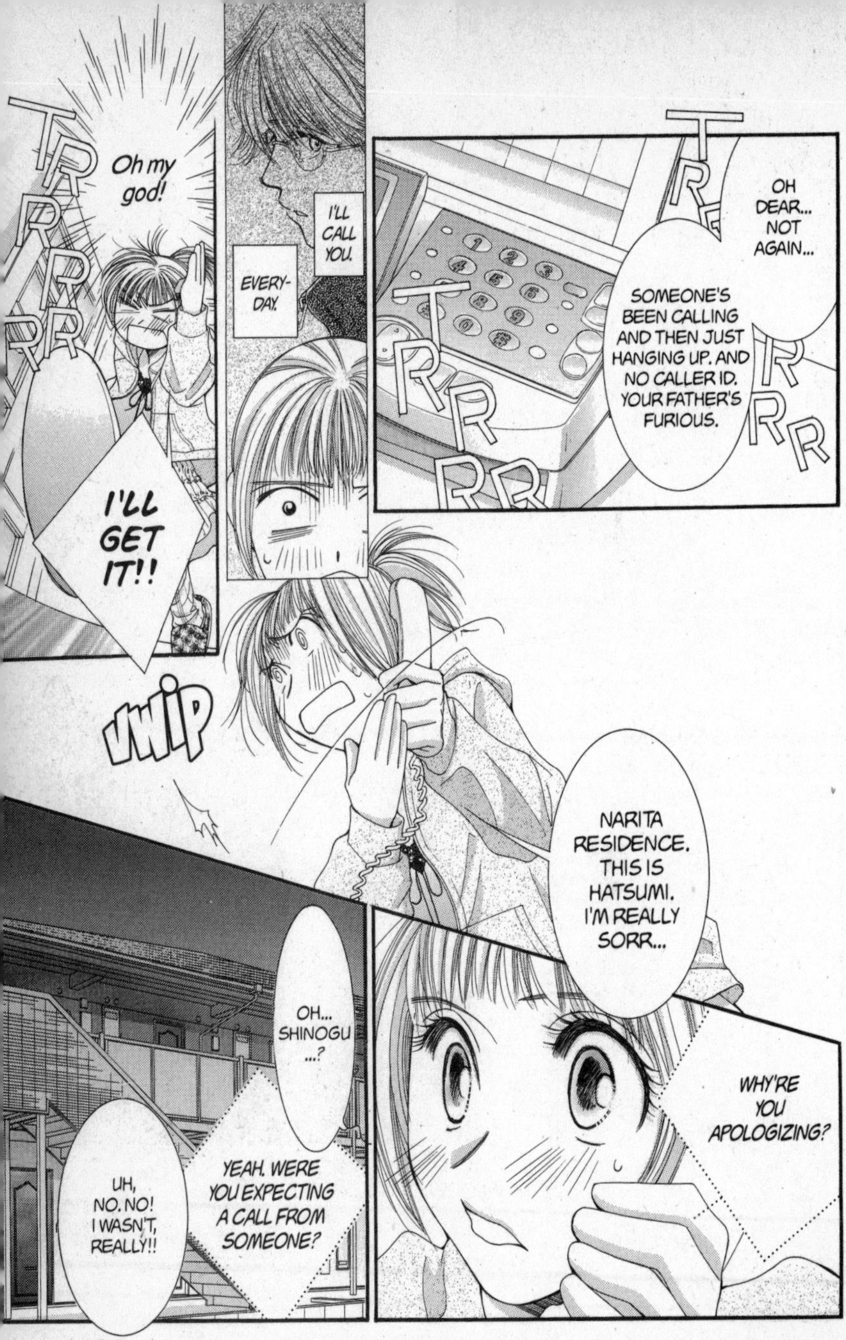
TRRRRRR
OH DEAR... NOT AGAIN...
SOMEONE'S BEEN CALLING AND THEN JUST HANGING UP. AND NO CALLER ID. YOUR FATHER'S FURIOUS.
I'LL CALL YOU.
EVERY-DAY.
Oh my god!
TRRRRRR
I'LL GET IT!!
VWIP
NARITA RESIDENCE. THIS IS HATSUMI. I'M REALLY SORR...
WHY'RE YOU APOLOGIZING?
OH... SHINOGU ...?
YEAH. WERE YOU EXPECTING A CALL FROM SOMEONE?
UH, NO. NO! I WASN'T, REALLY!!

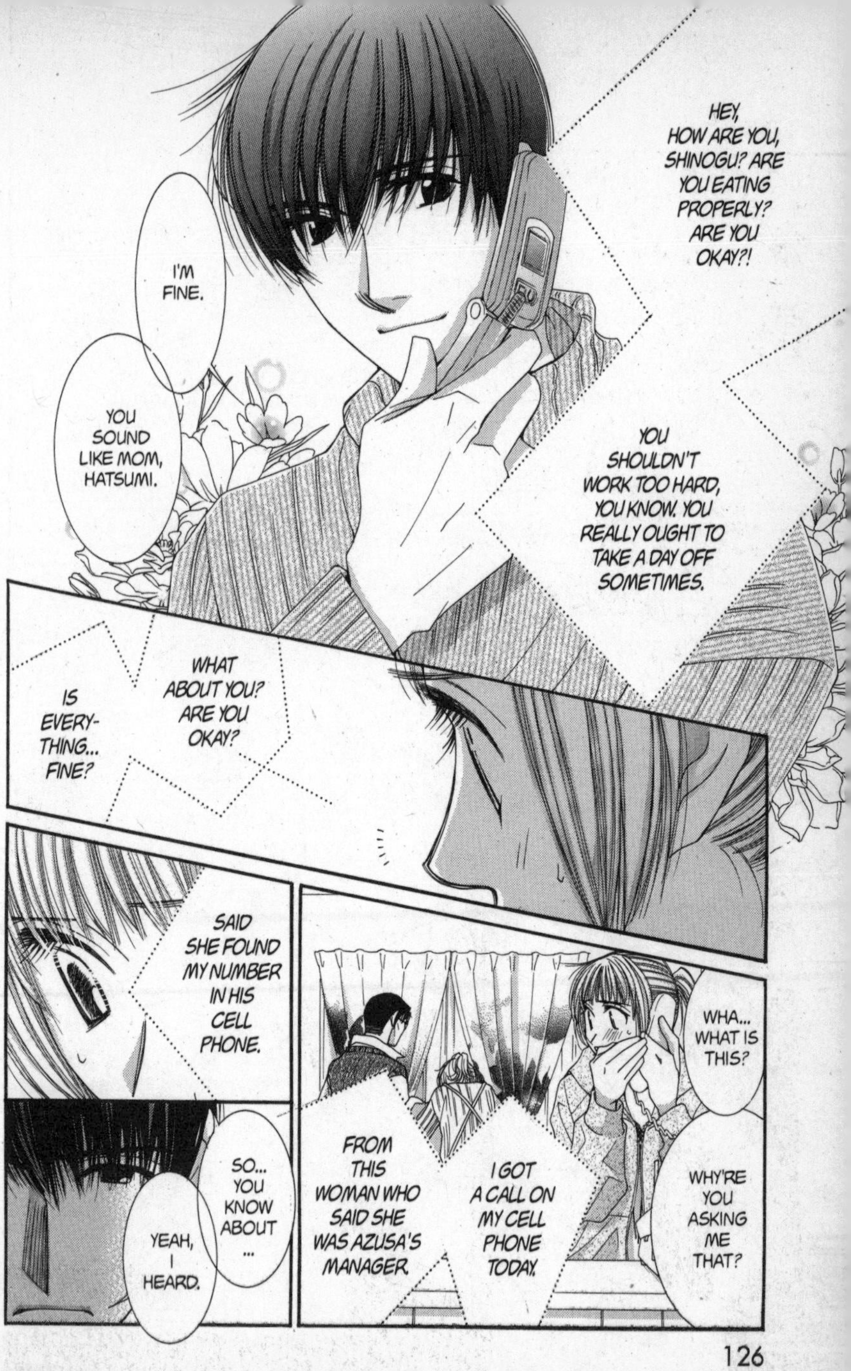
HEY, HOW ARE YOU, SHINOGU? ARE YOU EATING PROPERLY? ARE YOU OKAY?!
I'M FINE.
YOU SHOULDN'T WORK TOO HARD, YOU KNOW. YOU REALLY OUGHT TO TAKE A DAY OFF SOMETIMES.
YOU SOUND LIKE MOM, HATSUMI.
WHAT ABOUT YOU? ARE YOU OKAY?
IS EVERY-THING... FINE?
WHA... WHAT IS THIS?
WHY'RE YOU ASKING ME THAT?
I GOT A CALL ON MY CELL PHONE TODAY.
FROM THIS WOMAN WHO SAID SHE WAS AZUSA'S MANAGER.
SAID SHE FOUND MY NUMBER IN HIS CELL PHONE.
SO... YOU KNOW ABOUT ...
YEAH, I HEARD.

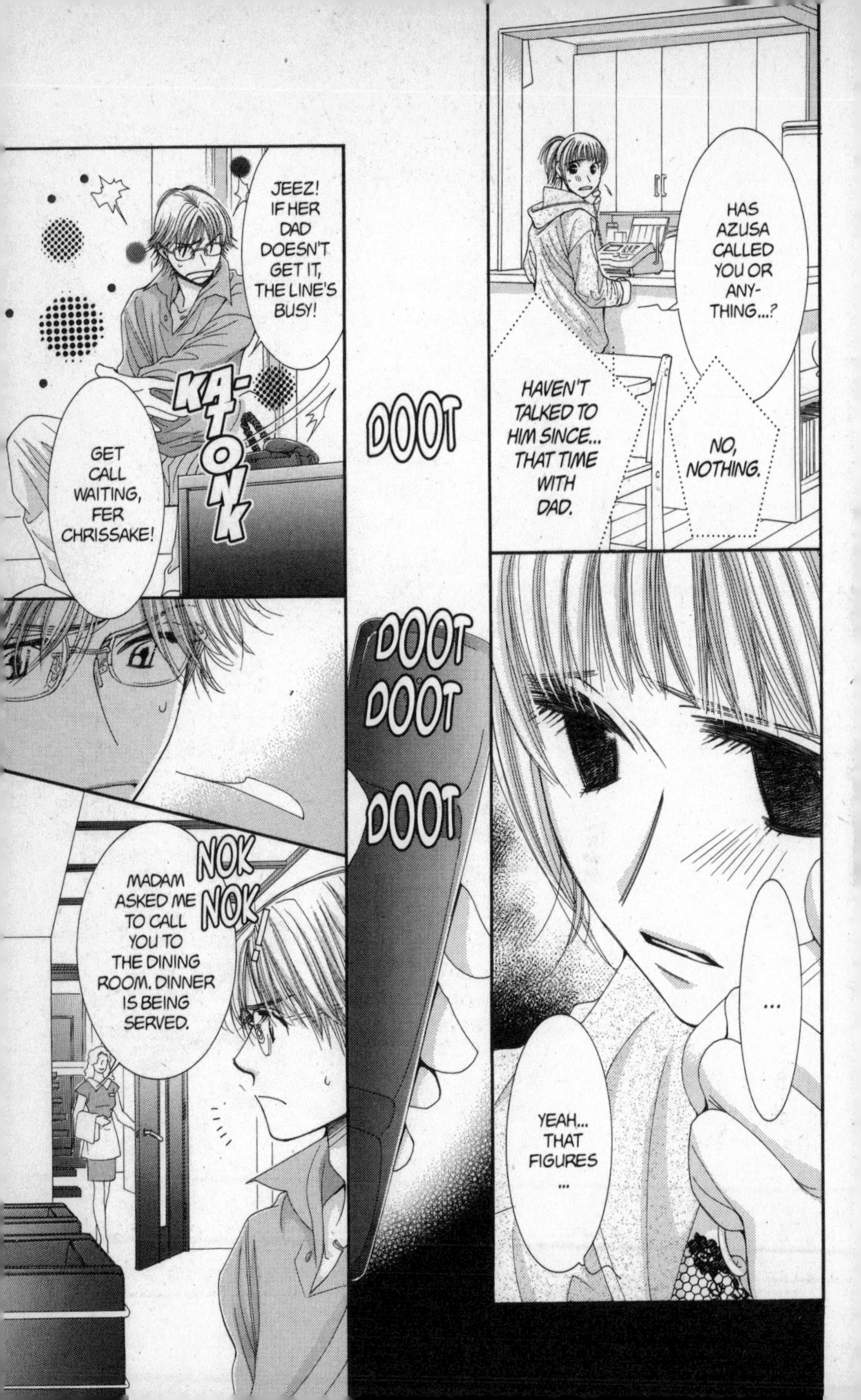
HAS AZUSA CALLED YOU OR ANY-THING...?
NO, NOTHING.
HAVEN'T TALKED TO HIM SINCE... THAT TIME WITH DAD.
...
YEAH... THAT FIGURES ...
DOOT
DOOT DOOT
DOOT
JEEZ! IF HER DAD DOESN'T GET IT, THE LINE'S BUSY!
KA-TONK
GET CALL WAITING, FER CHRISSAKE!
NOK NOK
MADAM ASKED ME TO CALL YOU TO THE DINING ROOM. DINNER IS BEING SERVED.

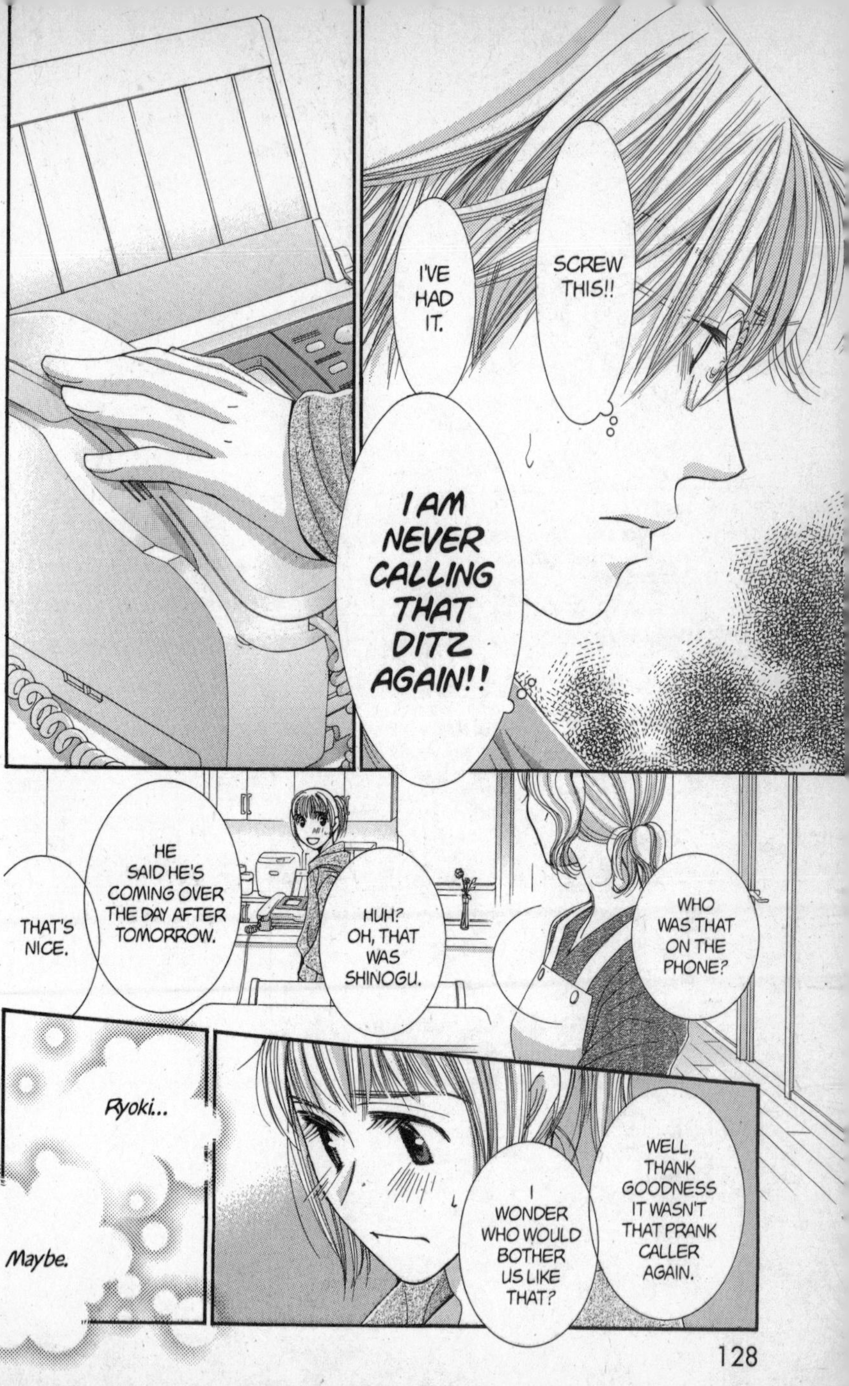
SCREW THIS!!
I'VE HAD IT.
I AM NEVER CALLING THAT DITZ AGAIN!!
WHO WAS THAT ON THE PHONE?
HUH? OH, THAT WAS SHINOGU.
HE SAID HE'S COMING OVER THE DAY AFTER TOMORROW.
THAT'S NICE.
WELL, THANK GOODNESS IT WASN'T THAT PRANK CALLER AGAIN.
I WONDER WHO WOULD BOTHER US LIKE THAT?
Ryoki...
Maybe.

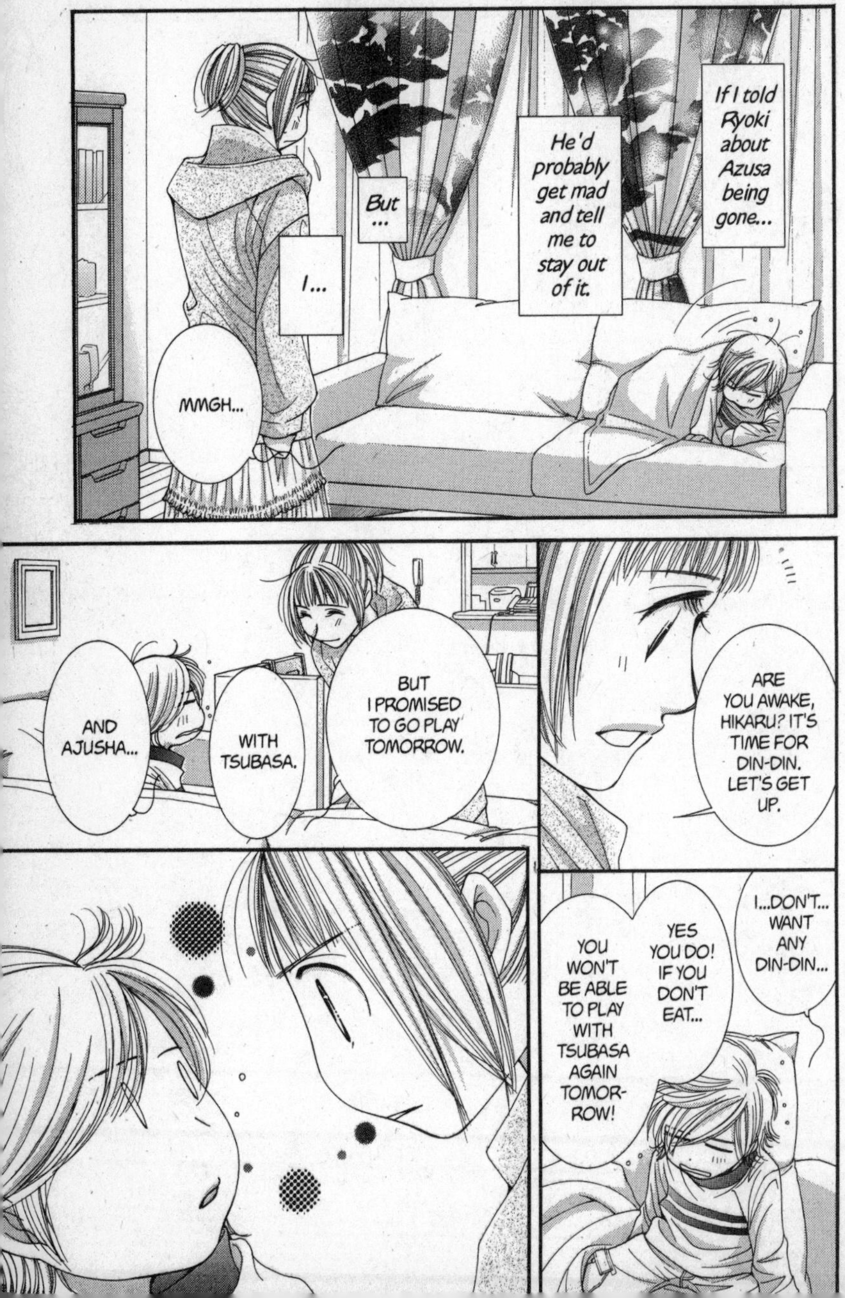
If I told Ryoki about Azusa being gone...
He'd probably get mad and tell me to stay out of it.
But...
I...
MMGH...
ARE YOU AWAKE, HIKARU? IT'S TIME FOR DIN-DIN. LET'S GET UP.
I...DON'T... WANT ANY DIN-DIN...
YES YOU DO! IF YOU DON'T EAT...
YOU WON'T BE ABLE TO PLAY WITH TSUBASA AGAIN TOMOR-ROW!
BUT I PROMISED TO GO PLAY TOMORROW.
WITH TSUBASA.
AND AJUSHA...

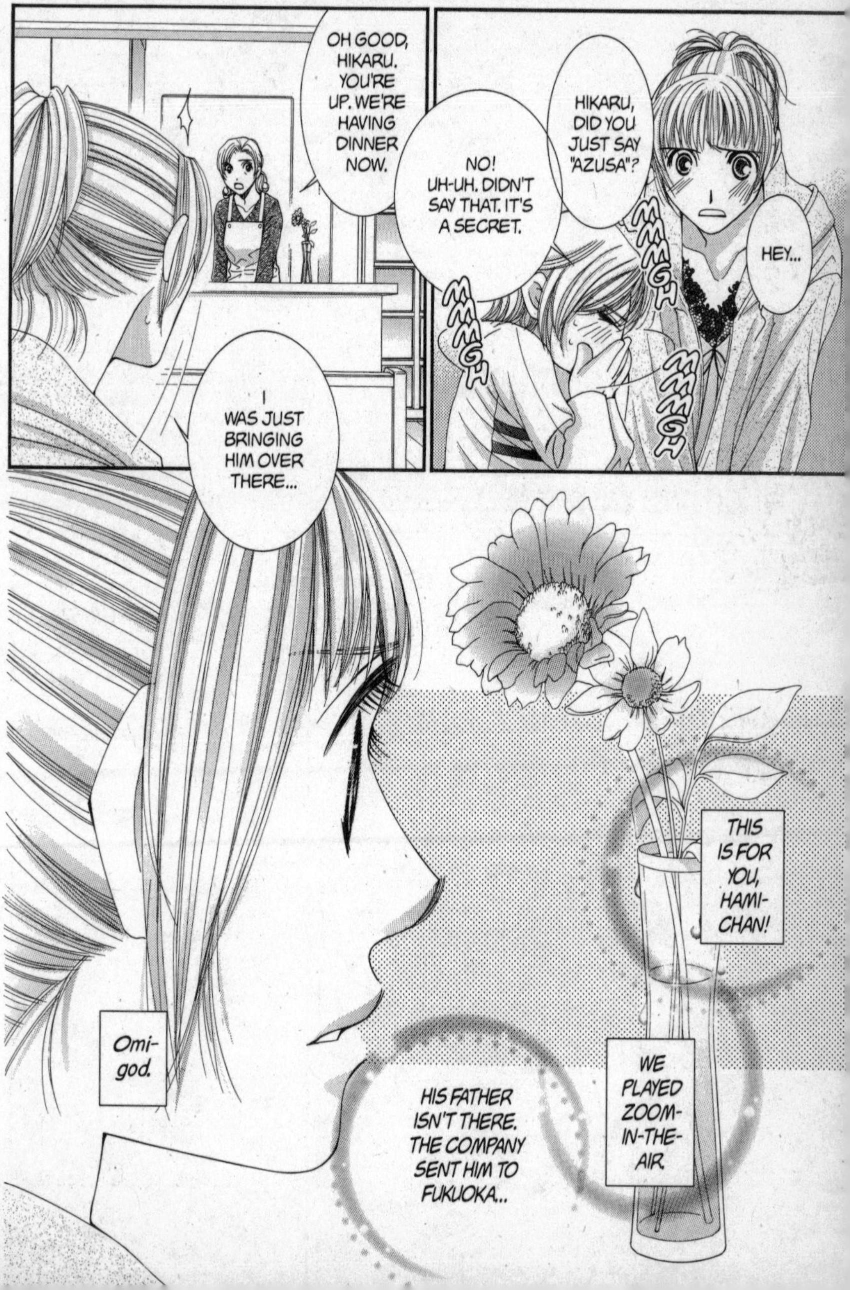
HIKARU, DID YOU JUST SAY "AZUSA"?
HEY...
NO! UH-UH. DIDN'T SAY THAT. IT'S A SECRET.
MMMGH
MMMGH
MMMGH
OH GOOD, HIKARU. YOU'RE UP. WE'RE HAVING DINNER NOW.
I WAS JUST BRINGING HIM OVER THERE...
THIS IS FOR YOU, HAMI-CHAN!
WE PLAYED ZOOM-IN-THE-AIR.
HIS FATHER ISN'T THERE. THE COMPANY SENT HIM TO FUKUOKA...
Omi-god.

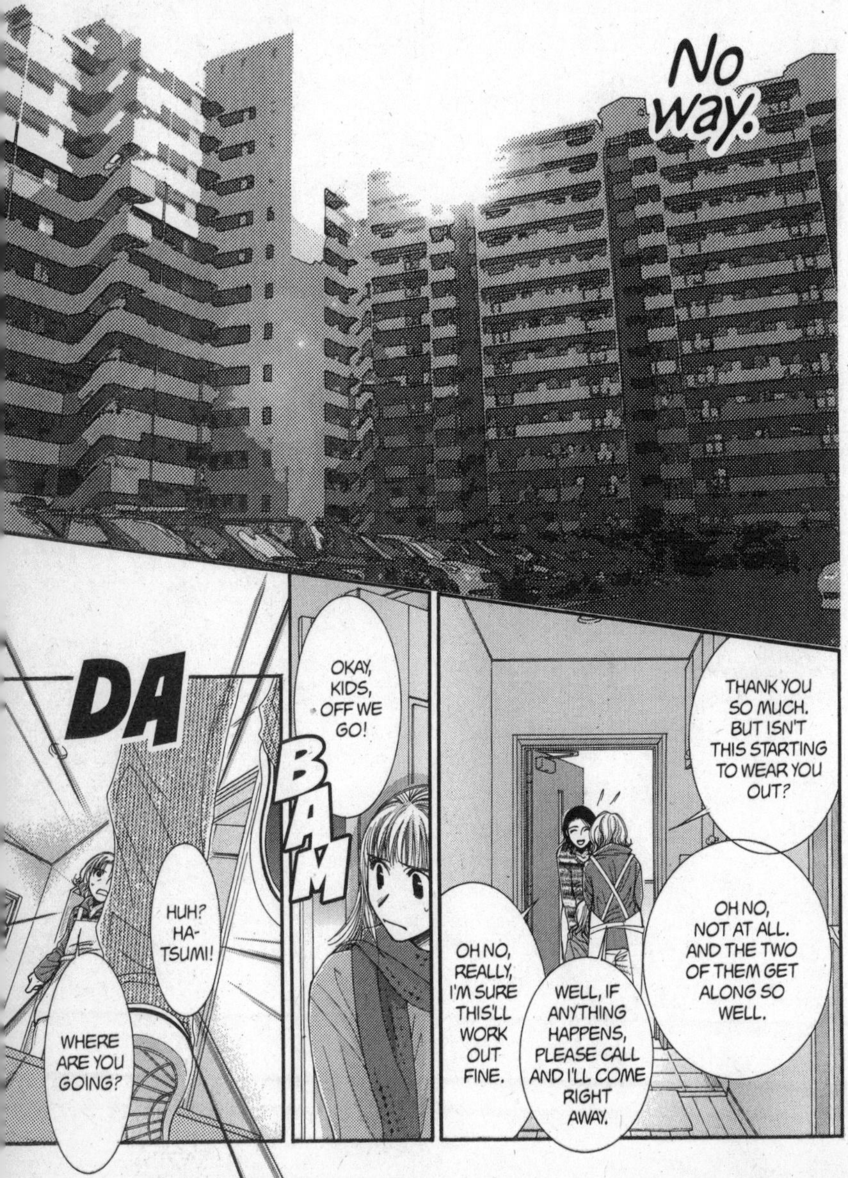
No way.
THANK YOU SO MUCH. BUT ISN'T THIS STARTING TO WEAR YOU OUT?
OH NO, NOT AT ALL. AND THE TWO OF THEM GET ALONG SO WELL.
WELL, IF ANYTHING HAPPENS, PLEASE CALL AND I'LL COME RIGHT AWAY.
OH NO, REALLY, I'M SURE THIS'LL WORK OUT FINE.
OKAY, KIDS, OFF WE GO!
BAM
DA
HUH? HA-TSUMI!
WHERE ARE YOU GOING?

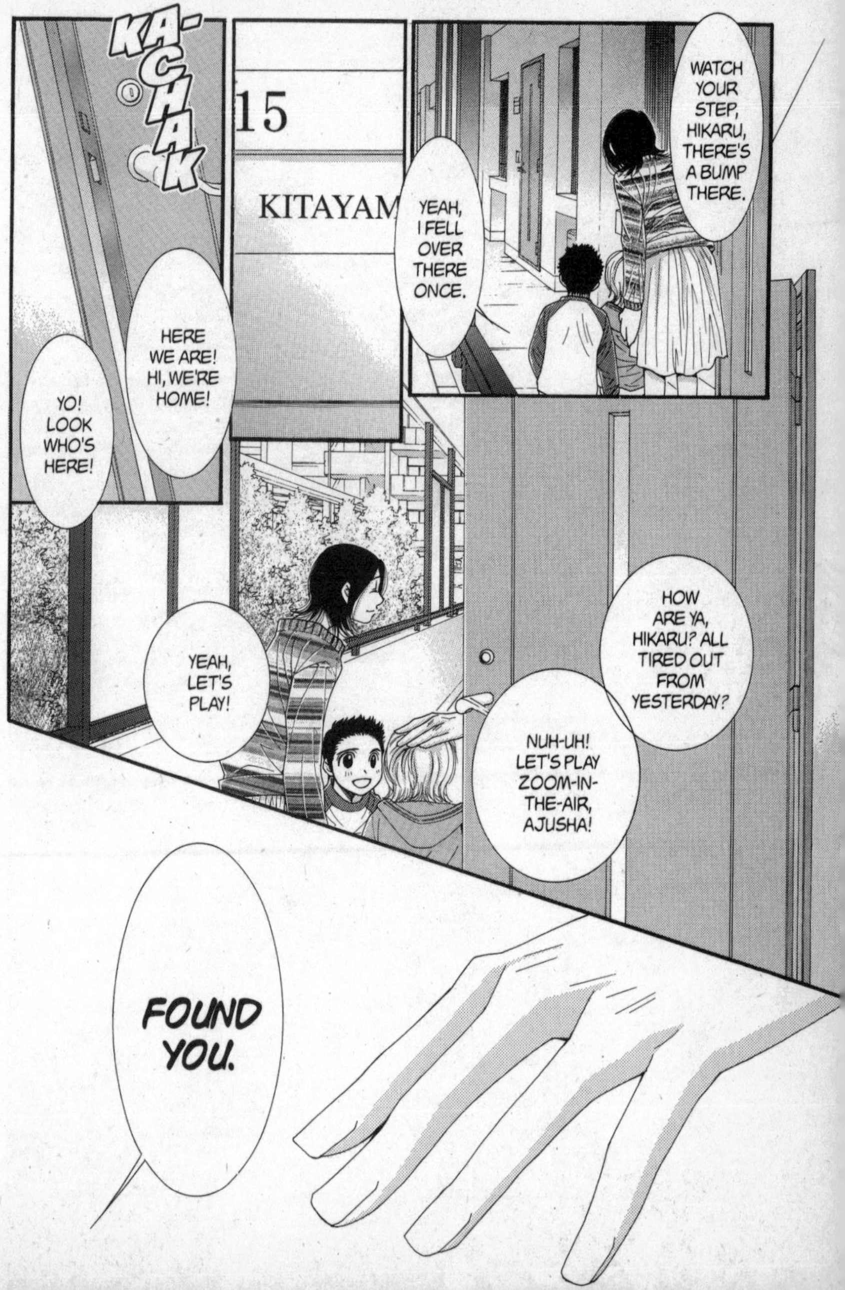
WATCH YOUR STEP, HIKARU, THERE'S A BUMP THERE.
YEAH, I FELL OVER THERE ONCE.
15
KITAYAM
KA-CHAK
HERE WE ARE! HI, WE'RE HOME!
YO! LOOK WHO'S HERE!
HOW ARE YA, HIKARU? ALL TIRED OUT FROM YESTERDAY?
NUH-UH! LET'S PLAY ZOOM-IN-THE-AIR, AJUSHA!
YEAH, LET'S PLAY!
FOUND YOU.

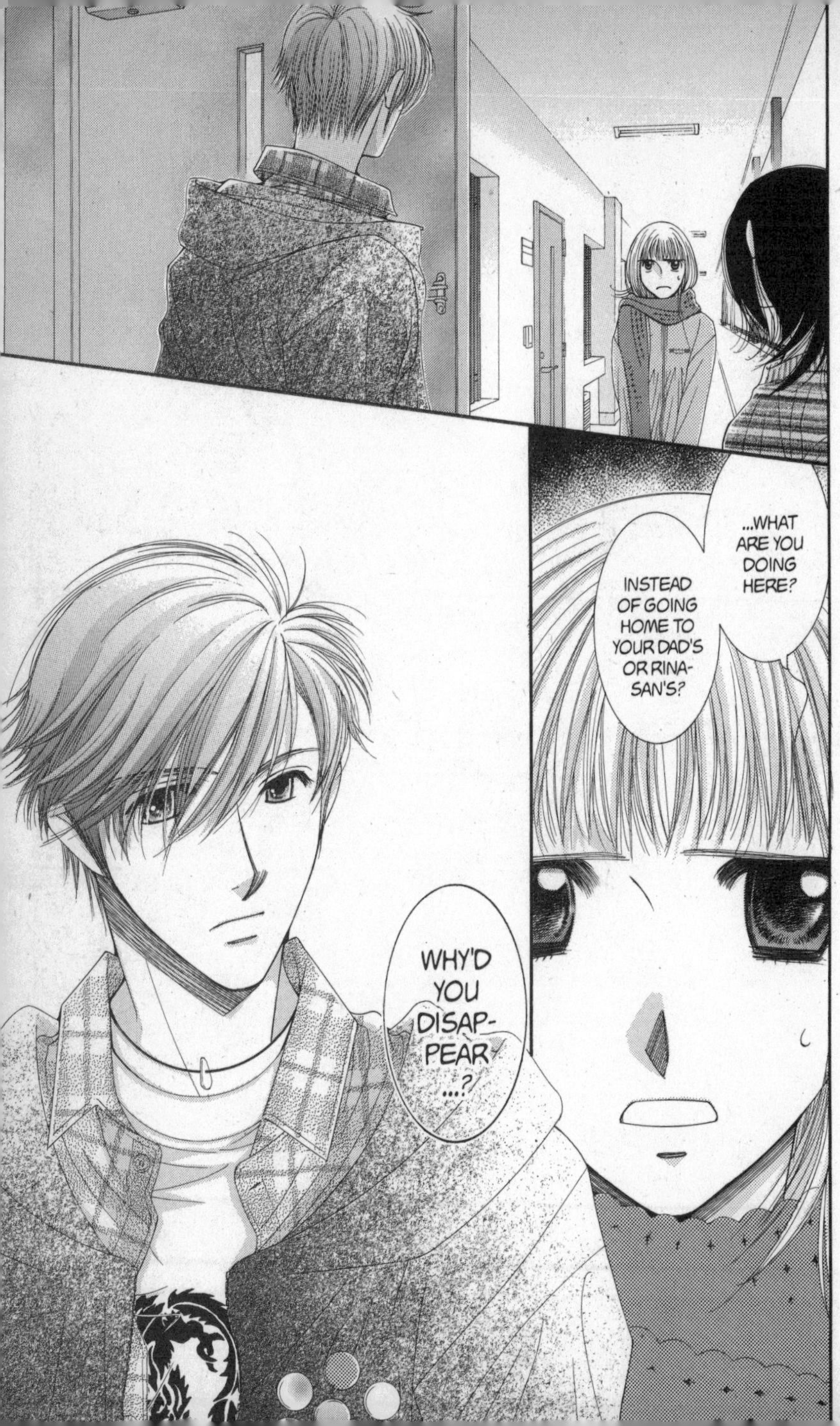
...WHAT ARE YOU DOING HERE?
INSTEAD OF GOING HOME TO YOUR DAD'S OR RINA-SAN'S?
WHY'D YOU DISAPPEAR ...?

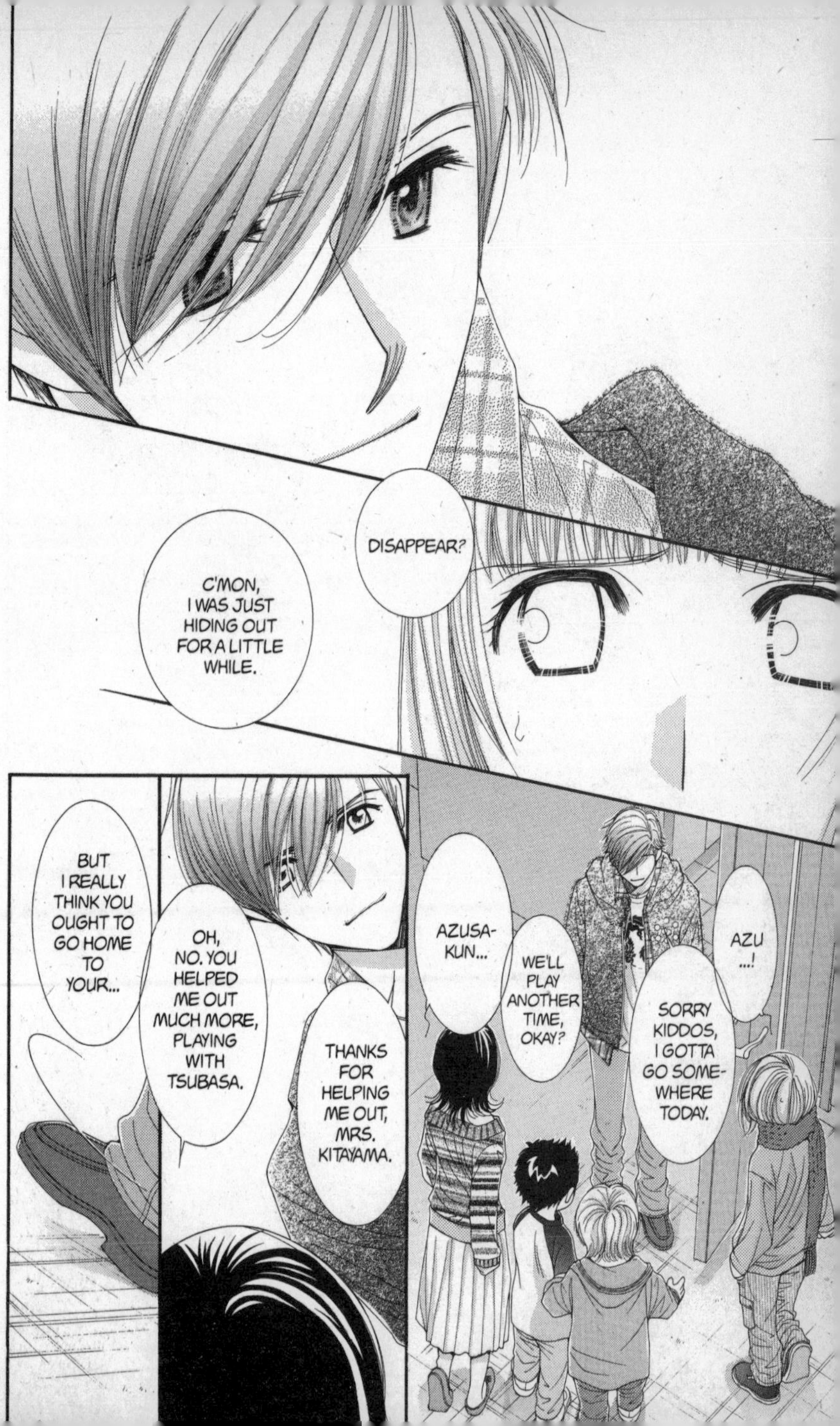
DISAPPEAR?
C'MON, I WAS JUST HIDING OUT FOR A LITTLE WHILE.
AZU ...!
SORRY KIDDOS, I GOTTA GO SOME-WHERE TODAY.
AZUSA-KUN...
WE'LL PLAY ANOTHER TIME, OKAY?
THANKS FOR HELPING ME OUT, MRS. KITAYAMA.
OH, NO. YOU HELPED ME OUT MUCH MORE, PLAYING WITH TSUBASA.
BUT I REALLY THINK YOU OUGHT TO GO HOME TO YOUR...

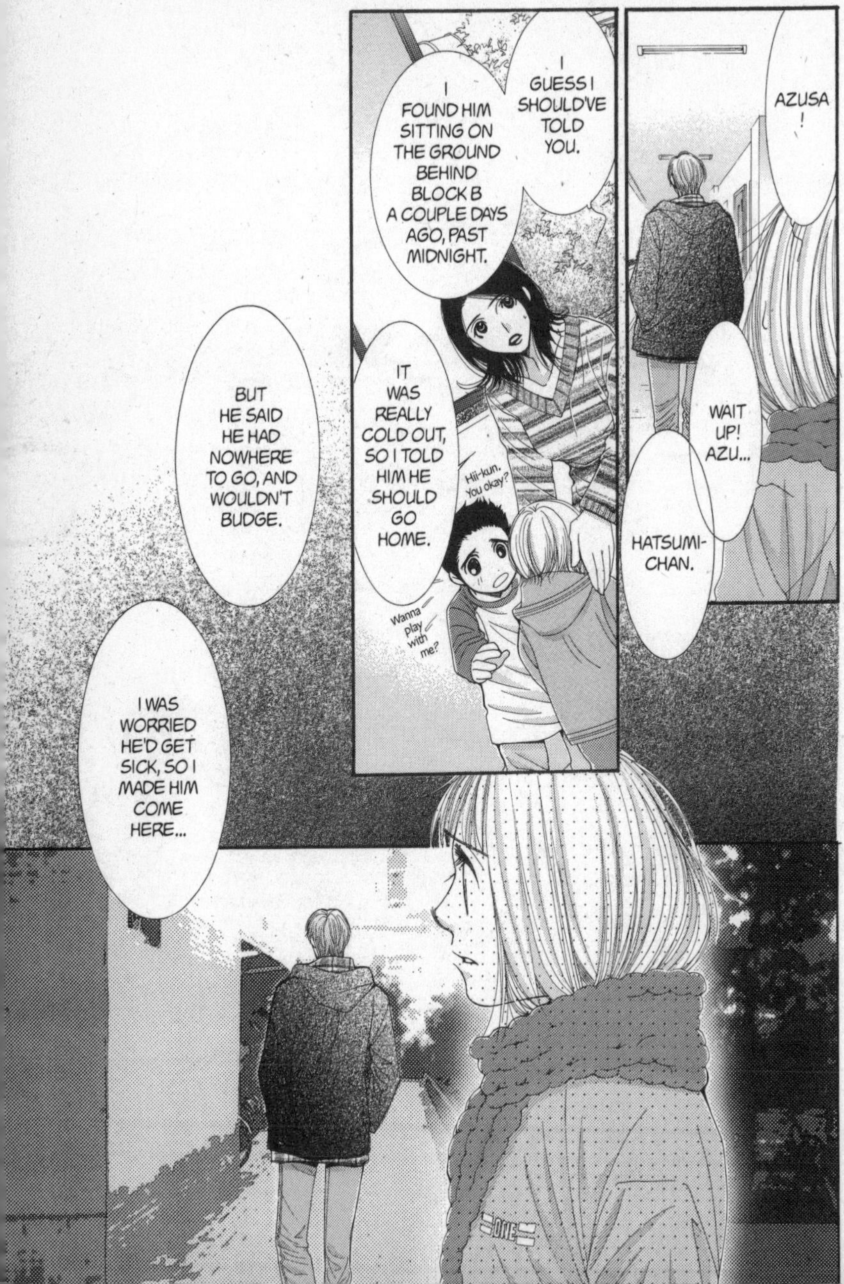
AZUSA!
WAIT UP! AZU...
HATSUMI-CHAN.
I GUESS I SHOULD'VE TOLD YOU.
I FOUND HIM SITTING ON THE GROUND BEHIND BLOCK B A COUPLE DAYS AGO, PAST MIDNIGHT.
IT WAS REALLY COLD OUT, SO I TOLD HIM HE SHOULD GO HOME.
Hii-kun. You okay?
Wanna play with me?
BUT HE SAID HE HAD NOWHERE TO GO, AND WOULDN'T BUDGE.
I WAS WORRIED HE'D GET SICK, SO I MADE HIM COME HERE...

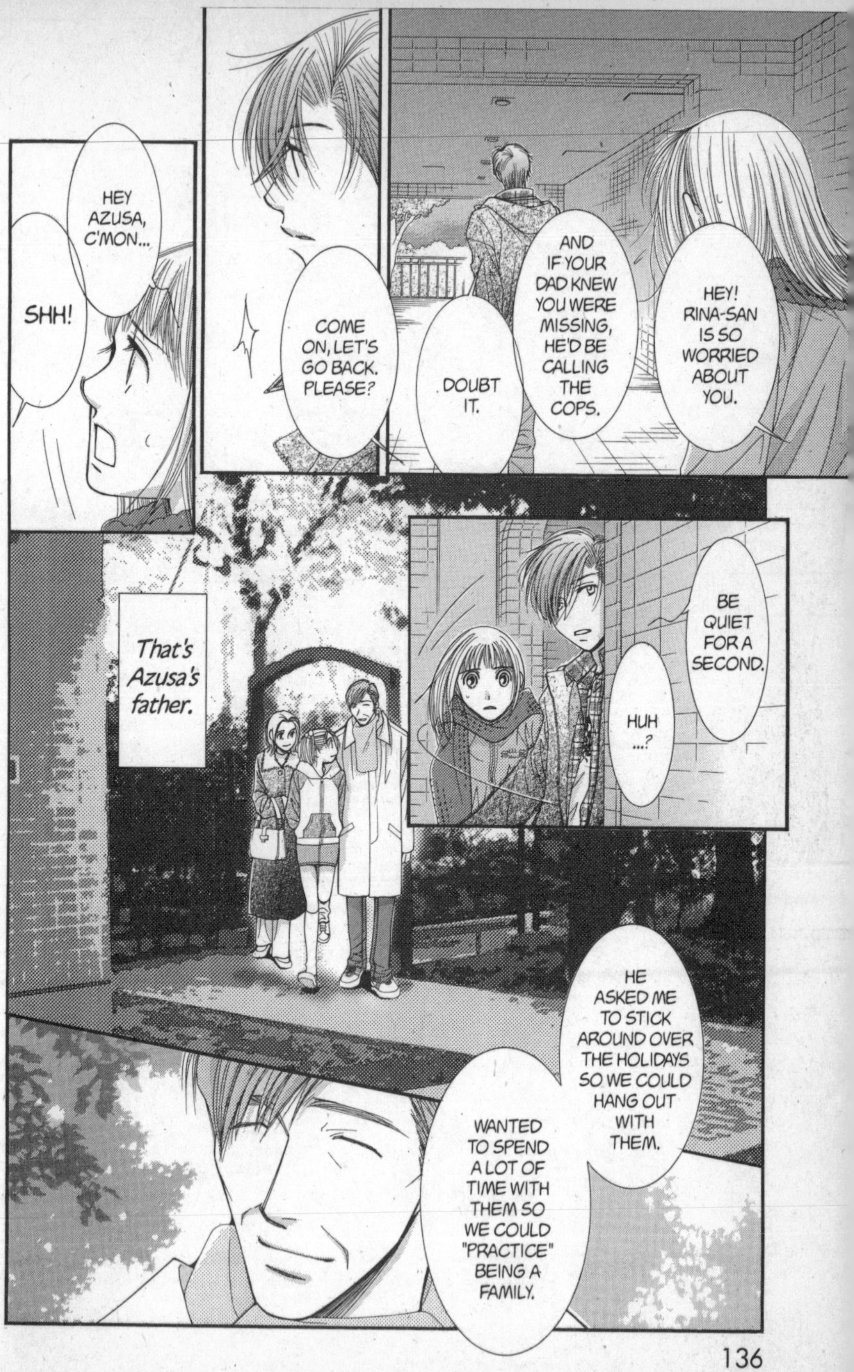
HEY! RINA-SAN IS SO WORRIED ABOUT YOU.
AND IF YOUR DAD KNEW YOU WERE MISSING, HE'D BE CALLING THE COPS.
DOUBT IT.
COME ON, LET'S GO BACK. PLEASE?
HEY AZUSA, C'MON...
SHH!
BE QUIET FOR A SECOND.
HUH ...?
That's Azusa's father.
HE ASKED ME TO STICK AROUND OVER THE HOLIDAYS SO WE COULD HANG OUT WITH THEM.
WANTED TO SPEND A LOT OF TIME WITH THEM SO WE COULD "PRACTICE" BEING A FAMILY.

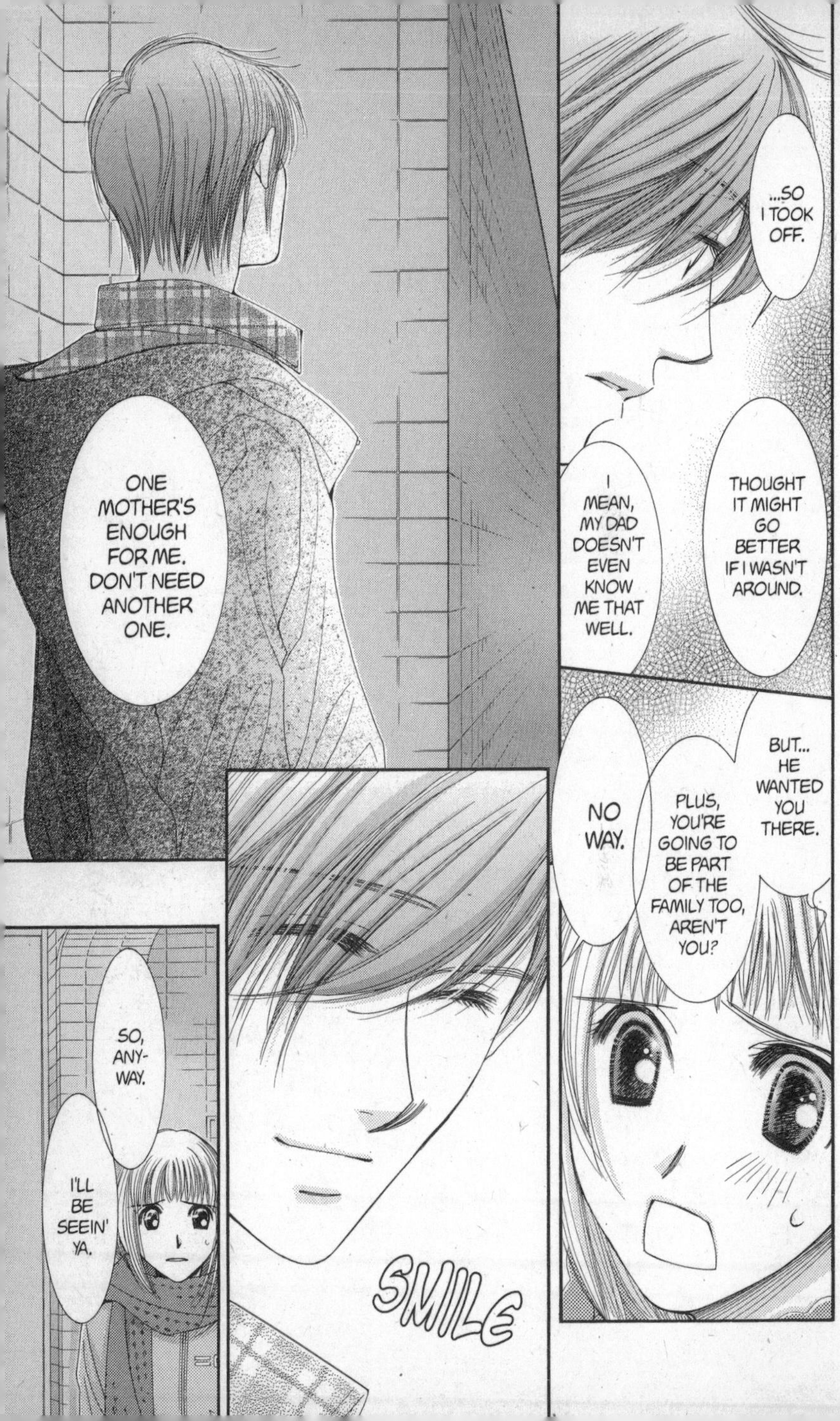
...SO I TOOK OFF.
THOUGHT IT MIGHT GO BETTER IF I WASN'T AROUND.
I MEAN, MY DAD DOESN'T EVEN KNOW ME THAT WELL.
BUT... HE WANTED YOU THERE.
PLUS, YOU'RE GOING TO BE PART OF THE FAMILY TOO, AREN'T YOU?
NO WAY.
ONE MOTHER'S ENOUGH FOR ME. DON'T NEED ANOTHER ONE.
SMILE
SO, ANY-WAY.
I'LL BE SEEIN' YA.

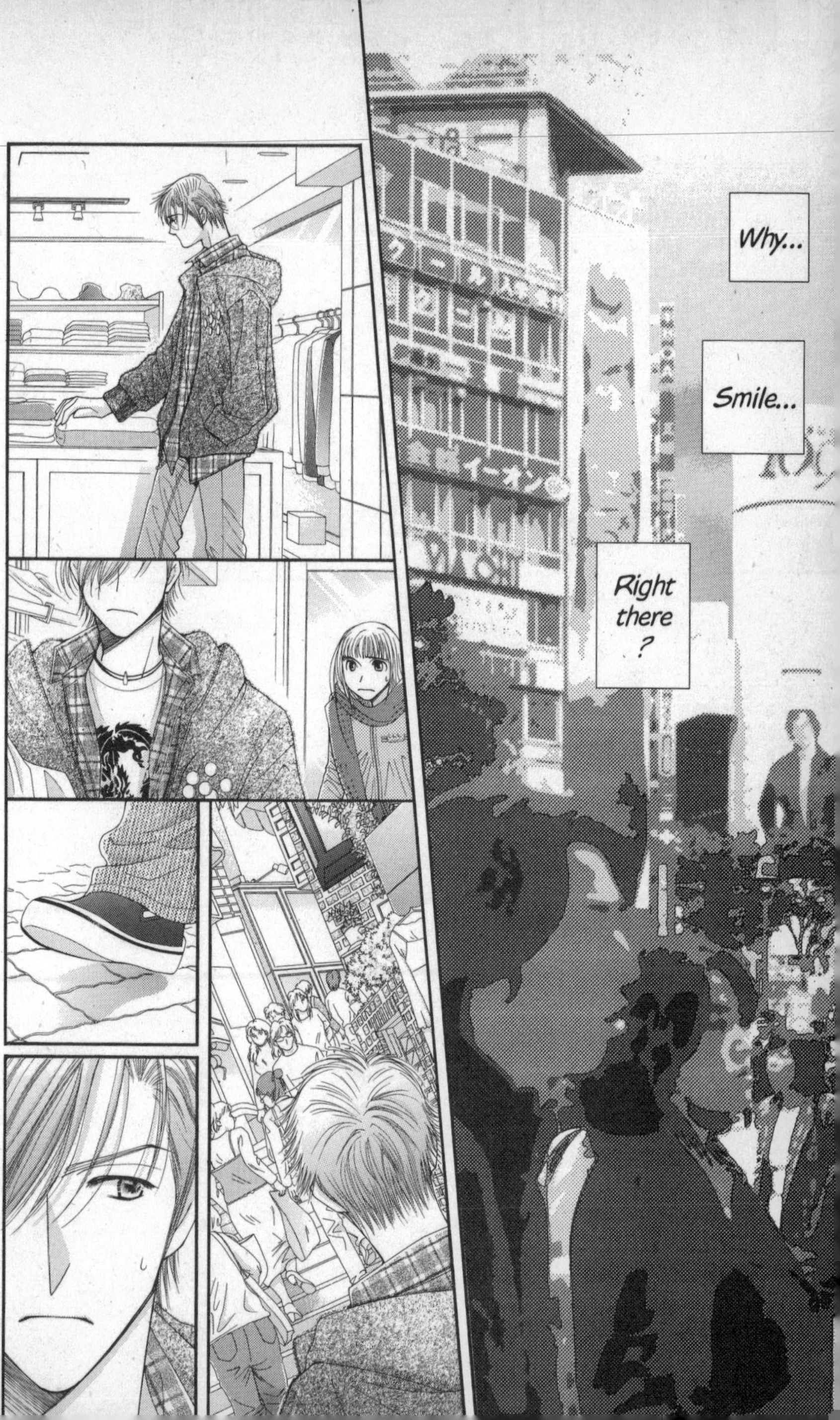
Why...
Smile...
イーオン
Right there ?

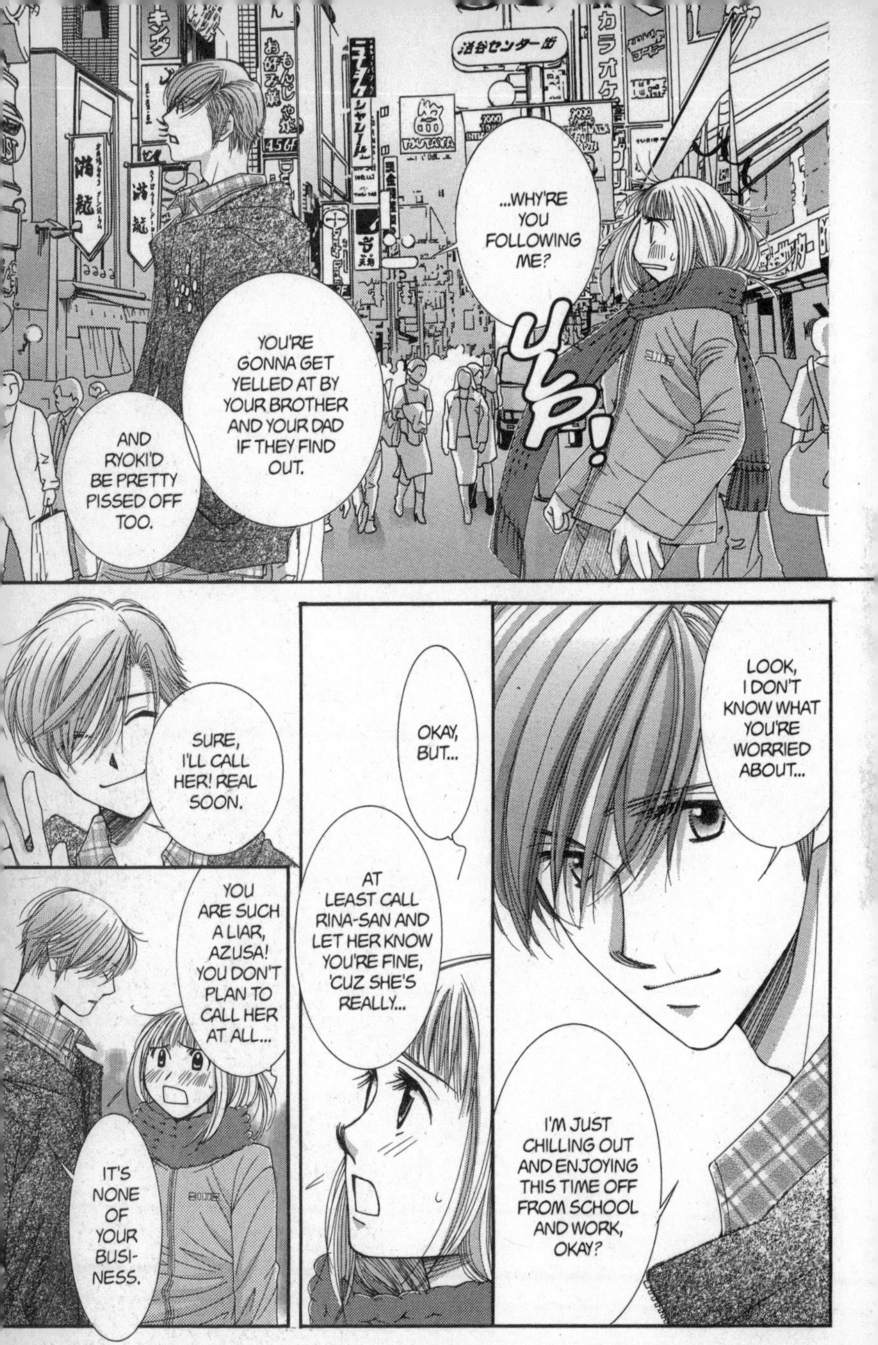
...WHY'RE YOU FOLLOWING ME?
ULP!
YOU'RE GONNA GET YELLED AT BY YOUR BROTHER AND YOUR DAD IF THEY FIND OUT.
AND RYOKI'D BE PRETTY PISSED OFF TOO.
LOOK, I DON'T KNOW WHAT YOU'RE WORRIED ABOUT...
I'M JUST CHILLING OUT AND ENJOYING THIS TIME OFF FROM SCHOOL AND WORK, OKAY?
OKAY, BUT...
AT LEAST CALL RINA-SAN AND LET HER KNOW YOU'RE FINE, 'CUZ SHE'S REALLY...
SURE, I'LL CALL HER! REAL SOON.
YOU ARE SUCH A LIAR, AZUSA! YOU DON'T PLAN TO CALL HER AT ALL...
IT'S NONE OF YOUR BUSINESS.

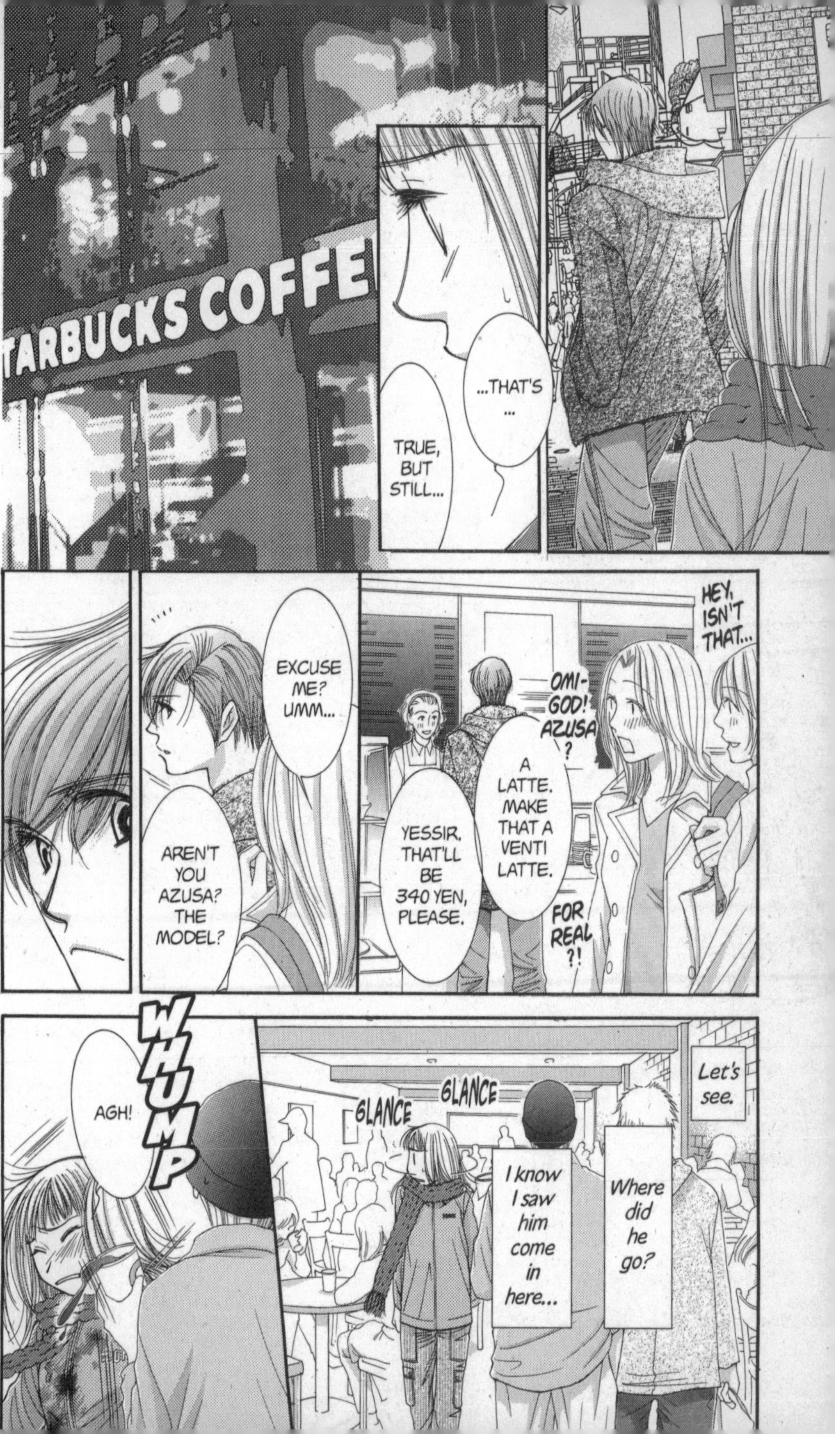
...THAT'S ...
TRUE, BUT STILL...
TARBUCKS COFFE
HEY, ISN'T THAT...
OMI-GOD! AZUSA?
A LATTE. MAKE THAT A VENTI LATTE.
YESSIR. THAT'LL BE 340 YEN, PLEASE.
FOR REAL?!
EXCUSE ME? UMM...
AREN'T YOU AZUSA? THE MODEL?
Let's see.
Where did he go?
I know I saw him come in here...
GLANCE
GLANCE
WHUMP
AGH!

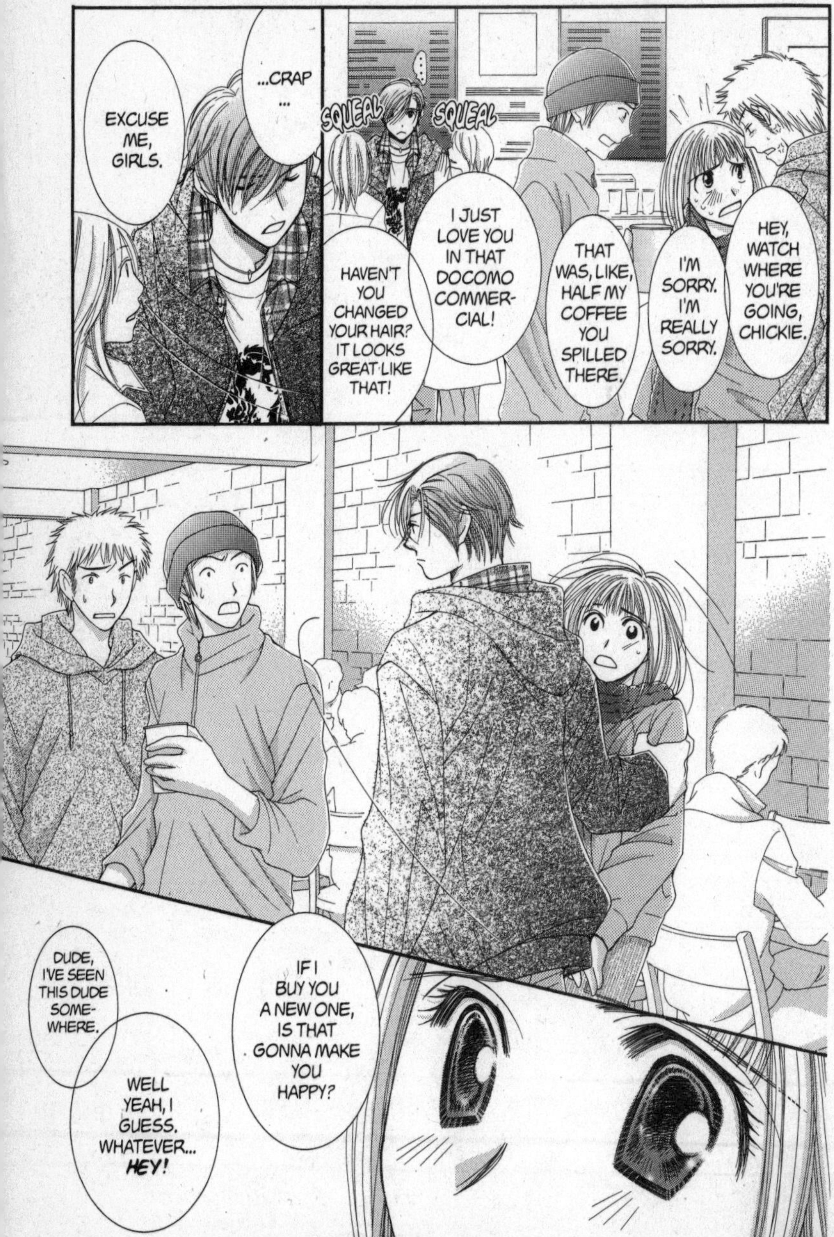
HEY, WATCH WHERE YOU'RE GOING, CHICKIE.
I'M SORRY. I'M REALLY SORRY.
THAT WAS, LIKE, HALF MY COFFEE YOU SPILLED THERE.
!
SQUEAL
SQUEAL
I JUST LOVE YOU IN THAT DOCOMO COMMER-CIAL!
HAVEN'T YOU CHANGED YOUR HAIR? IT LOOKS GREAT LIKE THAT!
...CRAP ...
EXCUSE ME, GIRLS.
IF I BUY YOU A NEW ONE, IS THAT GONNA MAKE YOU HAPPY?
DUDE, I'VE SEEN THIS DUDE SOME-WHERE.
WELL YEAH, I GUESS. WHATEVER... **HEY!**

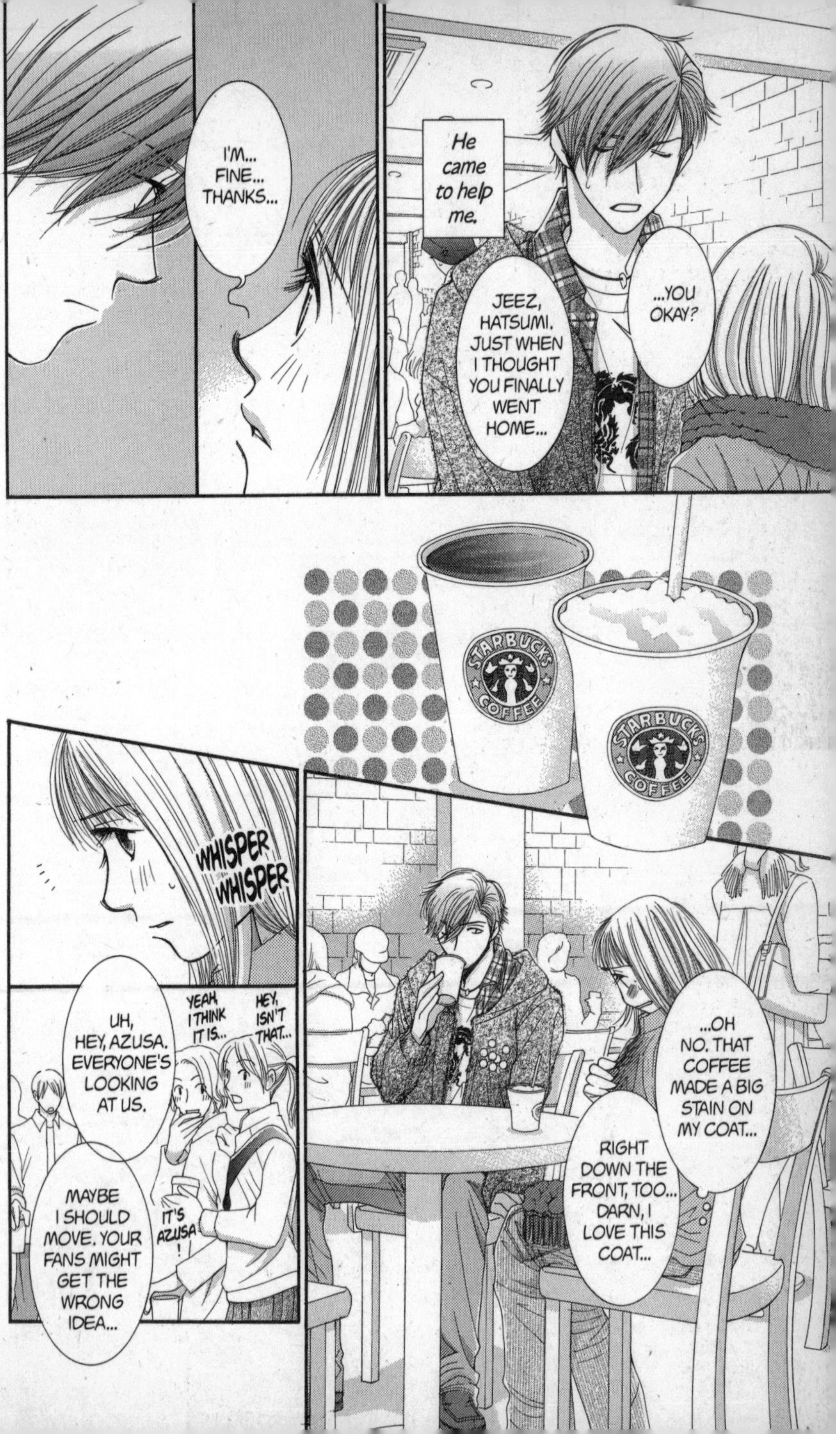
He came to help me.
...YOU OKAY?
JEEZ, HATSUMI. JUST WHEN I THOUGHT YOU FINALLY WENT HOME...
I'M... FINE... THANKS...
...OH NO. THAT COFFEE MADE A BIG STAIN ON MY COAT...
RIGHT DOWN THE FRONT, TOO... DARN, I LOVE THIS COAT...
WHISPER WHISPER
HEY, ISN'T THAT...
YEAH, I THINK IT IS...
UH, HEY, AZUSA. EVERYONE'S LOOKING AT US.
IT'S AZUSA!
MAYBE I SHOULD MOVE. YOUR FANS MIGHT GET THE WRONG IDEA...

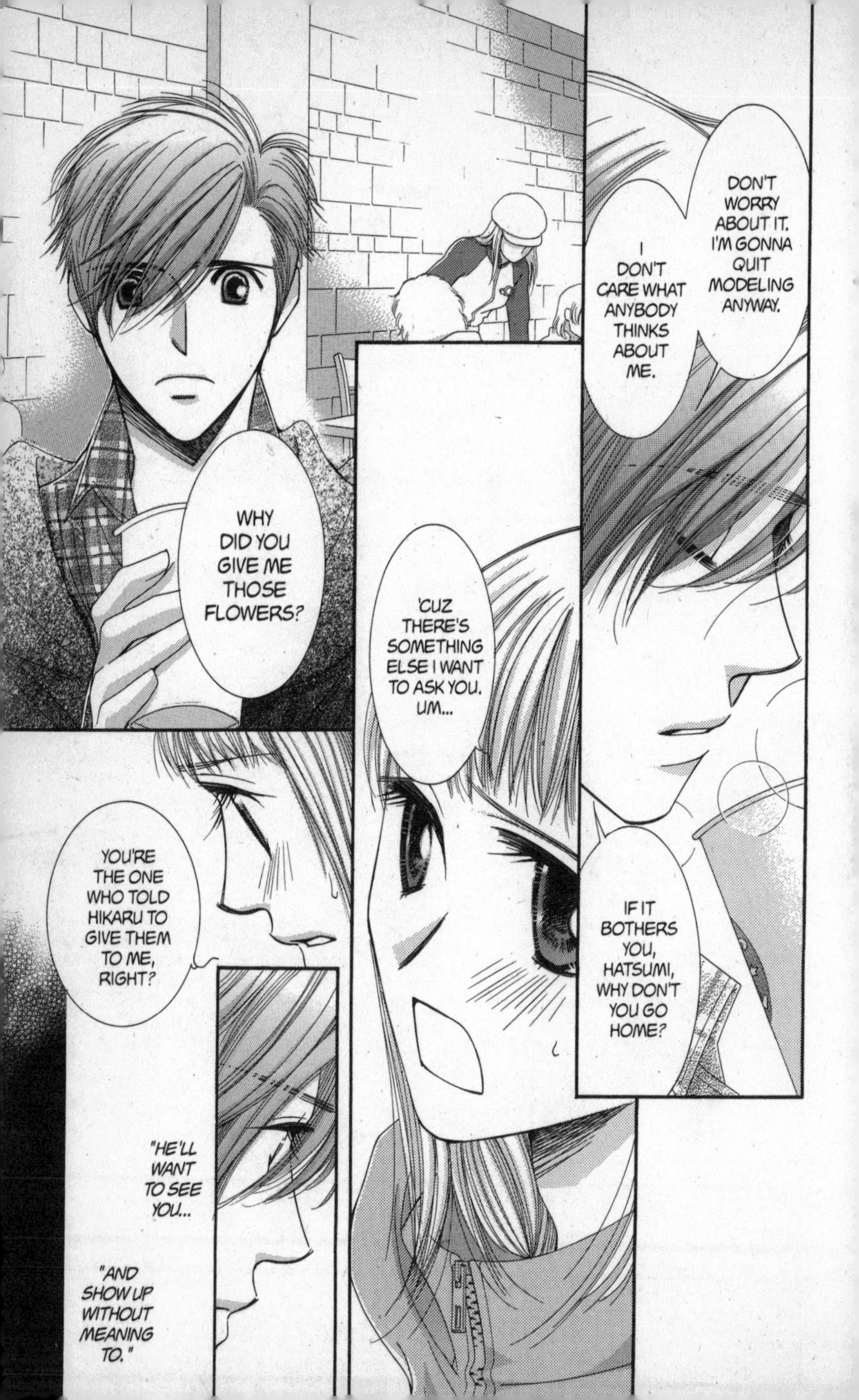
DON'T WORRY ABOUT IT. I'M GONNA QUIT MODELING ANYWAY.
I DON'T CARE WHAT ANYBODY THINKS ABOUT ME.
IF IT BOTHERS YOU, HATSUMI, WHY DON'T YOU GO HOME?
WHY DID YOU GIVE ME THOSE FLOWERS?
'CUZ THERE'S SOMETHING ELSE I WANT TO ASK YOU. UM...
YOU'RE THE ONE WHO TOLD HIKARU TO GIVE THEM TO ME, RIGHT?
"HE'LL WANT TO SEE YOU...
"AND SHOW UP WITHOUT MEANING TO."

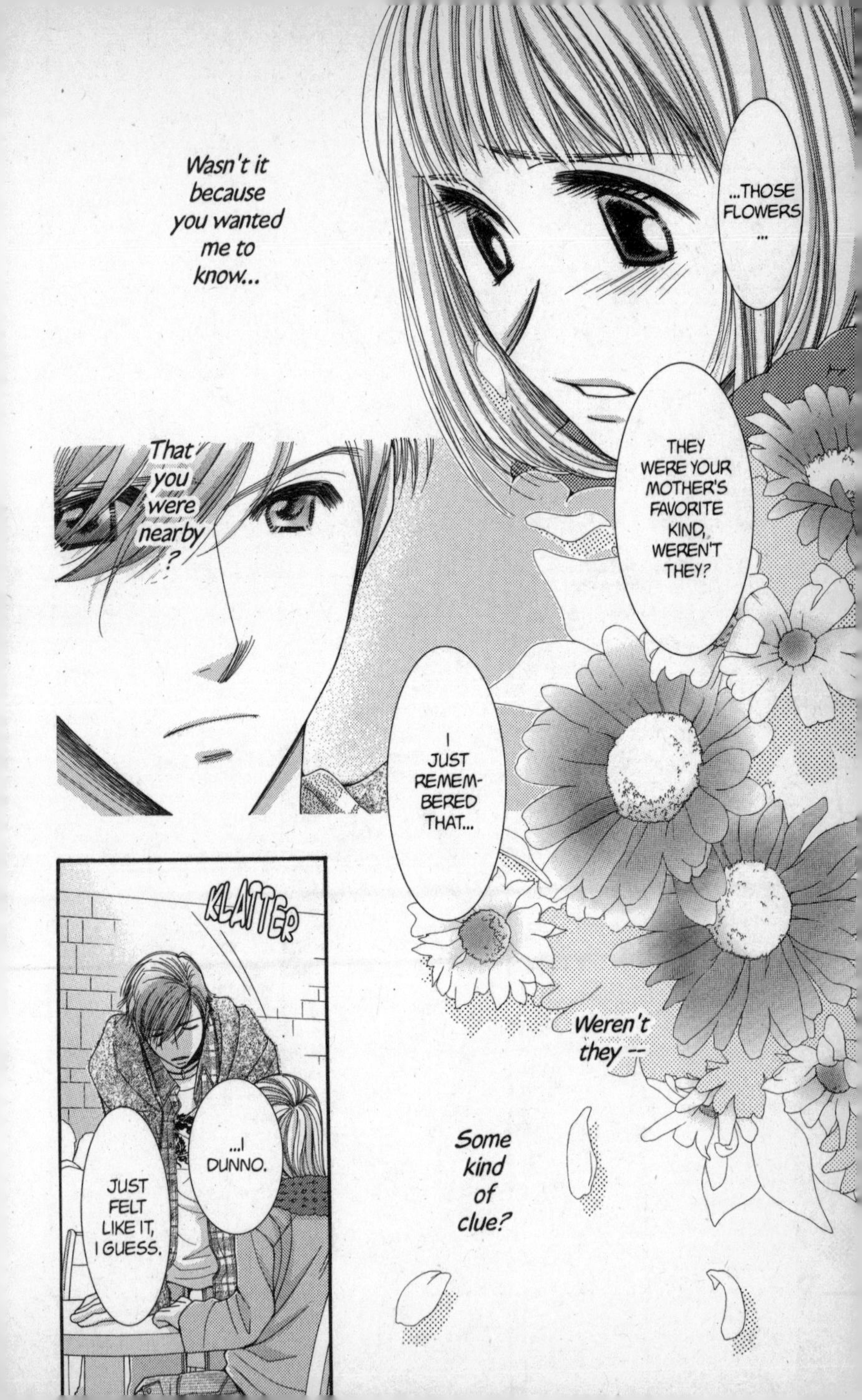
...THOSE FLOWERS ...
Wasn't it because you wanted me to know...
THEY WERE YOUR MOTHER'S FAVORITE KIND, WEREN'T THEY?
That you were nearby?
I JUST REMEMBERED THAT...
Weren't they --
Some kind of clue?
KLATTER
...I DUNNO.
JUST FELT LIKE IT, I GUESS.

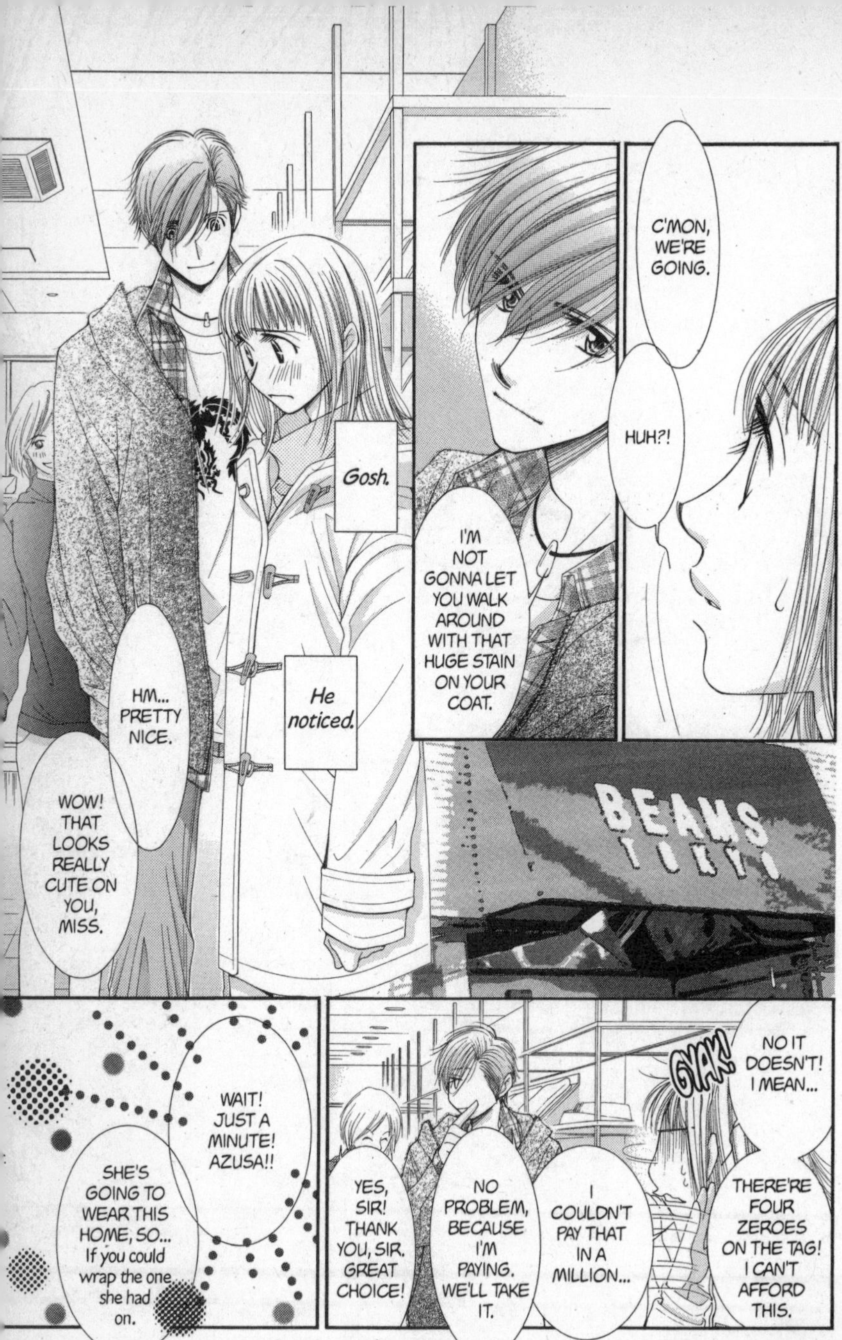
C'MON, WE'RE GOING.
HUH?!
I'M NOT GONNA LET YOU WALK AROUND WITH THAT HUGE STAIN ON YOUR COAT.
BEAMS TOKYO
Gosh.
He noticed.
HM... PRETTY NICE.
WOW! THAT LOOKS REALLY CUTE ON YOU, MISS.
NO IT DOESN'T! I MEAN...
GYAK!
THERE'RE FOUR ZEROES ON THE TAG! I CAN'T AFFORD THIS.
I COULDN'T PAY THAT IN A MILLION...
NO PROBLEM, BECAUSE I'M PAYING. WE'LL TAKE IT.
YES, SIR! THANK YOU, SIR. GREAT CHOICE!
WAIT! JUST A MINUTE! AZUSA!!
SHE'S GOING TO WEAR THIS HOME, SO... If you could wrap the one she had on.

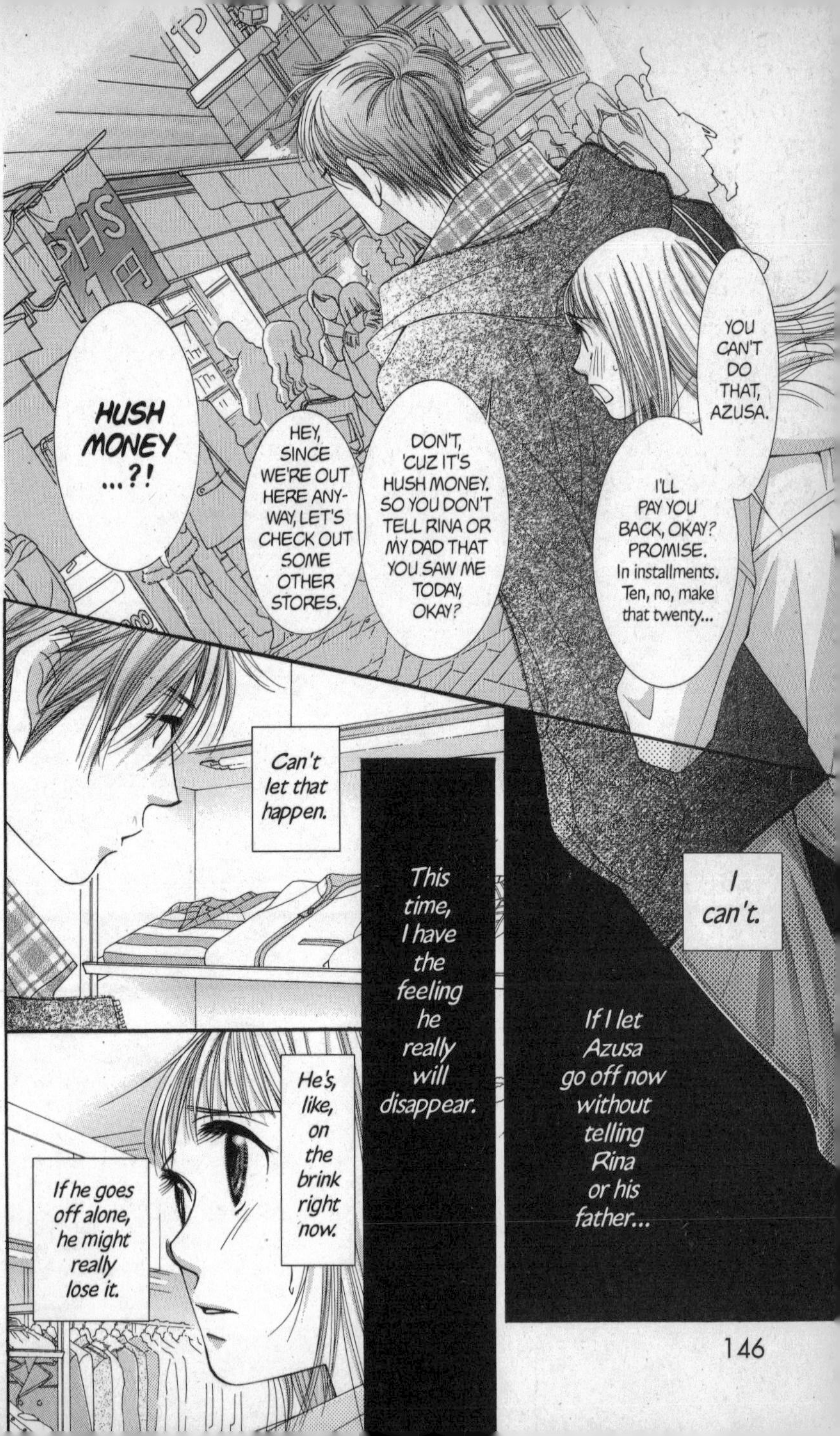

YOU CAN'T DO THAT, AZUSA.
I'LL PAY YOU BACK, OKAY? PROMISE. In installments. Ten, no, make that twenty...
DON'T, 'CUZ IT'S HUSH MONEY. SO YOU DON'T TELL RINA OR MY DAD THAT YOU SAW ME TODAY, OKAY?
HEY, SINCE WE'RE OUT HERE ANYWAY, LET'S CHECK OUT SOME OTHER STORES.
HUSH MONEY ...?!
I can't.
If I let Azusa go off now without telling Rina or his father...
Can't let that happen.
This time, I have the feeling he really will disappear.
He's, like, on the brink right now.
If he goes off alone, he might really lose it.

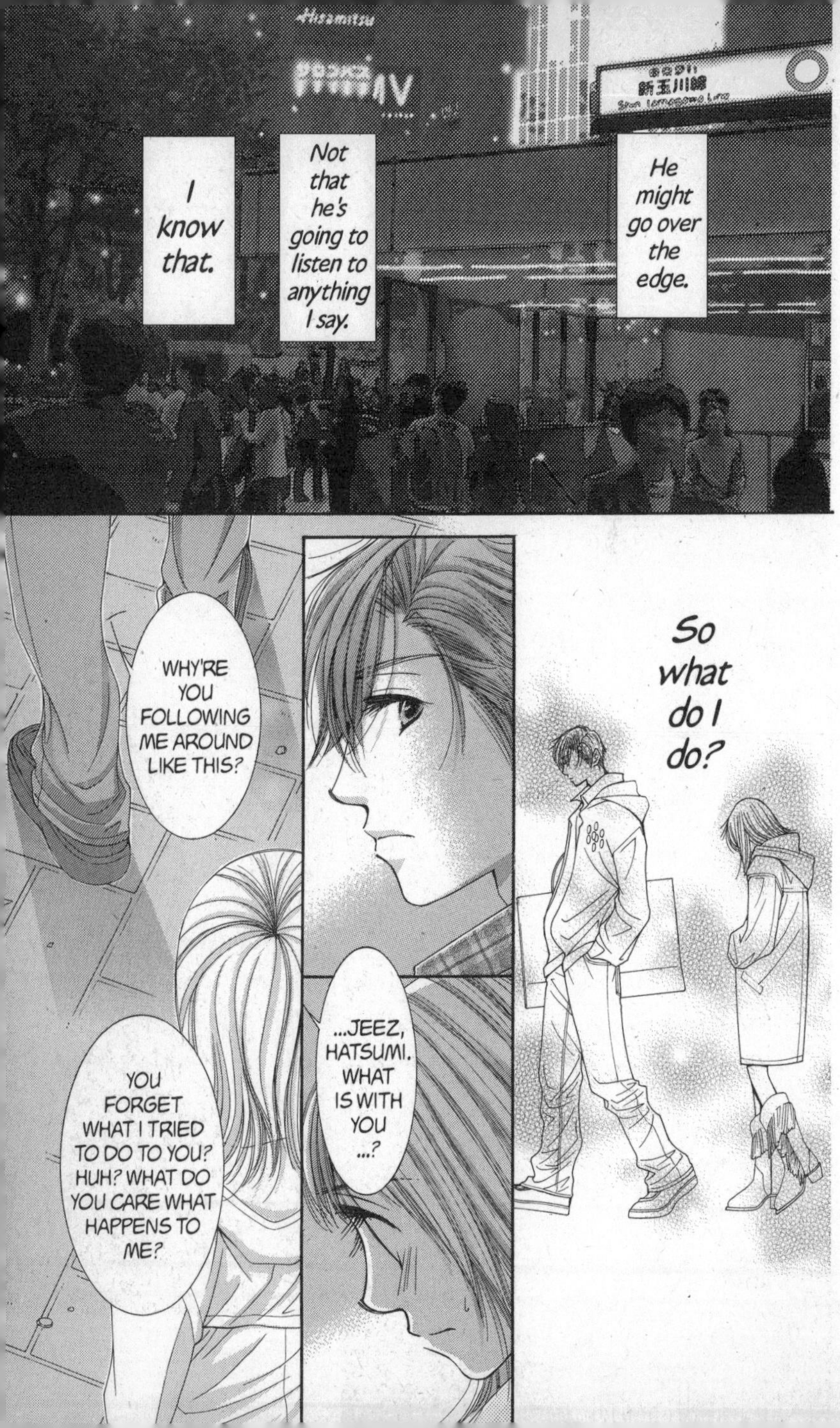
Hisamitsu
新玉川線
He might go over the edge.
Not that he's going to listen to anything I say.
I know that.
So what do I do?
...JEEZ, HATSUMI. WHAT IS WITH YOU ...?
WHY'RE YOU FOLLOWING ME AROUND LIKE THIS?
YOU FORGET WHAT I TRIED TO DO TO YOU? HUH? WHAT DO YOU CARE WHAT HAPPENS TO ME?

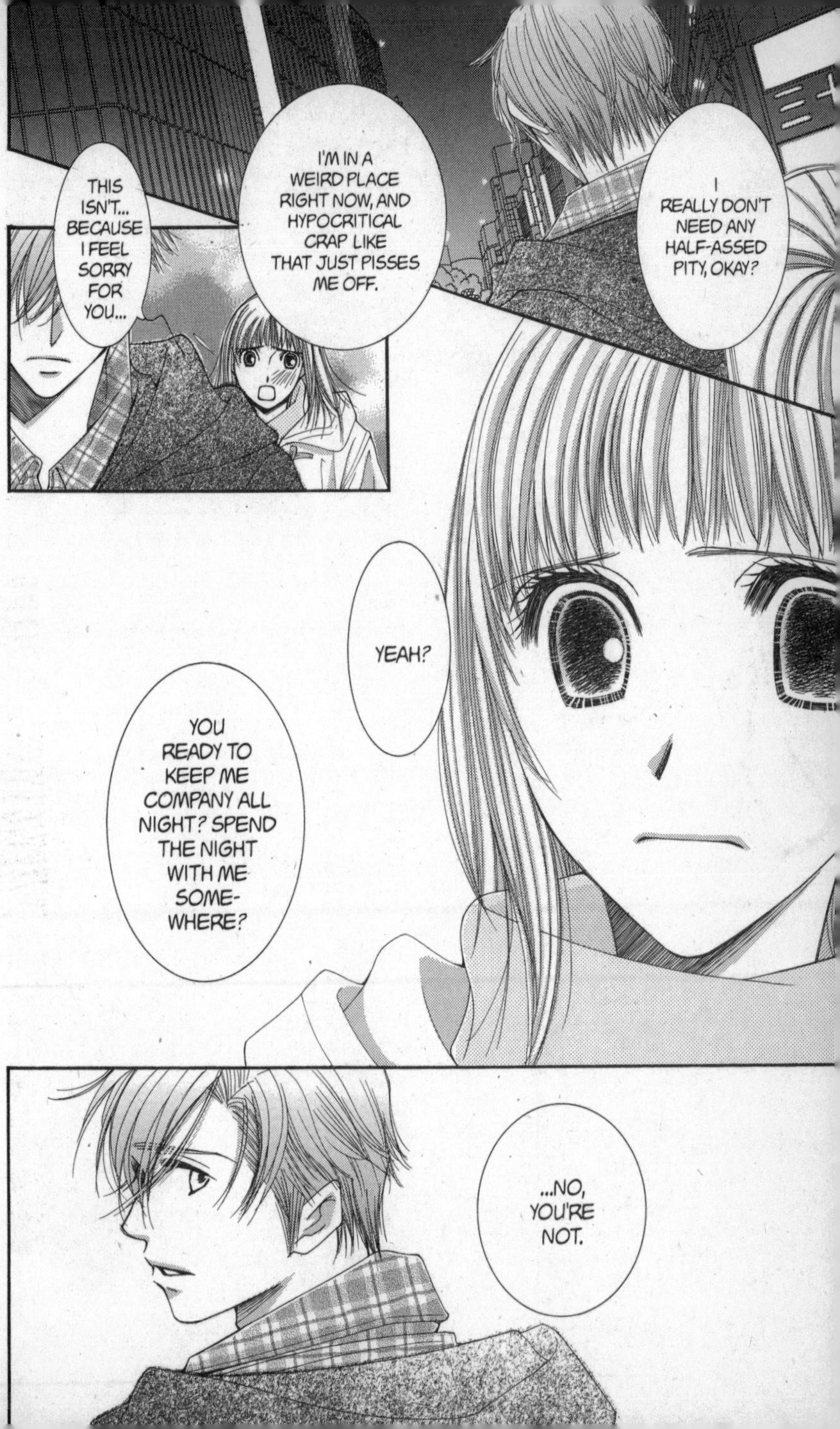
I REALLY DON'T NEED ANY HALF-ASSED PITY, OKAY?
I'M IN A WEIRD PLACE RIGHT NOW, AND HYPOCRITICAL CRAP LIKE THAT JUST PISSES ME OFF.
THIS ISN'T... BECAUSE I FEEL SORRY FOR YOU...
YEAH?
YOU READY TO KEEP ME COMPANY ALL NIGHT? SPEND THE NIGHT WITH ME SOME-WHERE?
...NO, YOU'RE NOT.

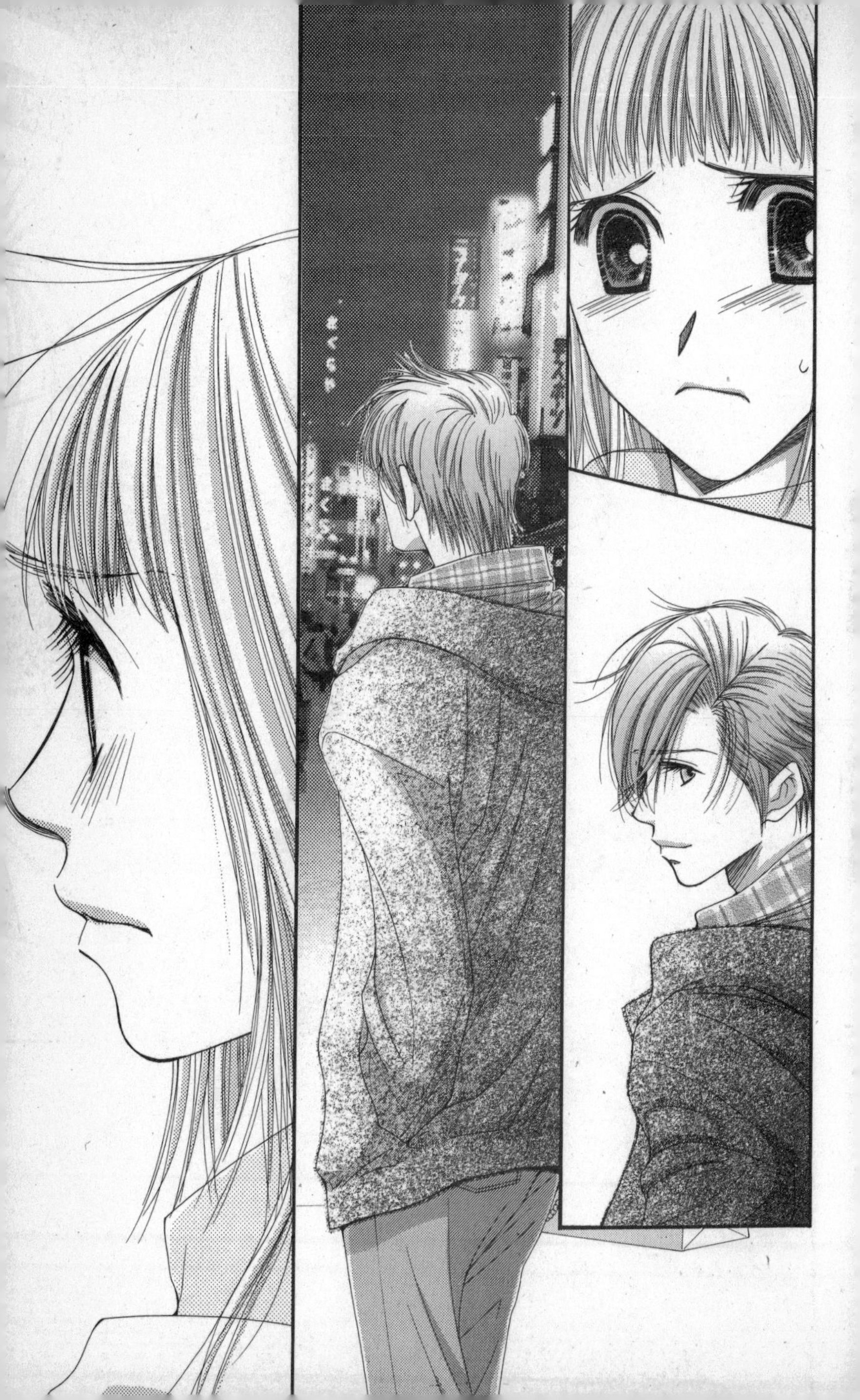

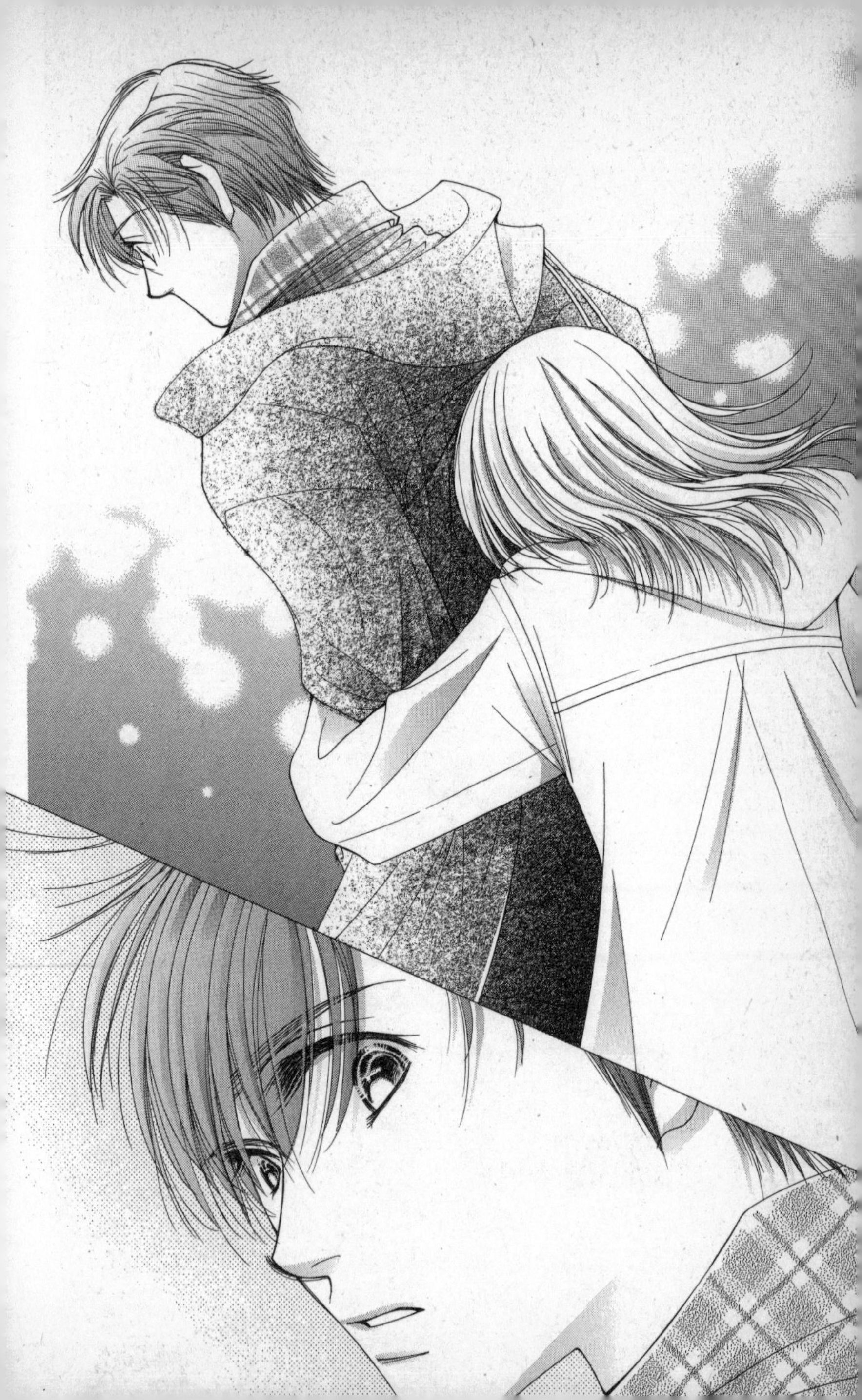

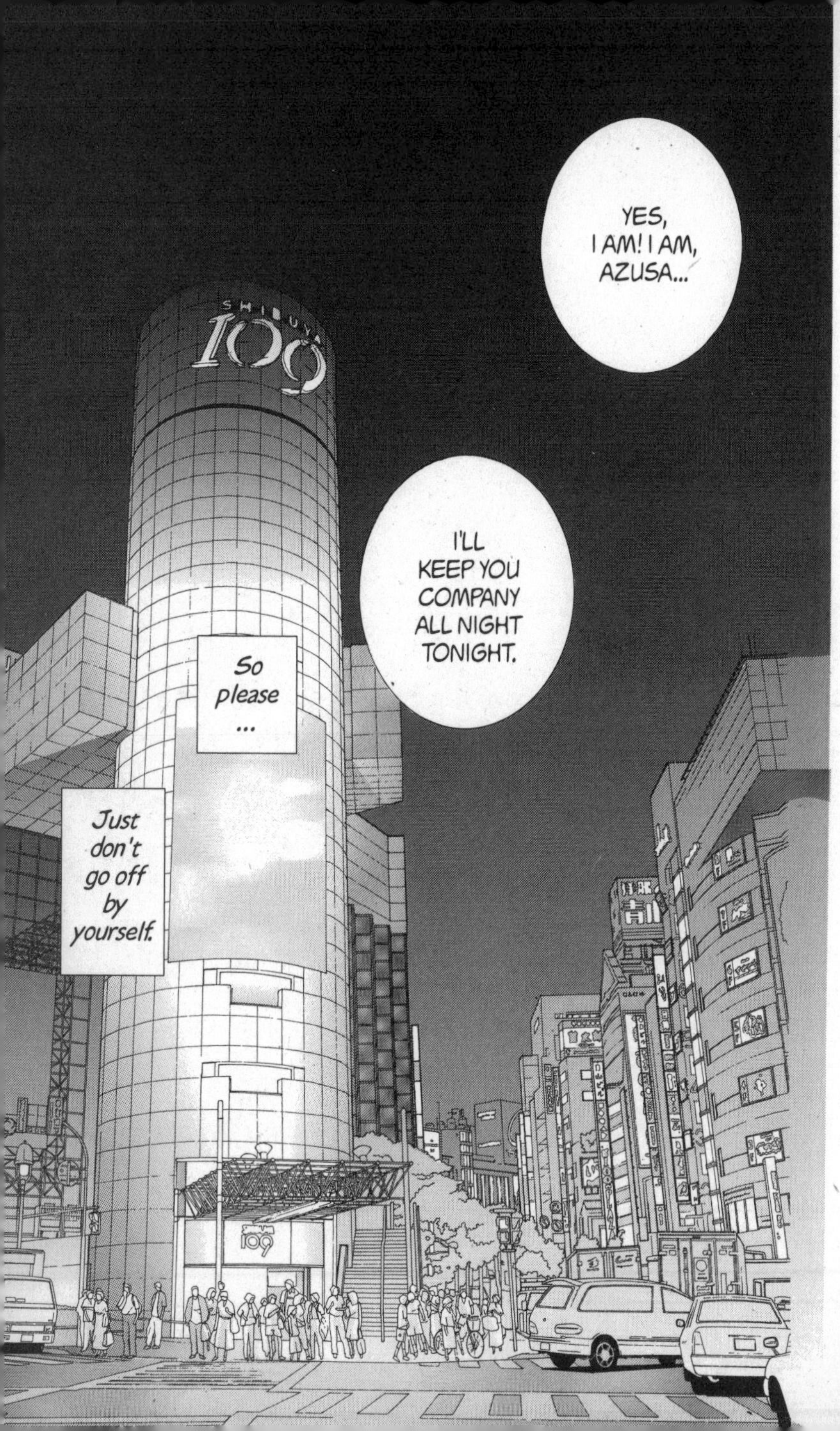
YES, I AM! I AM, AZUSA...
I'LL KEEP YOU COMPANY ALL NIGHT TONIGHT.
So please ...
Just don't go off by yourself.
SHIBUYA 109

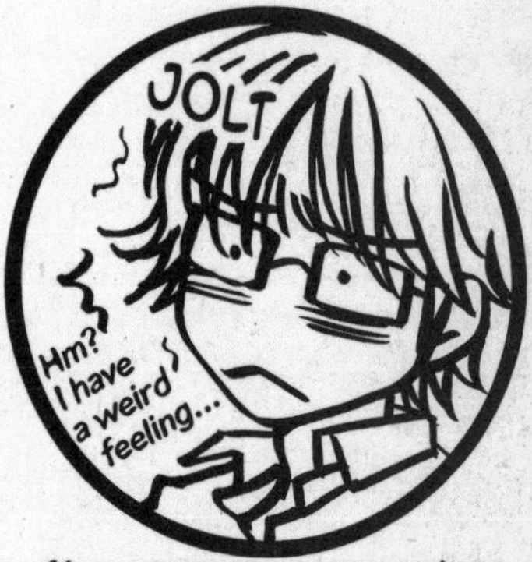
JOLT
Hm? I have a weird feeling...
Meanwhile, on the other side of the planet...

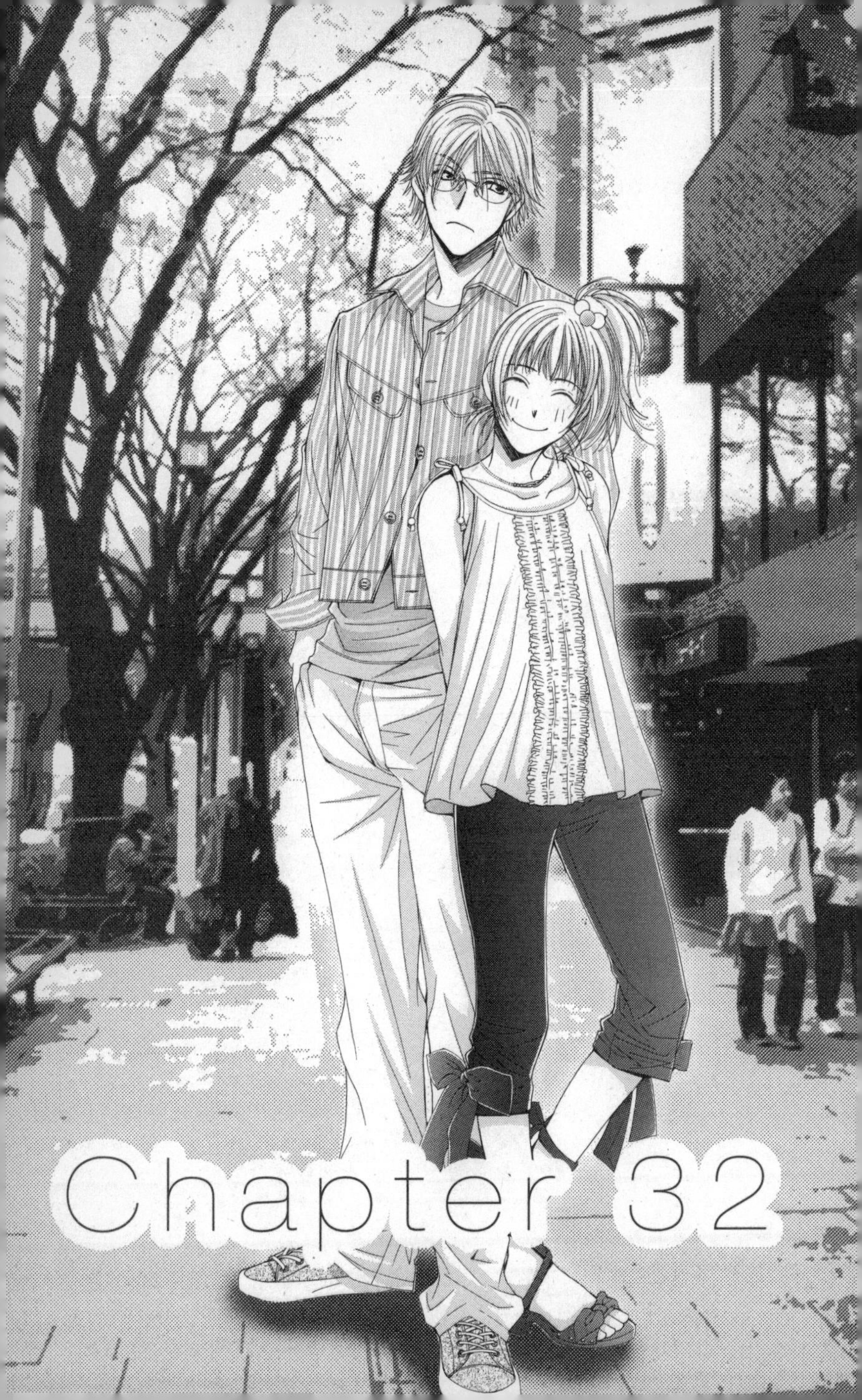
Chapter 32

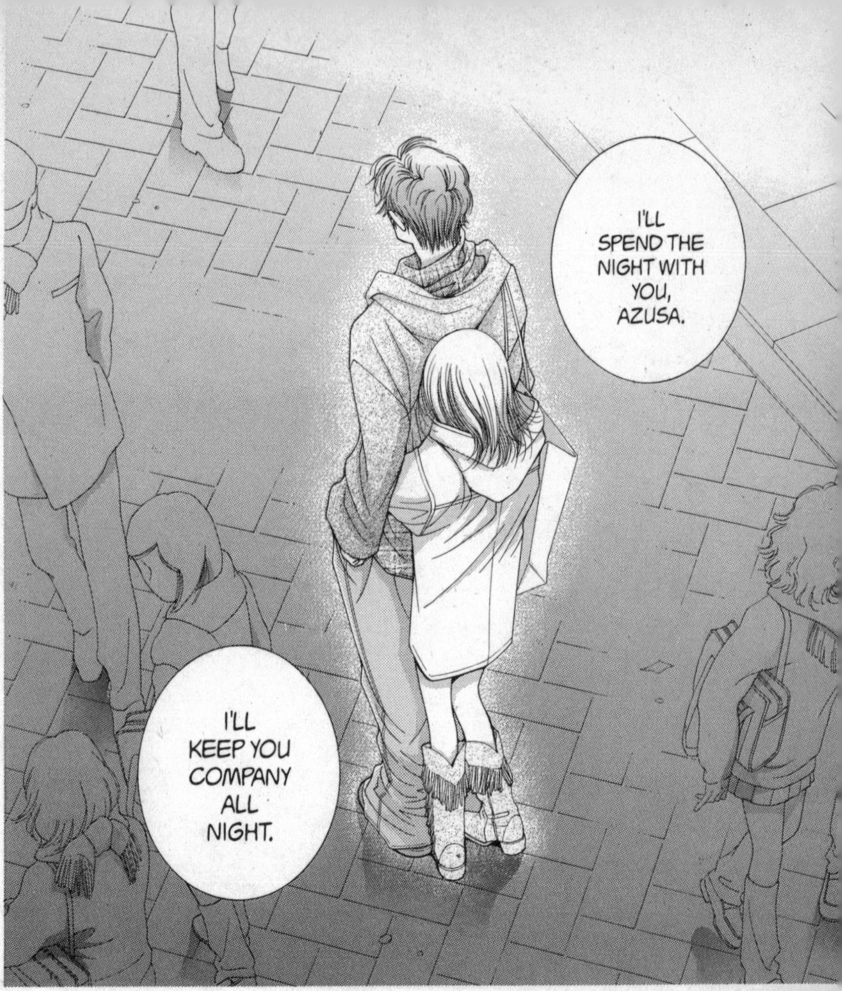
I'LL SPEND THE NIGHT WITH YOU, AZUSA.
I'LL KEEP YOU COMPANY ALL NIGHT.

hot gimmick

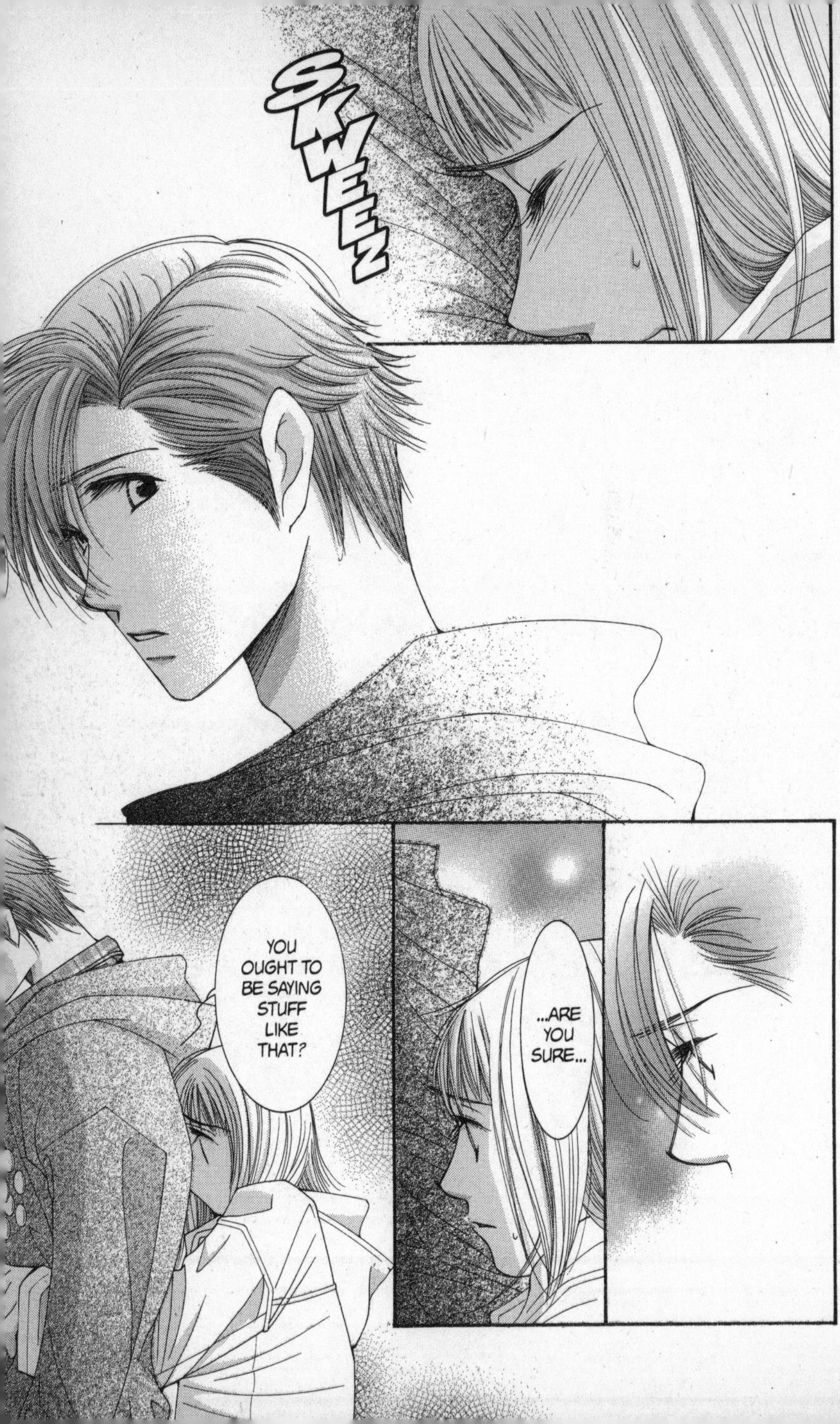
SKWEEZ
...ARE YOU SURE...
YOU OUGHT TO BE SAYING STUFF LIKE THAT?

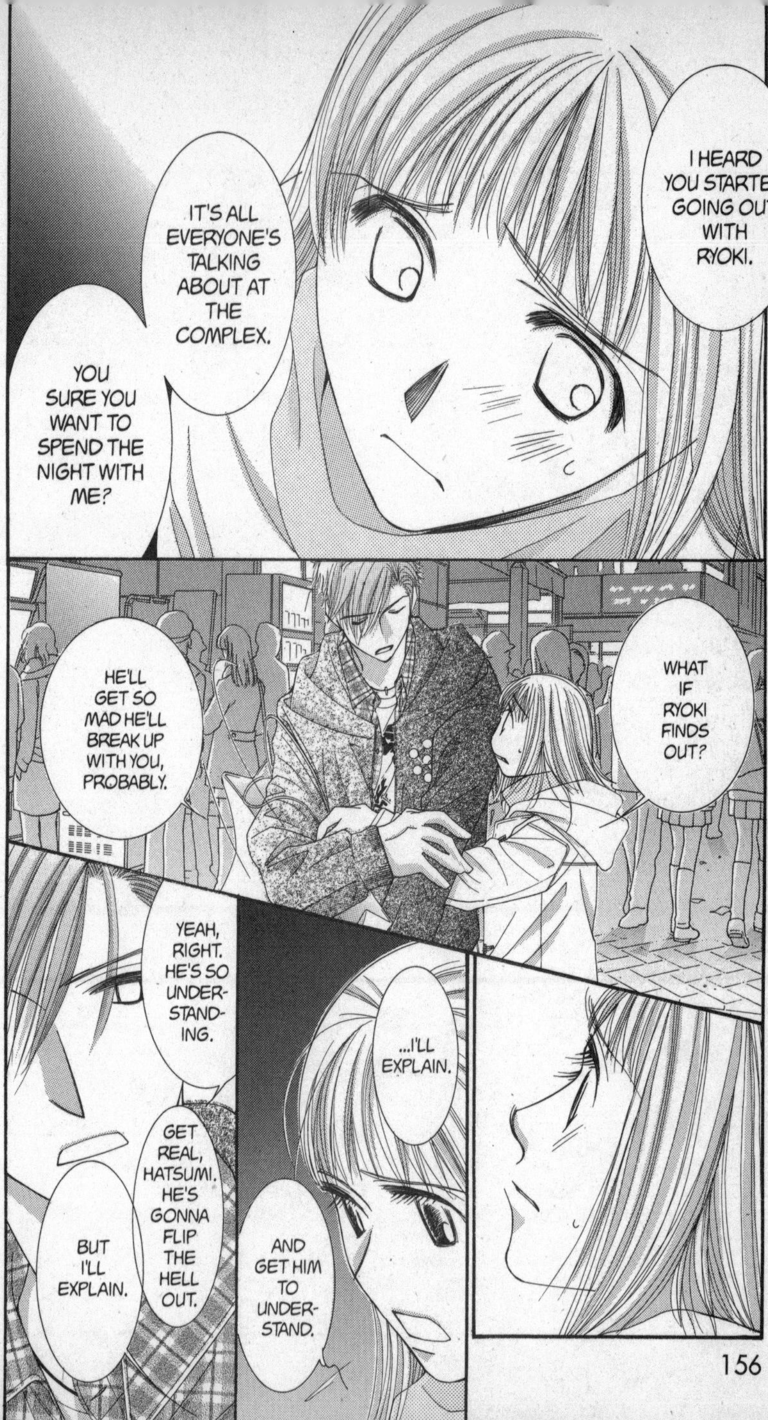
I HEARD YOU STARTED GOING OUT WITH RYOKI.
IT'S ALL EVERYONE'S TALKING ABOUT AT THE COMPLEX.
YOU SURE YOU WANT TO SPEND THE NIGHT WITH ME?
WHAT IF RYOKI FINDS OUT?
HE'LL GET SO MAD HE'LL BREAK UP WITH YOU, PROBABLY.
...I'LL EXPLAIN.
YEAH, RIGHT. HE'S SO UNDER-STAND-ING.
GET REAL, HATSUMI. HE'S GONNA FLIP THE HELL OUT.
BUT I'LL EXPLAIN.
AND GET HIM TO UNDER-STAND.

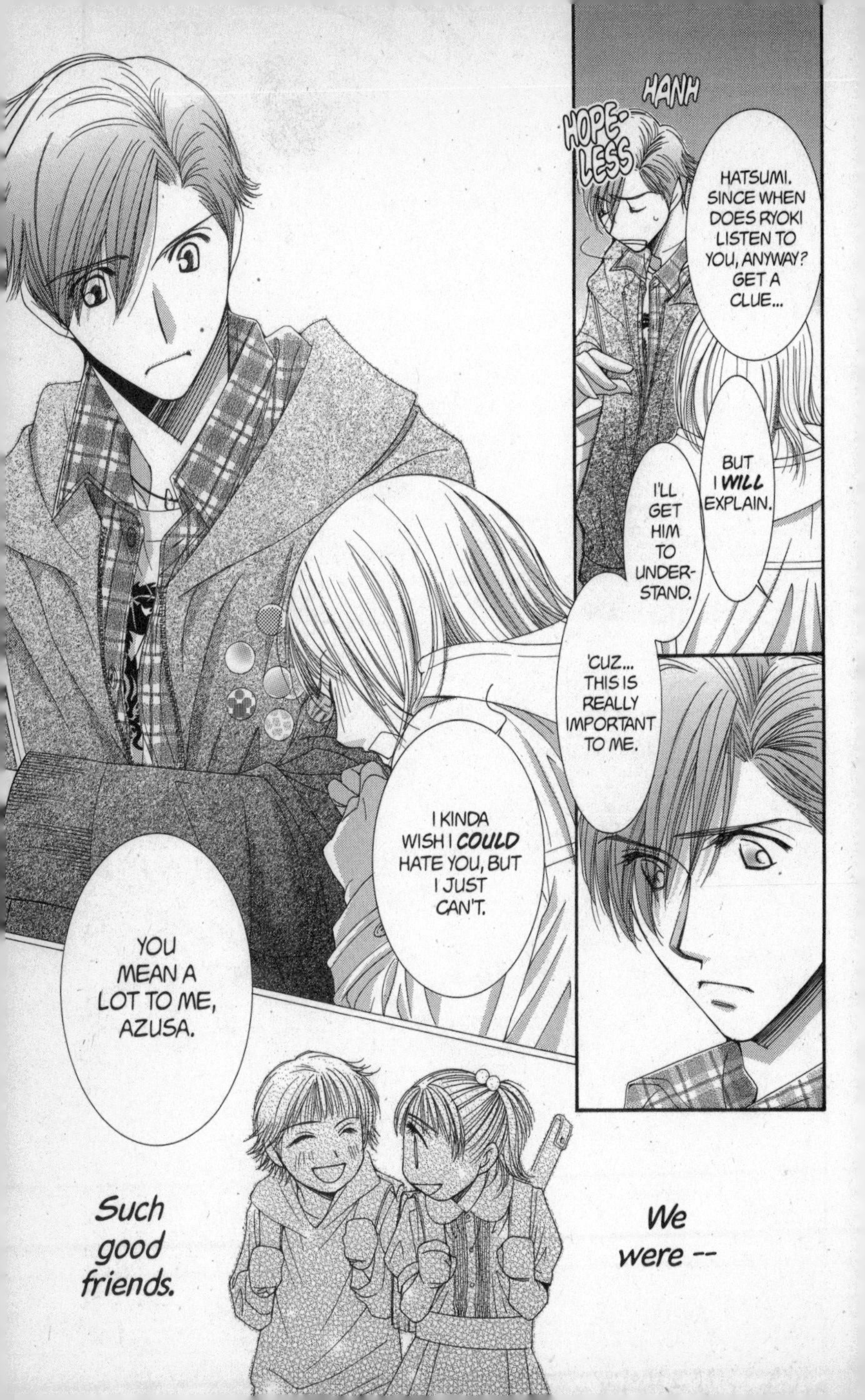
HANH
HOPE-LESS
HATSUMI. SINCE WHEN DOES RYOKI LISTEN TO YOU, ANYWAY? GET A CLUE...
BUT I **WILL** EXPLAIN.
I'LL GET HIM TO UNDER-STAND.
'CUZ... THIS IS REALLY IMPORTANT TO ME.
I KINDA WISH I **COULD** HATE YOU, BUT I JUST CAN'T.
YOU MEAN A LOT TO ME, AZUSA.
We were --
Such good friends.

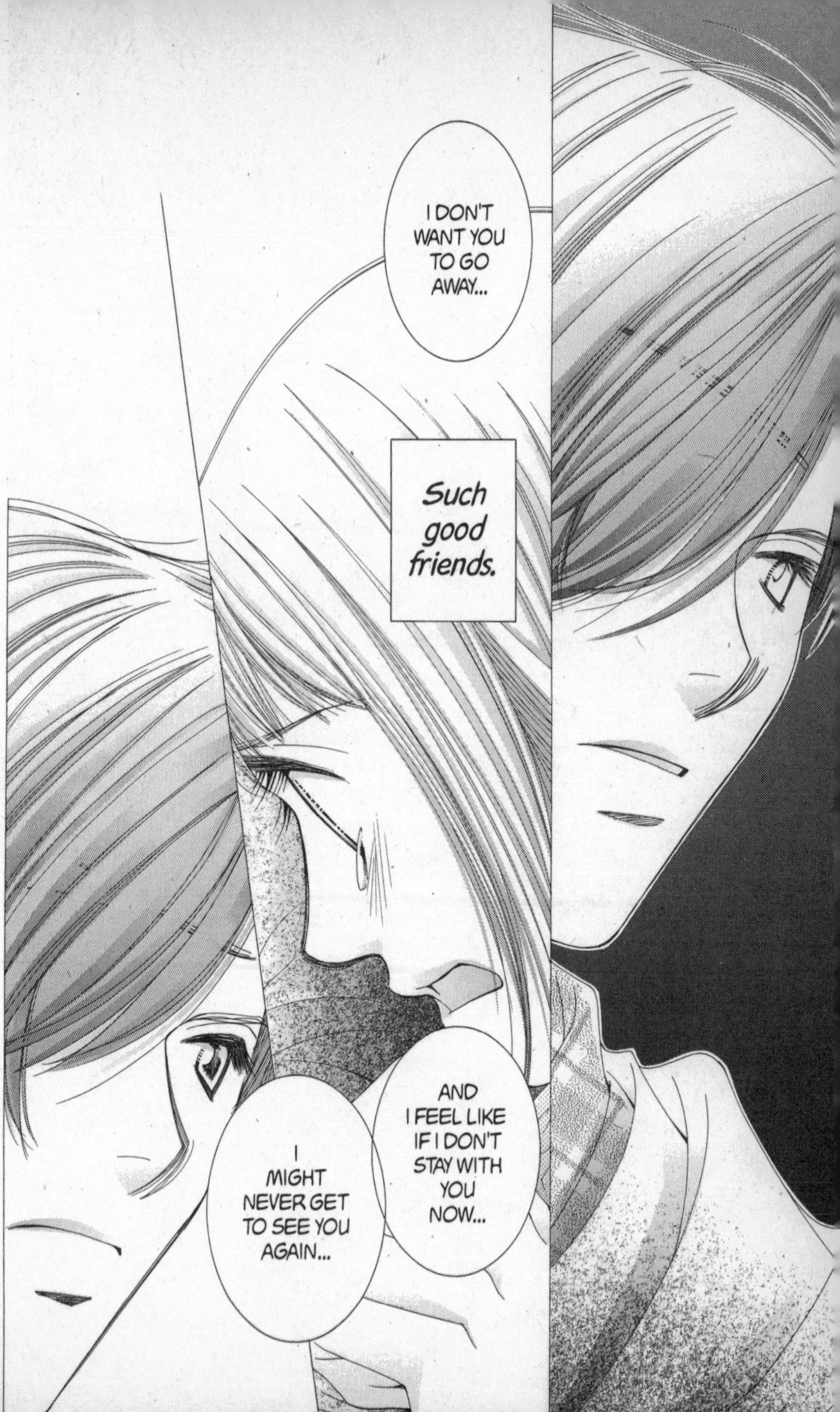
I DON'T WANT YOU TO GO AWAY...
Such good friends.
AND I FEEL LIKE IF I DON'T STAY WITH YOU NOW...
I MIGHT NEVER GET TO SEE YOU AGAIN...

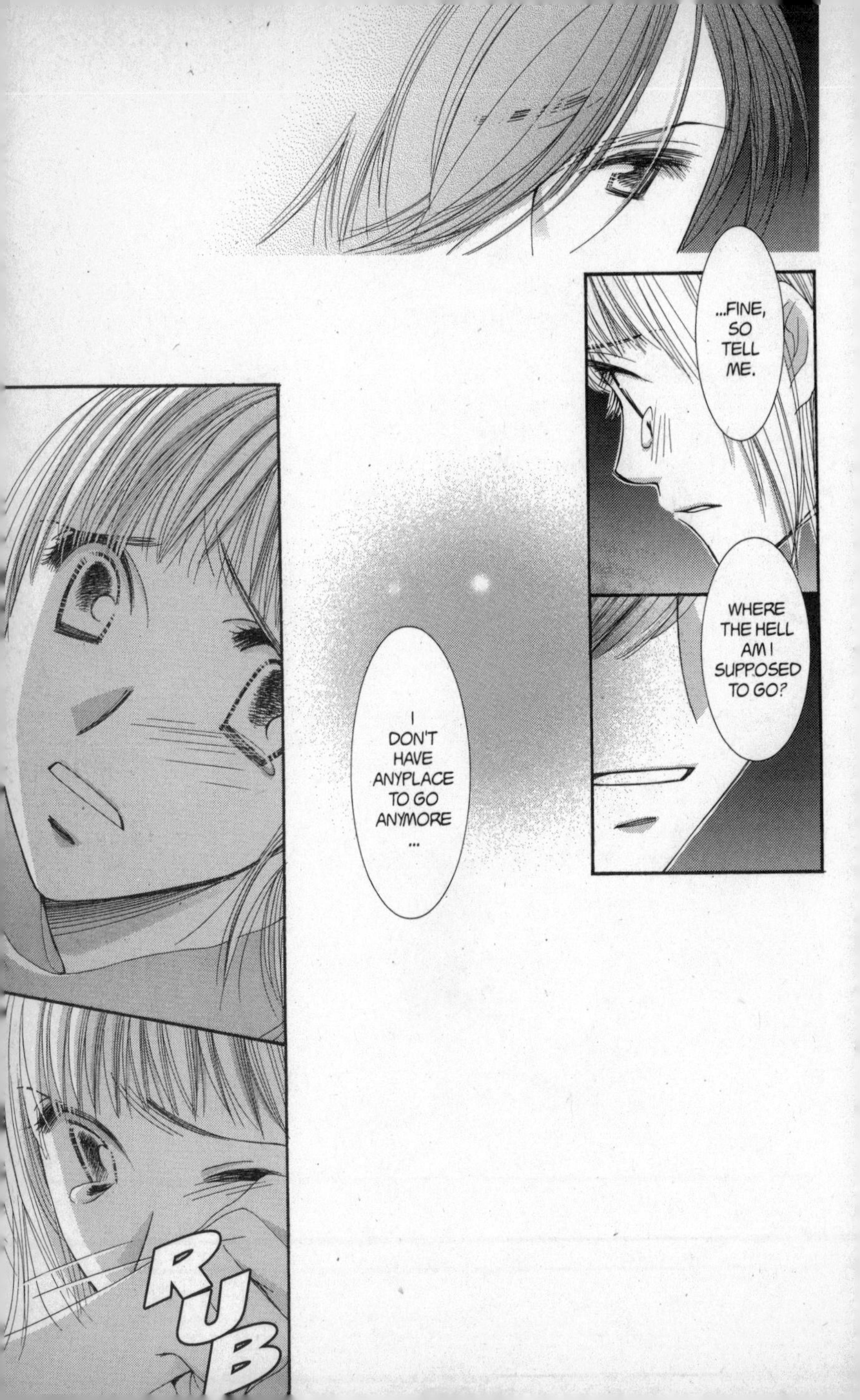
...FINE, SO TELL ME.
WHERE THE HELL AM I SUPPOSED TO GO?
I DON'T HAVE ANYPLACE TO GO ANYMORE ...
RUB

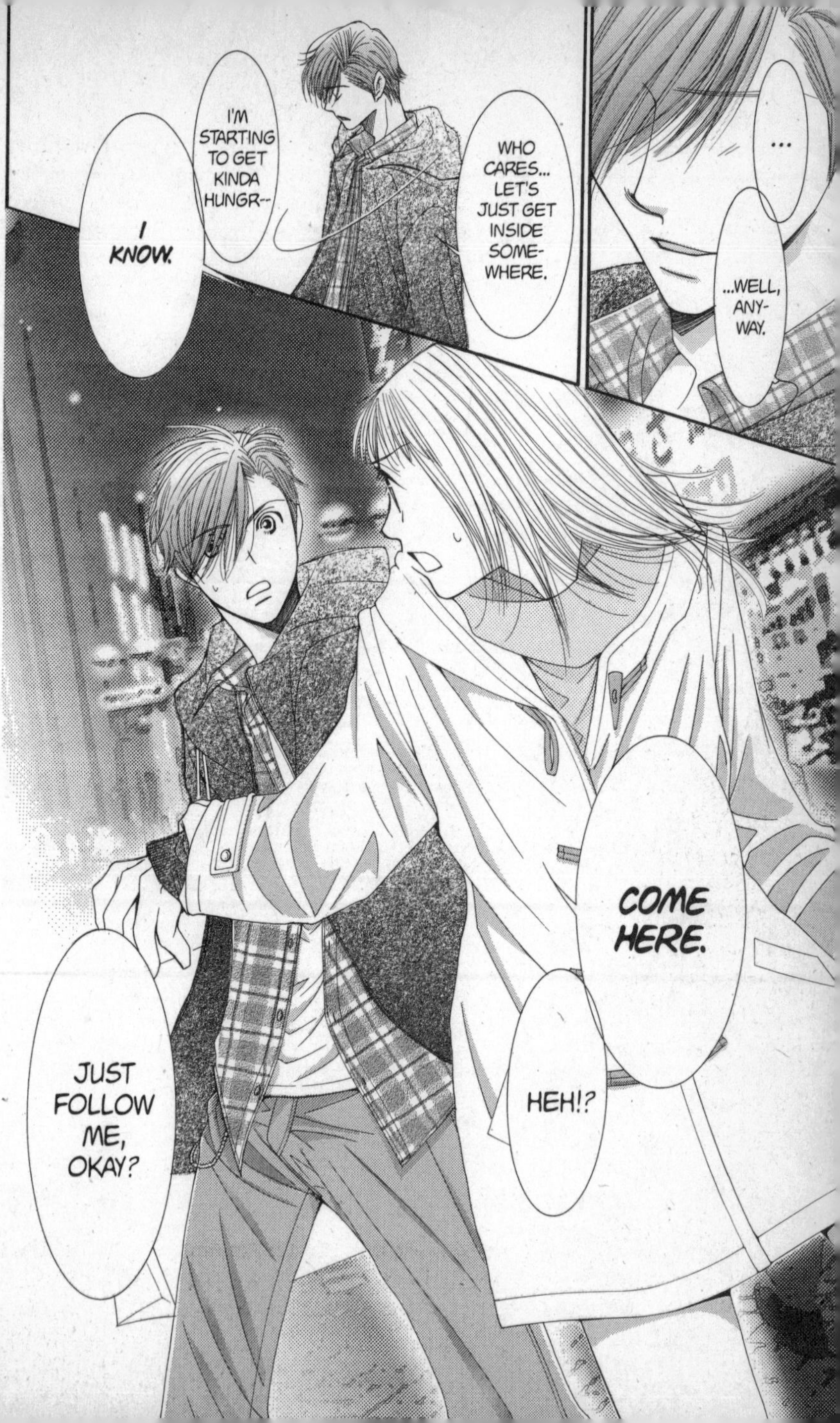
...
...WELL, ANYWAY.
WHO CARES... LET'S JUST GET INSIDE SOMEWHERE.
I'M STARTING TO GET KINDA HUNGR--
I KNOW.
COME HERE.
HEH!?
JUST FOLLOW ME, OKAY?

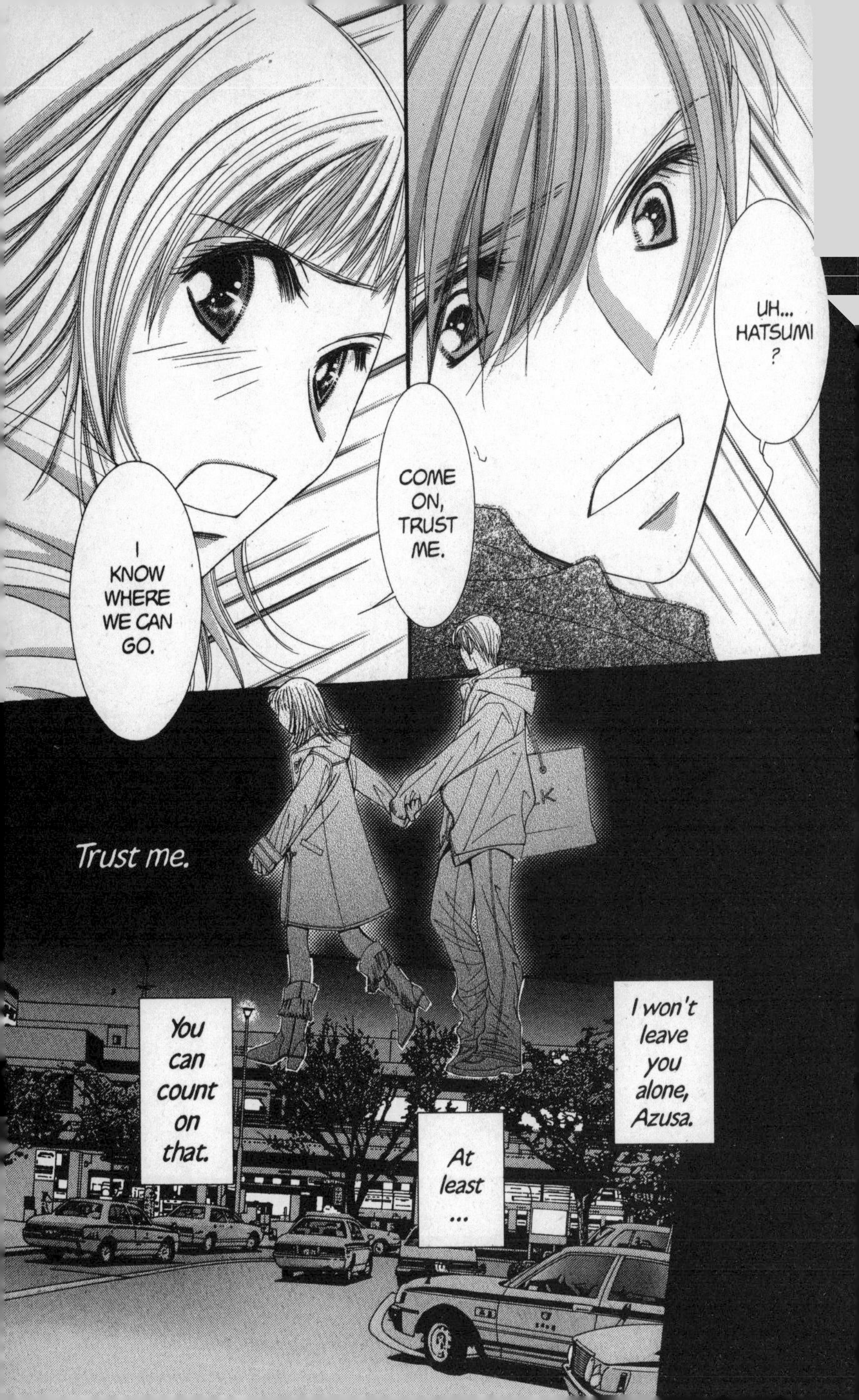
UH... HATSUMI ?
COME ON, TRUST ME.
I KNOW WHERE WE CAN GO.
Trust me.
I won't leave you alone, Azusa.
At least ...
You can count on that.

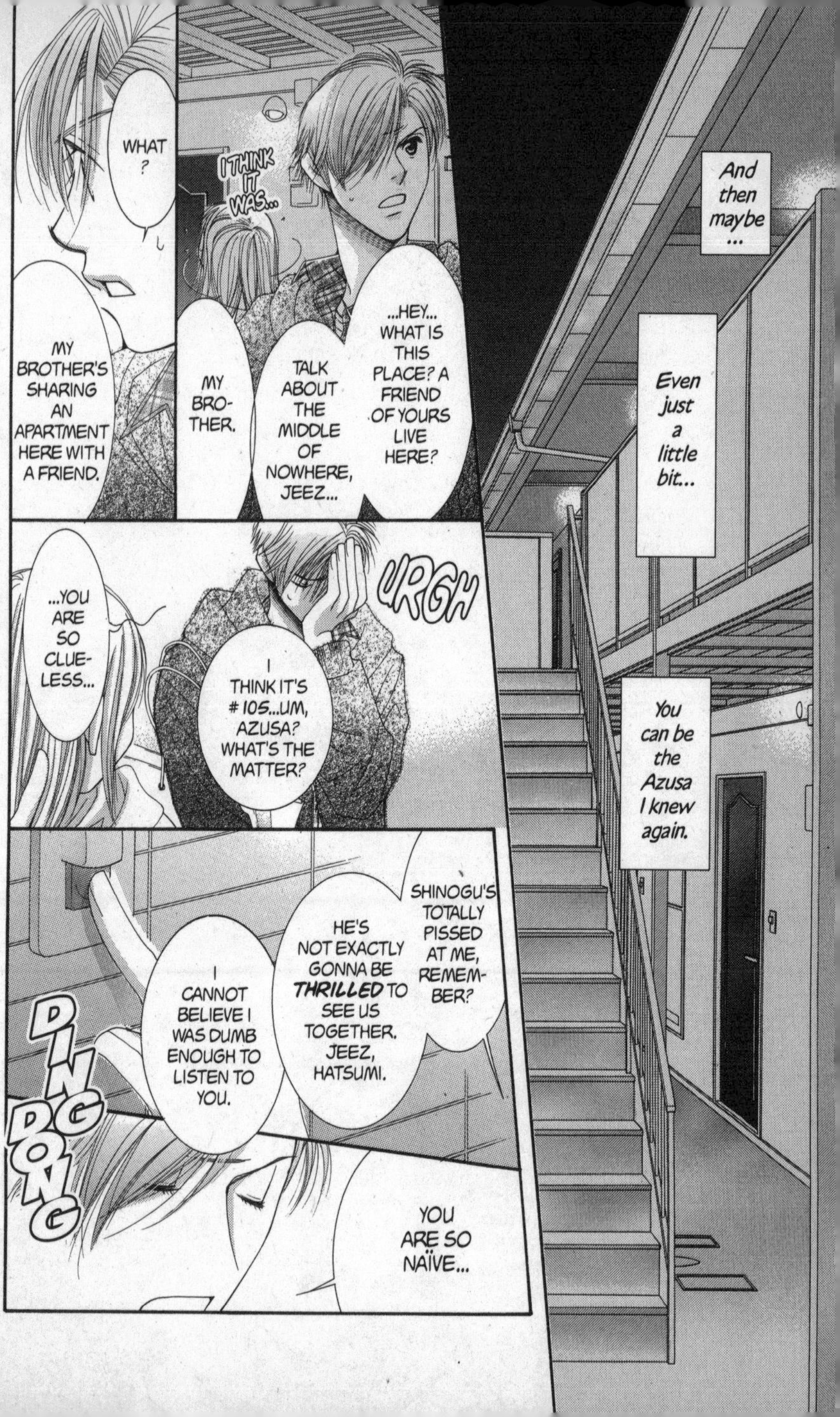
And then maybe ...
Even just a little bit...
You can be the Azusa I knew again.
I THINK IT WAS...
...HEY... WHAT IS THIS PLACE? A FRIEND OF YOURS LIVE HERE?
TALK ABOUT THE MIDDLE OF NOWHERE, JEEZ...
MY BROTHER.
WHAT?
MY BROTHER'S SHARING AN APARTMENT HERE WITH A FRIEND.
URGH
I THINK IT'S #105...UM, AZUSA? WHAT'S THE MATTER?
...YOU ARE SO CLUELESS...
SHINOGU'S TOTALLY PISSED AT ME, REMEMBER?
HE'S NOT EXACTLY GONNA BE THRILLED TO SEE US TOGETHER. JEEZ, HATSUMI.
I CANNOT BELIEVE I WAS DUMB ENOUGH TO LISTEN TO YOU.
DING DONG
YOU ARE SO NAÏVE...

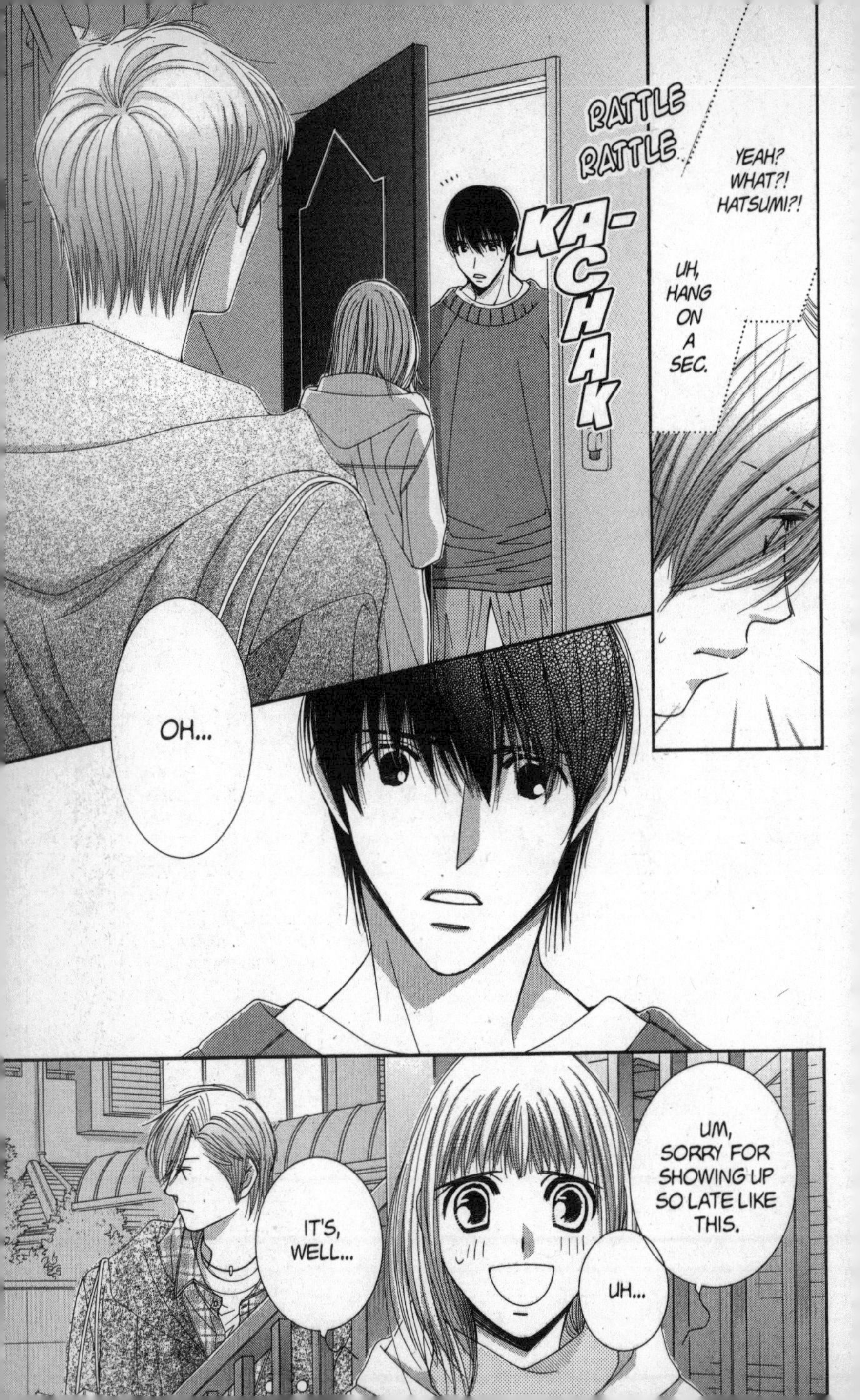
YEAH? WHAT?! HATSUMI?!
UH, HANG ON A SEC.
RATTLE RATTLE
KA-CHAK
OH...
UM, SORRY FOR SHOWING UP SO LATE LIKE THIS.
UH...
IT'S, WELL...

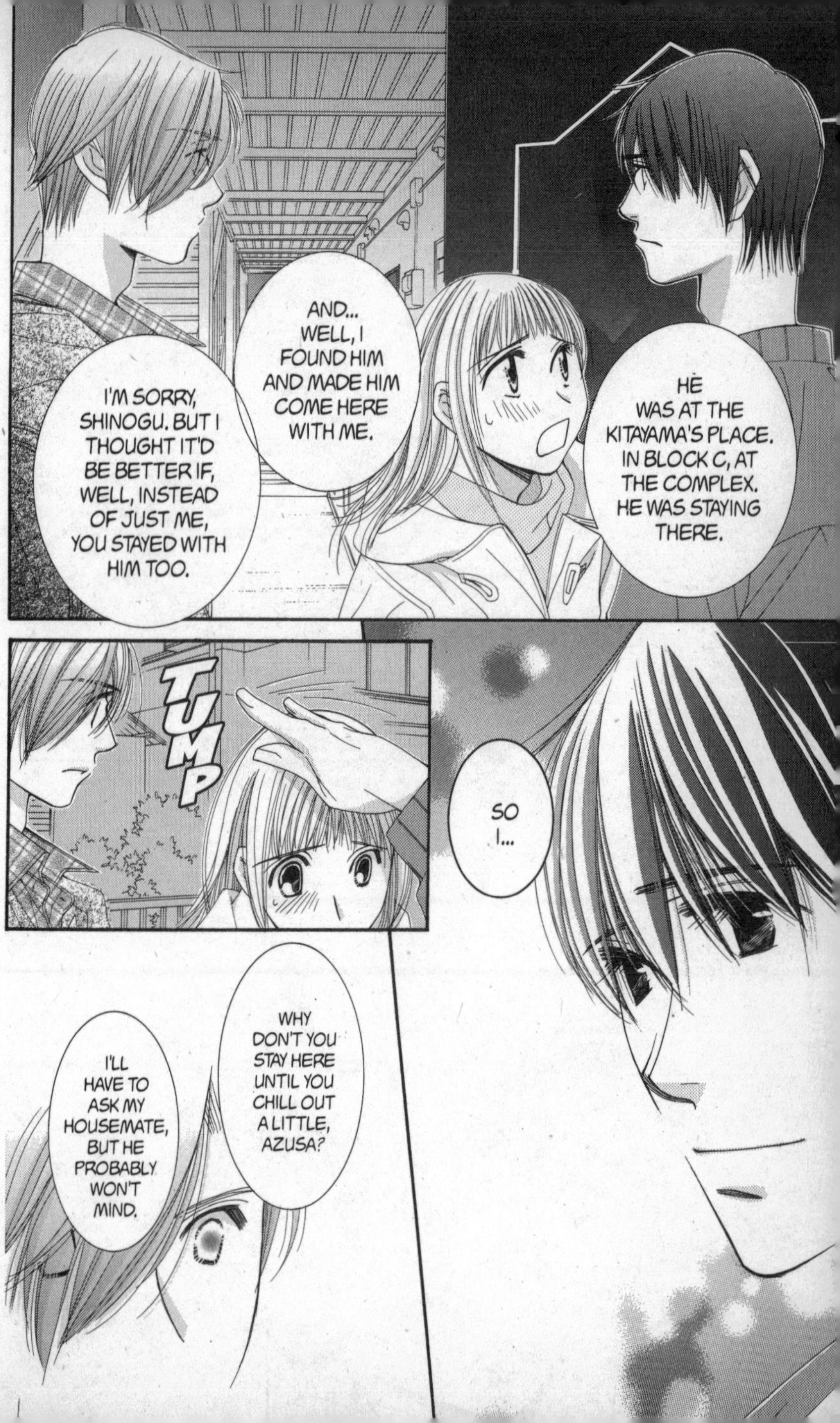
HE WAS AT THE KITAYAMA'S PLACE. IN BLOCK C, AT THE COMPLEX. HE WAS STAYING THERE.
AND... WELL, I FOUND HIM AND MADE HIM COME HERE WITH ME.
I'M SORRY, SHINOGU. BUT I THOUGHT IT'D BE BETTER IF, WELL, INSTEAD OF JUST ME, YOU STAYED WITH HIM TOO.
SO I...
TUMP
WHY DON'T YOU STAY HERE UNTIL YOU CHILL OUT A LITTLE, AZUSA?
I'LL HAVE TO ASK MY HOUSEMATE, BUT HE PROBABLY WON'T MIND.

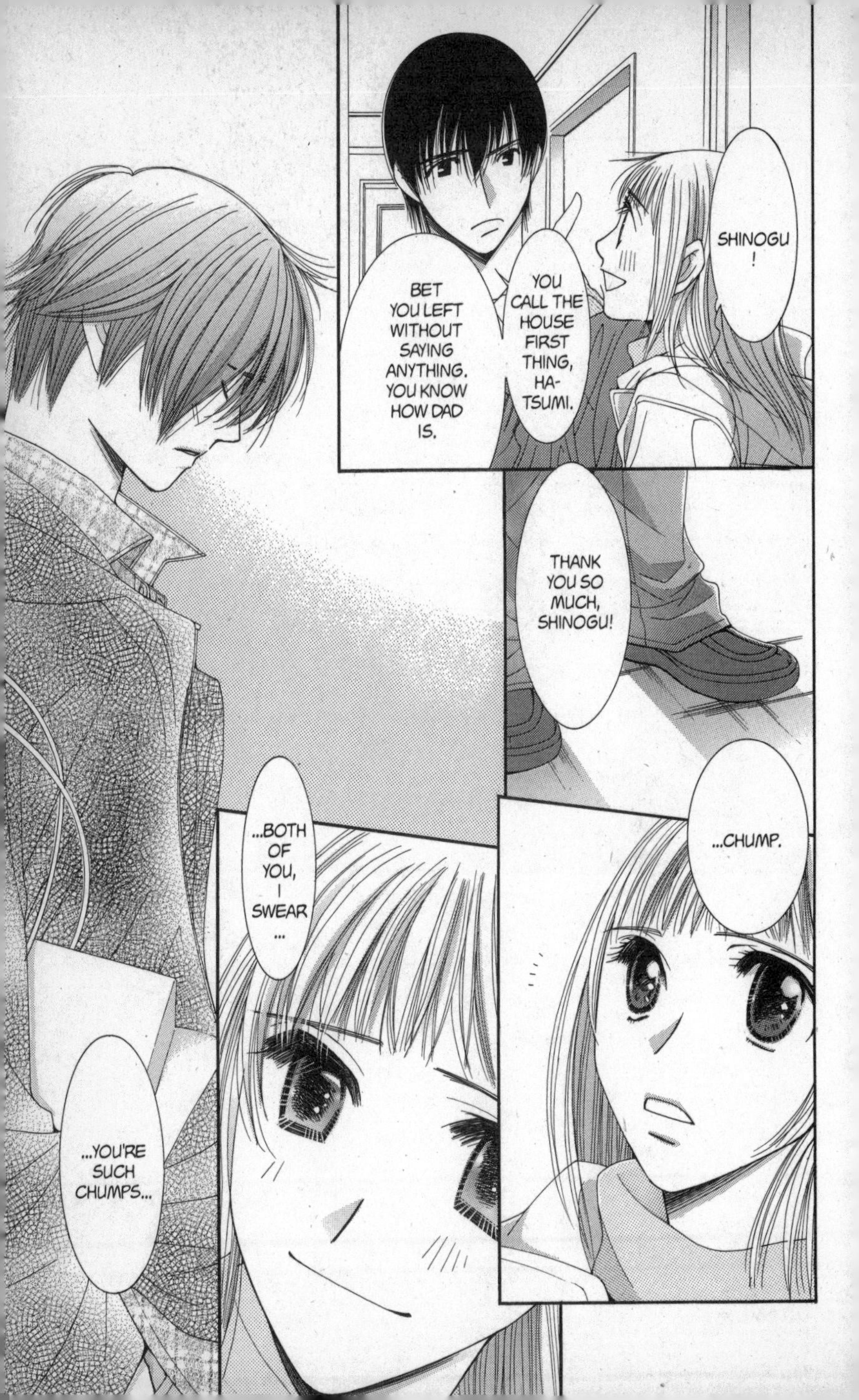
SHINOGU!
YOU CALL THE HOUSE FIRST THING, HA-TSUMI.
BET YOU LEFT WITHOUT SAYING ANYTHING. YOU KNOW HOW DAD IS.
THANK YOU SO MUCH, SHINOGU!
...CHUMP.
...BOTH OF YOU, I SWEAR...
...YOU'RE SUCH CHUMPS...

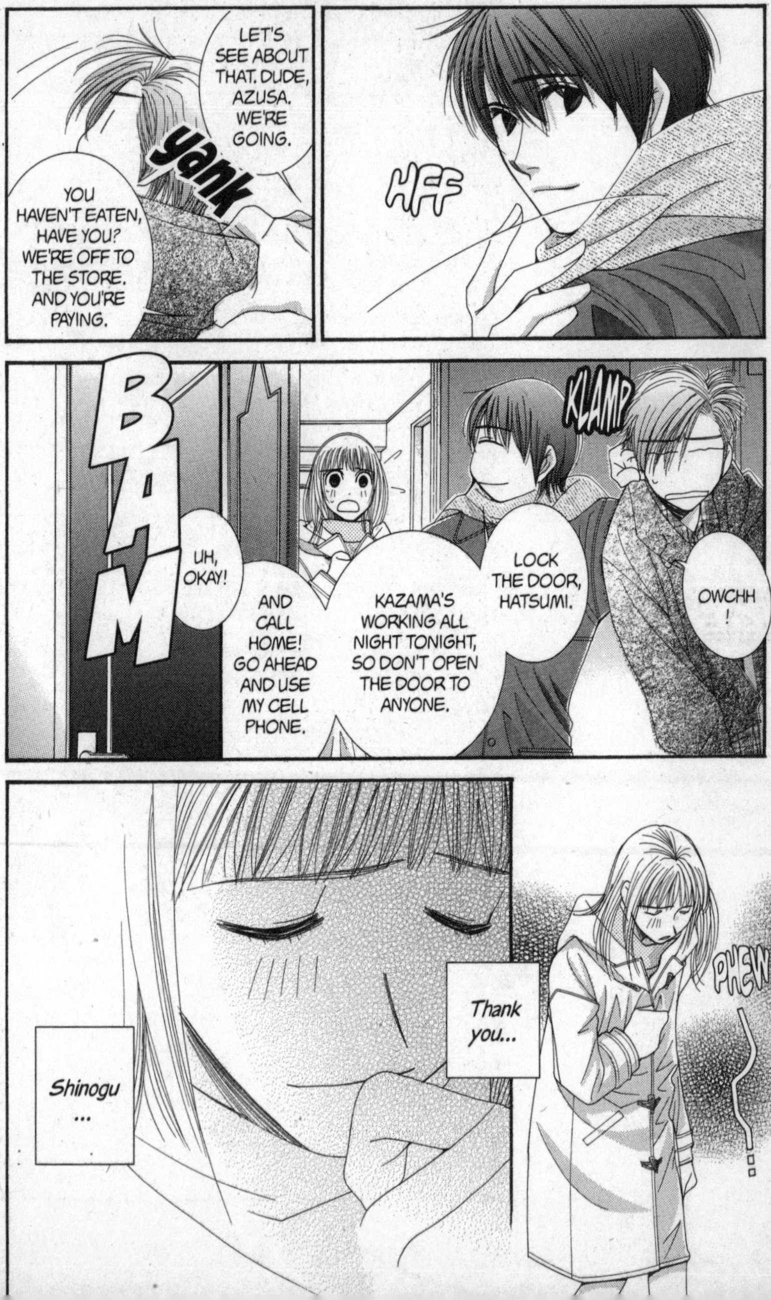
HFF
LET'S SEE ABOUT THAT. DUDE, AZUSA. WE'RE GOING.
yank
YOU HAVEN'T EATEN, HAVE YOU? WE'RE OFF TO THE STORE. AND YOU'RE PAYING.
KLAMP
OWCHH!
LOCK THE DOOR, HATSUMI.
KAZAMA'S WORKING ALL NIGHT TONIGHT, SO DON'T OPEN THE DOOR TO ANYONE.
AND CALL HOME! GO AHEAD AND USE MY CELL PHONE.
UH, OKAY!
BAM
PHEW
Thank you...
Shinogu ...

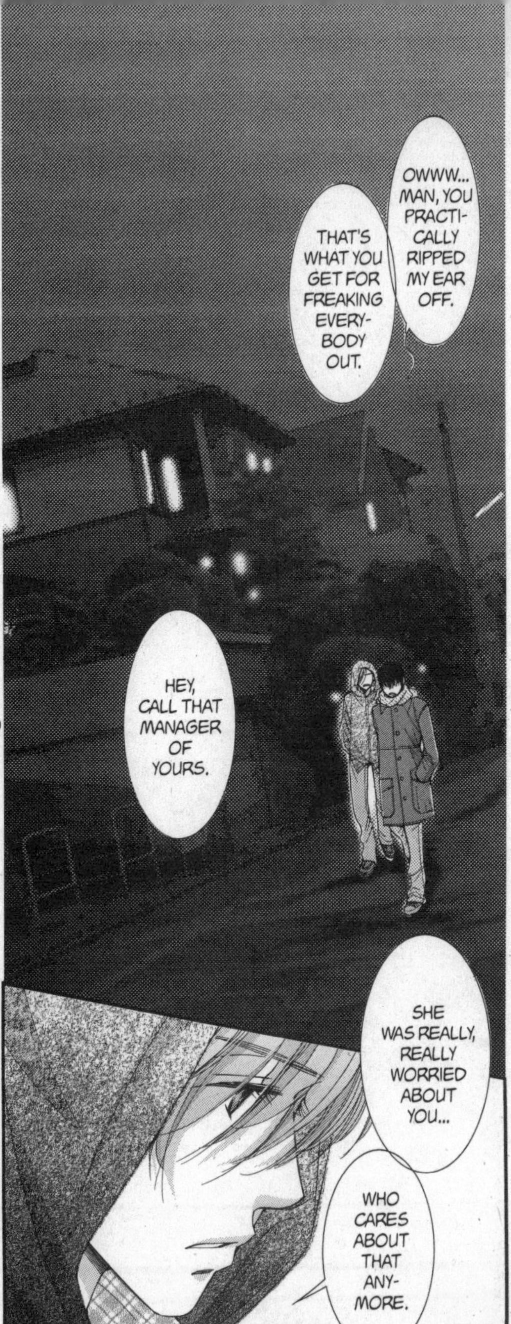
OWWW... MAN, YOU PRACTI-CALLY RIPPED MY EAR OFF.
THAT'S WHAT YOU GET FOR FREAKING EVERY-BODY OUT.
HEY, CALL THAT MANAGER OF YOURS.
SHE WAS REALLY, REALLY WORRIED ABOUT YOU...
WHO CARES ABOUT THAT ANY-MORE.

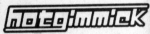

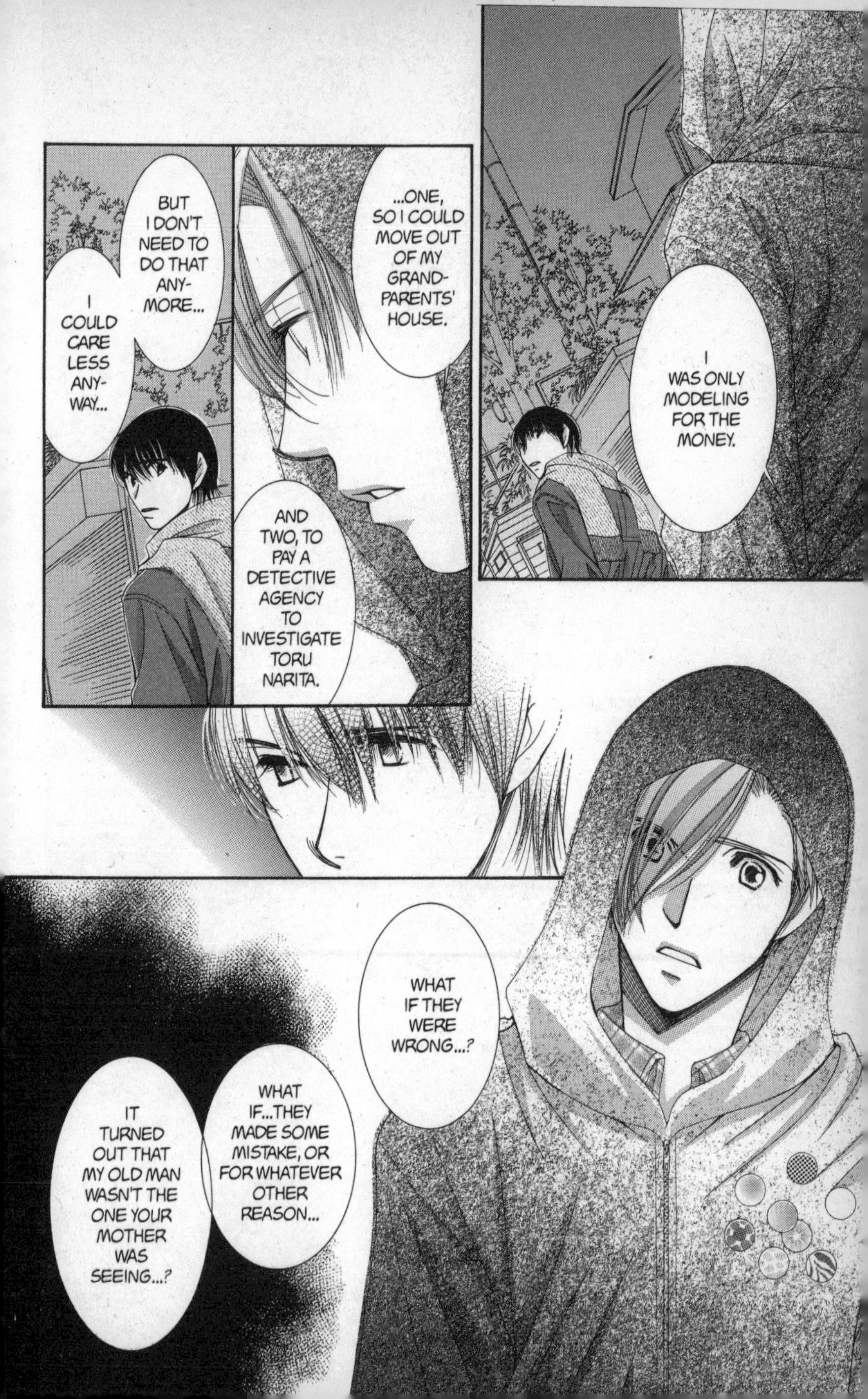
I WAS ONLY MODELING FOR THE MONEY.
...ONE, SO I COULD MOVE OUT OF MY GRAND-PARENTS' HOUSE.
AND TWO, TO PAY A DETECTIVE AGENCY TO INVESTIGATE TORU NARITA.
BUT I DON'T NEED TO DO THAT ANY-MORE...
I COULD CARE LESS ANY-WAY...
WHAT IF THEY WERE WRONG...?
WHAT IF...THEY MADE SOME MISTAKE, OR FOR WHATEVER OTHER REASON...
IT TURNED OUT THAT MY OLD MAN WASN'T THE ONE YOUR MOTHER WAS SEEING...?

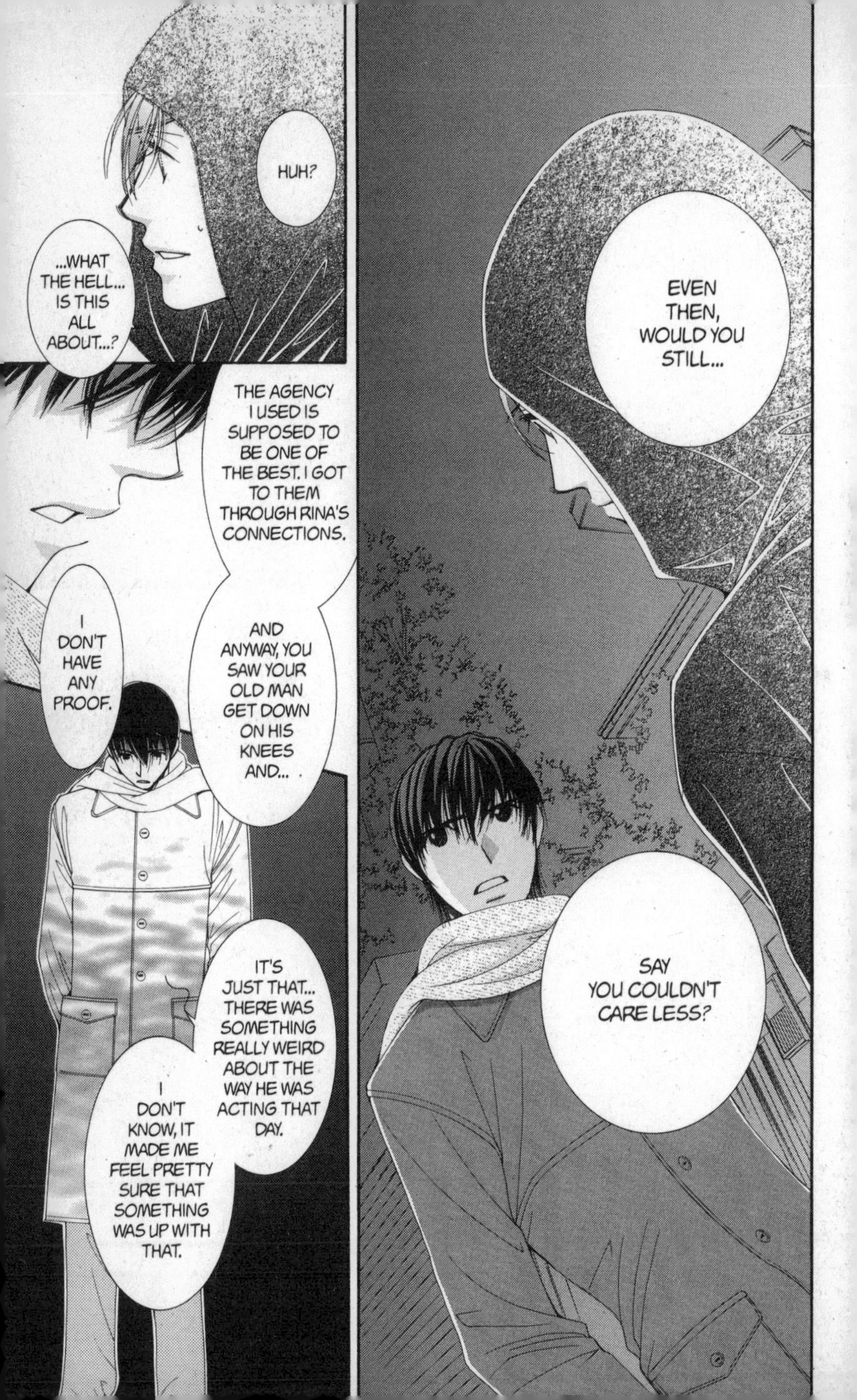
EVEN THEN, WOULD YOU STILL...
SAY YOU COULDN'T CARE LESS?
HUH?
...WHAT THE HELL... IS THIS ALL ABOUT...?
THE AGENCY I USED IS SUPPOSED TO BE ONE OF THE BEST. I GOT TO THEM THROUGH RINA'S CONNECTIONS.
I DON'T HAVE ANY PROOF.
AND ANYWAY, YOU SAW YOUR OLD MAN GET DOWN ON HIS KNEES AND...
IT'S JUST THAT... THERE WAS SOMETHING REALLY WEIRD ABOUT THE WAY HE WAS ACTING THAT DAY.
I DON'T KNOW, IT MADE ME FEEL PRETTY SURE THAT SOMETHING WAS UP WITH THAT.

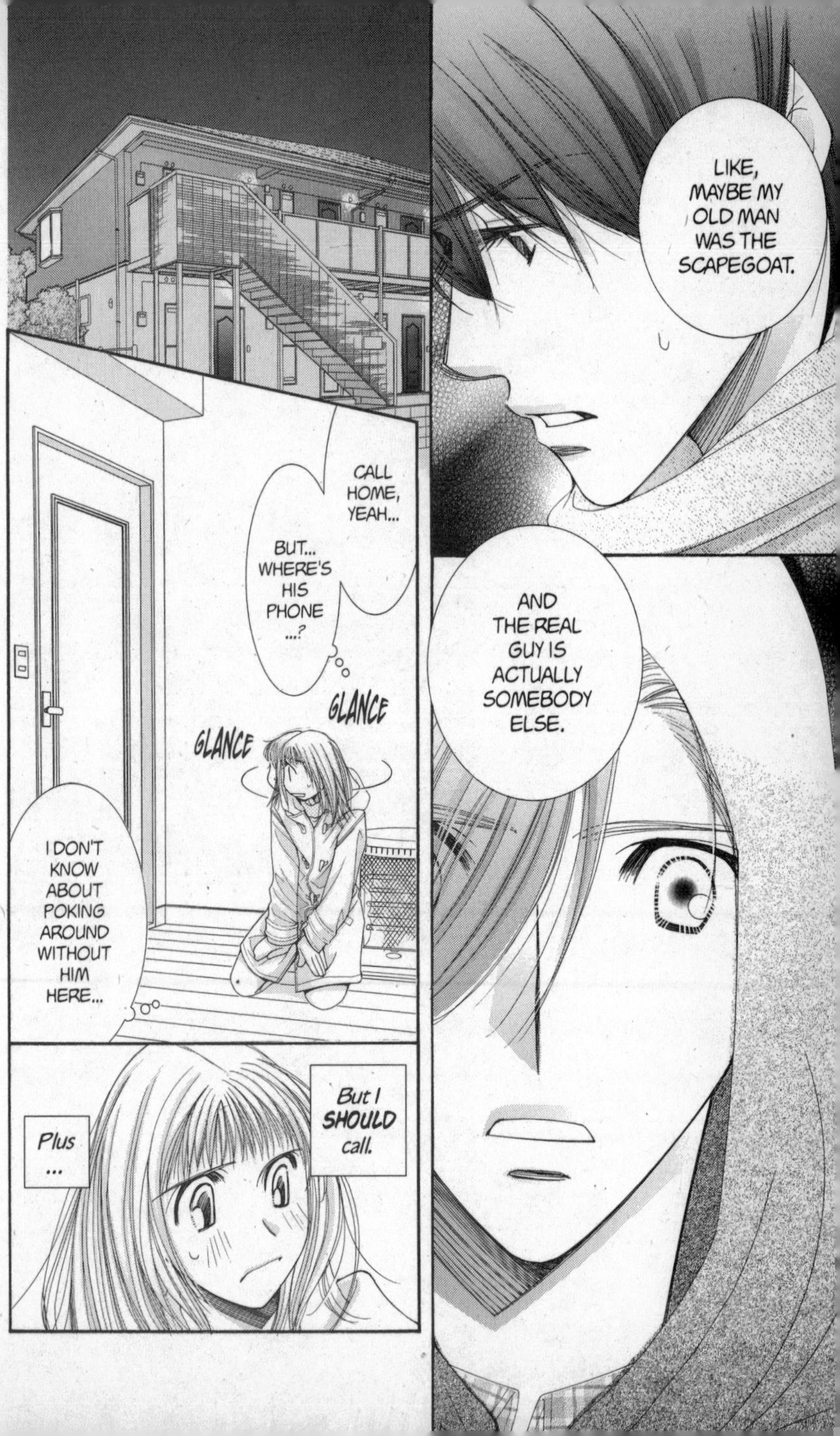
LIKE, MAYBE MY OLD MAN WAS THE SCAPEGOAT.
AND THE REAL GUY IS ACTUALLY SOMEBODY ELSE.
CALL HOME, YEAH...
BUT... WHERE'S HIS PHONE ...?
GLANCE
GLANCE
I DON'T KNOW ABOUT POKING AROUND WITHOUT HIM HERE...
But I SHOULD call.
Plus ...

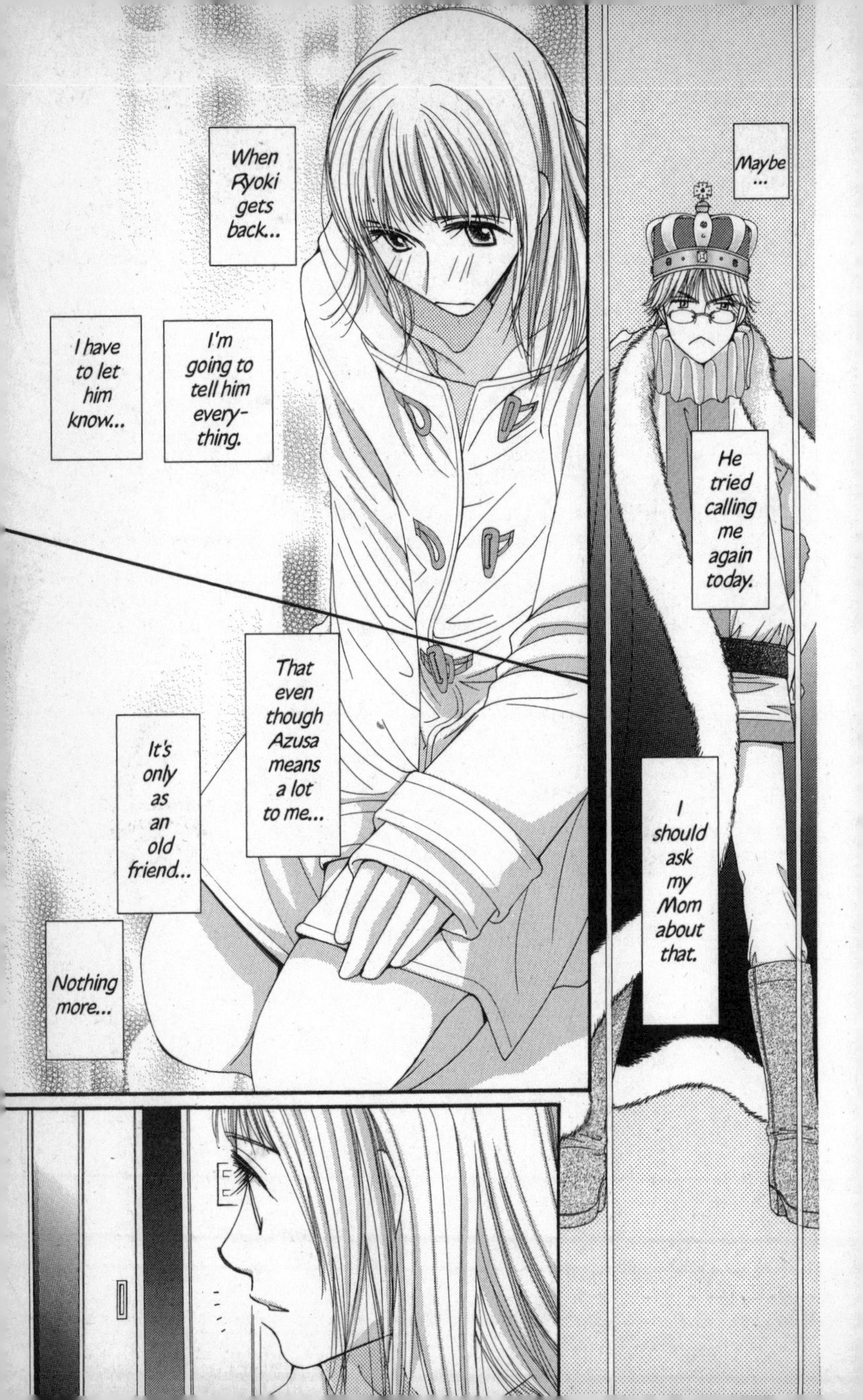
Maybe...
He tried calling me again today.
I should ask my Mom about that.
When Ryoki gets back...
I'm going to tell him every-thing.
I have to let him know...
That even though Azusa means a lot to me...
It's only as an old friend...
Nothing more...

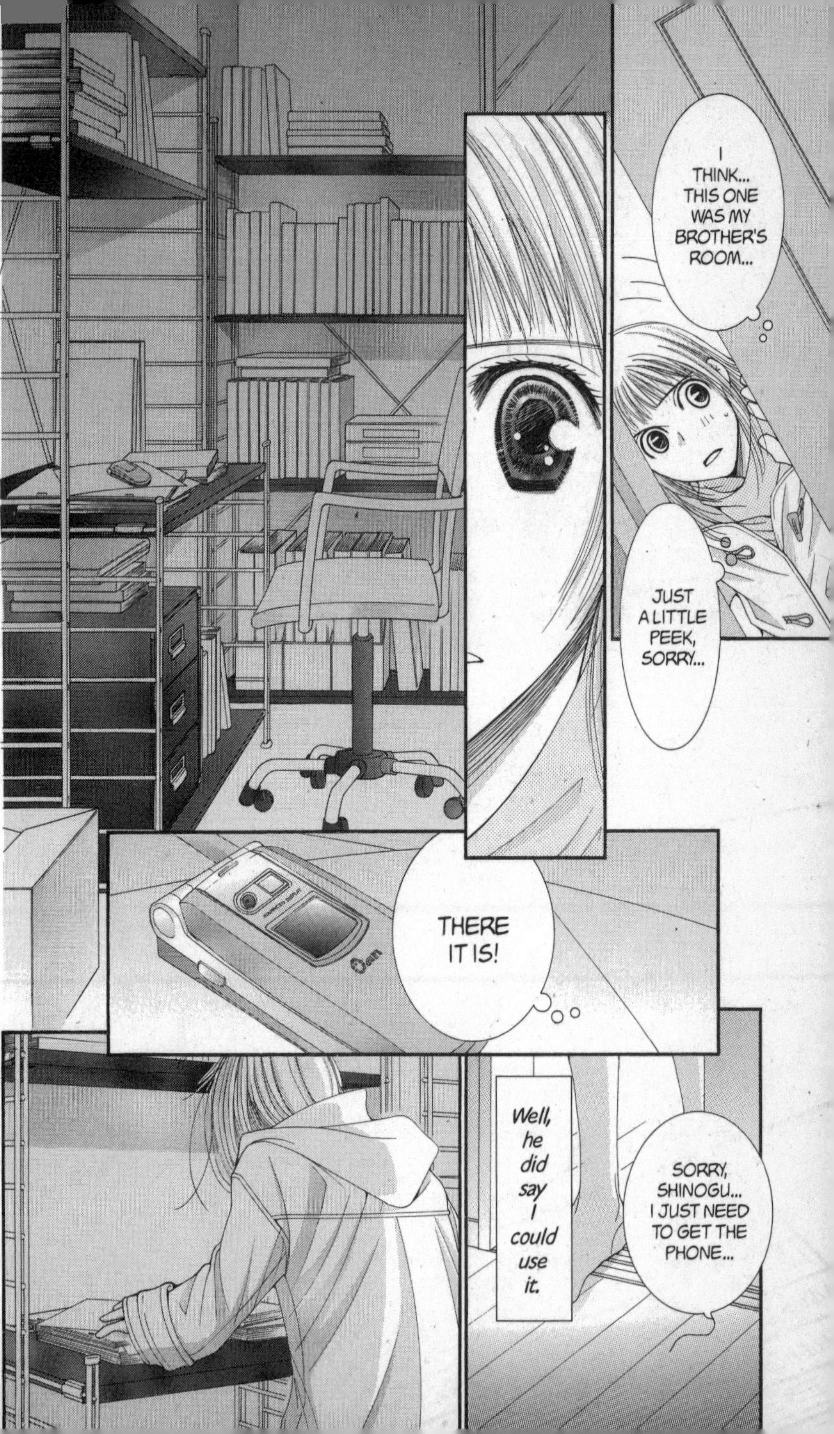

I THINK... THIS ONE WAS MY BROTHER'S ROOM...
JUST A LITTLE PEEK, SORRY...
THERE IT IS!
SORRY, SHINOGU... I JUST NEED TO GET THE PHONE...
Well, he did say I could use it.

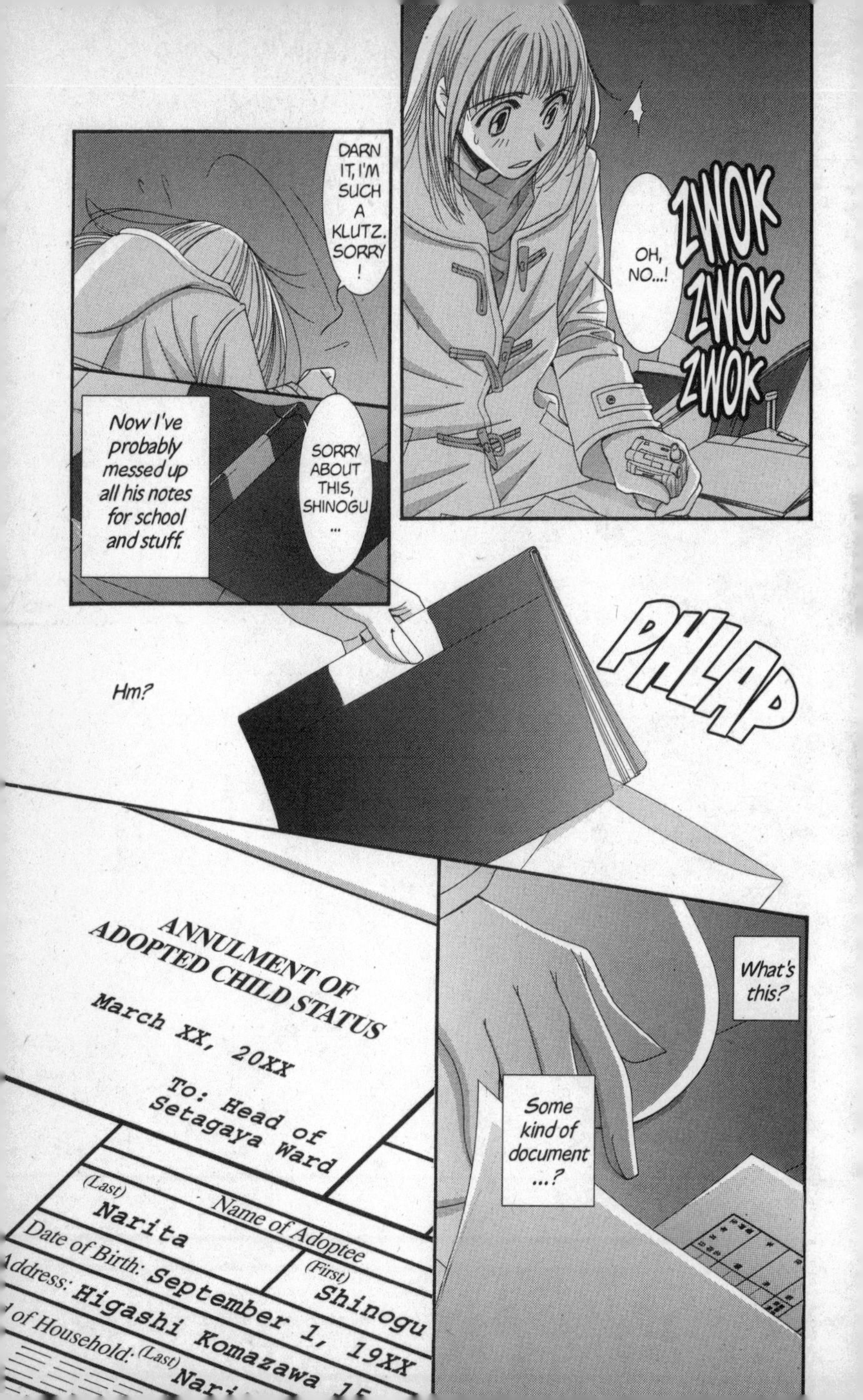

OH, NO...!
ZWOK ZWOK ZWOK
DARN IT, I'M SUCH A KLUTZ. SORRY!
SORRY ABOUT THIS, SHINOGU...
Now I've probably messed up all his notes for school and stuff.
PHLAP
Hm?
What's this?
Some kind of document...?
ANNULMENT OF ADOPTED CHILD STATUS
March XX, 20XX
To: Head of Setagaya Ward
Name of Adoptee
(Last) Narita
(First) Shinogu
Date of Birth: September 1, 19XX
Address: Higashi Komazawa 15
of Household: (Last)

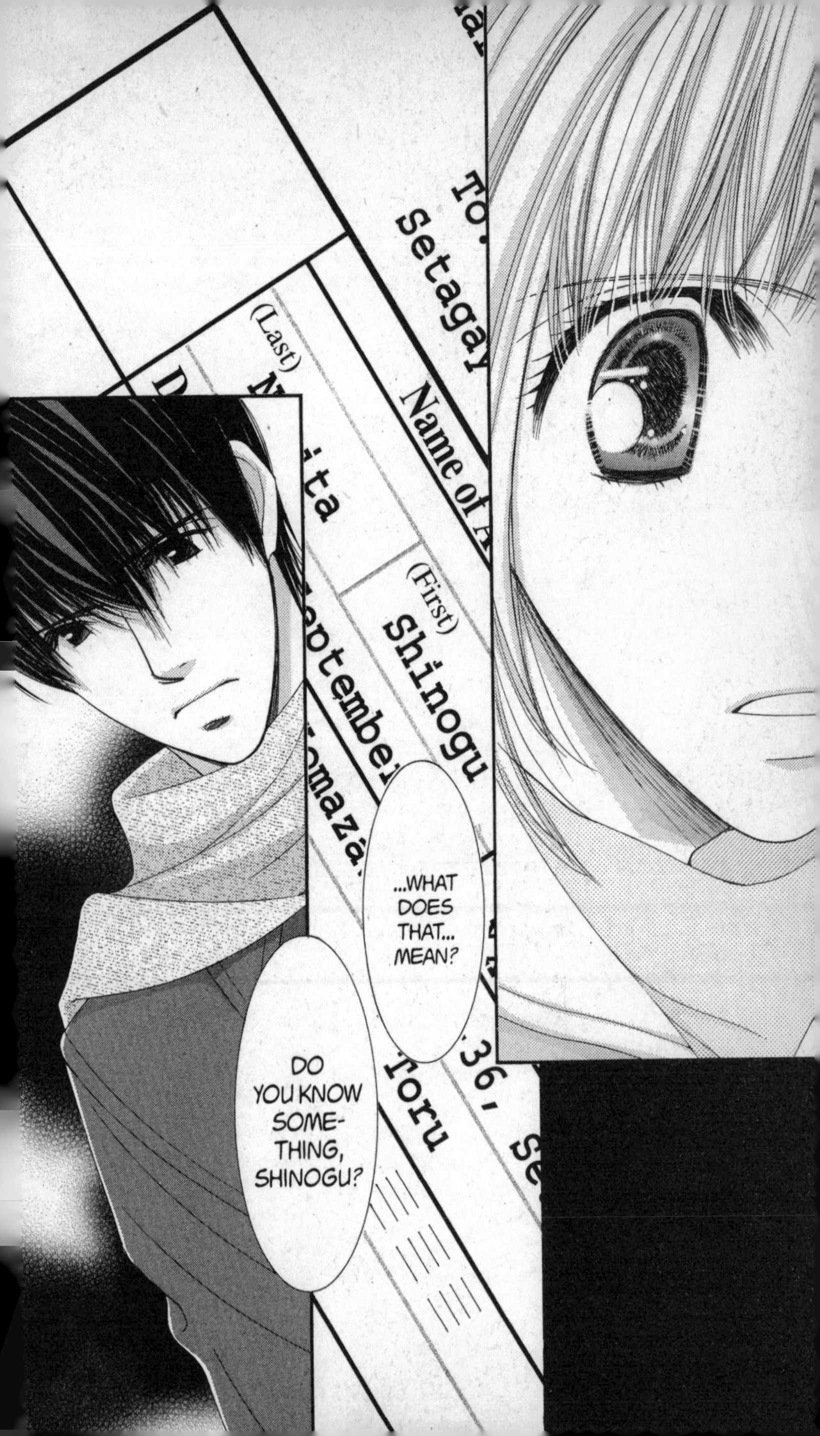

(First)
Shinogu
(Last)
Toru
...WHAT DOES THAT... MEAN?
DO YOU KNOW SOME-THING, SHINOGU?

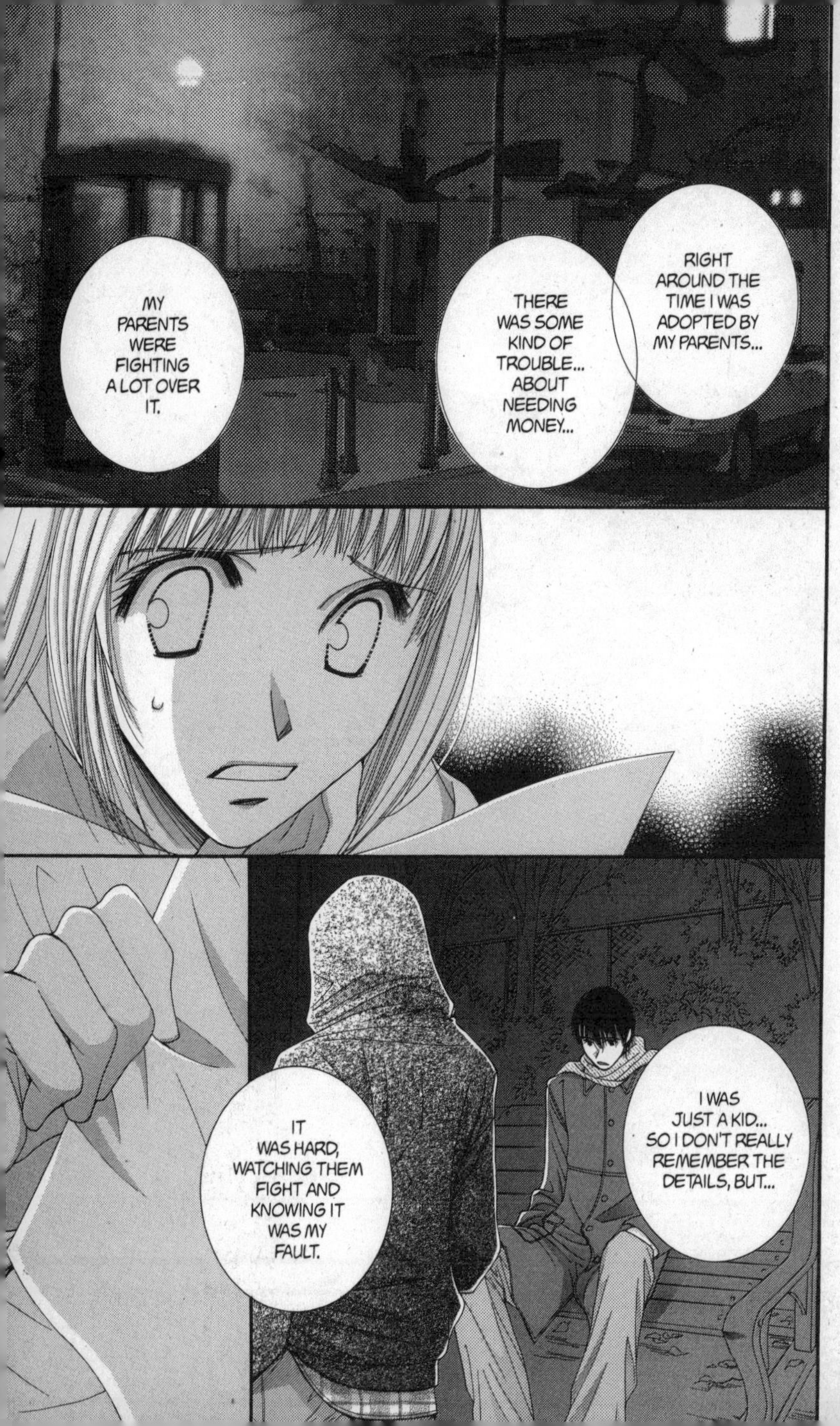
RIGHT AROUND THE TIME I WAS ADOPTED BY MY PARENTS...
THERE WAS SOME KIND OF TROUBLE... ABOUT NEEDING MONEY...
MY PARENTS WERE FIGHTING A LOT OVER IT.
I WAS JUST A KID... SO I DON'T REALLY REMEMBER THE DETAILS, BUT...
IT WAS HARD, WATCHING THEM FIGHT AND KNOWING IT WAS MY FAULT.

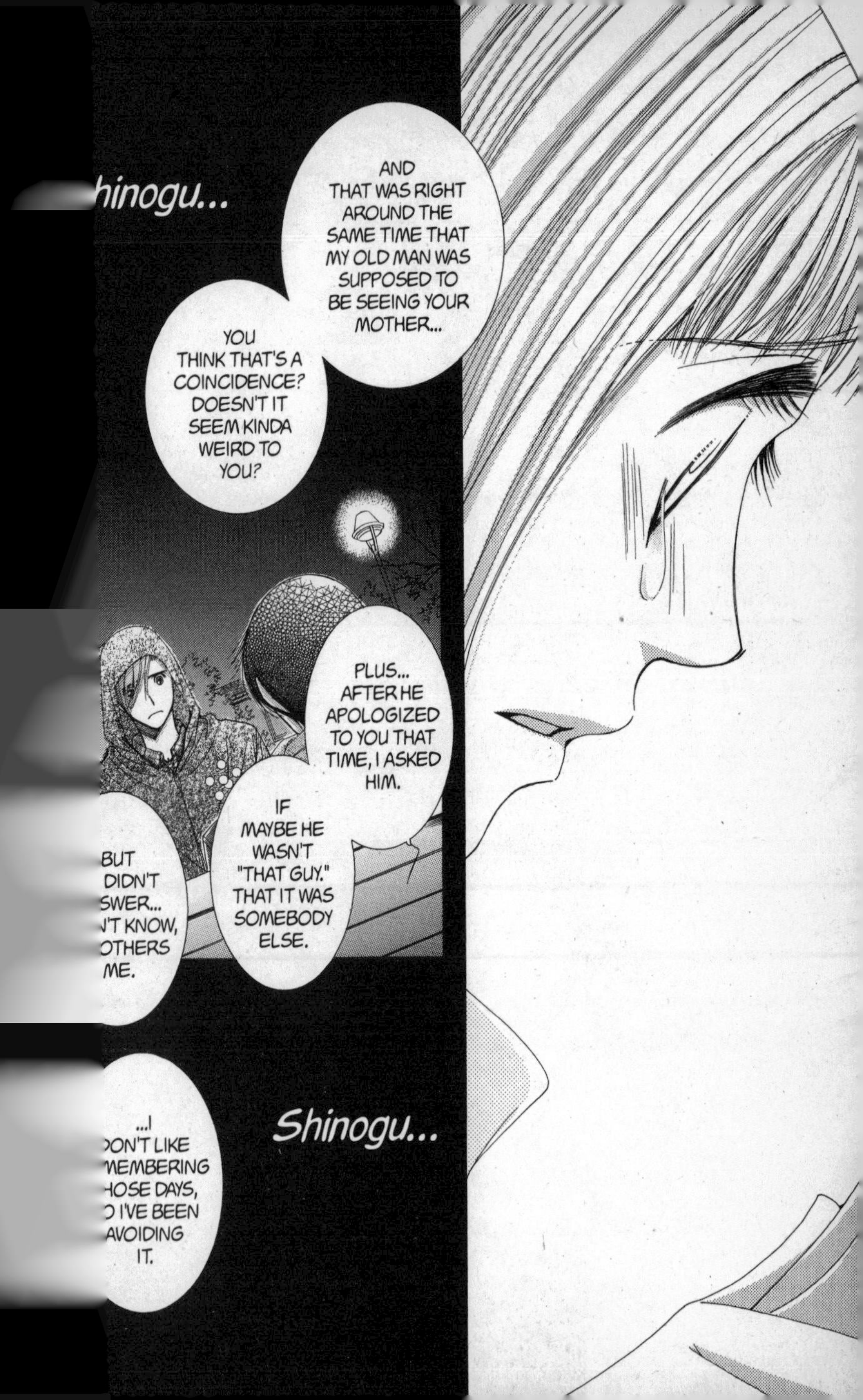
AND THAT WAS RIGHT AROUND THE SAME TIME THAT MY OLD MAN WAS SUPPOSED TO BE SEEING YOUR MOTHER...
hinogu...
YOU THINK THAT'S A COINCIDENCE? DOESN'T IT SEEM KINDA WEIRD TO YOU?
PLUS... AFTER HE APOLOGIZED TO YOU THAT TIME, I ASKED HIM.
IF MAYBE HE WASN'T "THAT GUY." THAT IT WAS SOMEBODY ELSE.
BUT DIDN'T SWER... N'T KNOW, OTHERS ME.
Shinogu...
...I ON'T LIKE MEMBERING HOSE DAYS, O I'VE BEEN AVOIDING IT.

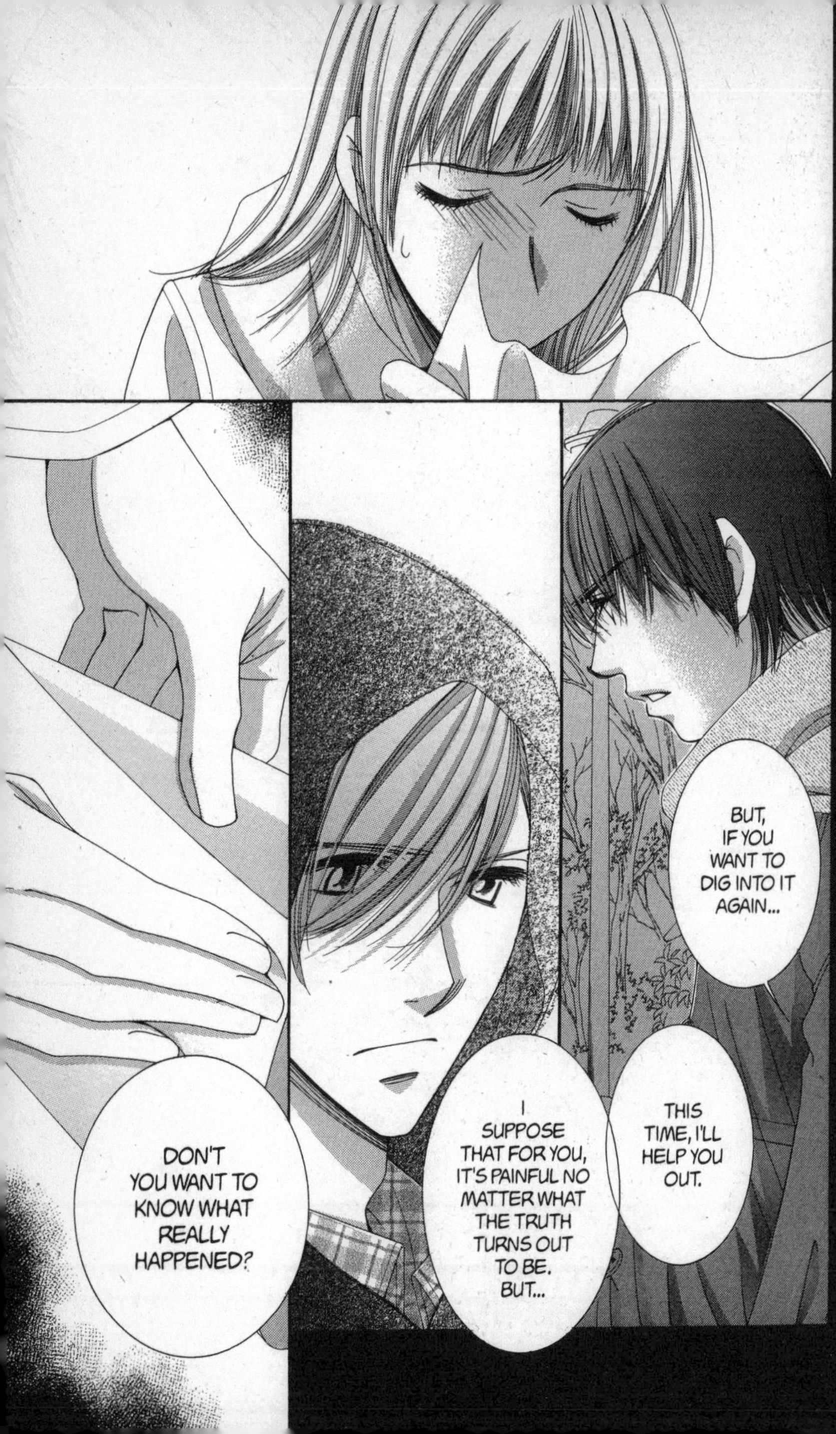
BUT, IF YOU WANT TO DIG INTO IT AGAIN...
THIS TIME, I'LL HELP YOU OUT.
I SUPPOSE THAT FOR YOU, IT'S PAINFUL NO MATTER WHAT THE TRUTH TURNS OUT TO BE. BUT...
DON'T YOU WANT TO KNOW WHAT REALLY HAPPENED?

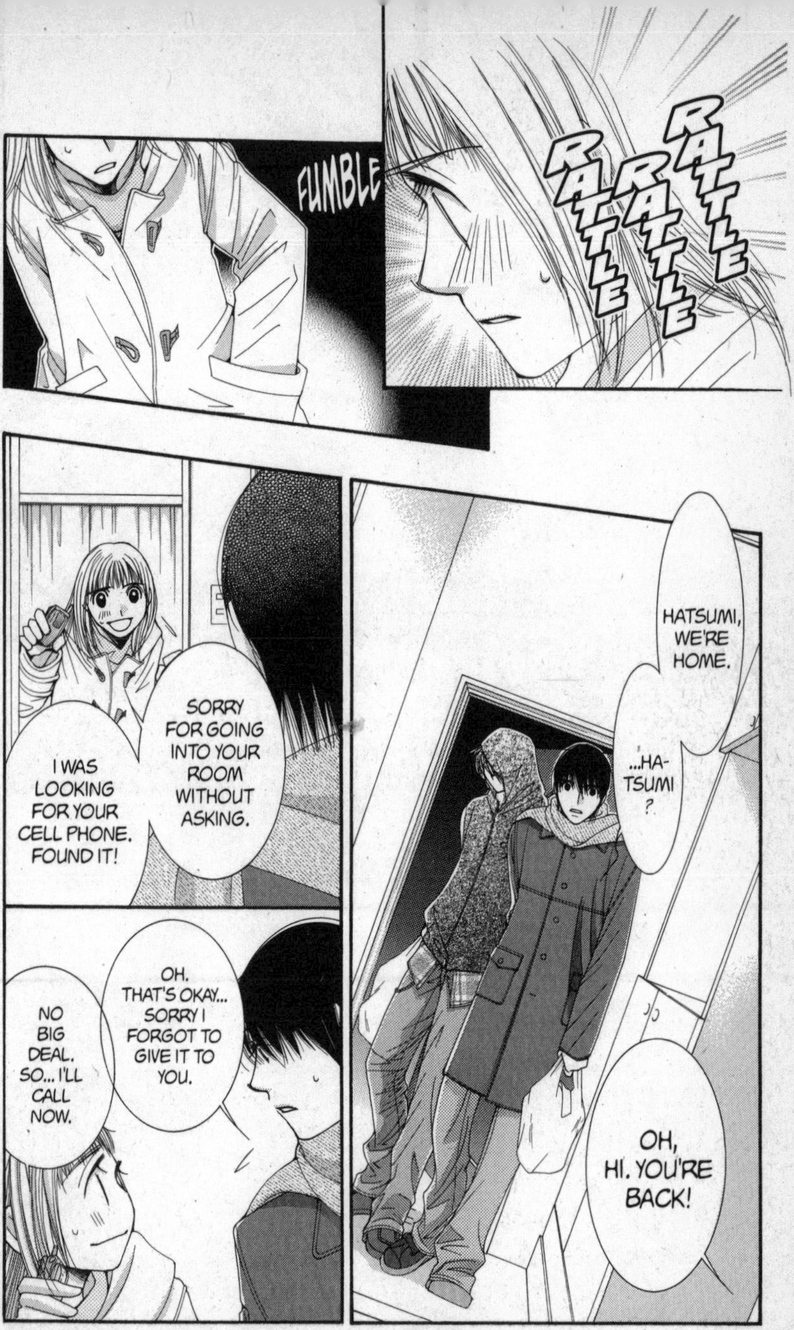
RATTLE RATTLE RATTLE
FUMBLE
HATSUMI, WE'RE HOME.
...HA-TSUMI?
OH, HI. YOU'RE BACK!
SORRY FOR GOING INTO YOUR ROOM WITHOUT ASKING.
I WAS LOOKING FOR YOUR CELL PHONE. FOUND IT!
OH. THAT'S OKAY... SORRY I FORGOT TO GIVE IT TO YOU.
NO BIG DEAL. SO... I'LL CALL NOW.

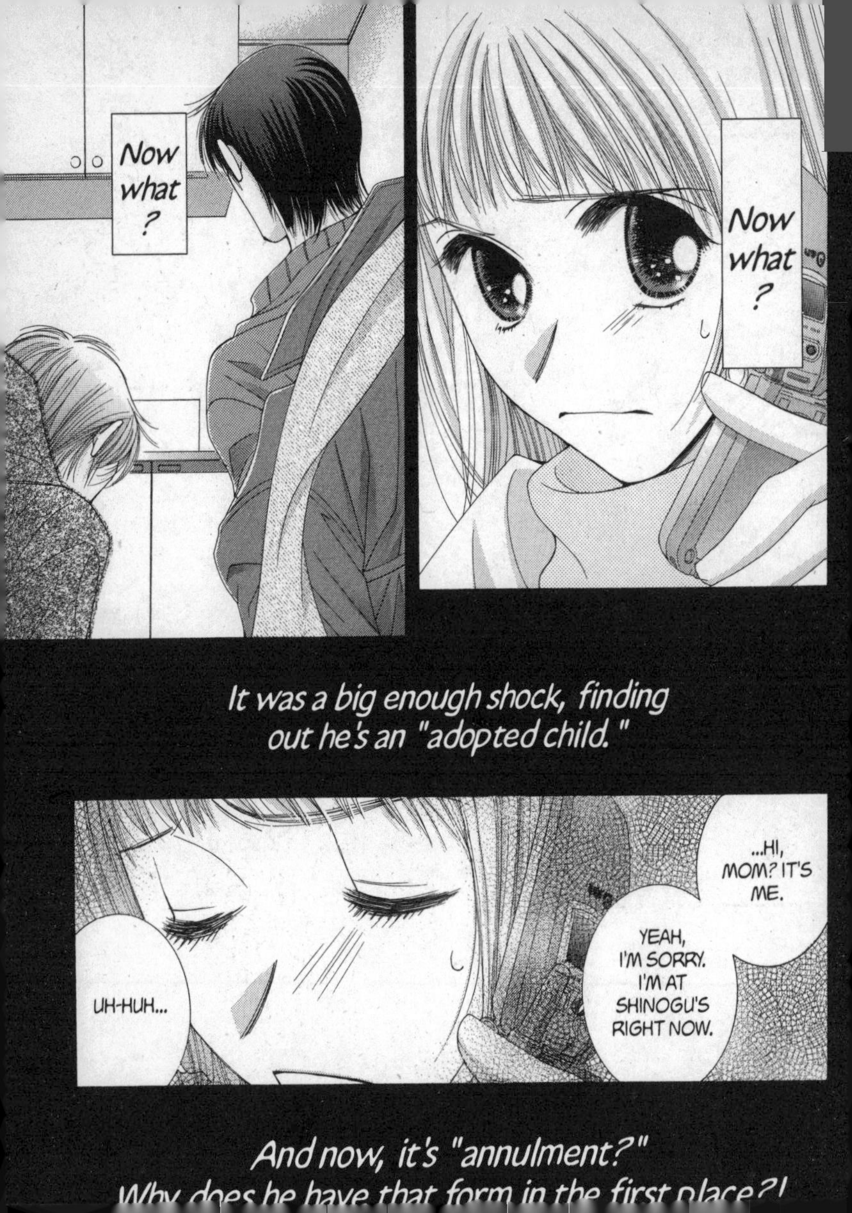
Now what?
Now what?
It was a big enough shock, finding out he's an "adopted child."
...HI, MOM? IT'S ME.
YEAH, I'M SORRY. I'M AT SHINOGU'S RIGHT NOW.
UH-HUH...
And now, it's "annulment?"
Why does he have that form in the first place?!

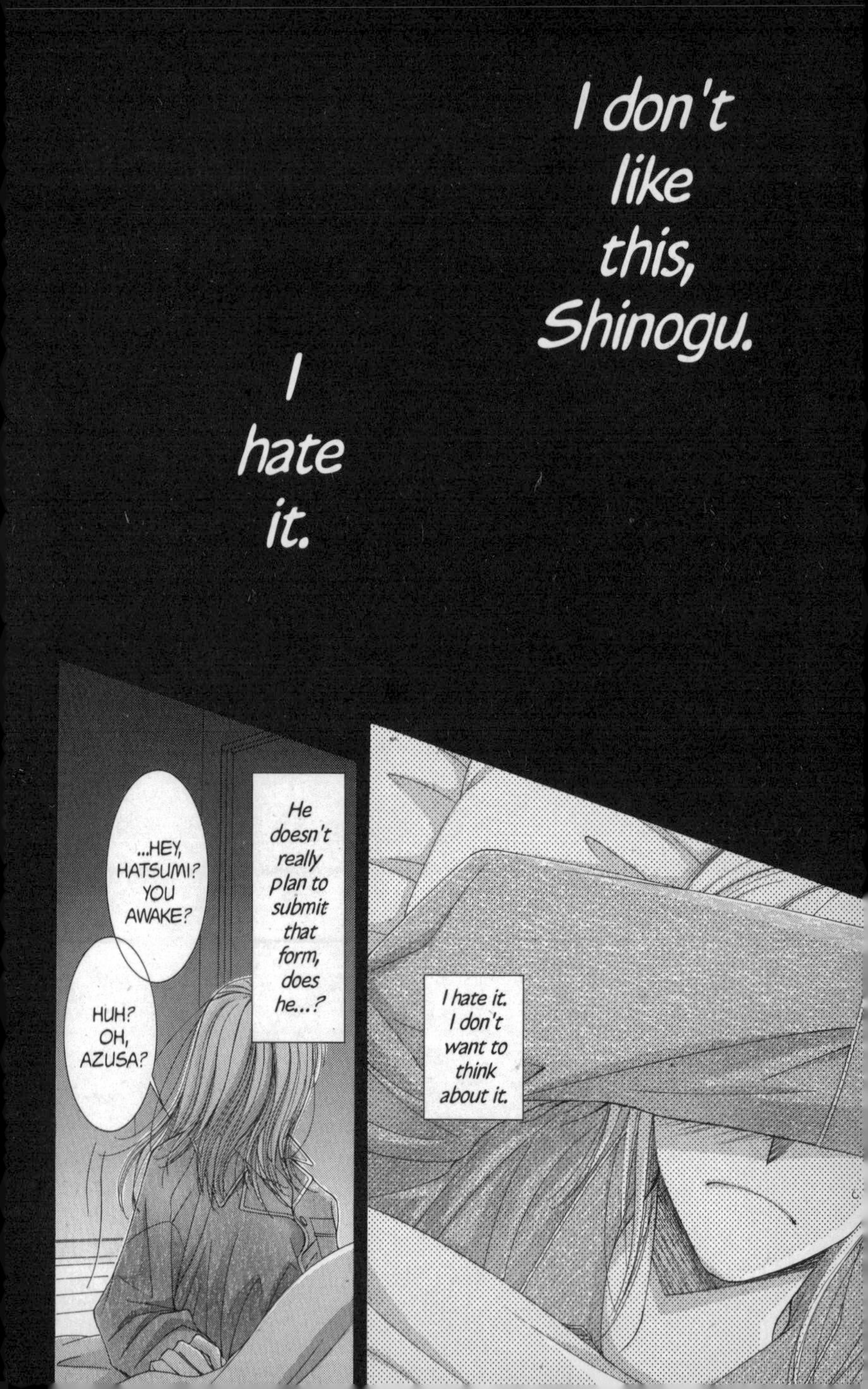
I don't like this, Shinogu.
I hate it.
I hate it. I don't want to think about it.
He doesn't really plan to submit that form, does he...?
...HEY, HATSUMI? YOU AWAKE?
HUH? OH, AZUSA?

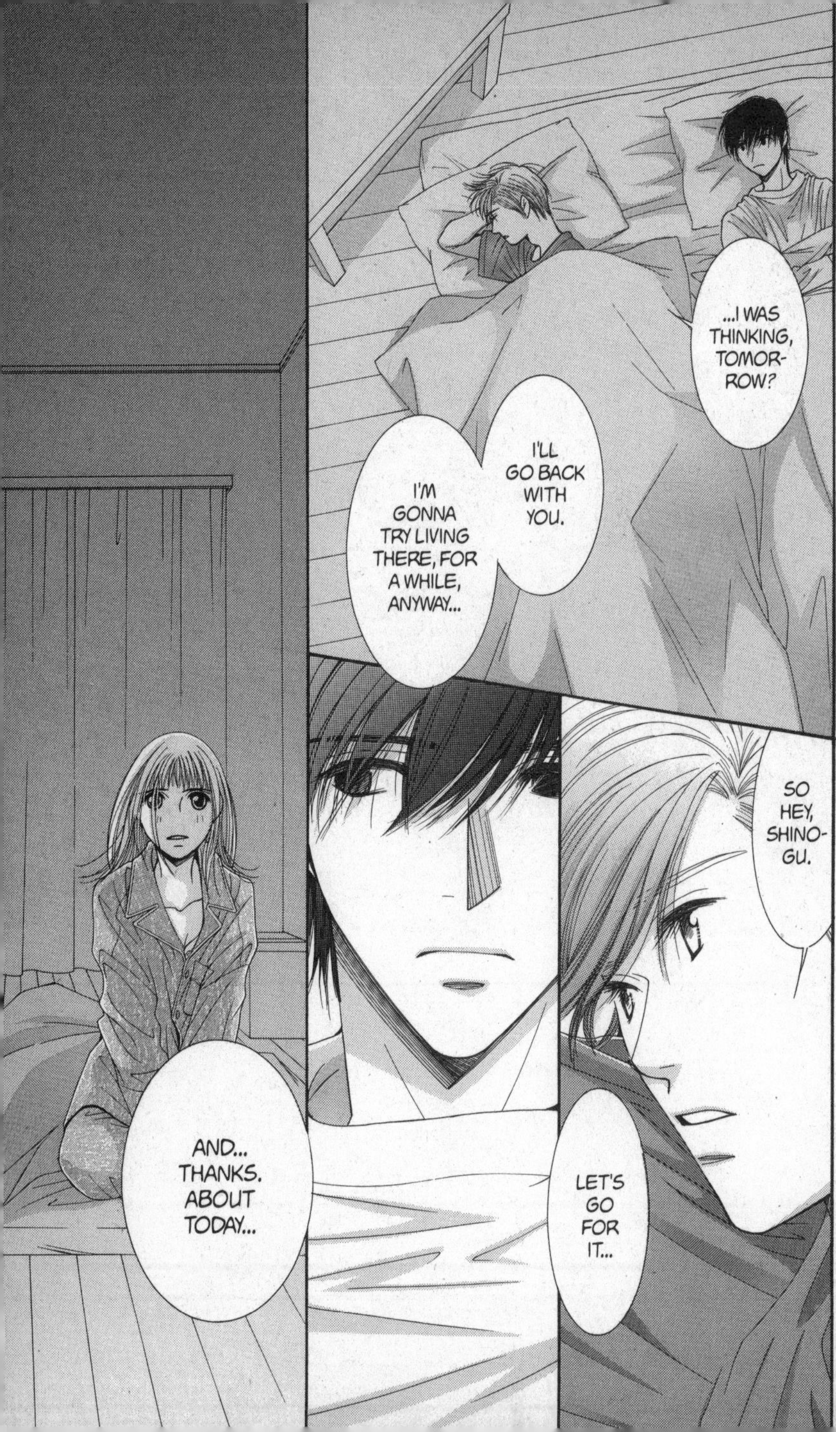
...I WAS THINKING, TOMORROW?
I'LL GO BACK WITH YOU.
I'M GONNA TRY LIVING THERE, FOR A WHILE, ANYWAY...
SO HEY, SHINOGU.
LET'S GO FOR IT...
AND... THANKS. ABOUT TODAY...

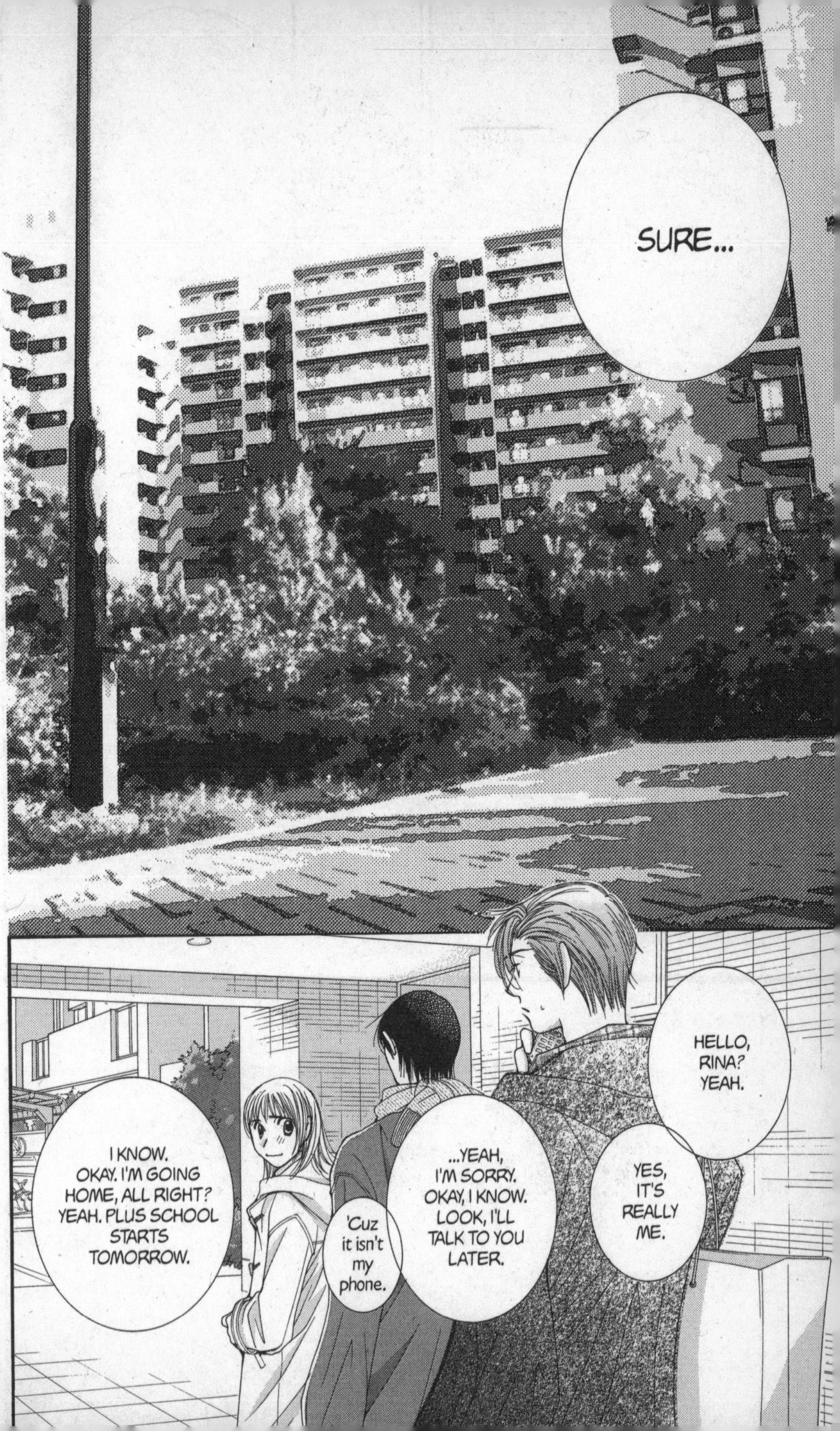
SURE...
HELLO, RINA? YEAH.
YES, IT'S REALLY ME.
...YEAH, I'M SORRY. OKAY, I KNOW. LOOK, I'LL TALK TO YOU LATER.
'Cuz it isn't my phone.
I KNOW. OKAY. I'M GOING HOME, ALL RIGHT? YEAH. PLUS SCHOOL STARTS TOMORROW.

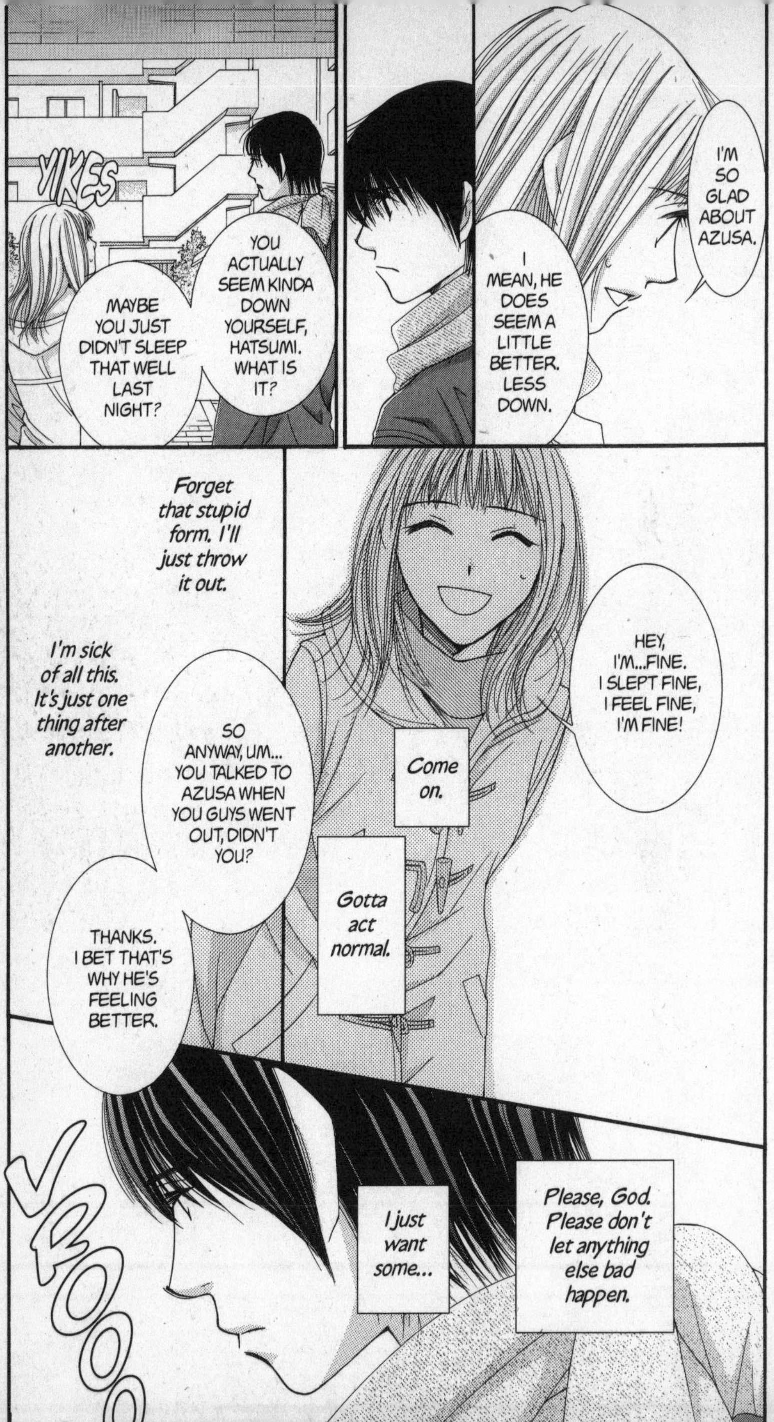
I'M SO GLAD ABOUT AZUSA.
I MEAN, HE DOES SEEM A LITTLE BETTER. LESS DOWN.
YIKES
YOU ACTUALLY SEEM KINDA DOWN YOURSELF, HATSUMI. WHAT IS IT?
MAYBE YOU JUST DIDN'T SLEEP THAT WELL LAST NIGHT?
HEY, I'M...FINE. I SLEPT FINE, I FEEL FINE, I'M FINE!
Come on.
Gotta act normal.
Forget that stupid form. I'll just throw it out.
I'm sick of all this. It's just one thing after another.
SO ANYWAY, UM... YOU TALKED TO AZUSA WHEN YOU GUYS WENT OUT, DIDN'T YOU?
THANKS. I BET THAT'S WHY HE'S FEELING BETTER.
Please, God. Please don't let anything else bad happen.
I just want some...
VROOO

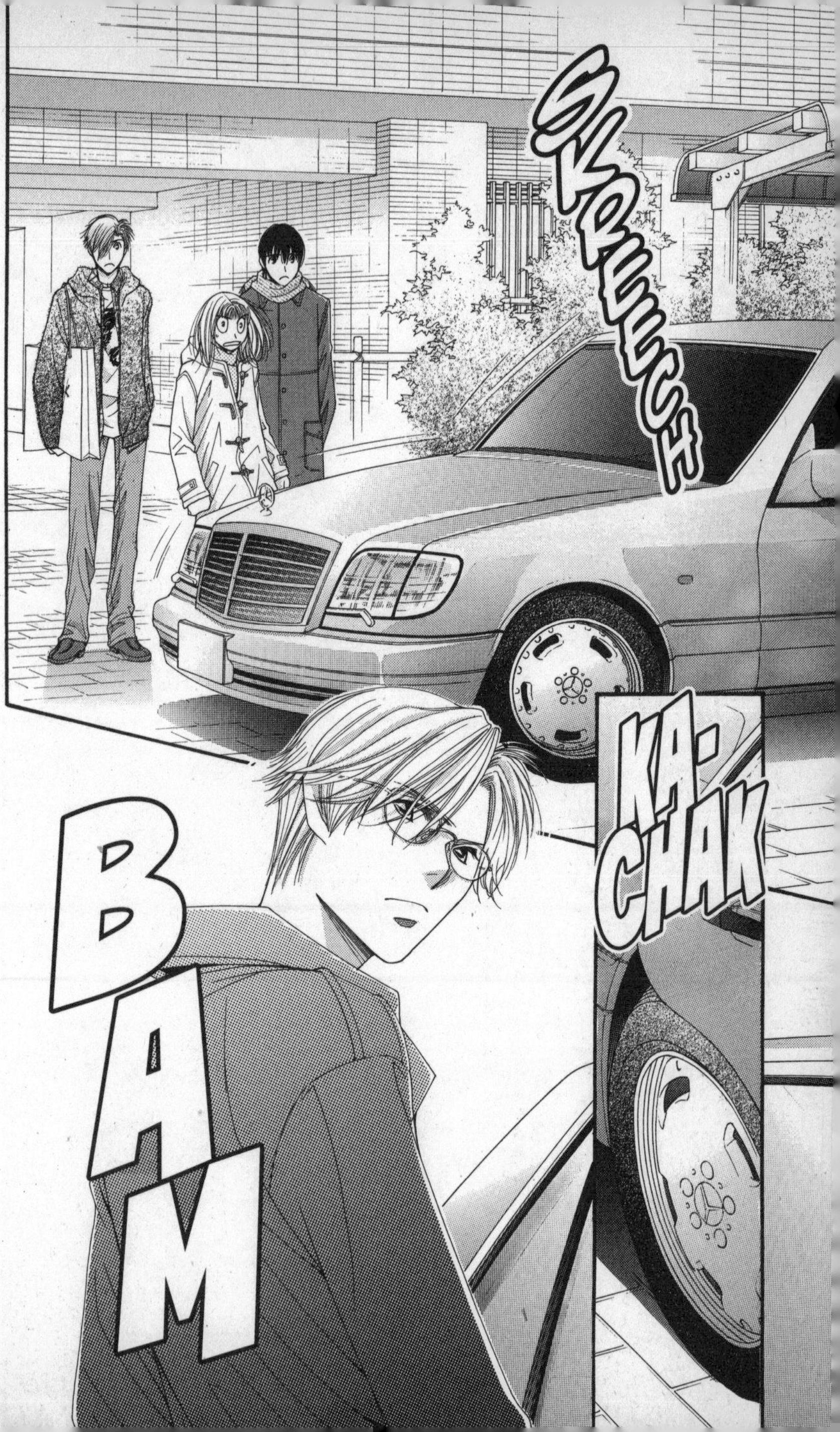
SKREECH
KA-CHAK
BAM

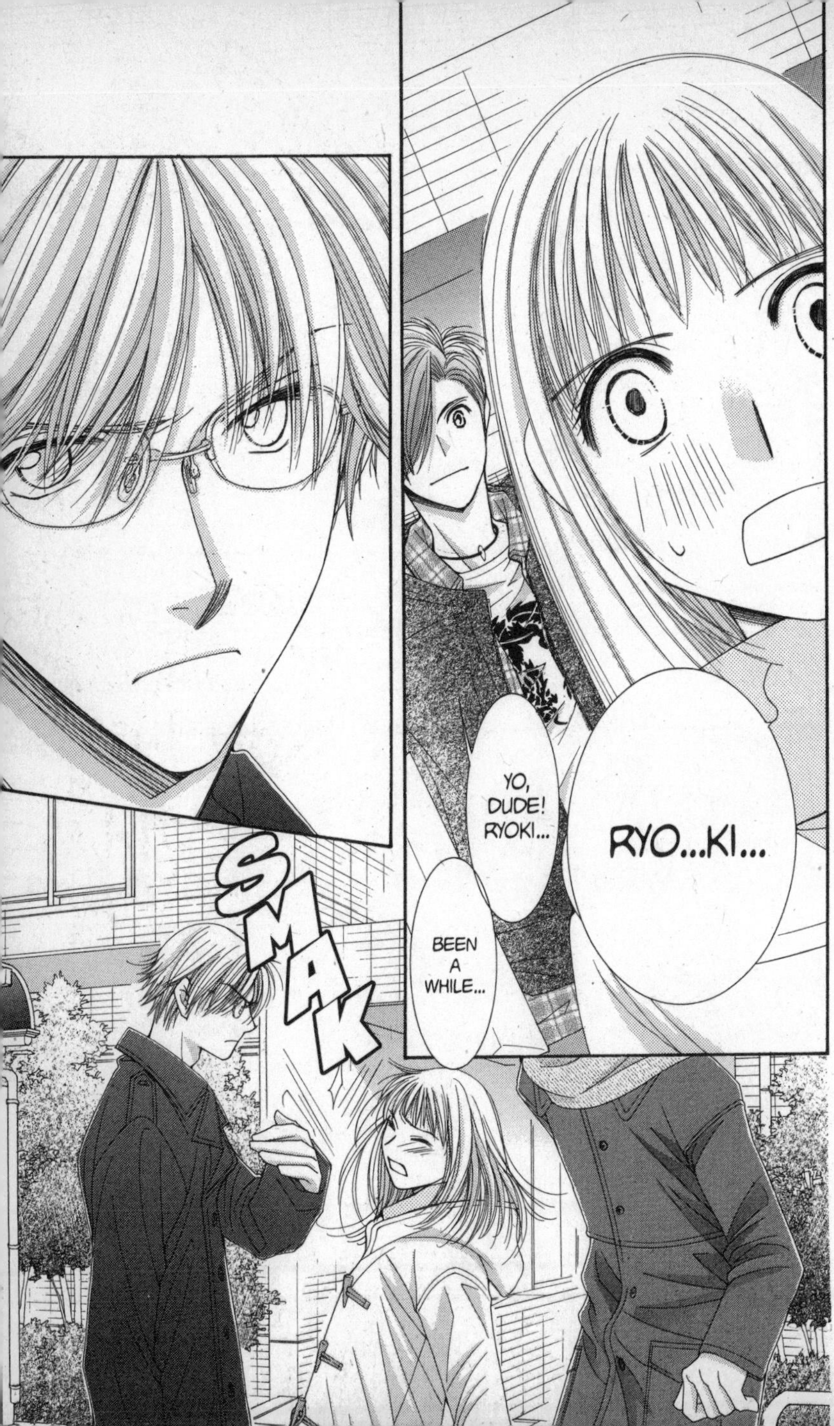
RYO...KI...
YO, DUDE! RYOKI...
BEEN A WHILE...
SMAK

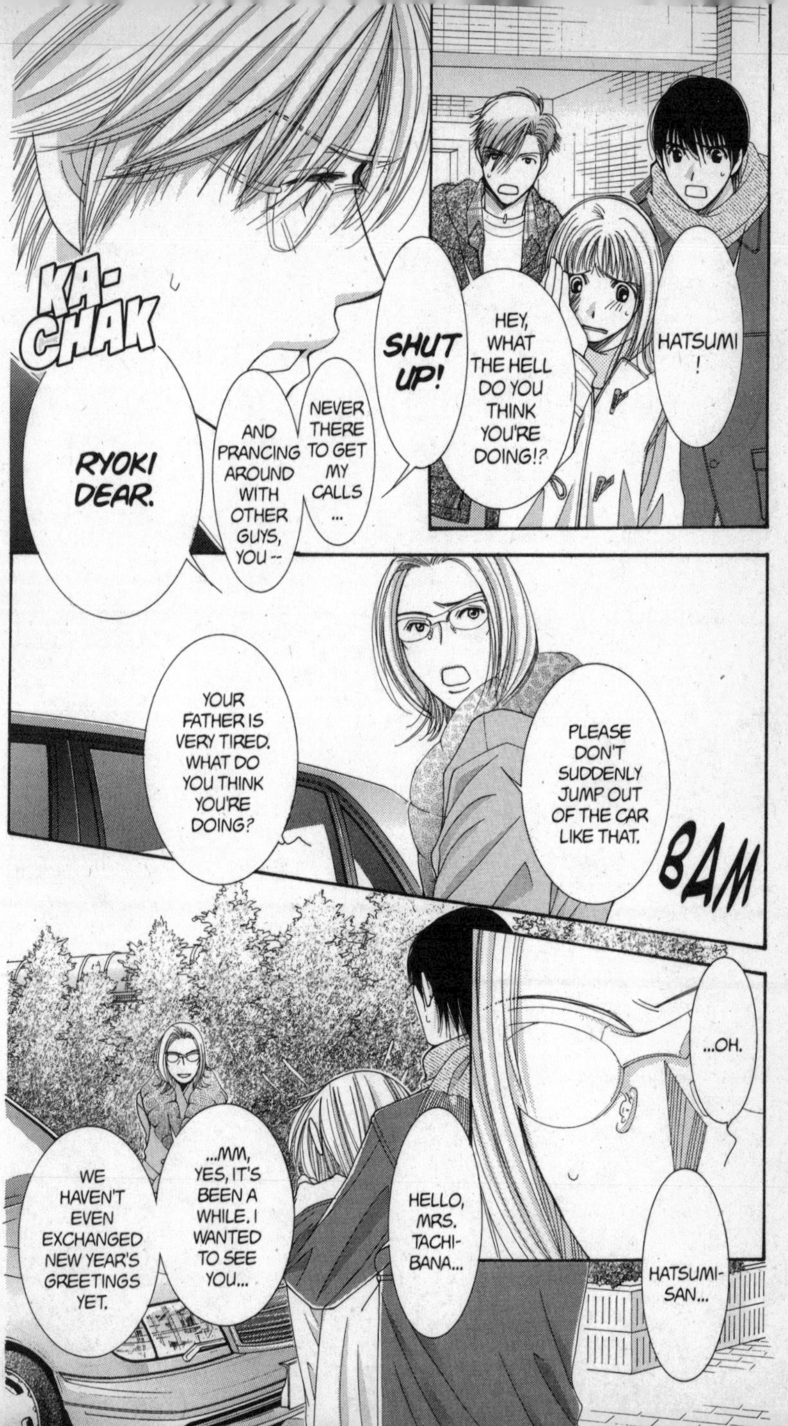
HATSUMI!
HEY, WHAT THE HELL DO YOU THINK YOU'RE DOING!?
SHUT UP!
KA-CHAK
NEVER THERE TO GET MY CALLS ...
AND PRANCING AROUND WITH OTHER GUYS, YOU --
RYOKI DEAR.
PLEASE DON'T SUDDENLY JUMP OUT OF THE CAR LIKE THAT.
BAM
YOUR FATHER IS VERY TIRED. WHAT DO YOU THINK YOU'RE DOING?
...OH.
HATSUMI-SAN...
HELLO, MRS. TACHI-BANA...
...MM, YES, IT'S BEEN A WHILE. I WANTED TO SEE YOU...
WE HAVEN'T EVEN EXCHANGED NEW YEAR'S GREETINGS YET.

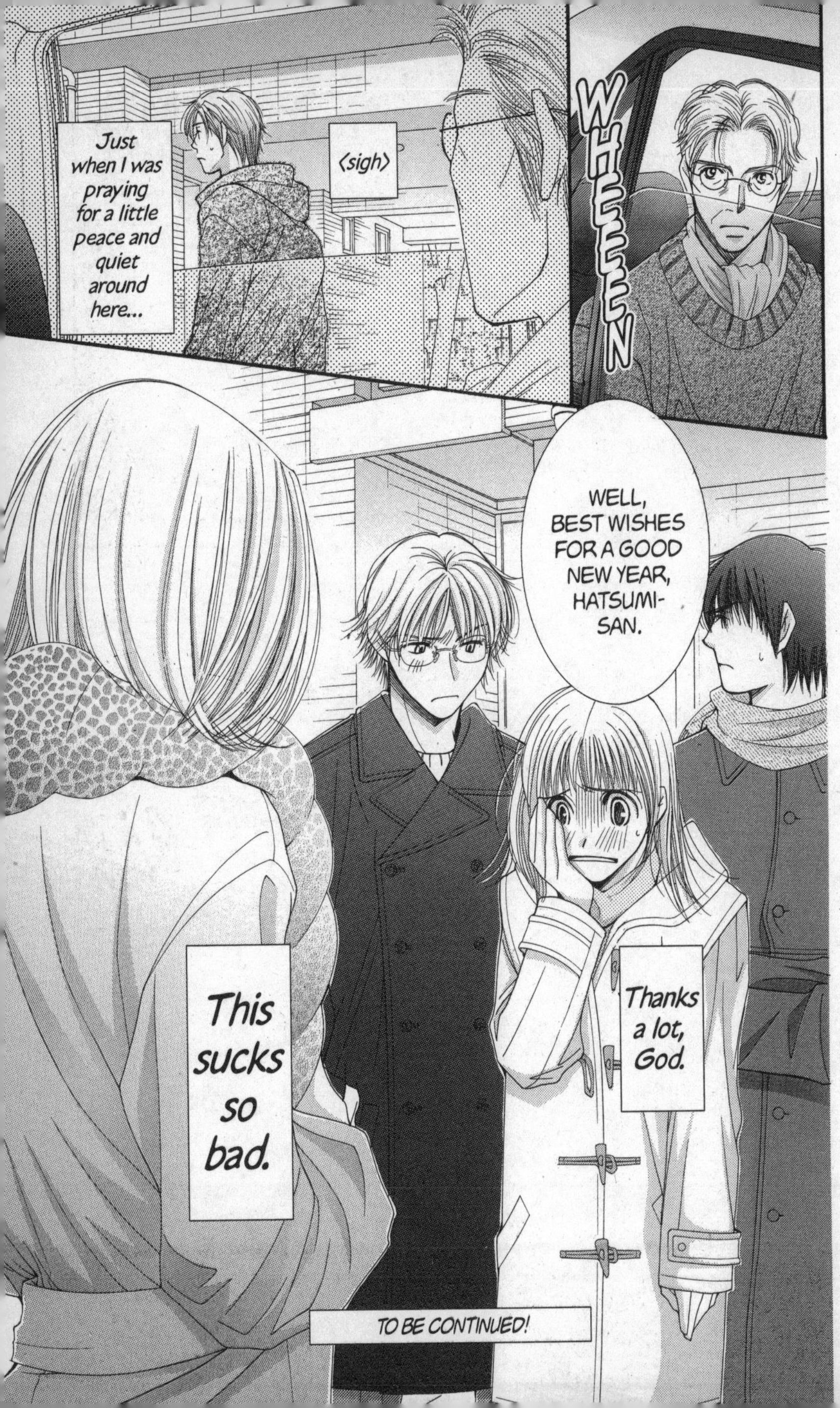
WHEEEEN
<sigh>
Just when I was praying for a little peace and quiet around here...
WELL, BEST WISHES FOR A GOOD NEW YEAR, HATSUMI-SAN.
Thanks a lot, God.
This sucks so bad.
TO BE CONTINUED!

JUST A LITTLE

EXTRA

GIMMICK

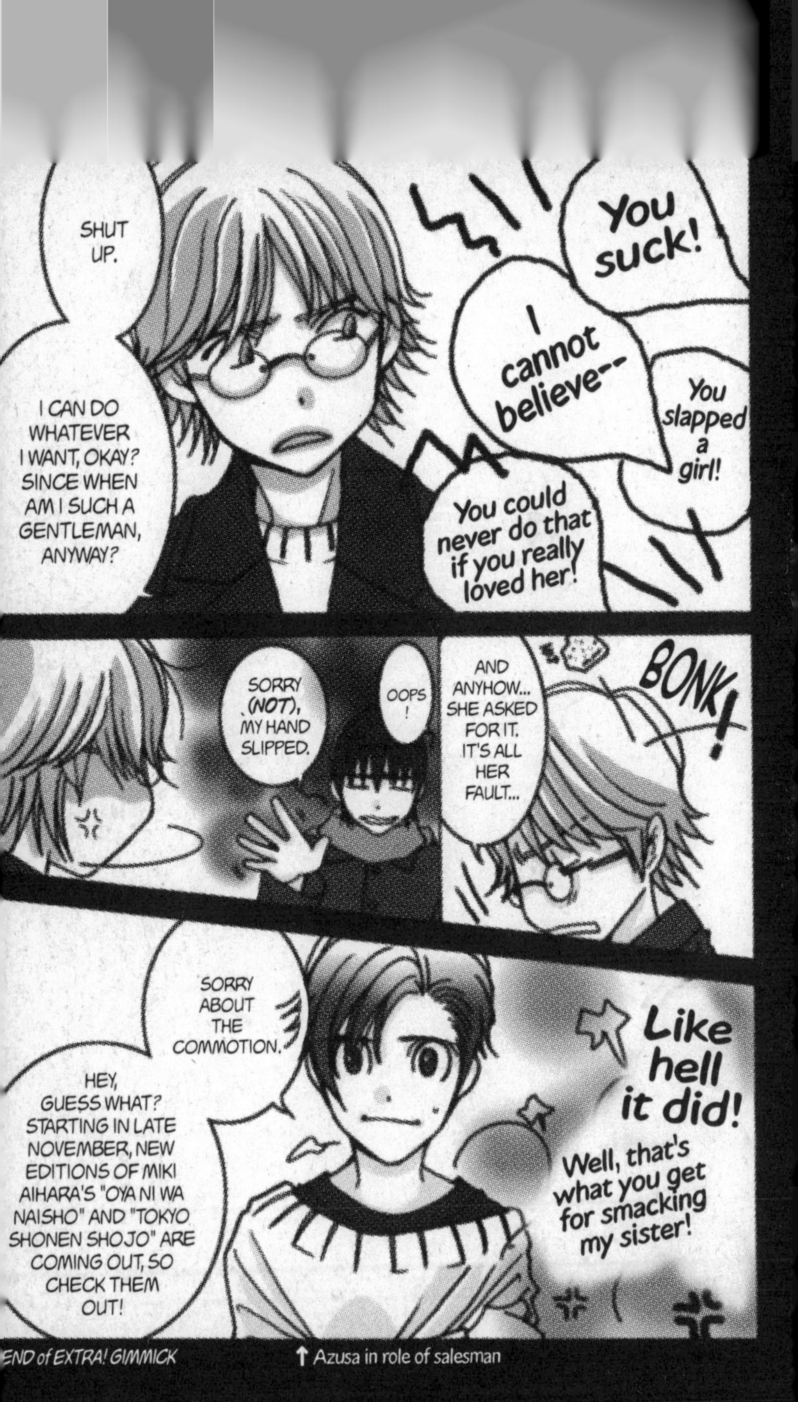
You suck!
I cannot believe--
You slapped a girl!
You could never do that if you really loved her!
SHUT UP.
I CAN DO WHATEVER I WANT, OKAY? SINCE WHEN AM I SUCH A GENTLEMAN, ANYWAY?
BONK!
AND ANYHOW... SHE ASKED FOR IT. IT'S ALL HER FAULT...
OOPS!
SORRY (NOT), MY HAND SLIPPED.
Like hell it did!
Well, that's what you get for smacking my sister!
SORRY ABOUT THE COMMOTION.
HEY, GUESS WHAT? STARTING IN LATE NOVEMBER, NEW EDITIONS OF MIKI AIHARA'S "OYA NI WA NAISHO" AND "TOKYO SHONEN SHOJO" ARE COMING OUT, SO CHECK THEM OUT!

END of EXTRA! GIMMICK ↑ Azusa in role of salesman

HOT GIMMICK
Vol. 7

Shôjo Edition

STORY & ART BY MIKI AIHARA

ENGLISH ADAPTATION BY POOKIE ROLF

Touch-up Art & Lettering/Rina Mapa
Cover Design/Izumi Evers
Editor/Kit Fox

Managing Editor/Annette Roman
Director of Production/Noboru Watanabe
V.P. of Publishing/Alvin Lu
Sr. Director of Acquisitions/Rika Inouye
V.P. of Sales & Marketing/Liza Coppola
Publisher/Hyoe Narita

Printed in Canada.

Published by VIZ Media, LLC
P.O. Box 77010
San Francisco, CA 94107

10 9 8 7 6 5 4 3 2
First printing, October 2004
Second printing, June 2005

RATED T+ FOR OLDER TEENS

PARENTAL ADVISORY
HOT GIMMICK is rated T+ for Teen Plus.
Contains strong language and sexual themes.
Recommended for older teens (16 and up).

VIZ media

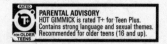

www.viz.com